To: Ad

With every good wish from Sam Silverling.

(author)

14 December 2019.

Nation, Tradition & Liberty

SAM SWERLING

Nation, Tradition & Liberty

— A POLITICAL MEMOIR —

My 50-year campaign (1966-2016)

First published 2017 in the UK by TAW Design and Print

ISBN: 978-0-9567753-3-7

Typeset in Palatino Linotype by TAW Design and Print (01271 314455)

Printed and bound by Gomer Press Ltd, Llandysul, Ceredigion SA44 4JL

1 2 3 4 5 6 7 8 9 10

Dedicated to:

My mother and father:
Sybil
(d 29 April 1995)
and Mark
(d 4 December 1984)

My brother:
Graham
(d 24 December 2013)

My sisters:
Ruthie, Sarah-Anne, Pamela and Penelope

My wife:
Anne
and our children:
Victoria, Thomas and George

Our grandchildren:
Charlotte, Francesca, Cosima and Marlowe

PICTURE ACKNOWLEDGEMENTS

All images are from the author's personal collection, with the exception of the following:

David Cameron's official portrait from the 10 Downing Street website – by Unknown – Meet the PM (direct image link) from the 10 Downing Street Website, OGL, https://commons.wikimedia.org/w/index.php?curid=21357999

Marie-France Stirbois with her sash of member of European Parliament, at the Front National's march in honour of Joan of Arc, 1 May 2004 in Paris, France – by Novosti yu – self-photographed, CC BY-SA 3.0, https://commons.wikimedia.org/w/index.php?curid=16106790

Penny Mordaunt, MP – by HM Government – https://www.gov.uk/government/people/penny-mordaunt, OGL, https://commons.wikimedia.org/w/index.php?curid=41830829

Portrait of Alexander Graham Bell – by Moffett Studio – Library and Archives Canada / C-017335, Public Domain, https://commons.wikimedia.org/w/index.php?curid=1559

Map of former Yugoslavia including Kosovo independence – by Ijanderson977 – derived from File: Former Yugoslavia 2006.png by Dudemanfellabra at en.wikipedia, CC BY-SA 3.0, https://commons.wikimedia.org/w/index.php?curid=7523932

Angela Merkel at the EPP Summit in Brussels, March 2016 – by https://www.flickr.com/photos/eppofficial/ – https://www.flickr.com/photos/eppofficial/25738722632/, CC BY 2.0, https://commons.wikimedia.org/w/index.php?curid=47997163

Former Watford FC manager and chairman Graham Taylor, pictured at a football match on 9 May 2010 – by Clurr – http://www.flickr.com/photos/clurr/4593254642/in/set-72157623902070077/, CC BY 2.0, https://commons.wikimedia.org/w/index.php?curid=20338709

Acknowledgements

I would like to thank Allan Robertson, Chairman of the Swinton Circle, for his input to some of the material on Northern Ireland, upon which he is an expert.

My thanks also to Radomir Putnikovic for permission to reproduce several letters to MPs and others on the subject of the Balkan Wars. Likewise my thanks to Alec Kendall, a politics graduate from Oxford University, who accompanied me to the national archive centre in Kew and did some of the research into the secretive background to the Lisbon Treaty 2007 upon which I have written at length in this book.

I am very grateful to my publisher, Jeremy Paxton, for everything he has done in putting the book together and making it, as I hope, a readable and useful production.

Contents

Foreword

I was delighted to hear from my old friend and long-time political colleague, Sam Swerling, that his retirement years had not been given over to gardening and other forms of just passing time, but instead had been devoted to the writing of a major new book: an account of his 50 years of political action and thought – half-a-century, *not out*.

I first met Sam in the spring of 1985, at a Monday Club meeting held in a committee room in the Houses of Parliament. I was but 20 years old. I am now 52. My recollection of the evening is strong – not because of the speaker or subject matter of the event, but because of Sam's "stage presence", and the impression he left and continues to leave of hard-hitting eloquence. During the meeting's question time, I succeeded in asking the sort of question that was designed to ingratiate myself with the audience (twenty-year olds, especially in politics, have a peculiar need to make waves ...). I recall a broad smile from Sam and an approving nod, and knew instantly that I had found a new ally. The alliance has stood the test of time – indeed, knowing Sam has not just been a conventional friendship, but a privilege and a unique chance to spend part of 30 years learning much about European political philosophy (especially the esoterica of pre- and post-war French Right-wing doctrines); how to approach the art of speech-making (Sam is surely one of the finest orators the British Right has ever produced); and – just as importantly – to keep things in their place, to enjoy all the vital experiences life has to offer: cricket at Lord's, classical music, football matches, expertise in solving *The Times* cryptic crossword puzzles, days on the English south coast, the importance of friends and family – and I fondly remember being admitted to Sam's family circle at his daughter's wedding, memorably held in the glorious South Devon countryside.

Sam (by training and profession, a lawyer) began his political quest in the mid 1960s, proving to be an effective committee man, orator at Speakers' Corner, local councillor and – by the 1970s – an official Conservative Party Prospective Parliamentary candidate, although the winning line just eluded him. The resounding speeches that Sam *would* have made in the House of Commons – against mass-immigration, and in the early 1990s, the disastrous Maastricht Treaty as championed by the then Prime Minister, John Major – were, therefore, made at public meetings and rallies across the country. Ironically, his message probably reached a far wider audience: the standing of our parliamentarians has never been lower.

Britain's vote to leave the European Union in June of last year seemed to be a vindication of all the great causes to which Sam dedicated his political life; and – typically for a man of high ideals – he now talks of the new opportunity that awaits the people of France and continental Europe following Brexit, to create a replacement cultural community of sovereign nation-states – imbued with serious, noble ideals, instead of the present EU's dull obsession with control and uniformity.

Sam Swerling's new book is a memoir of political life, which began in the St. Marylebone Conservative Association – "a much-coveted constituency at the heart of London, a safe Conservative seat, famous for many notable landmarks such as ... Lord's Cricket Ground." This was the era of Gerald (later, Sir Gerald) Nabarro, Macmillan and Lord Hailsham, and the author gives a clear view of the political landscape of the time – taking us further into his own political pathway, with a piece for the 1970 Monday Club journal, *Monday World*. The piece concerns the United Nations, its formation, good intentions – and inability to act in relation to the Soviet invasion of Hungary, not to mention the organisation, in the case of Katanga, overlooking its own "domestic jurisdiction" clause (which, theoretically, precludes it from interference in the affairs of a state). There is also much discussion on the fate of Rhodesia, with the then Prime Minister, Harold Wilson, referring the "naughty Rhodesians" to the high counsels of the United Nations.

Other invasions feature in the book: such as Militant's incursion into the Labour Party (Sam Swerling is as detailed in his analysis of socialist politics as he is of his own Conservative Party); and the bewildering situation in the Balkans which preoccupied British foreign policy in the 1990s. The reader also gains an insight into the author's interest in legal affairs – and students of the politics of the early 1970s will find much to absorb in his 1972 piece on the Rudi Dutschke affair; a civil liberties / national security case, in which a German extreme left-winger, dedicated to the overthrow of capitalism was admitted to Britain for medical treatment.

Continental political developments feature heavily in the pages ahead, and as we survey (here in 2017) the beginning of Brexit and the loss of faith among European electorates in the parties of "consensus", the chapter concerning the rise of the French *Front National* is as compelling as it is instructive. Writing about the FN's *Bleu, Blanc, Rouge* festival in 1997, we learn that the party had already exceeded the size of the Gaullist UDF – "with support levels in some regions of France (particularly in the south and the industrial north-east) running at over 35%." I know of no other writer in Britain today who has chronicled the politics of France and the FN with such dedication and understanding.

Educational policy in Britain; the need for a Tory Right (and the inherent weaknesses of Toryism); the legacy of Enoch Powell, the Europe of Maastricht, of Major – and the Tory High Command's vendetta against the Monday Club; the post-Communist cocktail of Eastern Europe – of Serbs and Croats and international disarray; to the future of football – Sam Swerling offers us an unmissable sweeping view of his half-century in politics.

Stuart Millson
Kent
March 2017

Early Years in Marylebone

My introduction to politics was fairly belated. I had shown no interest either at school, where mock elections were held from time to time with a good deal of cynicism and wry amusement, or at university where my law degree studies involved an enormous amount of reading, including case studies and yearly examinations leaving only time for sporting endeavours where I was in the first team at soccer and lawn tennis, both for two years. In the vacation during the autumn and winter months I continued to play Eton Fives in London for Old Reptonians, a wonderfully skilful court game which happily is being gradually developed outside the milieu of a small number of independent schools.

It was in the summer 1964 that I met a long-time member of St Marylebone Conservative Association[1], Bob Skinner, who invited me to accompany him to the association headquarters, then in Grove End Gardens, St John's Wood, London NW8 to listen to a talk to be given by Gerald Nabarro (later Sir Gerald), a colourful and very popular MP who was to address around 100 members on 'economy and taxation'. He proved to be a wonderful public speaker – no notes, an engaging manner and an evident ability to enthuse his listeners on what might otherwise have been a somewhat dry subject.

Sufficiently impressed, I joined the young conservative branch of the association shortly afterwards and set about reading as

---

[1] St Marylebone, a much coveted constituency at the heart of London, a safe Conservative seat, famous for many notable landmarks such as London Zoo, Madame Tussauds and Lord's cricket ground.

much as I could on political structures, Conservative policy on as many subject-areas as possible as well as learning about the party's history and leading thinkers and philosophers such as Disraeli, Maynard Keynes, Joseph Chamberlain and others. It was a form of disciplined education because unless you become knowledgeable about such antecedents you are in no position to make any sort of critical appraisal or judgment, nor indeed to identify or understand whether your views will lead you to becoming left-of-centre, centrist or right-wing.

By the time I had joined Marylebone Tories, a by-election had been held in early December 1963 after the then MP, Wavell Wakefield, (an international rugby player and England captain among many more cerebral attributes) became a hereditary peer. The seat was retained for the Conservatives by Quintin Hogg who had renounced his peerage as Lord Hailsham in order to enter the House of Commons in the hope of being chosen as party leader following the resignation of Harold Macmillan, and thereby becoming Prime Minister, in which bid his boisterous behaviour at the Conservative Party Conference of October 1963 made him many significant political enemies. Hogg went on to hold the seat in the 1966 and 1970 General Elections. Like his predecessor, Hogg would leave the seat on being given a life peerage. Forty years earlier the constituency had been represented by Hogg's father, Douglas.

Meanwhile, the YCs in Marylebone were becoming far more politically interested and independent-minded (and that continued to be so for several years – certainly up to the time I became Chairman in 1969) than most branches where the popular perception of the YC movement was to offer young ladies an opportunity to engage in plenty of social life and the chance to meet 'respectable' young men – possibly even to be seen as an early-day marriage bureau!

My own political acumen grew exponentially and proportionate to the time and effort I was able to put in. Briefing notes published by the Conservative Research Department were always very useful in this regard. My particular interest in this early period centred around housing, defence and foreign affairs. I was soon to be invited to join 'Impact' panels which would travel to other YC branches in the Greater London area for question and answer sessions, designed to impart policy knowledge and generate enthusiasm.

At Marylebone the YCs always had a regular programme of speakers, usually on Wednesday evenings. Our constituency agent, Billy Ball, an air force hero of the Second World War, always generous with his time, a consummate professional steeped in all the intricacies of Conservative Party management and organisation, maintained a particularly good relationship with me and I admired him tremendously. He had been kind enough to tell me that I was "capable of going places" in the Conservative Party, a most generous comment and one that filled me with optimism for the future.

Another dominant figure in the constituency was our President, Sir Louis Gluckstein[2], a man of great distinction, universally popular and highly respected with a long and successful career both in politics and law behind him.

A highly visible figure in the association was Margaret Challis (who for many years worked as secretary to Sir Louis's business affairs. She was here, there and everywhere, a buzzing bee, always exhorting members to ever greater efforts. She was, if you like, a Tory *grande dame*, a party loyalist of the first rank. A ward chairman for many years she would often be heard calling upon the more idle to pull their weight for the cause, describing them disdainfully as "slackers" if they fell short. Margaret would never hear of defeat at election times. An example of her indefatigability was amply illustrated at a Church Street, Marylebone, ward council election in April 1968. The Conservative candidates were Jonah Walker-Smith (later Sir Jonah), a barrister; Ken Hamer, also a barrister and myself, a solicitor.

Realistically, we had no chance of winning. It was a strong Labour ward. An hour before polls closed she declared joyfully in the committee rooms that everyone must get out to the streets and do a final "knocking-up" of voters since she had worked it out that we could win, for which optimism there was not a shred of evidence and certainly not from the canvassing card

---

2 Sir Louis Gluckstein, educated at St Paul's School and Lincoln College, Oxford. Commissioned into the Suffolk regiment during the First World War and saw action as a captain in the Second World War. Elected as Member of Parliament for Nottingham East in the 1931 General Election until his defeat at the 1945 General Election. Conservative Councillor on the Greater London Council (GLC) from 1964 to 1967, becoming an Alderman from 1967 to 1973. Appointed King's Counsel in 1945 and knighted in the Coronation Honours of 1953. Became CBE in the 1964 New Years Honours List and promoted to King's Grand Cross in the 1969 Queen's Birthday Honours.

returns. The result showed a resounding win for Labour. Margaret was mortified. She needed to be consoled. All her hard organisational work had failed to come to fruition. This rather splendid lady, known to many at the time as 'the queen of Grove End Gardens', where she lived fairly modestly , finally bit the dust at the grand old age of 97. God bless her.

Membership of the association offered not only friendship and camaraderie amongst like-minded people but also many exciting, even dangerous moments. One such was a General Election campaign public meeting held in Seymour Hall Marylebone, in October 1966 in support of our candidate, Quintin Hogg. About 600 people turned up. One of them was the ubiquitous and well-known local figure, George Smith, a resident of Penfold Street, Marylebone. He was no ordinary attender. He had a history of interrupting Conservative meetings with his comrade, Alan Thompson, both Communist Party members (CPGB) of long-standing. Smith, who worked as a Thames Board gas meter collector but whose principal occupation was security officer at the CPGB's headquarters at 16 King Street, London WC1, acted as a formidable deterrence to anyone who might have been an interloper or undesirable at that venue. Even party members were careful not to upset him lest they should be on the receiving end of one of his tempestuous outbursts. At the Seymour Hall meeting he met his match. Three burly YC activists bundled him out of the hall when his heckling had become tiresome and threatening.

One of Smith's regular haunts was Speakers' Corner in Marble Arch where Hyde Park Tories held regular open-air meetings championing the Tory cause before overseas visitors, party supporters, the general public and the simply curious. Smith's function was to heckle the platform. I was a member of the speaking team for 10 years (1969 – 1979). On one occasion, I was so irate that I referred to him in less than dulcet tones as a "boring old bolshevik". I should have known better. I had to be rescued from my speaker's stand by other speakers' timely intervention, preventing thereby a nasty incident.

The only other meeting I can recall where the smell of violence hung in the air was at the Albert Hall, in March 1966. The Monday Club (which I had joined in April 1965) in conjunction with the Anglo-Rhodesian Society held a public meeting attended by over 1,500 people. Its purpose was to protest vigorously about economic sanctions imposed against Rhodesia after that country's unilateral declaration of independence in November 1965[3].

The speakers were to be Lord Salisbury, in the chair, John Biggs-Davison MP, Patrick Wall MP, Julian Amery MP Stephen Hastings MP and Ronald Bell MP, described by the media as "the Rhodesia lobby" and all of them members of the Monday Club.

Shortly after the start of the meeting, a youngish man with urgent step and more than a hint of menace, approached the platform clearly intent on causing physical violence. He had not counted on the presence of Barrington Saunders, a former Army boxing champion and well-known in right-wing circles as a protector and bodyguard. Saunders intercepted the would-be assailant, one Manny Carpel, just before he mounted the steps, a member of the '62 group of *soi-disant* anti-fascists, with a solid punch to the jaw which sent him reeling, a sight to behold. Carpel was duly thrown out of the elegant surrounds of the Albert Hall in double-quick time, together with a couple of his associates. No messing about there. The meeting went on for 2½ hours. I remember it as if yesterday.

I continued being active in St Marylebone YCs, involved in both organisation and public speaking. My views on most subjects had 'firmed up' as identifiably right-wing which had made my Monday Club membership little more than a formality. I would then, as now, describe myself as a Tory nationalist, dedicated to the ideals of nationhood, patriotism, economic freedom so as to support the small business sector and private enterprise generally but within a framework of government intervention capacity to counter monopoly capitalism, cartels and globalisation with its catastrophic effects on manufacturing industry and as a harbinger of austerity and poverty.

None of the above inhibited my advance in the voluntary side of politics so that after ceasing to be eligible as a Young Conservative, I spent four years as Chairman of St Marylebone

---

3 This had been a controversial step but should have been considered in the light of Northern Rhodesia becoming independent as Zambia under Kenneth Kaunda and Nyasaland becoming independent as Malawi under Hastings Banda (both events in 1964) and the implicit understanding made known to Winston Field, and after him Ian Smith, that Southern Rhodesia would shortly follow course – added to the fact that excellent race relations had existed between white and black Rhodesians for many years.

Conservative Political Centre (CPC) where I developed a cordial relationship with our MP, Kenneth Baker[4], as a Conservative councillor on Westminster City Council, and later Hertsmere Borough Council and as Chairman of the Monday Club. I also had the honour of being Conservative parliamentary candidate at Stalybridge and Hyde and Nottingham East. On three occasions I was runner-up for safe Conservative seats between 1976 and 1979. If I had softened my views I might have made it into Parliament. But I wouldn't, so I didn't.

Much of the debate is now carried forward into those appointments, the various articles I have written and speeches I have made covering the numerous political events of significance that have taken place between 1966 and 2016.

---

[4] Kenneth Baker, MP for Acton, 28 March 1968 – 18 June 1970; MP for St Marylebone, 22 October 1970 – 9 June 1983 (hereafter constituency abolished); MP for Mole Valley, 9 June 1983 – 2 May 1997; Secretary of State for the Environment, 2 September 1985 – 21 May 1986; Secretary of State for Education and Science, 21 May 1986 – 24 July 1989; Chairman, The Conservative Party, 24 July 1989 – 28 November 1990; Home Secretary, 28 November 1990 – 10 April 1992; Assumed office as Lord Baker of Dorking CH PC, 16 June 1997.

Differences with the GLYC leadership

St Marylebone Young Conservatives set up their own magazine in March 1970. We called it *Bastion*. It was edited by myself and my lifelong friend, Reay Wood. My piece appeared in May of that year. Reay's clear insights and political conviction on most issues over 45 years have been a guiding light to me and very many others down the years. His deep and abiding traditionalist Catholic faith has shown that politics and religion need not conflict. We were the only YC branch to have a quarterly magazine and it had a readership beyond the confines of the constituency itself, suggesting some people must have liked it!

Readers of *The Marylebone Mercury*, the main local newspaper of our constituency, may have noted in the letters column recently a marked difference of opinion on current issues between, on the one hand, the Chairman and a majority of the Committee of St Marylebone Young Conservatives, and on the other the Executive of the Greater London Young Conservatives, to whom the Marylebone branch is affiliated.

It has become quite clear over the past three years, although it was apparent a long time before then, that the GLYC Executive on virtually all the important political issues of the day has adopted a position which generally may fairly be described as left of centre, and in certain specific instances well to the left of centre.

Perhaps the rationale of GLYC attitudes is best expressed in the closing speech made at the London Area Conference in Margate last March by GLYC Chairman, Gerry Wade, when he said that the YC movement in a changing world must itself be geared to change. If by change Councillor Wade meant that we should change, for instance, outdated methods of industrial management and gear ourselves to the new processes which modern science has required us to adopt to make ourselves economically more competitive we would not dispute his notion of change for one moment. But Councillor Wade was not so specific. He appeared to place the idea of change on a conceptual basis, as if it were a value in itself. To those who would consider change in itself a value it is simple to label an opponent as a reactionary and we have had our fair share of opponents among the liberal consensus who have attempted to pass us off among the unthinking as reactionaries.

We consider that change for change's sake is as utterly alien to Conservative thinking as private enterprise is to doctrinaire socialism. Indeed, change in that sense is the very stuff of perpetual revolution. If this sounds trite and self-evident we offer no apology whatsoever because the lesson does not appear to have been learned by certain people in the Conservative Party.

If the word 'conservative' means anything it means conserving the best of our traditions and institutions which we hold in trust for future generations until they have been shown beyond any doubt to have outlived their usefulness and until they can be replaced by better ones. Concepts of continuity, certainty, stability and patriotism should weigh very heavily in the Conservative conscience within a system which guarantees liberty under the law. They are as important to young conservatives as they are to our seniors, and no less worthy of emphasis.

For our part, we are not interested in sheltering under our Tory umbrella people and organisations who have no basic understanding of conservatism. We are very much at variance with the GLYC executive for their recent decision to affiliate to groups who cannot be regarded as specifically conservative. It is no reason to affiliate to such groups in the hope that they will come round to our way of thought, or at least to what ought to be our way of thought. The opposite will in fact be the case and we would have thought experience and events have proved this time and time again.

The most extraordinary affiliation made by the GLYC executive is to the National Council for Civil Liberties, an organisation which would find it hard to refute allegations that it has been partly infiltrated by the Communist Party and several Communist Front organisations in the past five years. Anyone who recalls the October 1968 street riots in Grosvenor Square will testify to how NCCL observers strained every muscle to find evidence of 'police brutality'. In fact the police have always been a special target of the NCCL and many an agitator or potential revolutionary has reason to be grateful for NCCL advice on how to make the policeman's job as difficult as possible. Of course the NCCL would never admit that it directly impedes the police, and perhaps in fairness it does not have that intention, but no-one who has made a study of some of the causes that it champions can avoid the inescapable conclusion of its hostility to the police and the necessary methods which the police sometimes have to use in the execution of their duty.

At the present moment, the high priests of liberaldom are hammering away at the eminently wise decision of Home Secretary Maudling to refuse the German left-wing revolutionary, Rudi Dutschke, an extension of his temporary permit (which was granted for the purposes of his convalescence from gunshot wounds suffered not in this country, mind you, but in Germany on condition that he refrained from all political activity). Mrs Joan Robinson, Professor of Economics at Cambridge, has described the decision as "a serious attack on academic freedom". This lady would have been Dutschke's supervisor on his intended post-graduate study at Cambridge into revolutionary theory. Presumably she would have also helped him with his "academic freedom" to facilitate his task. Mr Michael Foot has spoken of it "as a miserable piece of inhumanity". We cannot recall, incidentally, Mr Foot or anyone else of his ilk describing the Red attacks on the police in the student disorders of 1967 and 1968 as "miserable pieces of inhumanity". And, significantly, for the purposes of this article, the NCCL General Secretary Mr Tony Smythe wades in with this pompous pronouncement on the Home Secretary's edict: "This is a dangerous precedent which threatens Britain's reputation as a refuge for the distressed". Certainly, we regret that Mr Dutschke was shot and is still feeling the effects of his wounds but why should Britain be made responsible for that? Just who are the distressed people today? Those who foment violence in the furtherance of revolutionary causes and suffer the consequences or the long-suffering public who have with seemingly unlimited tolerance seen the streets of London on more than one occasion turned into battlefields between the forces of constitutional authority and those striving to upturn the existing order?

The NCCL should be judged by the company it keeps. It seems more concerned with civil licence than civil liberty. We should disaffiliate from it forthwith and with no regrets.

The second strange decision is that of affiliating to the United Nations Youth Association. If this had been done at a time when the UN was vaguely pro-West some good may have come from it but, as has been shown on another page, the UN's interests have become largely identifiable with Afro-Asian interests and the Third World and no amount of pressure exerted by Greater London YCs through affiliation can alter that fact.

The third affiliation is more easily justifiable, but we are still critical. It is the decision to work closely, wherever possible, with Shelter. We do not deny the tremendous service Des Wilson has done in highlighting the appalling housing conditions under which many people have been living for three decades or more, but the fact remains that Shelter is short, in our view, of any practical solution on how to remedy the situation. Indeed, the solutions which they do advocate would tend to derogate from the powers of local government and concentrate on further centralisation. This in principle must be resisted although we admit so far as slum clearance is concerned it may be necessary but it is certainly not Tory Party policy at the moment. We therefore have reservations concerning the Shelter affiliation.

Perhaps the biggest single issue, however, with which we find ourselves in disagreement with the GLYC Executive is the vexed subject of Ulster. Whether the GLYC Executive likes it or not our party is the Conservative and Unionist Party and Northern Irish representation in the Westminster Parliament is as fundamental to our constitutional position as the representation of any other proportionate area in England, Scotland or Wales. That is an undeniable truth to which the GLYC executive, in our view, appears to have paid scant regard in issuing their recent memorandum on the subject of Northern Ireland to the Home Secretary. This memorandum stated that: "The Home Secretary should publicly recommend to the Orange Order that, in the interest of good community relations they voluntarily cancel the 12 July commemorations". The memorandum also stated that "there should be an insistence upon publicly declared deadlines for the completion of reforms in the fields of housing and local government".

We have some general observations to make on this memorandum. We consider that the problems of Ulster are primarily political and that a solution to them would automatically lead to greater religious toleration and acceptance of the Catholic minority with the same rights and opportunities as the Protestants. The GLYC executive on the other hand seems quite certain that religion is the predominating factor. To accept their viewpoint is to misunderstand the whole nature of Irish constitutional development since the creation of the Irish Free State in 1916. The border was created, and the Government of Ireland Act 1920 passed, with the express intention of preserving for the Northern Irish their historic links in allegiance to the British Crown. The division was seen as the best solution to a seemingly intractable problem and the two Irelands today are no different in constitutional status than the two Germanys.

If there is to be a re-unification of Ireland, as with Germany, it can only come by express agreement of the two sovereign parliaments of both states without outside pressure. This is why the GLYC memorandum is absurd because it seriously contemplates the exertion of pressure by Westminster to bring about reforms which can only be implemented by Stormont. Westminster has no power in the matter; it therefore has no responsibility.

Accepted that the root of the problem is political, the religious side of the issue has only taken on a growing significance because the Northern Irish Protestants are convinced, rightly or wrongly, that forces are at work, and always have been at work, which seek to overthrow the State of Ulster by unconstitutional means from outside and to destroy the fabric of that State and by necessary implication its Protestant heritage.

To the extent that subversive organisations such as the IRA and People's Democracy are at work in the Republic the fears of the Northern Irish Protestants are well founded, and it explains why successive Northern Irish Governments have been slow to accede to the just demands of the Catholics in the North for better housing conditions and the improved political status which goes with it.

The solution to the problems of Northern Ireland are less complex than many consider. A firm and unequivocal declaration of intent by the Northern Irish Catholic minority to work the Government of Ireland Act 1920 and to convince the Stormont Government of their sincerity would go a long way to bringing about the redress of many of their grievances. It is, it seems, vital that the political framework for a settlement first be established. That done, the religious differences which now loom large would considerably diminish, if not disappear altogether.

Postscript comment: December 2016

In my article (above) I have written that the biggest issue upon which the St Marylebone YCs differed from the Greater London YC leadership was that of Northern Ireland. My reasons, including other vexed matters, are set down therein. Harold Wilson, former Labour Prime Minister (1964 – 1970; 1974 – 1976) once famously stated: "A week in politics is a long time". How true, particularly when a long passage of time is accompanied by factionalism and unending violence. This has, of course, been the experience of warfare throughout history. A fundamental re-think was required. My own trenchant views would need to change. The Anglo-Irish Agreement of November 1985, signed at Hillsborough Castle, was the catalyst. It conferred upon the Republic of Ireland, a foreign power, a consultative rôle in the affairs of Northern Ireland, part of another foreign power, Great Britain.

This was not only remarkable in itself but also in that it appeared to be paving the way for establishing a condominium/joint sovereignty solution. Both governments would participate in planning. Certainly the London and Dublin governments expressed their intentions to work closely together. Essentially, the agreement was formalisation of inter-governmental co-operation motivated by the need to secure a lasting peace, however complicated and difficult. One of the preliminary aims was to draw Irish nationalist support away from Sinn Fein.

The Agreement was not without its casualties. Ian Gow, a Treasury Minister (murdered by an IRA car bomb at his home in Sussex on 30 July 1990), resigned in protest over the A-IA and Enoch Powell was highly critical of Prime Minister Thatcher. Having given her strong parliamentary praise over her conduct of the Falklands War in 1982, Enoch declared in a press release that the Iron Lady appeared to have lost much of her "ferrous qualities".

Unionist opinion was firmly opposed but the agreement weathered the storm that erupted and within three years Sinn Fein and the SDLP began talks with a view to achieving a common nationalist position. Entrenched views were giving way to the need for compromise. I supported this development because the alternatives could only mean unending violence and misery. It is unconstructive and myopic to hold fast to an intractable and untenable position. The sentiment behind John Lennon's adage: "Give peace a chance", turned into a song, in my opinion had a profound meaning in the context of the need for a cessation of conflict.

The Anglo-Irish Agreement was assuredly the precursor of the Good Friday Agreement, signed on 10 April 1998. It could not have seen the light of day without the 1985 accord. By the end of 1997 an IRA ceasefire was in place. Prime Minister Blair and Secretary of State for Northern Ireland Mo Mowlam with President Clinton and Irish Prime Minister Bertie Ahern all used their good-offices to bolster the 'peace process'. All-party talks re-started. A strictly ideological outcome was no longer appropriate. As with Vietnam, this was a 'no-win' war.

The Good Friday Agreement was unquestionably the most important document ever signed in Northern Ireland, bringing with it a devolved assembly; power sharing; representation of all the main parties, with a framework of committees dealing with specific content. The value of the work of George Mitchell and General de Chastelain cannot be overstated. Northern Ireland had become a happier place. Nor should the part of Dr Ian Paisley and Martin McGuinness be underplayed – an astonishing and remarkable change of heart by both and a triumph of reason and good faith over the hopelessness of the blind alley.

The UN – Idealism thwarted by ineffectiveness

I wrote this piece for the Winter 1970 quarterly journal *Monday World*, published by the Monday Club. The United Nations organisation has always interested me. One of my degree subjects was international law for which a detailed knowledge of the content and application of the UN charter was required. I have always been opposed to war, my views bordering on pacifism. Securing the peace of the world is more than a mere option. It has sometimes seemed otherwise, for instance the Blair/Bush gung-ho attitude towards Iraq. Despite its efforts, an overall assessment 46 years on is that the UN has been largely unsuccessful. A major deficit has been the lack of a sanction to enforce its will. This has been one of several failings which I describe in my article. It is difficult to see a way forward for the UN without major changes to its charter including, possibly, a revised view of the need for the veto. A future realisation of world peace will be more likely if the processes of conciliation, and for that matter reconciliation, are pursued with greater urgency and passion as much within nations as between nations, something which currently is inhibited by the UN's lack of authority under its charter because of domestic jurisdiction barriers.

In the aftermath of the Second World War it was inevitable and right that an attempt should be made to finally win for the world a lasting peace in the realisation that, with the development of modern science, a Third World War would destroy civilisation as we know it. In the preamble to the United Nations Charter the signatory nations recognised this factor and declared their intent "to save succeeding generations from the scourge of war which twice in our lifetime has brought untold sorrow to mankind …."

In this article an examination is made of the extent to which the United Nations has succeeded, if at all, in achieving its primary objective of maintaining international peace and security.

The initial drafts of the Charter were prepared by the Soviet expert Molotov with the assistance of an American, Alger Hiss, at Dumbarton Oaks in 1944. In February 1945, at the Yalta Conference, further progress was made and the final draft was completed at San Francisco in June 1945. Alger Hiss, a Harvard University graduate, had a succession of American Government posts culminating in his appointment as Director of the Post-War Planning Division in the State Department. He was instrumental in recruiting most of the former employees of the United Nations Secretariat. When President Roosevelt died on the eve of the San Francisco Conference it was Hiss who attended as Acting Secretary-General. The full story of Hiss' imprisonment for perjury before a Grand Jury while being questioned about his Communist activities is well known and does not need recounting in full here. Suffice it to say he had been a leading Soviet agent for some time as indeed had the Treasury Department's representative at the San Francisco Conference, Harry Dexter White, convicted of having transmitted stolen documents belonging to the American Government to the Kremlin. Also well documented is the fact that many Americans employed by the United Nations in its early days took the Fifth Amendment when questioned about their Communist affiliations by the American Senate's Sub-Committee on Internal Security.

Such then was the background to the framing of the UN Charter. It would be accurate to deduce from these facts that the Charter reflected in its wording basically anti-Western attitudes but it would be unrealistic to conclude that *ipso facto* such attitudes were all-pervasive for the good reason that the Great Powers (Russia, America, Great Britain, France and

Nationalist China) were accorded a privileged position in view of their status by being given permanent seats at the Security Council and therefore it was always in their power to veto any decision at variance with principles of national sovereignty or national interest as they saw it.

Under the Charter the authority for decision-taking is Article 39 which provides that the Security Council shall determine the existence of any threat to the peace, breach of the peace, or act of aggression and shall make recommendations or decide what measures shall be taken .... to maintain or restore international peace and security. We might recall that the Soviet Union as a so-called 'peace loving nation', a requisite for UN admission, had prior to 1945 already swallowed up Estonia, Latvia and Lithuania, and taken the Karelian Isthmus from its potentially dangerous neighbour, Finland. The Security Council had thus been forewarned. Yet it did precisely nothing between the years 1946-1950 when Soviet acts of aggression included: the occupation of the Sakhalin and Kurile Islands in the Pacific, the illegal creation of the Peoples Republic of Mongolia, the subjugation of Albania, Yugoslavia, Rumania, Bulgaria and Czechoslovakia.

Was there some escape clause whereby the UN was prevented from taking action in these instances? Did they come within the 'domestic jurisdiction' clause of Article 2(7), which provides that "Nothing in the present charter shall authorise the UN to intervene in matters which are essentially within the domestic jurisdiction of any State or shall require the members to submit such matters to settlement under the present Charter"? The answer is a clear negative. The UN allowed these flagrant breaches of its Charter to occur without the slightest promise of effective action.

On the other hand the UN action in Korea can be regarded as a success. With a strong contingent of European infantry supporting American infantry, the war would have been effectively ended in December 1950 but for Chinese intervention on the side of North Korea prolonging it for a further 2½ years. The UN achievement in the face of aggression was remarkable, moreover, because the Soviet delegate at the UN, Vishinsky, by his absence from the meeting convened to pass the resolution under Article 39, claimed that absence was the equivalent of abstention and that therefore the UN action had been illegal for want of the "concurring vote of all the Permanent Members" as required by the Charter. This tactic failed and it is to the UN's credit here that it was not deterred from taking effective action.

Since the Korean war, however, the UN has reverted to form and its efforts have been decidedly unhappy. The year 1956 witnessed two events of immense consequence, the one immediately following the other. First the Suez crisis which really marked the turning point in British foreign prestige. The British and French delegates to the Security Council had vetoed the Security Council's resolution and national interest demanded that the concept of national sovereignty in a just cause take preference over internationalism. Confronted with the veto the Security Council could do nothing but under heavy American pressure and the 'Uniting for Peace Resolution' the General Assembly was enabled to effect a cease-fire. The full calamitous result of British and French submission is seen today in the present confusion and unrest in the Middle East.

The second event was the Soviet onslaught on Hungary. The UN's inability to act during the Hungarian Crisis fully demonstrated its principal weakness – its lack of an effective sanction to enforce its will. In October 1956 the heroic Hungarians for nine days threw off the yoke of Soviet oppression until the Soviets returned with tanks and artillery to crush the Hungarian resistance, shooting women and children in the streets in one of the greatest crimes ever committed against a civilian population. What did the UN do? Admittedly it was pre-occupied with the Suez crisis but if the world's foremost so-called peace-keeping organisation is incapable of giving sufficient attention to two matters at once it is unworthy of its high calling. It is true that the General Assembly eventually passed a resolution "calling upon the Soviet Union to desist forthwith from all armed attack" and "requests the Secretary-General to investigate the situation" but by then it was too late and ineffectual.

The UN operation in Katanga was a classic example of illegality. If ever there was an instance of the 'domestic jurisdiction' clause of Article 2(7) precluding the UN from interfering it was here. A similar factual situation has occurred in Biafra where the UN, correctly, deemed the matter one of 'domestic jurisdiction' between Nigeria and Biafra and kept out. So they should have done in Katanga where Moise Tshombe, the only outstanding statesman yet produced from

Independent Africa, was merely asserting the right of Katanga to secede from the utterly corrupt pro-Communist régime of Lumumba in the Congo.

The UN sent troops, tanks and bombers with a crushing display of military might against little Katanga. Why did the UN do this? The reason is quite clear. Tshombe represented Western interests in the Congo. He was unyielding in his anti-Communism and forthright in his demands that the Katangese be allowed a measure of self-determination. This was too much for the biff-boys of the UN force whose brutality in this operation should never be overlooked. The full story has been told by the Swedish General Van Horn who from his position at the front admitted how ashamed he was to have at his command such an undisciplined rabble of an Army conscripted largely from Afro-Asian countries hostile to the West.

The UN action in Katanga created the precedent for its shameful intervention, albeit in the economic and not military sense, in Rhodesia. On 11 November 1965, Ian Smith, Prime Minister of Rhodesia, after protracted and unproductive negotiations with successive British governments unilaterally declared Rhodesia independent of Britain. Rhodesia was already virtually independent as she had been a self-governing colony since 1923. At first, Labour, confident of the expertise of Wilsonian diplomacy, decided that this was a dispute between two countries, Britain and Rhodesia. Mr Wilson clearly preferred to gain some personal prestige from the inevitable collapse, according to his fatuous boast, of the Rhodesian economy 'in a matter of weeks, not months'. It was only when it became apparent that these naughty Rhodesians were beating sanctions by the application of nationalist economic principles that Wilson referred the matter to the UN. The extent of the illegality with which the UN assumed jurisdiction should not be understated. It was mammoth.

First, it was claimed under Article 39 that Rhodesia was a "threat to international peace" – clearly utter nonsense. As Lord Conesford observed in the House of Lords debate shortly after the imposition of UN sanctions: "The action taken under Article 39 was wrong. No precedent whatsoever can be found for the action of the Security Council in this case. I doubt whether the precedent set is yet understood and appreciated by some of the Great Powers who either concurred in or voted for that action.

To give an example I wonder whether it is generally understood in the United States that should there be unfortunately, at some future occasion, racial riots in Los Angeles, there is no reason whatsoever why the matter should not be brought before the Security Council on the precedent that is now being set." A chilling thought indeed.

Secondly, Article 32 provides that "Any member of the UN which is not a member of the Security Council or any State which is not a member of UN, if it is a party to a dispute under consideration by Security Council, shall be invited to participate, without vote, in the discussion relating to the dispute. Was Rhodesia invited to participate? No, she was not.

Thirdly, if, as was claimed, Rhodesia was a British colony then the matter was within the 'domestic jurisdiction' clause of Article 2(7) and outside the UN's jurisdiction.

Fourth, the conciliation procedures required by Article 33 were not observed, nor was the dispute referred to the International Court as recommended by Article 36(3).

Fifth, the resolution calling for mandatory sanctions did not receive the concurring votes of all the permanent members of the Security Council as required by Article 27(3).

The United Nations' 25 years history has, it seems, been marked with no greater distinction than that of its shorter-lived predecessor, the League of Nations. Its lack of effective sanction has already been noted but more startling is its apparent readiness to breach its own charter in the pursuit of internationalist ideology. Perhaps this is more readily explicable when we consider that of three Secretaries-General all three have been dedicated socialists: Trygve Lie, the Norwegian socialist, Dag Hammarskjold, the Swedish socialist, and U Thant, the Burmese socialist.

If the continent of Europe should ever become politically federated one of the fruitful products will be the creation of a third Power bloc in the world which may, and we hope will, be able to maintain the balance of power in the world – something which the UN for reasons we have seen, despite its pretence of lofty idealism, has signally failed to do. The UN's role in such an event could then be revised. It would remain as a venue for the letting off of political steam but the power of decision-taking would by force of the new power structure be removed from it.

Subversion on a grand scale

For three years, from the beginning of 1972 to the end of 1974 I made a detailed study of the left in Britain. I had become convinced of two things: that the Conservative Party knew very little about the subject and seemed content to rely upon other independent organisations to do their own research; and, secondly, that most people would tend to mutter to themselves, if confronted with suggestions of communist influence in the unions and public life, that this must be some sort of re-run of the McCarthyite[5] witchhunts of the late 1940s and early 1950s in America and that the entire issue was small-scale and not likely to threaten our own democratic way of life or our national institutions.

At least Harold Wilson seemed to know otherwise. He was Prime Minister at the time in 1966 during the national seamen's strike of that year. He declared that the strike was run by "a tightly-knit group of politically-motivated men" under the control of the Communist Party's industrial organiser, Bert Ramelson. The Labour Party itself was sufficiently aware of the high possibility of infiltration from outside elements that it had long established its own

---

5 A reference to Senator Joe McCarthy's search, often unscrupulous, for communists within key positions in America and therefore considered to be a danger to national security. Real or alleged demeanours came within the ambit of McCarthy's Senate House Un-American Activities.

proscribed list of organisations, all of them with enticing and benevolent-sounding names such as the British Peace Committee. The phrase 'fellow travellers' had become firmly embedded in popular parlance.

I had the good fortune to meet up with a remarkable man by the name of Jack Hill, a former Labour Party agent who used the pseudonym David Williams to write articles on subversive influences for an organisation called Common Cause. They were dedicated to publishing commentaries on how the left were punching well above their weight. Other organisations in this field were Industrial Research and Information Services (IRIS) and the Economic League, which was mainly an employer's information service.

Hill had an astonishing memory for names, places and organisations which he stored in his head. A huge amount of material was retained there by him. He told me one day that he knew the names and history of the 4,000 Communist Party members living in London. I used to see him twice a week to help with his work, usually for one hour.

I was delighted when before long he said to me: "your memory is beginning to rival mine". He was almost certainly in touch with Special Branch and probably MI.5 which he used to knowingly refer to as DI.5.

At this time, I was speaking on the subject of 'subversion', as it was then known, to many Conservative Party constituencies. In May 1974 I was invited by Ian Gilmour MP, Chairman of the parliamentary Home Affairs Committee, to address its members on the extent of the problem. I had also become a contributor of articles and was responsible for the 1974 document *The Hidden Face of the Labour Party*. Some of my writing in this field of work I have reproduced in this book which reflects the scale of the problems, including the rôle played by Trotskyist organisations, ideologically to the left of the Communist Party, so named after Leon Trotsky, who was expelled from the Politburo of the Communist Party on Stalin's orders for 'ideological deviation' in November 1927.

(i) Militant's invasion of the Labour Party

Hereunder, is my first piece concerning the *Militant* Group's involvement with the Labour Party, being an entire booklet written by me for Movement for True Industrial Democracy (TRUEMID), published by Trueline Publications in September 1975.

Events of the past year within certain constituency Labour parties where concerted attempts have been and are still being made to dislodge incumbent MPs points to the fragile nature of our democratic system and the importance which we must attach to the preservation of our constitutional freedom from the attacks of those who would seek to destroy it.

The immediate impact of the struggles inside the Newham North-East Labour Party and the pressures being brought to bear upon moderate Labour MPs from unrepresentative minorities in recent months has had the salutary effect of highlighting and alerting the silent majority to the true nature, degree and extent of the subversive challenge.

According to *The Times* [6], even the Prime Minister, Mr Callaghan, at one point declared his intention to challenge left-wingers in the management committee of his Cardiff South-East constituency, and informed his local party that if dissidents succeeded in gaining a majority on the management committee he would resign both as Foreign Secretary and MP. The campaign against Mr Callaghan, which received less publicity than that against Mr Prentice but which was no less sinister in its implications, was organised by a lecturer and former Young Socialist officer, Andrew Price. Price claimed that 14 members of the management committee had signed a letter of support to their counterparts in Newham North-East supporting the decision to drop Reg Prentice.

The ostensible reasons for dissatisfaction with Mr Callaghan were his failure to support the beleaguered Clay Cross councillors; his support for membership of the Common

---

6 Report – 29 August 1975.

Market; his failure to speak up for the imprisoned Shrewsbury pickets (now only one, Des Warren), and his association with the Julian Hodge Commercial Bank of Wales.

These reasons illustrate that the nature of the attack is not upon the abilities, competence or effectiveness of an MP in serving his constituents but because of an unwillingness to defer to marxist aspirations; in other words, the attack is purely ideological. The Labour MP for Hammersmith North, Frank Tomney, who succeeded the late marxist D N Pritt QC in 1950, is under sustained attack for much the same reasons. After four or five attempts to depose him the militants have won the first round at management committee level.

The Minister of State for Defence, William Rodgers, in a speech to constituents at Stockton on 28 August 1975 spoke of an "ugly threat to the party which required a tough response". He put the matter in perspective: "There is no denying that a relatively small number of activists, many of them new to the party but rich in experience of fringe politics are now seeking positions of power. They do not share the democratic assumptions of the legitimate left. They will use them, however, as allies and front men. But they despise their values and are contemptuous of their record".

Although a number of suggestions have been made for placating extremist opinion, including the setting up of a joint NEC – Parliamentary Labour Party conciliation committee to find common ground between an MP and his constituency party, majority moderate opinion takes the view that while the National Executive has a standing in such disputes, the very nature of his representative capacity means that an MP's first obligation is to his parliamentary colleagues and, in the last analysis, he cannot be seen merely as a mandated delegate.

Moreover, conciliation may be possible where there is a dispute on policy providing there are certain shared common assumptions between MP and management committee; it becomes impossible where a divergence of view is such as to go to the very nature of the role of the Labour party in democratic society. And it is this factor which has such ominous portents in the present struggles within constituencies and which is so unrelated to the earlier debate between Aneurin Bevan and Hugh Gaitskell which could be, and was, solved within a broad framework of shared aims.

It is noteworthy that the Social Democratic Alliance, a strong force for moderation, is unimpressed by attempts to reconcile the irreconcilable. In its first newsletter [7] it called upon Transport House to put an end to Trotskyist infiltration: "Anyone who has knowledge of these groups will know the extent to which they will go to misrepresent and distort the views of loyal Labour MPs and the difficulty of dealing with them in political arguments because of the phoney means they use to conceal their real views".

Identifying the nature of the problem and the extent of the penetration is one thing: taking effective remedial action is another, not least because of the extreme difficulty in democratic society of justifying what would in practice amount to proscription. Nevertheless the seriousness of the position of a number of MPs is such as to warrant a drastic re-assessment of the available options in dealing with the threat. Amongst those MPs faced with Trotskyist elements on their management committees are: Sir Arthur Irvine (Liverpool Edgehill), Jack Dunnett (Nottingham East), Eric Ogden (Liverpool, West Derby), Neville Sandelson (Hillingdon), Ben Ford (Bradford North), Edward Lyons (Bradford West), Richard Crawshaw (Liverpool, Toxteth), Roy Hattersley (Birmingham, Sparkbrook) and Pat Duffy (Sheffield, Attercliffe).

Conflicting opinions as to the true danger to democracy posed by Trotskyism has inhibited Transport House hitherto from conducting its own internal investigation. One faction is reported [8] as asserting that a very serious penetration of the Labour Party Young Socialists and constituency management committees has, in fact, taken place. Another faction is more sceptical. Transport House views with particular concern [9] the activities of the Revolutionary Socialist League, which it admits to being a clandestine organisation within the Labour Party, dedicated to the destruction of parliamentary democracy through the break-up of the party and the creation of a mass revolutionary party in its place round a left-wing rump. Headquarters officials say [10] they have no direct evidence that those in the league hold dual membership of the Labour Party

---

7 Report *The Times* – 21 August 1975.

8 Report *The Times* – 2 September 1975.

9 Ibid.

10 Ibid.

but there can be little doubt that in some areas this is the case and unquestionably many of those associated with the Trotskyist paper *Militant* are active in constituency Labour parties. Transport House puts a figure of 1,000 active Trotskyists within 10 of the 11 regional organisations of the Labour Party.

The process of penetration and infiltration is inextricably tied up with the Fourth International, the foundations for which were laid by Leon Trotsky in 1938. At its Third World Congress in 1951 in Paris the Fourth International was reformed with 27 affiliated sections. The prime mover in re-establishing the movement was Michael Pablo, a Greek who worked as a factory employee in Britain throughout the war.

Arising out of the post-war tensions between European Communist Parties and the Soviet Union which it sought to exploit to the full, the Third Congress adopted a number of political objectives. It decided that the existing Trotskyists in each country should group themselves into an 'experienced cadre' and become fully integrated in the real mass movement. The view taken was that where the revolutionary spirit was independent of either 'reformism' or 'Stalinism' they could form the core of an authentic revolutionary party, for example as in America. In England and Australia they must become integrated in the social-democratic movement, i.e. the Labour Party. In 'Stalinist' dominated countries their place would be in the Communist Party.

This approach, and the theory behind which it was sustained was rejected by Gerry Healy, leader of the then Socialist Labour League, Britain's largest Trotskyist Party, and is the reason why that movement was never accredited as the official British Section of the Fourth International. Healy considered it revisionist and a capitulation to 'Stalinism'. Those who came to accept it were described by SLL supporters as 'Pabloites'.

The major question of how best to achieve permanent infiltration was not effectively resolved until 1963 at the Seventh (Re-unification) World Congress of the Fourth International. The solution adopted was that of 'deep entry' or 'entryism' into the Labour Party, for which the Congress gave the following rationale [11]:

---

11 Papers on the problems of **entryism**. Seventh (Reunification) World Congress of the Fourth International – 1963.

> "The purpose of entryism is not to construct a pressure group, but to build a mass revolutionary Marxist Party in the real conditions that must be faced in a number of countries. The tactic is mined with dangers and difficulties and cannot be successfully carried out unless these are constantly borne in mind. But for a certain stage of work, no practical alternative remains open. Owing to national peculiarities, the tactic has many variants. It must be applied with great flexibility and without dogmatism of any kind. The moral for those engaging in it is to maintain a sector of open public work including their own publication".

So far as Britain was concerned one of the resolutions adopted declared: "The return to power of a Labour government will occur under conditions in which the masses and the militants will not tolerate without revolt a mere continuation of Tory militancy and economic policy; after a brief interval a new push will without doubt be given to the Left in the Labour Party".

The Fourth International's work in Britain during the Second World War was centred on its official British section, the Revolutionary Communist Party [12] which was wound up in 1949. The successor movement was known as the "Grant group", named after its leader, Ted Grant, a post office employee, activist in the East Islington Labour Party and formerly theoretician of the RCP.

Grant claimed that Healy and the Socialist Labour League had sacrificed many years of patient work by coming out into the open to form a political party, to which allegation Healy says that the "entryists" have become hopelessly swallowed up in the Labour Party, devoid of real influence and stripped of any identity.

There is no doubt that the Fourth International wanted its British section to have a journal, public face, and yet keep itself clandestine in accordance with theoretical requirements. It

---

12 The Revolutionary Communist Party was never proscribed to members of the Labour Party. The immediate past Chairman of the Tribune Group, Mr Sidney Bidwell MP, was a wartime member according to the Journal *International Socialism*. In the *Morning Star* of 27 March 1969, Bidwell admitted that he was a "former Young Trotskyist". On 12 March 1972 he shared a platform with the Trotskyist leader of the Workers' Revolutionary Party (then Socialist Labour League), Gerry Healy. And see further the *The Hidden Face of the Labour Party*, published by Foreign Affairs Publishing Co., February 1974, written by myself.

has been conjectured that the "Grant group" is the same organisation as the Revolutionary Socialist League but there is no conclusive evidence of this and, in a recent survey [13], the political correspondent, Nora Beloff, reported that Grant had categorically denied any association with the League and that continued assertions to this effect would lead to defamation proceedings.

Nevertheless, Grant has built around him and his paper, *Militant*, a powerful Trotskyist grouping which has been able, as will be shown, to exert pressure in several constituencies.

Associated with Grant at the inception of his group were: Arthur Dean, an administrative officer of the Chemical Workers' Union who published in the late 'fifties a monthly journal, *Socialist Fight*, which ceased publication in October 1963; Patrick Jordan, a Nottingham publisher of left-wing books, who became a close associate of Tariq Ali, leader of the International Marxist Group (which succeeded the "Grant group" as the Fourth International's British section); Ellis Hillman, a former election agent of the West Lewisham Labour Party; Peter Taafe, formerly of Hackney Central Young Socialists who used to run the *Workers' International Review (WIR) Publications*, at an address in King's Cross Road, London WC1 (now the headquarters of "Rising Free"). Taafe is the editor of *Militant*; Julian Atkinson, a former secretary of the National Association of Labour Students' Organisation; Bob Pennington, now an activist with the International Marxist Group and regular contributor to that movement's journal, *Red Weekly*; Roger Protz, former editor of *Keep Left* and later *Socialist Worker* when he transferred his allegiance to the International Socialists; Edward Mooney, of the Bootle Branch of the AEU and Colin Penfold of the Birkenhead Labour Party.

According to Miss Beloff [14], Grant made representations to Frank Chapple, General Secretary of the Electrical Telecommunications and Plumbing Union, when Chapple had just announced his retirement from the Communist Party in 1959. "Both Mr and Mrs Chapple clearly recall the visit, during which Grant tried to recruit Mr Chapple into his supposedly non-existent organisation but succeeded only in persuading him to write a few articles for the Trotskyist Press".

---

13 In **'Trot' conspirators inside Labour Party**, *Observer* – 31 August 1975.

14 Ibid.

In order to fully appreciate the position of the "Grant group" it is instructive to analyse the differences between it, the International Marxist Group and the (then) Socialist Labour League, especially since all are Trotskyist in aspiration.

The International Marxist Group became the official section of the Fourth International at the same time as the French Ligue Communiste in May 1969 at the 9th Congress of the Fourth International. In the first issue of *International*, May 1968, the IMG rationalised its position.

> "We have always stood for the united front. The method is best expressed in the creation of non-exclusive organs of struggle on important and principled issues – Vietnam Solidarity Campaign, Workers' Control Campaign. We believe that these bodies have helped to establish a new mood in the British Left, one in which people with very differing views can work together. Such a mood is vital, if we are to reverse the tendency towards fragmentation and instead work for regroupment" (that is, on the principles of the 1938 founding programme of the Fourth International)".

In contrast to the philosophy of the IMG, the position of the "Grant group" in its early formative years (which it still maintains through its organ *Militant*) shows its firm adherence to the concept of "entryism". It is summarised by the Communist Party's expert on the ultra-left, Betty Reid[15].

a) No association with such campaigns as that on Vietnam since this would divert attention from the main struggle on the economic front.

b) Trotskyists in the Vietnam Solidarity Campaign utterly failed to attack and expose the Communists in Vietnam.

c) The importance of *Militant* supporters going along to youth peace organisations and agitate for their transformations into socialist youth organisations.

d) The development of a mass movement concerned with pressure upon its government to implement

[15] In *Ultra-Leftism in Britain*, by Betty Reid, 1969 Communist Party, price 25p.

progressive policies is regarded as totally irrelevant. Appeal must be to the international working class for socialist revolution.

e) The setting up of separate Trotskyist organisations is sectarian and fruitless. The masses of the workers will need to re-learn all the lessons of the 'twenties and 'thirties by painful experience, and then they will turn to the traditional mass organisations – the Labour Party and the trade unions. It will then be for the Marxists to intervene in the mass left-wings which will be created in order to leaven them with Marxist ideas.

f) Criticism of other Trotskyist groups which soft-pedal their criticism of Communism and particularly of the Communist countries, the "Grant group" being firmly committed to constant attack upon governments and parties of these socialist states.

The Workers' Revolutionary Party's position was clearly outlined in an article in its daily journal, *Workers' Press*, of 29 April 1974 by Michael Banda[16]. On the subject of working class youth, Banda postulates two directions, mutually irreconcilable; first, "a principled and implacable struggle to build an alternative leadership to reformism and Stalinism: to break the working class and youth from their reactionary, collaborationist policies ... and building the Workers' Revolutionary Party as the essential condition for smashing the capitalist state and establishing a worker state in Britain" (the road charted out by the WRP Young Socialists at their April 1974 Conference in Blackpool); second, "the road of craven capitulation to reformism and bureaucracy, disguised by centrist phrases and a repudiation of Marxism and revolutionary leadership, so clearly expressed by the *Militant* Group.

Banda castigates Grant as an opportunist who sided with the Labour Party "witchhunt" of certain constituencies, in the late 'fifties, and voted for the expulsion of Bill Hunter, executive member, at that time, of the British section of the Fourth International, from the North Islington Labour Party.

---

16 Also known as Michael Vander Poorten, a Ceylonese. He was former editor of *The Newsletter*, the predecessor of the *Workers Press* which has itself been superseded by *Newsline*.

Banda dismisses [17] Grant "as a consummate distorter of Marxism and a barefaced and craven apologist for counter-revolutionary social-democracy". No less scathing in their attacks on Grant and his followers were the International Marxist Group. Nora Beloff [18] has written how Bob Pennington, in an updated handwritten memorandum of 1965, declared that "Grant & Co should be put out of the International (they haven't paid one penny in subs for years) because they refuse to accept the policies of a majority and because they are not really a Trotskyist tendency". And put out they were – four years later!

There is at present, among moderate opinion, considerable anxiety about the extent to which the *Militant* faction has penetrated the Labour Party Young Socialists. In a recent authoritative article [19] it is revealed that of the 18 regions, 17 are Marxist-dominated. As yet West Midlands region is not under Marxist control but 7 of the 11 Birmingham City's LPYS branches have so gone – Northfield, Perry Barr, Sparkbrook, Erdington, Sutton Coldfield, Handsworth and Edgbaston. The Marxists, supporters of the *Militant* faction, are concentrating behind the "Birmingham Labour Party Defence of the Manifesto Campaign". Labour Party officials are worried not only at the extent of the penetration but the speed at which it is taking place. In practical terms it can only serve to weaken the position of moderate MPs because, through the medium of the constituency management committee, LPYS representatives help to determine the type of MP which a constituency gets.

There is undoubtedly a fierce struggle going on in the LPYS about the role of the movement, its relationship with the senior party and the type of socialism which it wants to see introduced in Britain. Some of this debate took place in the correspondence columns of the left-wing weekly paper, *Tribune,* in May and June 1974.

The Editor of the LPYS paper, *Left,* Bob Labi, in an article in *Tribune* on 3 May 1974, wrote that over 1,600 were present at the National Conference in 1974, an increase of 50 per cent over the previous year. On the other hand the number of branches

---

17 Ibid.

18 In *The Observer* article – 31 August 1975.

19 **Marxist campaign to oust Labour's Midland moderates** by Gerard Kemp, 9 September 1975 – *The Daily Telegraph.*

had fallen from 385 to 346 during that year. He reported that Chairman for the year, Andy Bevan, had expressed utmost confidence that the LPYS's Marxist programme would find a larger and better reception inside the Labour movement, and that LPYS would be in the vanguard of the national battle for a socialist Britain.

In the 17 May 1974 edition of *Tribune*, Ian Davidson, of the Scottish Regional Committee of the LPYS expressed his extreme dissatisfaction with the movement's development and the strong Trotskyist influence. He wrote in a letter to the paper: "The group involved this time, the Revolutionary Socialist League, its existence denied of course, with its newspaper *Militant*, while somewhat more subtle than the Socialist Labour League, nevertheless exhibits all the classic signs of an entryist sect".

Davidson complained bitterly of the internal dissent, the constant bickering which had replaced reasoned discussion, and the upsurge of factionalism, disunity and the ultimate disillusion of those who believe the revolution should now be upon us.

Strong support for this view came in a letter to *Tribune* of 31 May 1974 from George Howarth, a member of the North West Regional Committee, LPYS Huyton. He wrote: "Let us not continue to delude ourselves; they (Militant faction) exist solely to smash the existing structure of the Labour Party and trade union movement, and their presence is in no way beneficial to our activities since they see themselves as an entirely separate force". Howarth claimed, however, that as they had as yet made no inroads into the factories and trade union branches they could hardly claim to be the broad base of the 'proletarian revolution'.

Yet further light on the internal rift within the LPYS was shed by a letter from Marie Bridge, of Tackley, Oxford, to *Tribune* in the same issue. She declared that she had joined the Labour Party four months previously and had been a regular subscriber both to *Militant* and *Tribune*; she could thus claim the status of impartial observer in stating that the fundamental philosophy of the socialist programme in Clause IV of the Labour Party's constitution was acceptable to both Tribunites and *Militant* supporters. She concluded that since the recommendations of the *Militant*-dominated National Committee were carried by a majority of around 10-1 democracy was seen to be working.

Both Labi, in answer to Davidson's attack, re-asserted the *Militant* argument in a letter to *Tribune* on 7 June 1974. He stated that Davidson's attack stemmed from Davidson's annoyance that *Militant* supporters had won a majority in the National Organisation of Labour Students, NOLS, of which he was an ex-chairman. Labi claimed that the organisation was growing fast and cites as evidence the fact that 3,000 people took part in the LPYS "March against racialism" in Bradford on 18 May 1975, an increase of 50 per cent on the previous demonstration. Labi goes on to bitterly attack Davidson for his personal unwillingness to sell *Left* when the NOLS Secretary asked him to do so during the April 1974 NUS London demonstration. "We believe (*Militant* faction) it is vital that the Labour Government stops trying to manage the capitalist system and carries out the socialist transformation of society", he concluded.

On 14 June a letter of support for Labi in the same paper came from Gerry Lerner, Chairman of the North West Regional Committee of LPYS, but the most devastating indictment of the whole *Militant* approach came in a letter from Frank Sykes, former Yorkshire organiser of LPYS, now active in the West Midlands. He claimed that the West Midlands was now the only region free from *Militant* domination, and that since the expansion of *Militant* influence in Yorkshire, branch membership had dropped by up to one-third. He went on: "relationships with the local parties have been soured for years to come, as they were by the infiltration of the former SLL in the early 1960s ... Many young trade unionists and students are repelled by the dogmatic policies of *Militant*. As a trade unionist I am particularly concerned about *Militant*'s new 'initiative' inside the trade union movement. Those of us who have spent years trying to build a viable youth movement are tired of seeing our work destroyed. We demand that there be a full NEC enquiry into the youth movement including NOLS so that our work will not have been in vain".

This slashing attack led to a letter in *Tribune* on 21 June 1974 from Paul Gerrard, Chairman of Yorkshire LPYS and secretary of its Huddersfield branch, defending the *Militant* position. He observed that Brian Ingham, a *Militant* supporter and regular contributor to the paper, had won the LPYS National Committee place by 14 votes to four, that not one LPYS branch had been closed down and that in Yorkshire alone eight new branches had been set up, including those at Leeds, Sheffield, Halifax, Dewsbury, Elland and Bridlington. Gerrard claimed, moreover, that relations between the LPYS and the party at regional and local level had never been better, and that suggestions that the NEC should institute an enquiry into the youth movement were absurd and frivolous.

Whatever the arguments and counter-arguments revealed in this correspondence may prove, official statistics show that LPYS branches have seriously declined in a short space of time – 485 in 1972, 366 in 1973 and 346 in 1974. Further, the attendance of delegates at National Conference has declined, the figures in those three years being respectively 202, 181 and 182. According to a member of Edgware LPYS, M V Shuck in a letter to *Tribune* of 21 June 1974, the figure of 182 would have been much lower had not regional delegates gone round pleading with people to come. Shuck declared: "Clacton 1974 was not so much a conference as a ritual gathering of *Militant* hacks dancing a pow-wow round the LPYS funeral pyre".

That the *Militant* faction has a very strong influence within LPYS is demonstrably proven. Undoubtedly it could not have achieved its position without a journal, as predicted by Trotskyist theorists. For many years, however, the relationship between Grant and his followers and the Revolutionary Socialist League has been clouded in obscurity. Much of the evidence is intangible although Nora Beloff [20] confidently asserts: "Not all the young enthusiasts who sell *Militant* and go to *Militant* meetings belong to the inner circle of conspirators and until they have done at least nine months, or a year, of dedicated work they are unlikely even to be told that the RSL even exists".

Whether or not the Revolutionary Socialist League exists or does not exist is largely immaterial. What is significant is that a co-ordinated group of Trotskyists, dedicated to the practice of 'entryism', united in their leadership and with an ideology fundamentally opposed to social democracy, upon which the Labour Party was founded, has seriously penetrated that party.

The *Militant* Group in 1971 moved from their original headquarters at 197 King's Cross Road and bought their own press and premises. *Militant* is currently edited by Peter Taafe, has as its business manager Dave Galashan, and is printed by Cambridge Heath Press Ltd (TU) at 375 Cambridge Heath Road, London E2.

---

20 *The Observer* article – 31 August 1975.

The 29 August 1975 edition of *Militant* advertised a meeting to be held at the annual TUC Conference at Blackpool on 3 September, under the theme: "No redundancies – no wage curb", to be addressed by Ray Durman, the AUEW Staff Side Convenor at Norton Villiers Triumph, Wolverhampton, and Councillor John Dunn, Secretary, Clay Cross Labour Party, with Brian Ingham of *Militant* in the chair. The same issue carries an advertisement for a public meeting of Hendon South Labour Party on 9 September 1975 addressed by Joan Maynard MP[21].

An organiser of the Birmingham Labour Party Defence of the Manifesto Campaign, Lewis Jones, wrote a letter in the same issue: "By patient debate and patient comradely argument the supporters of *Militant* have gained the majority of the LPYS to their political perspectives and their socialist programme".

In his letter Jones announced that a meeting of his campaign would be held at 7.30 pm on Tuesday 23 September at 211 Broad Street, Birmingham. Amongst those billed to speak were Judith Hart MP and Eric Heffer MP, together with Fred Griffiths, divisional organiser of the AUEW/Engineering Section, and Peter Taafe. (In his letter, however, Jones does not mention the names Judith Hart and Eric Heffer but instead says that Dennis Skinner MP will be the star speaker).

Most of the articles in *Militant* adopt a strident tone. For instance, in the 29 August edition under the heading: "Wage cuts do not save jobs", the writer declares: "Wilson, instead of going

---

21 The Left-wing Labour MP for Sheffield, Brightside, in which seat the Communist Party in the October 1974 election failed to put up a candidate for the first time since the war. Miss Maynard, a member of the NEC of the Labour Party, is the Chairman of the British Peace Committee, a Communist-front organisation which shares an office with the British-Hungarian Friendship Society in Claverton Street, London SW1. Of its 44 Council members the British Peace Committee has 30 Communists. Miss Maynard has spoken at *Morning Star* birthday rallies. In the 17 July 1975 edition of the International Marxist Group journal, *Red Weekly*, Miss Maynard, asked about her attitude to the then Prime Minister, Mr Wilson, answered: "He is not the leader I would vote for. He has never been a socialist". Stating her view about parliament she declared "... that place in London is very insidious. It's not a place, it's the other people's place, and it would be easy to forget the people you go there to represent". In the 15 August 1975 edition of *Militant*, Miss Maynard, in answer to a question by her interviewer, Brian Ingham, said: "I see my job as a Labour MP to fight against the Government policies in here, but much more important to fight these policies outside by explaining what the alternative policies must be". In answer to a question about the role of the LPYS, she declared: "They have decided, generally speaking, not to have any truck with this society ... they do a tremendous job in the Labour movement.

on TV to tell the workers to accept cuts in necessary services and real wages, could use his time on the box to really campaign and expose the rottenness of the system he has created".

Apart from propaganda through its journal, the *Militant* Group has a wide range of Trotskyist books and pamphlets. It calls these 'World Books'. It also arranges '*Militant* Readers Meetings' which are intended to develop political consciousness among readers. The 29 August edition, for example, reports that on 15 August 1975 36 people attended a meeting at East Ham Town Hall to hear Nick Bradley, of the Labour Party's NEC, and Peter Taafe speak on the theme – "No retreat – carry out Socialist Policies". It was reported that a Newham Borough Councillor expressed the sentiments of the seven delegates to Newham North-East General Management Committee when he said – "I hope that Newham North-East will not be on its own in the action that we've taken over the Prentice business. This is the type of thing that we need to see repeated in many other constituencies". The meeting, chaired by Tom Jenkins of Newham North-East LYPS, yielded £38.62 for the *Militant* Fighting Fund.

In the 15 August 1975 edition of *Militant*, a meeting was advertised to be held at Gosport, where Keith Morrell [22] was billed to speak on: "No retreat from socialist programme".

Growing evidence of *Militant*'s involvement in the unions has been the prominence given to Trade Union Day Schools. One such Day School was held, again in East London, in August, sponsored by Hawker Siddeley (Walthamstow) Shop Stewards, Hackney District Labour Shop Stewards and *Militant*, for whom Jim Brookshaw spoke on Capitalism.

Militant is no less equivocal in its attitude towards the Armed Forces. In the 29 August edition there appears a letter from Kevin Ramage, of Brentwood and Ongar LPYS – "Military forces exist for the protection of capitalism's interests from the masses, capitalism's interests being based on the exploitation of those masses ... I am sure all *Militant* readers would like to see the abolition of armed forces of any kind as soon as possible, but as long as capitalism exists, so will workers' militias, to defend the workers".

---

22 Morrell was Labour Party Candidate at St Marylebone in the June 1970 General Election and the October 1970 by-election.

Other contributors to *Militant* in recent editions have included: Pat Craven, of Queens Park Labour Party, on "Ladbrokes, Scottish workers need support urgently", an unnamed GLC Councillor on "The Cuts and London's Crisis"; Martin Ward, of Wolverhampton LPYS "The fighting mood at NVT" and Glennys Bithell, Chairman of NOLS, on the campaign by Labour students. Reporting an increase in clubs and a 100 per cent increase in membership, Miss Bithell emphasises the importance of giving more attention to the NUS As the Broad Left dominated NUS executive fails to solve the acute problems facing students many are now turning to the socialist ideas of NOLS. We have followed a policy of working closely with the LPYS, turning students towards the Labour movement where the power and strength for change solidly lies. Miss Bithell further states that a campaign will start to get the NEC of the Labour Party to re-appoint the NOLS Chairman as a full-time Officer. It has the broad support of a number of NEC members, constituency Labour parties, Labour Party regional executive committees, and LPYS and NOLS branches throughout the country. Miss Bithell emphasises that the Labour Party is the only major party without at least one full-time student officer.

Associated with *Militant* is *Militant Irish Monthly,* edited by Peter Hunt, and published by Militant Irish Monthly, 32 Brickfield Drive, Dublin 12. Its business manager is John Throne. Hunt is the author of the pamphlet, *Northern Ireland – for workers' unity*.

Concerned chiefly with industrial problems in the Irish Republic, this eight-page journal is also 'entryist' in ideology and strives to achieve an all-Ireland workers state as an integral part of a socialist revolution. The July/August 1975 edition contains an article on the Northern Ireland Convention by Eileen Cullen who asserts that it will not end sectarianism and that no solution is possible under capitalism.

The overall threat posed by Trotskyist groupings such as *Militant* ought not to be minimised. Non-believers in parliamentary democracy, they use the classic tactic of infiltration by taking advantage of the electoral processes which the system offers. By campaigning tirelessly for their own people, often by cloak-and-dagger methods, they serve to show how dedicated individuals, or groups of individuals, can find their way into key positions of influence at branch, local and national level. It is an urgent necessity that the Labour Party's internal enquiry in November takes positive action to rid the party of malign Trotskyist influences, not merely for the cause of social democracy inside the party but also for the cause of social peace and constitutional freedom.

(ii) Labour's Red Maiden

Joan Maynard's arrival in parliamentary politics is described in my article published in *Free Nation* journal, May 1977 edition. Her adoption as Labour candidate for Sheffield, Brightside, in 1974 was nothing short of a disgrace. It was less than a year earlier that the Labour Party's Executive Committee decided to abandon the proscribed organisations list. How many Trotskyists entered the Labour Party in support of Jeremy Corbyn's leadership I ask?

"That place in London is insidious" – Miss Maynard, speaking of Parliament , in an interview with *Red Weekly*, journal of the International Marxist Group (IMG), British section of the Trotskyist Fourth International.

No Member of Parliament represents so accurately, both in thought and deed, the left-wing element of the Parliamentary Labour Party as Joan Maynard, even if not in such extreme terms.

Her political career at national level first blossomed in 1956 when she was appointed agent for the constituency of Thirsk and Malton in the North Riding of Yorkshire. In the same year she achieved prominence in trade union activity when appointed Yorkshire Area Secretary of the National Union of Agricultural Workers.

In April 1970 Miss Maynard was one of four trade union leaders who gave their support to a meeting convened by the British Peace Committee (a Communist-front organisation which is the affiliate of the Moscow-sponsored World Peace Council) on the theme: "Co-operation and Security in an Undivided Europe". At the time the British Peace Committee was one of 36 movements proscribed by the Labour Party (by 1972, the year before the removal of the ban, the number of proscribed organisations had dropped to 31: in 1962 it had been 46).

In September 1970 Miss Maynard was a member of the first trade union delegation to visit Communist North Vietnam in company with Ken Gill, a leading Communist official and trade unionist in the draughtsmen's union, then known as DATA, later to become TASS. In the following February she wrote a laudatory article about North Vietnam, its people and government in *World Trade Union Movement*, the official journal of the international Communist-front World Federation of Trade Unions, whose operations are directed from Prague and channelled through the good offices of the Communist Party's industrial department, the Labour Research Department (no relation of the Labour Party Research Department) and the Communist-dominated Liaison Committee for the Defence of Trade Unions.

On 3 March 1971 the ubiquitous Joan Maynard spoke glowingly of the Vietnamese struggle against "American imperialism" at a protest meeting organised by the Communist-dominated British Campaign for Peace in Vietnam.

On 29 May 1971 she was re-elected to *the* Council of the Institute for Workers' Control, a Trotskyist foundation whose printing facilities in Nottingham are shared by the Bertrand Russell Peace Foundation and National Council for Civil Liberties.

On 10 August 1971 Miss Maynard, in one of her not infrequent incursions into the columns of the Communist *Morning Star*, wrote an article urging the Labour Party to "get rid of the ridiculous bans and proscriptions which exist in the Labour Movement ... in particular we suffer from the Marxist wing being hived off from the main body".

Two years later, on 6 August 1973, the *Morning Star* reported that Miss Maynard had been the official guest, representing the Labour Party, at the Communist World Youth Festival held in East Berlin (the British Youth Festival Committee was at that time proscribed by the Labour Party). In November 1973 the

National Executive Committee of the Labour Party, of which Miss Maynard became a member in 1970, responded to her (and others) promptings and duly lifted the ban on all hitherto proscribed organisations, which thus became 'acceptable' overnight to Labour Party members.

In January 1974 Miss Maynard became Chairman of the British Peace Committee, which has for some years shared an address with the British-Hungarian Friendship Society in Victoria. Of the BPC's 44 Council Members, 30 are known to be Communist Party members. In the same month she spoke at a Troops Out Movement rally in Manchester demanding the immediate withdrawal of British troops from Northern Ireland. The significance of this is that TOM is dominated by the International Marxist Group, the British Section of the Trotskyist Fourth International (founded in 1938). TOM, moreover, maintains very close, if unofficial, links with Official Sinn Fein and the Communist Party of Ireland.

Joan Maynard's ambition to enter parliament took a major upward turn when, as a result of constant left-wing pressure within the constituency Labour Party of Sheffield, Brightside, the sitting member, Eddie Griffiths, was ousted. Miss Maynard was adopted as official Labour candidate in his place in preparation for the October 1974 election. It is not insignificant that the Communist Party, which had put up a parliamentary candidate in that constituency in every election since the war and which had nominated as its official candidate for this election Violet Gill, a member of the 42-strong Communist Party executive committee, instructed her to withdraw (which she was pleased to do) in order to allow Joan Maynard a straight contest against Eddie Griffiths and the Conservative and Liberal candidates.

On 27 October 1974 Miss Maynard, now an MP of less than a month's standing, took part as a speaker at yet another joint-sponsored meeting of Troops Out Movement and British Peace Committee in London. She handed in a letter to 10 Downing Street calling upon Mr Wilson "to implement immediately a policy of political and military withdrawal from Ireland". As a member of the rally's organising committee she demanded the imposition of an early date for the withdrawal of British troops, a theme to which she returned in an article in the *Morning Star* of 13 August 1975 in which she declared: "The only real problem for Britain is how to relinquish power in Ireland, not how to cling to it ... there should be a clear Declaration of Intent ... that spells out the intent to dissolve the Act of Union and to withdraw all British troops".

In February 1975 Miss Maynard was due to speak at the 45th *Morning Star* Birthday Rally at the Royal Festival Hall, but illness prevented her from doing so. Sydney Bidwell, MP for Ealing, Southall, filled the breach admirably.

In the September 1975 issue of the Communist publication, *Labour Monthly*, for years edited by the Communist Party's elder statesman and leading intellectual, Rajani Palme Dutt, Miss Maynard stated that the House of Commons personified 'elitism and the establishment', and expressed the view that the Party leader should be elected at the Party conference and that all MPs should be required to submit themselves for re-selection.

She is currently President of the Campaign for Labour Party Democracy which has as its central aim the re-selection of MPs.

In an interview in the 17 July 1975 edition of *Red Weekly* Miss Maynard, asked about her attitude to Mr Wilson as Prime Minister, answered: "He is not the leader I would vote for. He has never been a socialist". Stating her view about parliament she declared "... that place is very insidious. It's not our place, it's the other people's place, and it would be easy to forget the people you go there to represent".

In the 15 August edition of the Trotskyist journal *Militant*, in answer to a question put to her by Brian Ingham, Miss Maynard stressed: "I see my job as a Labour MP to fight against the Government policies in here, but much more important to fight these policies outside by explaining what the alternative policies must be".

One might well ask what it is about Miss Joan Maynard that impels her to retain her links with the British Labour Party when she appears so avowedly to reject the essential principles and policies which inform that party's thinking. The good people of Sheffield, Brightside, should be given the opportunity to say whether they support an MP, whose views on many political issues are indistinguishable from those of the Communist Party and who has shown by her words and actions her apparent contempt for the institution wherefrom she purports to represent her constituents.

(iii) Rudi Dutschke: Multiple reasons for rejecting his claims

This article is drawn from a section of my pamphlet *Some Uncivil Liberties* written in September 1972 and published by the Monday Club. Rudi Dutschke was an extreme left-winger of German nationality who was admitted to Britain in December 1968 for medical treatment to injuries sustained from his being shot in Berlin in April 1968. He had been a long-time advocate of the use of force to overthrow capitalism. He had been granted extensions to his stay.

The crucial question had become whether the Immigration Appeals Tribunal's assessment that Dutschke's continued presence in Britain placed our national security in jeopardy was correct. Although not involved in violence himself, Dutschke supported groups with proven violent records at a time when student unrest was widespread throughout Europe. The National Council for Civil Liberties waged a substantial propaganda campaign in favour of Dutschke.

This article attempted to put into sharper focus the conflicts which arise when individual liberty is met head-on by the state's duties to the larger public interest in ensuring security and safety. My researches were lengthy and, I believe, balanced as far as they could be. I claimed that Dutschke's case was fundamentally weak for all the reasons given.

NCCL regarded the way in which the Government handled the Rudi Dutschke affair as evidence of the arrival of "McCarthyism" into this country and a classic example of retreat from normal standards of British democracy. It was, apparently, yet a further instance of the erosion of individual liberty.

It is as well to recount the full story surrounding the circumstances of Dutschke's arrival in the United Kingdom and his ultimate departure. He was admitted in December 1968 for the sole purpose of receiving medical treatment to injuries sustained when shot in Berlin in April 1968 although in October 1968 application had been made for him to pursue a university course. Dutschke himself volunteered that he would not engage in political activities were he to be admitted. Mr James Callaghan, who was then Home Secretary, agreed that Dutschke could come here for one month for medical consultations subject to that condition and, further, that he would not study at a university. These conditions had been imposed on Dutschke in the light of his known extremist political activities and his open advocacy of the use of force to overthrow capitalist society. The Dutch and French Governments had already forbidden his entry into their countries for this reason.

In January 1969 Mr Callaghan was again asked to allow Dutschke to remain in the United Kingdom for a further period of six months to continue his convalescence on the continued understanding that he would abstain from all political activity. Permission was given for this extension as it was for another extension on the same basis. Dutschke readily accepted these conditions. In January 1970 application was again made on Dutschke's behalf to Mr Callaghan for him to take a University course, which, it was freely admitted, would involve a major alteration from the conditions originally imposed upon his entry. Yet another six months extension was permitted and Dutschke was informed that if he sought at the end of this period to continue with his application for a place at a British university he should let the Home Office know the details.

It was abundantly clear that if Dutschke were to be granted permission to remain in this country it would arouse considerable misgivings amongst a substantial section of the public which was not disposed kindly towards the type of action with which he had been closely associated elsewhere. In the event Mr Callaghan was not prepared to state definitively whether or not he was willing to vary the terms on which the original permission for Dutschke's entry had been granted. In the House of Commons debate on 19 January 1971, Mr Callaghan came to expound some of the arguments which he had heard expressed in favour of Dutschke's departure from the United Kingdom: that we were in national danger; that our traditions were in danger of being undercut; that our values were being undermined; that this man should not be allowed to continue that process. All of these fears and apprehensions in the event were well founded but Mr Callaghan preferred to think of them as irrational prejudices. He was, however, prepared to admit that in the final analysis, and in different circumstances, the safety of the state is the supreme law: "I take the view that a democracy is entitled to take undemocratic action to preserve itself if the threat is at the gates. I firmly believe that a democracy cannot sit back and allow itself to be raped and destroyed by those who merely wish to use it". (Hansard H of C 1971, Vol 809, p.754).

On 13 July 1970, Mr Reginald Maudling who was now Home Secretary in the new Conservative Government received a letter of application on behalf of Dutschke for him to remain in the United Kingdom and to pursue a course of study in aspects of marxist theory at Cambridge University, under the tutelage of Professor Joan Robinson FBA, herself a veteran marxist and prominent figure in the Society for Cultural Relations with the USSR and the ultra-left Society for Anglo-Chinese Understanding, an off-shoot of the (strangely enough) pro-Moscow British-China Friendship Association. Mr Maudling took the broader view that it was wrong in principle that people who come to this country should do so on the basis that they refrain from activities which would be lawful for the ordinary citizen to engage in and accordingly decided that Dutschke should not be permitted to remain here any longer. At this point Dutschke exercised his right of appeal against Mr Maudling's decision and a special tribunal was set up under the Immigration Appeals Act and the Aliens Appeals Order made thereunder, presided over by Sir Derek Hilton, Kt, MBE, a former President of the Law Society. The Tribunal found that Dutschke had held meetings which exceeded normal social activities and that whatever his intentions may have been he did not abide by the assurances, given by him and on his behalf that he would not engage in political activities. It further found from evidence given by Dutschke himself that he had held meetings and discussions with a wide variety of people involved in political activities, some of whom he had not met before. Most of these persons, the Tribunal found, were British nationals while others were persons from overseas who had come to consult him. He had, for instance, paid a visit to Swansea during a steelworkers' strike at Port Talbot at which he sought to meet some of the strikers. His stay lasted for four days and was arranged by a Mr Sabby Sagall, a wealthy Trotskyist, prominent with the International Socialists. He had also been frequently in contact with Dr Christopher Pallis, a London neurologist, who uses the pseudonym Martin Grainger, a member of the Trotskyist Socialist Labour League's executive until 1960 when he joined the rival Trotskyist *International Socialism*'s editorial board.

On the other hand, the Tribunal found that Dutschke's presence in the United Kingdom constituted no immediate appreciable danger to national security but that it might do so could not be ruled out and indeed was a distinct possibility. Particularly, the Tribunal found that if Dutschke were to remain a student there might be serious risk in his continued presence here.

It is instructive to consider some of Dutschke's connections and associations in assessing the validity of the Tribunal's contention that he might constitute, at some future date, a danger to national security. He was Leader of the left-wing revolutionary German SDS student movement, and many of his close associates had been prominent in the Paris street riots of May 1968 which all but brought the French Government to its knees. The SDS, which is now dissolved, had played a major part in assisting deserters from the US Army and Air Force, numbering several thousand, to pass through Scandinavia. In 1967 the SDS's part in violent confrontations with the Police became even more marked, and although Dutschke himself did not take part in street violence, he made a number of inflammatory speeches asserting the right to use violence "in the fight against capitalism and imperialism". In February 1968 he addressed a large student gathering in Amsterdam where he underlined the importance of combating capitalism by anarchy and large scale internal subversion stating that "mass action might have to include the burning of NATO bases and warships in Germany".

After Dutschke had come to England to convalesce from his injuries, his political associates embarked on even more violent action. In April 1968 a large department store was gutted in Frankfurt as a result of which the perpetrators of this outrage, including Andreas Baader, a journalist on an underground newspaper, were apprehended, found guilty of arson and imprisoned. On 14 May 1970, Baader who continued his studies in prison was allowed to visit the library of the Institute for Social

Science in Berlinen-Dahlen. A group of men and women led by a Trotskyist extremist, Ulrike Meinhof, and a close friend of Dutschke, Irene Goergens, burst into the library, fired several shots wounding a librarian and two prison warders who had accompanied Baader. While the search for the gang who had escaped was going on, the groups defiantly announced in letters to newspapers that "the Bonnie and Clyde actions would be stepped up". Armed raids were carried out on an American tourist office, two banks and a supermarket and more than £50,000 was stolen. Meanwhile Dr Horst Mahler, Dutschke's West German lawyer who had by that time abandoned his legal practice after arranging Baader's escape, fled to Beirut where for many months the two of them were guests of the Palestine Liberation Front in Northern Jordan. Eventually both returned via Italy and Germany, using false passports. Mahler, Irene Goergens and four other members of the gang were arrested on 6 October 1970 in Berlin. During all these happenings, although there is no evidence that Dutschke knew of these actions or plots, it is firmly established that when Mahler's hide-out in Berlin was searched letters from Dutschke were found from which it became clear that not only had he maintained contact with Mahler and Irene Goergens when they were engaged in their armed violence but that he had known also about Baader and Mahler's visit to the Palestine guerrillas and their trips to Beirut and Jordan.

The effect of the tribunal's findings in essence was to confirm the Home Secretary's decision not to vary the original conditions which Dutschke himself had voluntarily undertaken to observe on his entry. It showed that the Home Office had abided strictly by the original agreement and sought no changes from it.

In its Annual Report for 1971 NCCL accused the Immigration Appeals Tribunal of allowing itself by "double-talk, defamation, and downright dishonesty to become the instrument for the suppression of civil liberties", a view which had received overwhelming acclaim at a meeting organised in Central Hall, Westminster, on 14 January 1971 by NCCL in conjunction with the left-wing Council for Academic Freedom and Democracy at which over 700 persons were present. The assembled faithful had come to hear the Rt Hon Richard Crossman, MP; Mr Michael Foot, MP (who five days later in one of his less happy performances was to allege in the parliamentary debate on the issue that the Home Secretary had committed an outrageous defamation of character against Mr Dutschke); Mr Jack Straw, then President of the National Union of Students; Des Wilson, then of Shelter; Mr John Pardoe, MP, of the Parliamentary Civil Liberties Group; Professor John Griffith, Chairman of CAFD and Professor of Public Law at London University; Professor Raymond Williams, a lecturer at Jesus College, Cambridge, formerly a director/shareholder of New Left Review Ltd (whose registered office at 7 Carlisle Street, W.1., used to be the Headquarters of 'Black Dwarf') and prominent in the Bertrand Russell Peace Foundation; and the Rev Paul Oestreicher, a South London vicar who is the joint author with James Klugmann, the Communist Party theoretician, of "What Kind of Revolution – a Christian-Communist dialogue".

The consensus of the meeting was forcibly expressed by NCCL's General Secretary, Tony Smythe; "There are too many frightened, disturbed people around who think that the way to defend their kind of freedom is to use the methods of dictatorship. Part of the growth of political intolerance which is now being fostered by the Home Secretary rests on the comfortable assumption that if there are problems, unrest, dissent, the causes lie not with those who make the decisions, not with what Dutschke describes as 'the critical elements', but the foreign, the insignificant number of immigrants who rightly claim equal rights for freedom of speech, thought and action while living in our society ... We have gone a long way since Britain was regarded as the traditional refuge for the victims of political and religious persecution. The next move will be the Government's new Immigration Bill. If it contains what I think it will contain, it will place thousands of people in the same precarious position as Dutschke found himself .... political violence must be opposed but judicial violence (sic) will not make that opposition any easier".

NCCL's indignation continued unabated for some weeks and in its February 1971 *Bulletin* it re-affirmed all the massive objections which it had raised at the Central Hall meeting: "The smears, the misrepresentations, the confusion between political thought and action, the trial that was not quite a trial, the telephone tapping, bugging and other activities of our own CIA. All that has been lacking is the brazenness of the senator but instead we had had Mr Maudling's speech in the House of Commons which John Pardoe, MP, called 'a monstrous performance that did no kind of honour to his office'." (Others had described it as a masterly exposition of the essential issues).

Some rather more specific objections were made by the NCCL in a Memorandum entitled "The Rudi Dutschke Case: Civil Liberty on Trial". First, it was contended that if the authorities were given power to expel Dutschke unchallenged, the way is clear for a repetition again and again. The point missed is that there was no question of Dutschke being expelled or deported. He was admitted on compassionate grounds for the specific purpose of receiving medical attention and the Home Office was unprepared to change the basis upon which he came once his treatment had been successfully completed. It was not as if Dutschke was a Commonwealth student registered as a British citizen; to that extent there was no deprivation of liberty involved.

Secondly, NCCL claimed that a new definition of 'political activity' had emerged from the Dutschke case. It could, it was argued, include meetings and discussions with a wide variety of persons involved in political activities. "If this definition prevails, and there is little indication that it will not, the threat to freedom of thought and opinion, the threat to academic life, the threat to the whole spectrum of civil liberty is very grave indeed". But can it be seriously doubted that the paramount duty of Government, subject always to Parliamentary scrutiny, is to decide who can reside in this country if he is not a British citizen? Is it now to be asserted that the overriding demands of "civil liberty" should ensure that anyone be given *carte blanche* to enter this country willy-nilly?

Thirdly, NCCL objected to the composition of the tribunal and the proceedings whereby it arrived at its decision ... "Here was the establishment and here was its very own 'Star Chamber' encrusted in secrecy and dictating its own rules". It was alleged that the qualifications for membership and the appointment of its members could by no stretch of the imagination be considered satisfactory for an appellant with political convictions, although NCCL did not state what qualifications for membership of the tribunal it *would* deem to be satisfactory. Nor did it attempt to explain what it understood by the phrase 'political convictions'.

In fact the tribunal was set up by the Labour Government and NCCL does not appear to have directed any of its objections, which it would appear to have based upon matters of principle, to that Government. Indeed, four out of five members of the tribunal were appointed by the Labour Government.

It was further argued that there was growing concern about the fact that evidence had been put forward on behalf of the Government, which had not been made available to Dutschke. The essential factor, however, is that the relevant information comes from sources which cannot be disclosed without damage to the national interest, and this is precisely why the special tribunal was set up. No security service can possibly function effectively if its sources of information are made public. Whatever inroads this proposition may make on the abstraction of civil liberty very few people would care to gainsay it. Indeed it was the precise reason why the Government, in considering the Report of the Committee set up under the Chairmanship of Lord Radcliffe to investigate *Security Procedures in the Public Service* (1962 Cmd. 1681), felt that much of the material was of a nature which it would not be in the public interest to publish. Clearly so long as there is need for a security service, and no other country has yet to find there is not, it is absurd to disclose the sources of its information upon which its effectiveness is necessarily dependent. The point was reiterated to the House of Commons by Mr Maudling during the Dutschke debate: "As the House knows it is the constant tradition of Governments not to reveal the sources from which the security services obtain their information in any case. I should certainly not, nor would anyone else, dream of departing from that tradition ... I should make it absolutely clear that every scrap of information presented to me was collected under the personal authority and approval of my predecessor". Hansard H. of C. 1971 Vol. 809, p 754).

The fourth objection registered by NCCL was that the hearing was *in camera*. It was a point also raised by Mr S Clinton Davis, Labour MP for Hackney Central, and member of the Parliamentary Civil Liberties Group in the House of Commons debate, who wanted to know why it was possible in treason trials or trials involving breaches of the Official Secrets Act, when evidence has to be given *in camera*, for it to be given in such a way that the defendant can answer it and cross-examine witnesses, and yet for Dutschke to be denied these elementary rights of the judicial system. The answer is perfectly clear. There was no question of there being a trial. The Home Office was at no point seeking a change in Dutschke's position and the case arose only because he sought to challenge the decision to refuse variation of the original terms of entry. If sources of information cannot be disclosed without substantial damage to the national interest *a fortiori* it is important that provision be made for the reference of such matters to an independent and judicially-minded body.

The fifth objection raised was that Dutschke's political freedom had been denied him. This cannot be so. Freedom had been upheld by Government for the benefit of the majority. In our modern open society where opportunities for subversion have never been greater the true threat to freedom comes from those who desire to overthrow or discredit democratic government itself, and all the available evidence showed that Dutschke fell into this category.

The sixth objection was that "the liberty of the subject was threatened". This cannot be so either. There is no question of the liberty of the subject being imperilled in the Dutschke case because he was not, and is not, a British subject and secondly his liberty was in no sense threatened.

The seventh objection is that peoples' "rights" are now being threatened as a result of the treatment meted out to Dutschke. So far as Dutschke himself is concerned he has no rights here and there is no country in the world which is prepared to recognise the right of an individual to come and settle in this country of his own free will, and the idea that the Dutschke decision has established a general principle restricting basic rights and liberties of British subjects is a manifest absurdity.

NCCL's antipathy to the conduct of the Dutschke enquiry springs partly from its underlying belief that conflict between competing concepts of individual liberty and national security should always be resolved in favour of the former. Its own phrase "civil liberty" has no precise meaning, no precise boundaries and no precise limitations, and is barely synonymous with individual liberty. In a sense this is convenient for adherents of the NCCL view because it means it can argue any case within the purely subjective interpretation of liberty which it alone recognises, and with a persuasiveness which is superficially compelling. Some of its allegations are so fanciful that it would presumably, on reflection, be prepared to disavow them. For instance, where is the evidence for the assertion that the Immigration Appeals Tribunal is guilty of "double-talk, defamation and downright dishonesty"? What can be made of the statement: "political violence must be opposed but judicial violence will not make that opposition any easier"? The use of the phrase 'judicial violence' to describe the proceedings of the tribunal, and presumably it was made in reference to the tribunal, is not only an unwarranted slur on the members of that tribunal but exemplary evidence of NCCL's tendency to use the most extravagant language to counter attitudes with which it is unable to agree.

The research arm of NCCL, the Cobden Trust, felt sufficiently incensed by the Dutschke decision and the implications which it contained for "civil liberty" that it announced its intention of investigating the methods by which the security services operate. The Trust's main concern is to know who controls them, who directs them, how much funds are available to them – something probably known to only a few civil servants in the Treasury – and the manner in which their activities and investigations intrude into privacy. Here again the conflict arises between the requirement that security should remain paramount and the freedoms and liberties which are available to all in an open society.

The identities of the men controlling MI5 and MI6 are covered by the D Notice system, which has always been regarded as an acceptable working code of what should or should not be published. There is nothing mandatory to restrict publication of material contained in these D Notices except for the legal sanctions imposed by the Official Secrets Acts which are generally confined to the protection of information about "prohibited places" and information obtained through some "wrongful communication" by or through an official. It has, however, been found that the Official Secrets Acts are not an effective instrument for controlling Press publications of that kind of information which, although perhaps not of great individual importance, it is nevertheless desirable to keep from hostile intelligence – Radcliffe Committee's Report on *Security Procedures in the Public Service* (Cmd. 1681, para 134, p 37). Such an instrument is provided by the D Notice system which is a means of voluntary censorship. The Radcliffe Committee found that the system suits both sides; it suits the Government side because it provides a centralised means of communicating requests and warnings to the Press before the damage is done and under the authority of a Committee upon which Press representatives are in a majority; and it suits the Press, because, without being mandatory, it enables an editor to know before publication that a news item is regarded by the Government as unfit for use without prejudice to the national interest (*Ibid.* para 135).

Further the system in practice has worked well. Apart from the findings of the Radcliffe Committee, the overwhelming consensus of opinion is against a change in the existing system. In view of the growing burden of the activities of Anarchists, Trotskyists, Maoists, and other revolutionaries upon our national economy is it unreasonable that aspects of national security should be placed in the category "Not open to inspection"?

The Special Branch, which comes in for so much criticism from NCCL allegedly because its necessarily secretive measures conflict with "civil liberty" is the executive arm of the Intelligence Service. It was referred to by NCCL's General Secretary as "the nasty grey area of our national life" during the course of his Central Hall, Westminster, speech on 14 January 1971. Many of the arrests made by Special Branch officers have been made on information supplied by MI5 officers. This became apparent in the trials of atom scientists Nunn May, Klaus Fuchs and also in the trial of George Blake. So far from the Special Branch being the "nasty grey area of our national life" it has provided Herculean service in tracking down the nasty grey area of espionage activity and subversive intrigue. Nor is there any evidence that the Special Branch intrudes upon the privacy of the individual.

Both NCCL and the Cobden Trust seem to ignore the indisputable fact that our security services are fighting in the dark; they often don't know their enemy. Is it the intention of the civil libertarians that the custodians of the Nation's security should fight with both hands tied behind their back, or perhaps not at all? Unquestionably foreign paid agitators have infiltrated student bodies and militant groups of ultra-leftists; a great deal of information is now finding its way into the hands of foreign intelligence. Can it be the wish of NCCL and the Cobden Trust that much valuable information acquired under the cloak of secrecy should be rendered nugatory by "democratising" the very sources who are employed to protect democracy itself?

(iv) The rigid theories of the Chartists

Written by myself for *East-West Digest* magazine in February 1976 this piece examines the work of The Chartists which drew their inspiration from the original version of the Socialist Charter drawn up by the Tribune Group of MPs in 1968. The Chartists saw themselves as the only revolutionary internationalist tendency in the Labour Party. In the 1970s, in particular, they were of some significance.

Some of the aspirations of the ultra-left in this country have received a serious setback in the last few weeks. The Parliamentary Labour Party in the elections to its liaison committee has effectively eliminated all the leading left-wingers, including veteran leftist MP, Ian Mikardo, its chairman of the past two years. Secondly, the Prime Minister has severely rebuked Mikardo, the Tribune Group's prime strategist in imposing left-wing disciplines on Labour MPs through local constituencies and the Party's National Executive Committee.

Added to this the defeat of the left in the elections to the Executive and National Committees of the Amalgamated Union of Engineering Workers, Britain's second largest union (which has totally vindicated that union's relatively new system of postal ballots) and the long-term prospects for a resurgence of moderate influence in our industrial and political affairs seems better than for some considerable time.

Yet there will, to be sure, be no slackening of effort or loss of appetite among those Trotskyist organisations which are striving to convert the Labour Party from its essential social-democratic base into a strident Marxist-oriented party bent on destroying our fundamental liberties and parliamentary institutions.

In a recent issue [23] this journal examined in depth the activities of the 'Militant' faction within the Labour Party in general and the Labour Party Young Socialists in particular. In this issue the spotlight is turned on a lesser known organisation, the Chartist

---

23 "Trotskyist Infiltration of the Labour Party by the Militant Group", *East-West Digest*, October 1975, No 19.

group, which if not so spectacular as its '*Militant*' rival, can boast a monthly newspaper superior in quality and a steadily rising membership, at present around 400.

The Chartist group of Trotskyists draw their inspiration from the original version of the Socialist Charter drawn up by the Tribune Group of MPs in 1968. This document emphasised the importance of government firmly holding the reins of power, not the City, organised business or the International Monetary Fund. The Chartists objection to the Tribune thesis lay not in the ultimate aim but in the means of its implementation. How, they argued, could a Labour Party govern when the entire economy and all the instruments of government are in the hands of the ruling capitalist class; in other words it would not only be necessary to learn how to govern but to capture the means of government.

It is instructive to examine a paper [24] prepared for the Chartists by Richard Stephenson and written in 1970 on the "degeneration" of the Fourth International, for it serves to illustrate how the group sees its own role in relation to national and international tendencies to the left and how its own approach would help to revive the sagging fortunes of the Trotskyist ideal.

Stephenson claims that the revolutionary international, as conceived and founded during the life of Trotsky, no longer exists and all that does exist in practice is a collection of disparate Trotskyist tendencies, in essence warring factions which have brought discredit on the left and served to prolong the capitalist nightmare.

The favourable conditions which existed for Trotskyism in 1938 when the Fourth International was founded – Stalinist degeneration (as they saw it) in Russia, the defeat of Republican Spain, the general retreat of the working class accompanied by the rise of fascism, ought to have been the signal for sustained victory in all the main struggles of political activity. That this was not so is attributed by the Chartists to the erroneous post-war perspective of social and economic instability arising from conditions of slump. They admit that Trotsky himself had made this miscalculation, which was supported by the economic theoretician Ernest Mandel. On the other hand the Revolutionary Communist Party (British Section of the Fourth

---

24 "The Fourth International, and our attitudes to it", Socialist Charter Publications.

International until 1949) and other groupings and personalities such as Tony Cliff [25], took an opposing view.

The Chartists own thesis on Trotskyism reflects the criticism of the Revolutionary Communist Party levelled at the Fourth International at its Second World Congress in 1948. At that time the RCP was alone in analysing the new Eastern European States as "deformed workers States". Moreover, whereas the Fourth International leadership supported immediate 'entryism' tactics on the grounds that slump would radicalise the Labour Party, the RCP supported the building of a revolutionary party by means of open recruitment. Gerry Healy, then closely linked with the RCP, supported this line and justified it in November 1973 when transforming his Socialist Labour League into the Workers' Revolutionary Party. The Chartists, for their part, are not so certain about the validity of 'entryism' and in any event see their own political outlook as indistinguishable from that which a Clause IV Labour Party would adopt.

The Chartists see themselves as the only revolutionary internationalist tendency in the Labour Party. Rigid in their application of Marxist principle they nevertheless concede certain technological advances made under capitalism. The whole system, however, is bound sooner or later to come to a grinding halt they argue, with catastrophic and uncontrollable inflation; mass unemployment; trade wars; hoarding of raw materials; and perpetual balance of payments crises caused by the "irrelevance" of the world trading system.

This is the prospect as presented in "The Socialist Charter – Labour Take the Power", a thirty-two page programme of action for the Labour Party. At the root of all evil lies the concept of the nation-state and the way capitalism organises property, the latter being the chief hindrance to the advance of progressive socialism. The document blames the "peaceful co-existence of so-called Communist States and collaborationist policies of Labour leaders as a major prop to imperialism and capitalism".

With some ten million trade unionists, six million members of the Labour Party and thirteen million attached to the

---

[25] Also known as Ygael Gluckstein, theoretician and founder of the International Socialists in 1951. IS, although regarded by the British Communist Party as Trotskyist, is not so regarded by most other groups claiming the Trotskyist tag. This is because Cliff has not always been over-enthusiastic in his adulation of Trotsky and has frequently criticised his economic analysis.

co-operative movement, embraced in a wide variety of organisations, the Chartists see a vast potential capacity to achieve socialism – a potential to overthrow the "dominance of rent interest and profit". Only weak, vacillating leadership prevents fulfilment of these tasks.

The Chartists, who take their name from the pioneers of Socialism, differ, they claim, from other movements in that they stand for taking the power of society into their own hands as a movement and as a class, whereas other groupings stand for reform which can only mean ultimate compromise with a "decaying capitalist system". For Chartists the struggle to gain Socialism is the life-blood of their work. It involves, in particular, two criteria: a) Recognition that workers must be won to the idea of taking power through effective action, not promises and appeals. b) Recognition that trade union militancy is not enough. Each struggle brings the worker up against State-power and a corrupt system which exercises that power. The need must be for the transformation of trade unions away from the traditional concept of collective bargaining and into the sphere of "full-blooded political activity". Significantly, the Chartists say this can be done through the Labour Party because the Labour Party was created as the political arm of the unions. Consequently, the trade union movement is the framework around which alone the working class must mobilise to secure the revolution.

While, therefore, the Chartist analysis is one of transforming the Labour Party itself into a revolutionary party, it is far more prepared to co-operate with other factions in securing its grand design. In the "Socialist Charter", a section is given over to the right of affiliation to the Labour Party, in which it is stated: "Chartists demand the right of all bodies pledged to common ownership, including the Communist Party, Socialist Labour League (as it then was), International Socialists and other groups to affiliate to the Labour Party if they so wish with delegates at Conferences, General Management Committees, etc., proportional to their paid-up numerical strength.

Chartists argue that the road to power lies in the strengthening of shop stewards committees, which being elected from amongst the workforce, provide a massive counter-weight to employers rule in a way which full-time union officials do not. Amongst some of the more strident policies advocated two years ago were:

1. TUC should insist on £35 minimum national wage (which it has now done).
2. Equal pay for women (which has now been achieved under the Equal Pay Act 1975).
3. Full pay for apprentices.
4. Proper system of wages for all students and pupils from the age of 16.
5. Pensions equal to the minimum wage.
6. Shop stewards committees should have the right to inspect the accounts of their firm in any dispute.

In the April 1974 edition of the monthly newspaper *Chartist,* an editorial declares: "If an insurrectionary General Strike is forced upon us, we will match up to the occasion in full. We would regard the present government as without a mandate and in that sense as illegal. We would declare our perfect right as a movement to defend ourselves with all necessary means, including physical force and an appeal to the troops".

Two political subjects which have much exercised Chartists have been the question of arms shipments to Chile and the Labour Party's response to the Clay Cross saga. Relying heavily on the decision of the 1973 Labour Party Conference to stop all arms shipments to Chile, the May 1974 edition of *Chartist* goes out of its way to congratulate Eric Heffer MP, on his denunciation of the deal and that his breach of ministerial responsibility has created a split and paved the way for left advance.

The same issue, noting that the 1973 Party Conference had accepted a resolution removing retrospectively all penalties, financial and otherwise, imposed upon councillors who had "courageously refused to implement the Housing Finance Act", expressed its full support for the Clay Cross councillors and announced that Mr Wilson's decision to require the Councillors to pay their £7,000 fine totally ignored: i) the "150 years of working class struggle against the law", and ii) "the total domination of the judiciary who come from the same public school background as the employers and bankers".

A third subject area to which *Chartist* has given considerable attention is Northern Ireland. The major burden of the Chartist agitation over Northern Ireland is to get the withdrawal of British troops, and this is being conducted through the Troops

Out Movement (TOM), which has had the support at rallies, meetings and demonstrations of several MPs including Andrew Bennett (Stockport North), Arthur Latham (Paddington), Miss Jo Richardson (Barking), Stan Thorne (Preston North), Ron Thomas (Bristol North-West) and, inevitably, Miss Joan Maynard (Sheffield Brightside).

At a weekend conference in early October of TOM, Chartist representatives attended and argued for TOM to be restructured on the basis of national affiliation. They were supported by delegates from International Marxist Group, Revolutionary Communist Group and Workers' Fight, a militant offshoot of the International Socialists. All these groups say that the first allegiance must be to an ideological left position. Other groups at the conference, such as the Big Flame group, saw in TOM the essence of a political revolutionary party.

Chartist has been currently using the trial of fourteen persons charged under the Incitement to Disaffection Act 1934 with conspiracy to incite troops to disaffection (of which charge they have just been acquitted) as a pretext for enlisting broad-based support for an extreme-left assault on our legal institutions and judicial administration. (Much the same tactic, it will be noted, was used to discredit the National Industrial Relations Court and the credibility of its presiding judge in a number of lawsuits over the Industrial Relations Act.)

The December 1975 edition of *Chartist* describes the trial of those associated with the British Withdrawal from Northern Ireland Campaign (BWNIC) as "further expression of escalating state repression of trade unionists and others", citing as other examples the imprisonment of Des Warren on a conspiracy charge and the imprisonment of fourteen Iranians who occupied the Iranian Embassy, likewise on a conspiracy charge.

Chartist will no doubt draw satisfaction from one newspaper editorial which described the Old Bailey trial as a farce, noting that the right to dissent had been preserved and that the 1934 Act should now be repealed. Fortified by this legal decision *Chartist* can be expected to continue to propagate the message that the army "grinds down the nationalist community, maintaining the confidence of loyalism, and keeps the whole of Ireland in the grip of Imperialism" and "that the Labour Party Young Socialists should open up discussions with TOM at all levels". (*Chartist* – November 1975).

The Chartists have been trying to make maximum capital out of the unemployment figures in recent months, and various meetings, particularly in the Greater London Area, have been held to draw attention to the crisis. Chartists in the LPYS at Hornsey, Wood Green, Hackney North and Stoke Newington, for instance, convened a Conference on 15 November on the theme "unemployment and how to fight it", protesting mainly about the steep rise in unemployment in the London Boroughs of Haringey and Hackney from 9,264 to 12,725 (35%) in the six-month period ending 1 October 1975.

The main objective was to organise an action campaign locally to unite employed and unemployed workers which could exert real pressure on the local labour council, union branches, trades councils and constituency labour parties, to combat unemployment, threatened redundancies and public expenditure cuts.

A prominent feature of the conference was the question of youth unemployment, with particular reference to women and black workers. Speakers included Tony Banks, Mike Davis (*Chartist*'s editor and member of Hackney Trades Council), Mary Corbishley (Working Women's Charter Campaign), and Roger Lofters (Black Unity and Freedom Party – with which the Chartist Group maintains close links).

The relationship between the Chartist Group and the 'Militant' faction of the LPYS is well illustrated by the Chartists' reaction to the LPYS/'Militant' unemployment campaign based around the slogan: "No return to the 1930s". It describes that campaign as "characterised by the usual propagandism and programmatic sterility which we have come to expect from the LPYS leadership, omitting to call for any support for the 26 November (1975) march and lobby of Parliament against unemployment in which the rest of the labour movement was participating".

The Chartists are also critical of the scant attention paid by the 'Militant' faction to the importance of the closed shop principle for all workers. "At a time when attempts are being made to drive down real wage-levels and redundancies are in the offering any exceptions to this right would be a foot in the door and a threat to the job security and living standards of all journalists ... for too long Labour governments have attempted to pack the Lords with ageing trade union bureaucrats instead of tackling the bastion of privilege at the roots", declares the

November *Chartist*, adding: "not even the Tribune Group has called for the scrapping of this parliamentary museum piece".

Although it cannot claim the same degree of success as 'Militant' faction in penetrating LPYS and gaining control over constituency management committees, the Chartists are clearly sympathetic to what has been going on in this direction. In its December edition, *Chartist* roundly condemns Mr Wilson for his attack on the "self-appointed Samurai" at this year's Labour Party Conference. They see the assault on the left from inside the Labour Party as an attempt to silence revolt in the trade unions and among party rank-and-files, against the leadership's brazen retreat from manifesto pledges.

The Chartists say that the Labour Right fear that workers will learn to link the economic struggle for "decent wages and jobs with a political perspective which opens the way for a struggle inside the Labour Party". The Chartists intend to fight for the right to recall and remove from office any MP or Councillor who refuses to carry out policies in the interests of the working class, and have already declared their firm opposition to the proposal of the London Labour Party's Regional Executive that at the next GLC election and each one thereafter a selection procedure in each constituency party will not be necessary and that the present councillor be re-adopted. This is seen as a right-wing manoeuvre.

One Parliamentarian who has been subjected to severe criticism from Chartists in the Labour Party has been Stan Cohen, MP for Leeds South East, well-known for his right-wing, pro-European views. On 7 October Chartists held a meeting in Leeds on the theme: "After Newham, what next for the Labour Left?" at which Tony Kelly, of Newham North-East Labour Party, was the main speaker. At that meeting the Leeds Evening Post reported *Chartist* editor, Mike Davis, as saying: "We've got to get Cohen out". This was duly denied by Davis in the November *Chartist*, describing the report as typical of "the right-wing press and scaremongers".

In a letter to the *Leeds Evening Post* of 24 October, quoted in the December *Chartist*, Graham Bash, who had been described as the prime mover with Tony Kelly behind plots to get rid of Cohen, firmly denied that there was any such plot. He said that he had voted against a motion of full confidence in Cohen passed by the Leeds South-East constituency Management Committee because he had had important political disagreements with him. These disagreements, said Bash, centre round:

a) the Common Market views of Cohen which went counter to the majority of his Association.

b) abortion; whereas he, Bash, supports free abortion on demand Cohen opposed a resolution for free abortion and took up a minority position in the Labour Party on this subject.

c) the reaction to the Prentice affair. What had happened to Prentice, according to Bash represented an important victory for democracy; "it was a blow against an extreme right-winger who had appeared on the same EEC platform as Ted Heath, and against someone who had spent more time attacking Clay Cross councillors than attacking the Tory Party". Cohen supported Prentice and thus took an opposed view to Bash.

Whilst not strong in terms of organisation or numbers the Chartists would appear to be a significant Trotskyist pressure group within the Labour Party if only for the fact that they are treated with unusual respect and esteem from fellow left and Trotskyist groupings. Now that a decision has been taken by the Labour Party's National Executive Committee to take no effective action to root out subversive influences within, the Chartists can be expected to go from strength to strength. Whether they will achieve the same degree of penetration as 'Militant' faction remains to be seen but their potential to this end seems unlimited, a prospect which is barely encouraging for parliamentary democracy.

(v) The Chile Solidarity Campaign – a broader base

In this article, which I wrote for *East-West Digest* in November 1976, I examine the work of the Chile Solidarity Campaign whose objective was to secure the downfall of the Chilean government which had replaced the government of Salvador Allende by military coup in August 1973. I do not defend what happened, my purpose being to look at the somewhat broader base of those supporting the Chile Solidarity Campaign.

In an earlier article [26] on the subject of Chile this journal analysed the unconstitutional actions of the Allende regime, as revealed in American congressional records and other unimpeachable documents of reference. In this article the spotlight is turned upon the British-based Chile Solidarity Campaign (CSC) which is the main irritant source of opposition to the Chilean Government and which serves as a meeting point for various Marxist groups to display their fraternal solidarity on issues not solely concerned with Chile or Third World countries.

In an article in *Socialist Worker* of 28 August 1976 the International Socialists, who are on the periphery of the Chile Solidarity Campaign without being deeply involved with it, argue in hostile vein that Allende's demise was caused by his fatal illusion of a parliamentary road to socialism, an illusion which is shared by the Communist Party of Great Britain in its prospectus: *The British Road to Socialism*. The International Socialists accuse Senator Luis Corvalan, General Secretary of the Communist Party of Chile, of the same heresy quoting him as stating [27]: "Some reactionaries have begun to seek new ways of driving a wedge between the people and the armed forces, maintaining little less than that we are intending to replace the professional army ... No, sirs, we continue to support the absolutely professional character of the armed institutions".

---

26 In *East-West Digest*, April 1976: Volume 12, No 8.

27 In an article in the Communist Party's theoretical journal, *Marxism Today*, September 1973.

The IS critique is that a social revolution cannot make progress by peaceful means or through accepted legal methods or through 'ingratiating the social-democratic officer corps'; on the contrary, legal powers, it contends, must be abolished at once, election of officers decreed and soldiers' councils established.

These arguments are of the type that are carefully rehearsed within the councils of the Chile Solidarity Campaign. Although necessarily subordinate to the Campaign's primary objective – which is to paint as black a picture as possible of the present Chilean administration and secure its downfall as speedily as possible – the theoretical aspects of power and, more particularly, power in a marxist context, are the subject of agonising debate and appraisal, and afford a classic example of how orthodox communists, trotskyists, broad leftists and other shades of marxist are prone to indulge in questions of less than immediate urgency.

The structure of the 'Chilean opposition' consists of three interlocking but independently-run movements. The Chile Solidarity Campaign is the political movement with close links with the trade unions. The second movement is the Chilean Committee for Human Rights (CCHR) a registered charity, whose brochure claim for it a 'deep concern for human rights problems', and the third is the Joint Working Group for Refugees from Chile (JWG), ostensibly a non-political body, upon which both CSC and CCHR are represented; this latter is concerned with organising the resettlement of refugees from Chile.

The Chile Solidarity Campaign was set up shortly after the overthrow of Allende in September 1973. It functions from offices let to it by the London Co-operative Society at 129 Seven Sisters Road, London N7. Its joint-chairmen are George Anthony and Brian Nicholson. Anthony, a member of the Communist Party, is a North London official in the Amalgamated Union of Engineering Workers (AUEW), and is prominent in the Communist-controlled Liaison Committee for the Defence of Trade Unions (LCDTU), set up in 1966 to oppose the Labour Government's prices and incomes policy. Anthony's knowledge of Chile or Chileans is indeterminate but his credentials would appear impeccable for on 20 October 1973 he addressed an LCDTU Conference [28] convened to protest against the fines

---

[28] See *East-West Digest*, November 1973.

imposed on the AUEW by the National Industrial Relations Court for non-compliance with the Industrial Relations Act.

The other joint-chairman, Brian Nicholson, is one of five members of the editorial board of *Voice of the Unions*, a communist-backed front journal which resumed publication in July 1976, despite a circular from 'Voice' newspapers admitting that it owed its printer over £1,000 and despite, moreover, an announcement in May 1976 that it would no longer be produced for financial reasons (attributed to the Communist Party withdrawing its support). Nicholson, a member of the Labour Party and active with the Institute for Workers' Control is on the executive of the Transport and General Workers Union. He was involved in the dock strike in early 1975 at the India and Millwall (London) dock and, according to *Workers' Press*, (forerunner of *Newsline*) the Workers' Revolutionary Party daily newspaper, was a leader of that strike, although he was off work himself because of a bad leg and had been drawing sick pay for seven months. Nicholson is currently chairman of Region No 1 Docks Group, T&GWU.

A Chile Solidarity Campaign brochure states that it is a leading element today in the long tradition of internationalism in the British Labour Movement. "This tradition had its most vital expression in the past in the brigades who went to fight on the republican side in the Spanish Civil War – still vividly remembered after 40 years". One such veteran of the republican cause in the Spanish Civil War is Jack Jones, leader of the Transport and General Workers' Union, who is one of the chief sponsors of the Chile Solidarity Campaign; other sponsors are Lord Allen, General Secretary of USDAW, Joe Gormley, President of the NUM, Judith Hart MP, Tony Benn MP, Alan Sapper, General Secretary of the ACTT, Hugh Scanlon, President of the AUEW and Alex Kitson[29], executive officer of the T&GWU (who is the Campaign's Hon Treasurer).

The joint-secretaries of the Campaign at its inception were Mike Gatehouse and Steve Hart, a Communist Party member, son of Judith Hart, and actively associated with Liberation, the successor to Movement for Colonial Freedom. Hart is no longer

29 One of Labour's 'Group of Eleven' set up to fight against the cuts in public services; the others are Frank Allaun MP, Barbara Castle MP, Eric Heffer MP, Joan Lestor MP, Ian Mikardo MP, Judith Hart MP, Renee Short MP, Lena Jeger MP, Joan Maynard MP, Tom Jones (socialist societies) and Nick Bradley (youth section).

joint-secretary, and Gatehouse remains the sole paid full-time officer of the movement. A decision was taken by the CSC executive committee in December 1975 to appoint a full-time secretary/technical worker additionally, for a period of six months subject to funds becoming available from an outside source of income to support a salary of £2,000 a year.

The annual report of the CSC for 1976 discloses that trade union branches, trades councils, smaller district committees and local political branches all pay £5 in affiliation fees to the Campaign; individuals contribute £5, student unions £10, regional organisations, larger district committees and local branches of the Campaign £12.50, while national bodies contribute £25.00. These figures were raised to their present levels in July 1975. All these contributions assist in supporting the rental of the Campaign's offices. According to the Campaign secretary's report the LCS political committee 'has made substantial contributions to the CSC from its inception'. £330 was made available in January 1975 for an IBM typewriter and a second-hand duplicator has also been purchased.

Affiliated unions at present include: ACTT, ASLEF, ASTMS, AUEW (engineering section), AUEW (Tass), G&MWU, NATSOPA, NUM, NUPE, NUR, NU Seamen, NU Sheet Metal Workers, NUTGWU, POEU, SLADE, SOGAT. Political organisations affiliated include the Labour Party (and sixty constituency Labour Parties), the British Communist Party, the International Socialists, the International Marxist Group, the Young Communist League, the Labour Party Young Socialists, London Co-Operative Society Political Committee (the Campaign's landlords) and Liberation. Other affiliates include 39 trade councils, Austin, BMC National, David Brown (Leigh), Rover Solihull, Rover Tyseley, Scotstoun Marine, T&GWU Heathrow, Vauxhall (Dunstable) Shop Stewards Committees. Youth affiliates include the National Union of Students and the National Union of School Students, brainchild of the Young Communist League.

According to the Communist *Morning Star* of 9 April 1976 Pedro Cornejo, a Chilean living in London was named as official representative in Britain of the Chilean TUC (founded in 1953). He is in close contact with most of the affiliated groups and his experience as President of RANQUIL, described in Campaign literature as 'the largest peasant federation which during the Popular Unity grew to a membership of 200,000', has been useful in acquainting the Campaign with much of the background material which gives it its essential impetus.

The principal activities of the Chile Solidarity Campaign are centred around boycotts and the blacking of goods. The value of this approach has, from its own viewpoint, been abundantly vindicated, as will be demonstrated. The *Morning Star* of 28 January 1976 reported that the Campaign had issued a poster under the banner: 'Don't keep Chilean torturers in business', calling upon trade unionists, co-operators, Labour Party members, students and others to ensure that all shops refuse to stock Chilean goods of any description. A national picket of the Ravel Shoe chain took place on 21 February 1976 in fulfilment of this pledge.

In early January 1976, the Chilean Ambassador to Britain under Allende, Dr Alvaro Bunster, took part in a four-day visit to Scotland to aid the Chile Solidarity Campaign. He urged the people of Scotland to 'intensity their solidarity with the Chilean people', alleging that the multi-national ITT had been instrumental in organising the coup and that British subsidiaries, notably Standard Telephones and Cables, were far from guiltless[30].

For their part, the National Union of Students were prominent in whipping up sentiment against the Chilean Government during the NUS 'Chile Week' from March 6-12 1976. Folk groups, theatre groups and exhibitions on Chile were featured up and down the country while many student unions 'adopted' allegedly political prisoners in Chile, campaigning for their release. At Portsmouth Polytechnic students picketed the naval dockyard in protest at the country's continued trading with Chile; plans were co-ordinated by the Campaign. March 11 1976 was set aside as fund-raising day and each student was asked to raise money on that day for the Campaign as part of an international student effort. Every national student union in Europe organised its own 'Chile Week' between March and June.

A notable achievement of the CSC was the discussion of Chile at the TUC Annual Congress in 1975. During the international debate George Anthony intervened to call for the halting of all submarine projects. This he did on behalf of the AUEW. At an evening meeting during the Congress Alex Kitson spoke to an audience of 40 about the 'manifold evils of present day Chile'.

---

30 Reported in *Morning Star*, 15 January 1976.

The agitation of the Campaign has undoubtedly been given a greater fillip by the support of left-wing MPs. On 18 February 1976 Maureen Colquhoun, Labour MP for Northampton North, and former member of Shoreham Port Authority, was reported by the *Morning Star* as stating that there was an overwhelming case for boycotts: "The export of food products from Chile is being increased at precisely the time when unemployment, desperate poverty and mass starvation confront the vast majority of the Chilean people", she declared in a press release. On the following day Robert Kilroy-Silk, MP for Ormskirk, was reported by the same newspaper as demanding the breaking-off of diplomatic relations with Chile as being "the only honourable course to take towards its despicable regime".

On 24 March 1976 a deputation of seven MPs led by Martin Flannery, (Sheffield Hillsborough) went to the Chilean Embassy in London to protest about the treatment of 'political prisoners' in Chile. Accompanying Flannery were Norman Buchan, Ron Thomas, Bob Cryer, Andrew Bennett, George Rodgers and Eddie Loyden. A Chilean Embassy spokesman forthrightly denounced the protest saying that in Chile only criminals were imprisoned.

Other pickets held and organised under the auspices of the Chile Solidarity Campaign included one of the Chilean Embassy reception at the United Services Club on the occasion of Chilean Navy Day (May 21); a demand for the release of Luis Corvalan and Anibal Palma, prominent Chilean Communist leaders, and a protest against the visit to London by Henry Kissinger; and there were pickets held in September 1975, on the 8th, 10th and 11th with the slogans, respectively: 'Stop the repression in culture and education', 'Stop the repression of women and children', and 'Stop military rule in Chile'.

At the annual general meeting of the Chile Solidarity Campaign on 5 February 1976 the assembled delegates heard Carlos Parra, an official of the Chilean Radical Party, call for the stopping of the increase in non-traditional exports from Chile. Beans, onions and shoes were the necessities of life for the Chilean people and must be stopped by developing the commercial boycott. This should not, however, deflect from the importance of the arms boycott or the training of military personnel. An emergency resolution called upon all affiliated trades unions to send messages of support to the National Union of Seamen in their refusal to work on Chilean ships, even if this cost them their jobs. Another resolution deplored the alleged harassment of the 150,000 Chilean refugees in Argentina.

One major consequence of the Chile Solidarity Campaign's activities was the Labour Government's decision not to approve any new arms contracts for Chile. Much of the agitation against arms supplies was conducted in Scottish ports. In March 1976, for instance, Rosyth naval dockyard workers urged the Transport and General Workers' Union to follow their example by instructing their members not to handle spare parts for the Chilean navy at Portsmouth, Devonport and Chatham. Rosyth stores workers had put on their embargo on 5 March when they discovered the destination of the spare parts.

The TUC has now urged that no military equipment, such as aero engines or naval vessels, should be sent to Chile 'until democracy is restored'. This has come about largely because of Chile Solidarity Campaign pressure but it has not brought about a reversal of the Government's decision that existing contracts should be honoured. The Campaign argues that the 'junta' has defaulted in payments for the submarines and is therefore breaking its contracts by strictly commercial criteria; an example of this defaulting, it is argued, is non-payment for submarines to Scott Lithgow and the private bank which extended credit under a government guarantee. The Campaign contends that since default in the sum of £1 million for 1975 has been made the government agency concerned, the Export Credits Guarantee Department is obliged to compensate the bank which provided the original credit. (The CSC was largely instrumental in leading the Labour Party to accept in principle a proposal that Chilean assets in Britain should be seized if alleged debts incurred by the Chilean Government were not paid on time. This proposal was endorsed at a meeting of the NEC in September 1975 and was fully discussed at the Labour Party's international committee in January 1976).

The Labour Government's attitude, however, in honouring existing contracts was rationalised by Edward Rowlands[31], Under-Secretary of State at the Foreign Office:

> "British Shipbuilders and manufacturers might effectively be excluded from a number of export markets if, in addition

---

31 In a letter to the Chile Solidarity Campaign of 4 November 1975.

> to the fierce competition they are now encouraging, they had to overcome the fears of potential foreign buyers that the British Government are ready to interfere with contracts. There are prospects for contracts worth over £200 million for constructing merchant marine and naval craft in Latin America alone ... to impound submarines might well increase the risk that overseas governments would entertain doubts concerning our reliability and endanger jobs at home".

Although much of the support for the CSC is centred on London several significant demonstrations in support of boycotts and embargoes have been held in other major cities. For instance on 15 March 1975 a national demonstration in Liverpool drew an attendance of between 4,000 and 5,000. Much of this support was mobilised by regional and local committees of the Campaign. The principal slogans were: 'Support the Peoples Resistance' and 'Isolate the Fascist Junta'. Speakers included Jimmy Symes, Brian Anderson, Martin Flannery MP, Joan Jara, Rene Plaza and Carmen Castillo.

Significantly, representatives of the Chilean TUC were busy in forging trade union links, particularly in the North. They attended the Scottish Trade Union Congress Annual Conference in 1975 as fraternal delegates; they were guests of the Scottish NUM in Edinburgh; met local trade unionists and shop stewards in Glasgow at a session chaired by Alex Ferry, AUEW Glasgow district secretary and chairman of the Scottish Chile Defence Committee; were guests of the Merseyside Docks Shop Stewards in Liverpool; met local trade unionists at the miners' institute in Leigh, Lancashire, and full-time officials from the principal unions in Manchester at a meeting chaired by Douglas Farrer, T&GWU regional secretary. They conveyed greetings to the National motor industry shop stewards conference in Birmingham and met the T&GWU regional secretary, Brian Mathers. Raul Caro remained to speak at the Swindon May Day march, was a guest at the AUEW national committee's dinner in Blackpool and was fraternal delegate to the AUEW – TASS annual conference in Edinburgh.

In late 1974 the Campaign initiated a consumer boycott of Chilean wine, printing posters and stickers; it claims this was largely successful, with local committees of the Campaign leading the way. The Annual Report for 1976 claims that the

Cumbernauld Committee obtained promises from several shops to cease stocking Chilean wine and Durham Committee organised pickets to support this venture. It is salutary that the Scottish TUC, and then the TUC itself, took up these causes and declared them official policy. The boycott was subsequently extended to include shoes, fruit and vegetables.

The Campaign see these boycotts and blacking actions as valuable, however limited and sporadic they may be, for a number of reasons. First, they have been reported back to the Chilean people and have thus been a considerable source of encouragement to them; secondly, they have raised the cost of trade with Chile; thirdly, they have had a deterrent effect, it is argued, upon those who would seek to trade with Chile (surely an extravagant claim), and, fourthly, they have served as an example to other trade unionists in Britain and abroad of an unselfish idealism which ought to be a model for all radical left-wing movements.

In a booklet 'Chile and the British labour movement'[32], the Chile Solidarity Campaign claims that the programme of boycotts, blackings and pickets during the two year period commencing October 1973 has yielded important and significant results. Some of these can be summarised as follows:

a) The Tory government was forced in September 1973 to send a telegram urging the 'junta' to spare the life of Chilean Communist leader, Luis Corvalan.

b) Half of Chile's Hawker Hunter jet fighters were grounded for lack of engines, Rolls Royce workers at East Kilbride in Scotland refusing to service them.

c) Because of concerted blacking of Rolls Royce by AUEW members the government was forced to cancel several Rolls Royce contracts.

d) 1,300 Chilean refugees have been settled in Britain; most have been found housing, English classes and jobs.

e) More than 10,000 demonstrated in Trafalgar Square in September 1974 on the first anniversary of the coup. Welsh miners and Merseyside trade unionists sent special trains.

---

32 At Page 8, published by the Chile Solidarity Campaign, and printed by the London Caledonian Press (TU) Ltd.

f) Britain withdrew her Ambassador from Chile in December 1975, following the (alleged) torture of Dr Sheila Cassidy.

g) NUR crane drivers at Newhaven refused to unload Chilean onions.

h) TUC demanded the cessation of all arms supplies to Chile and the training of Chilean military personnel.

i) Printing workers in Bristol refused to print labels for Chilean wine.

j) Workers involved in the copper industry demanded from management an undertaking to cease using Chilean copper.

k) 600 unemployed seamen in Liverpool refused to sign up for the PSNC ships sailing for Chile.

l) Liverpool dockers hid leaflets in cargoes destined for Chile with messages of greeting and solidarity to Chilean workers.

m) Welsh miners offered jobs, housing and support to 50 Chilean miners.

n) NALGO made adoption of Chilean prisoners its official policy.

Considerable pressure has been exerted by the Chile Solidarity Campaign upon trade unionists in Scotland to meet its demands. The export of essential foodstuffs, raw materials and other goods and products from Scottish ports to Chile has caused the Campaign to concentrate pressure in Scotland for boycotts and pickets. The *Morning Star* of 16 February 1976 reported that over 250 delegates attended the Scottish TUC's special conference on Chile in Glasgow. Delegates from every STUC affiliated organisation, several shop stewards and area Chile Defence committee heard T&GWU National Officer (and Campaign Treasurer) Alex Kitson, and Judith Hart MP outline the programme and objects of the Campaign. Also on the platform were Andrew Forman, STUC Chairman, and Enrique Vilanova, a former Chilean Naval NCO. Kitson, referring to Sheila Cassidy, exclaimed: "Thousands and thousands of Chileans were murdered and we should have taken action long ago ... organisations should send a flood of resolutions to MPs, trade unions and trades councils demanding action against the junta". Judith Hart, for her part, urged world solidarity to "speed the junta's demise". She expressed particular concern that delivery of two Chilean submarines being built at Scott Lithgow should be halted and asked for maximum pressure to secure this.

At its 'Red Festival' during the weekend, May 22-23 1976, members of the Young Communist League heard Viviana Corvalan express solidarity with her husband, Luis, and other allegedly political prisoners. She also addressed a large rally at London's Poplar Civic Theatre on 23 May where she called for a stepping-up of the international campaign to secure the release of prisoners, including Jose Vaibel, assistant general secretary of the Chilean Young Communist League.

The Chile Solidarity Campaign has not neglected the importance of maintaining close links with international organisations pursuing common objectives. It was instrumental in convening, together with the communist-inspired World Congress of Peace Forces, an international conference of solidarity with the people of Chile in Athens from 13-16 November 1975. The Conference met with the tacit support of the Greek Government. The British representatives were Susan Carstairs, of the Chile Committee on Human Rights, the ubiquitous Alex Kitson, Jenny Little – the official Labour Party representative, Judith Hart MP and Neil Caldwell for the National Union of Students.

One of the most significant and far-reaching events in the short history of the Chile Solidarity Campaign was its specially convened trade union conference on 25 October 1975. Some 440 delegates from all the major unions came to discuss ways in which trade union pressure could best be utilised to overthrow the Chilean Government. They declared their full support for Chilean trade unionists and urged them to oppose to the end ... "the brutal oppression of the fascist military dictatorship", to quote the words of Alex Kitson. Writing in the Communist journal *Labour Monthly* [33] in January 1976, Kitson recalled the October conference declaration that ..." what we can achieve in defence of the workers of a strange and distant country is a powerful demonstration of what a struggle we will wage in our own defence against the same forces that acted in Chile, and which, in more subtle ways, act here – imperialism, multi-national corporations and monopoly capital".

---

33 Founded in 1921 and for years edited by communist intellectual Rajani Palme Dutt until his death in 1975.

Harry Smith, an executive member of the Communist Labour Research Department (not to be confused with the Labour Party Research Department) prominent in AUEW/TASS and active Communist party member told the conference: "The engineers in this audience should remember ... that Babcock and Wilcox, British Leyland, EMI, Joseph Lucas, British Ropes are british-based companies which operate in Chile. Bowaters, British-American Tobacco Co., ICI, Lloyds Bank, Shell, Unilever, and many others are the same. These companies in which we sweat make profits out of the misery of the Chilean people. But beyond that they gather experience in exploiting a working class, stripped of all legal organisation and expression".

Similar sentiments were expressed by Sid Easton in a declaration of 27 November 1975. Easton, of the Transport and General Workers Union Region No 1, publisher of *Comment* and other Communist party literature, Communist representative on *World Marxist Review*, and executive member of the Communist-dominated Liaison Committee for the Defence of Trade Unions, declared emphatically: "I think we have got to review the situation of fascism in the world, not just as a question of what good news we can do for the people of Spain or Chile, or anywhere else but more particularly with regard to the defence of our own position".

The Chile Solidarity Campaign has attempted to derive maximum political capital from the internationally-orchestrated campaign to have Chile condemned in the public mind for torture and other inhumane practices. Much of the evidence is tenuous and inconclusive and where there has been some evidence of malpractices the Chilean Government has not been slow in condemning them and punishing those responsible. John Platts-Mills QC, for a long time actively associated with the National Council for Civil Liberties and prominent in the Communist-controlled Society for Cultural Relations with the USSR, is one who went to Chile on the Campaign's behalf to gather evidence of 'repression in the Universities' and to assist in the defence of Luis Corvalan.

He would have done well to have had in his possession an article in *Chile Today* of February 1976 by a non-political figure, the Rev F G Cave, a minister of the Union Church, Vina del Mar. He is an overseas representative of the Church of Scotland. He argues that it is impossible to present an adequate picture of

Chile today except against the background of Chile in the period 1970 to 1973. The constitution under Allende, when not totally ignored, became a means to imposing a Cuban-style dictatorship lacking in either efficiency or honesty. Persons with no qualifications but their Party membership cards were appointed to high administrative office and important industries were placed in the hands of the managers who were nothing other than regime toadies, concerned with personal enrichment and renowned for a capacity to overload their payroll with idle 'Companeros'. Rev Cave states that Chile is now enjoying the fruits of renewed effort and that its present rulers are honest, efficient and patriotic. The wild reports of wholesale torture and of people groaning under jackboots of fascist oppressors could be brushed aside as nonsense if they were not being used as purposeful and malignant propaganda.

In a leading article of 9 June 1976 in *The Times* it was contended that the announcement of the release of Chilean prisoners coincided with the visit of Mr William Simon, American Secretary of the Treasury to Chile (where he had said that credit would flow again from private banks and government agencies). This drew a strong retort from the Chilean Ambassador, Kaare Olsen, in a letter to *The Times* of 12 June 1976. He said that the programme for the release of detainees had been set in September 1975 and had absolutely nothing whatever to do with the programme of capital investment and credit for Chile upon which the United States Government had embarked. The truth was that the rate of inflation had been very substantially reduced since the Allende regime's overthrow. Further, in a combined report the World Bank and Agency for International Development expressed the considered view that the long-term policy adopted by the Chilean administration constituted a solid and coherent economic programme and the emergency measures taken in 1975 were, in practical terms, the only ones compatible with an anti-inflationary policy.

The malicious propaganda of the Chile Solidarity Campaign on the subject of Chile's foreign debt was further highlighted when the Minister of Finance, Mr Jorge Cauas, attending the International Monetary Fund meeting in Kingston, Jamaica, in January 1976, announced at a press conference that Chile was paying its foreign debt on schedule even with the current low copper prices. The Minister stated that unless copper prices fell drastically, Chile would not have to resort to negotiations with the 'Club of Paris'. The country was now evolving out of its dependence upon copper and with sugar production expanding and the whole agricultural sector improving, the economic prospects for Chile looked bright. The World Bank had reported very favourably on the economy and the National Recovery Campaign had been an unqualified success in curbing inflation and maintaining a healthy balance of payments.

Whether the CSC is able to maintain its impetus in the fourth year of its activities remains to be seen. The portents appear favourable, for as recently as 12 September 1976 it staged an effective demonstration in Trafalgar Square at which Madame Allende was the star attraction. Others who addressed the assembled faithful were Ron Hayward, Labour Party General Secretary, Cyril Plant, Chairman TUC, and Charles Clarke, President of the National Union of Students. The demonstration was the culmination of a week of action in all parts of the country.

Future plans are well advanced. They include a campaign against 'junta-nominated students coming to Britain on British Council Scholarships'; a campaign to raise the issue of multi-national corporations and their part in the coup; investigation of share-purchases in companies with Chilean interests in order to raise the issue at shareholders meetings and put pressure on these companies; the sending of a trade union delegation to Chile from Britain, and the extension of student contacts between Britain and Chile.

The Chile Solidarity Campaign is thus revealed as a constant thorn in the flesh of the present Chilean administration. To underestimate its influence is to misunderstand the nature and extent of subversion in this country. It is an error committed all too frequently by Western Governments; hopefully, it is not one which is irreparable.

(vi) Whose civil liberties?

I wrote a 56-page pamphlet in 1972 with the title *Some Uncivil Liberties* which was a critique of the National Council for Civil Liberties (NCCL) and the reasons why I thought it inappropriate for the Greater London Young Conservatives to have become affiliated to it, thereby suggesting common ideals.

In the article, written in the months earlier in the quarterly journal of the Monday Club, *Monday World*, in the Autumn 1971 I set down the background to the NCCL, the left and far-left composition over many years and my belief that it was not a credible organisation to be at the forefront of the movement to protect our liberties.

To an extent this may be less urgent and of historical interest only insofar as it has refashioned some of its targets and objectives, becoming less politically oriented and the fact that it has for many years operated under its changed name of Liberty.

Even though I find myself no longer interested in its activities, political researchers may find my own contributions of usefulness during the relevant period in any wider study of the rôle of pressure groups in influencing government and political opinion.

During 1970 Greater London Young Conservatives became affiliated to the National Council for Civil Liberties, a decision which I strongly opposed and contested at a meeting of Branch Chairmen of the Movement at its Council Meeting in the autumn of that year. My protestations and those of one or two others were rejected, it being suggested that we did not care about civil liberties because if we did we should not be objecting to an organisation, the only organisation it was said, which was non-political and certainly non-party political operating in this field. My researches into the origins, development and present attitudes of the NCCL reveals a rather different picture.

NCCL was founded in 1934 by a number of left-wing intellectuals, among them Kingsley Martin, H G Wells, Geoffrey Bing, Claud Cockburn and E M Forster, the latter of whom wrote an appreciation of the Council's first General Secretary, Ronald Kidd, in his *Two Cheers for Democracy*.

The Council represented a response to the manner in which it claimed the police were abusing their powers at a time of social unrest caused by large scale unemployment. The police were frequently accused of breaking up unemployment meetings and hunger marches with unnecessary severity, and NCCL developed the practice of sending observers to meetings to act as watchdogs on police behaviour, a practice which it still maintains today.

A major criticism levelled against NCCL is that it was founded in a spirit of opposition to established authority rather than as a result of a conscious and deliberate decision to promote the civil liberties of minorities against undue arbitrariness. In *Civil Liberty*, the monthly publication of NCCL, of June 1942, Kingsley Martin writing of Ronald Kidd confirmed the impression: "If he had not spontaneously resented authority he would never have founded the Council for Civil Liberties ..."

In one of his wartime pamphlets, *Civil Liberty and the Colonies*, NCCL could state as a general proposition that civil liberty is not an abstract or absolute value – "Those liberties which we know and enjoy in Britain owe their origin to a long course of struggle against tyranny of one form or another". And yet in the early days of the Second World War, and contrary to its self-proclaimed detestation of all forms of tyranny, NCCL responded to the International Communist Movement's call to oppose the war as "imperialist". It campaigned vehemently against wartime restrictions and in July 1942 sponsored a Press Freedom campaign for the repeal of Defence Regulation 2d, and the withdrawal of the ban on *The Daily Worker*, then mouthpiece of the Communist Party.

One of the leading figures in NCCL during the war years was D N Pritt, QC, who aspired to the Vice-Presidency of its Executive Committee. According to Victor Gollancz in his autobiography, *Reminiscences of Affection*, Mr Pritt was the most rigid Sovietist he had ever met; more rigid even than Palme Dutt (the Communist Party's leading theoretician). Although never himself a member of the Communist Party, Mr Pritt was expelled by the Labour Party in 1940 for associating with it. He has been connected with many front organisations, being sometime President of two of them, the benign sounding International Association of Democratic Lawyers, and the British Rumanian Friendship Association. Mr Pritt has also been President of the Society for Cultural Relations with the USSR, and is a member of two other organisations proscribed to members of the Labour Party, the British-Hungarian Friendship Society and the Society for Friendship with Bulgaria. He was also President of the British Peace Committee, condemned by the late Lord Attlee, Labour Prime Minister 1945-1951, when he said of it: "The British Peace Committee is an offshoot from the World Peace Council, an instrument of the Soviet Politbureau. More than 90 per cent of the members of its Permanent Committee are known to be Communists and fellow travellers. One of the duties of the 'peace movement' as stated in a Comintern directive of 22 September 1950 is to encourage evasion of military service by the youth of the USA, Britain, France, Belgium and Yugoslavia. Even the most woolly-minded pacifist can hardly be deceived into thinking that this injunction is due to a conscientious objection to taking part in military activities" – salutary words indeed, for it is just such a "woolly minded pacifism" which has inspired a fair number of supporters of NCCL to come to "civil liberties" via internationally famous pacifist bodies like the *War Registers International* and the *No Conscription Fellowship*. Tony Smythe, the energetic General Secretary joined NCCL from the WRI (War Resisters' International) taking on his present position when Martin Ennals, his predecessor, left to join Amnesty International. As a memorial to the pacifist ethos NCCL holds most of its annual meetings at Mahatma Gandhi Hall in Bloomsbury, London.

In the immediate post-war period NCCL became even further entrenched in left-wing attitudes. As Mr John Gretton, in an article in *New Society* of 1 October 1970 puts it: "When the war was over it became a left-wing platform, if not a Communist front, and compounded the impression by such acts as its opposition to the release of Mosleyites from prison". Trades Unions with strong Communist influence like the Clerical and Administrative Workers Union (CAWU) and the Civil Service Clerical Association (CSCA) became affiliated but as soon as non-Communists in these and other Unions responded to the Labour Movement's alert at the Trades Union Congress of October 1948, they took precipitate action in withdrawing their affiliation to NCCL, and both these unions have since been controlled by non-Communists.

From a period of relative inactivity in the early and mid-1950s NCCL became re-activated with its Mental Health Campaign which culminated in the Mental Health Act 1959. Martin Ennals took over in 1960 as General Secretary, a position which he held for six years before Amnesty International claimed his talents. During this period many affiliations took place from all manner of minority organisations climbing in on the civil liberties bandwagon; today NCCL can claim 3,000 members and over 550 affiliates, including 34 Trades Unions, most of them with a fairly strong left-wing bias such as the Musicians Union, Association of Cinematograph, Television and Allied Technicians (ACTT), Transport and General Workers Union, and the Draughtsman's and Allied Technicians Association (DATA).

There is also a Parliamentary Civil Liberties Group, comprising members of all three political parties; however the influence of these MPs on NCCL's general policy would seem to be minimal since none of them is now on the Executive Committee.

NCCL's major campaigns concern (a) maladministration of justice which is the largest single item of its work; (b) the rôle of the police and the Special Branch (which the General Secretary has referred to as "the nasty grey area of our national life"). Two of NCCL's well published booklets have been (i) *A Handbook of Citizen's Rights*, which, however well intended, was received with scathing criticism in legal circles; Lord Shawcross, for instance, has described it "as a useful guide for the inexperienced criminal", and (ii) *Arrest, a Guide to the Citizen's Rights*, which has been welcomed in odd places. For instance, Agit-Prop (Agitation-Propaganda, the Revolutionary Left's Information Service) in its *Bust-book* ("how we hate the Pigs") has described it as "short and useful". (c) Privacy, and the computer data bank . (d) Immigration Legislation; on the new Immigration Bill, the March-April bulletin of NCCL considers that "the (bill) poses one of the worst threats to civil liberty for a long time; it will put every new arrival on probation and prevent him from enjoying full welfare, social and political rights". (e) Academic Freedom; for which the Council for Academic Freedom and Democracy was recently set up under NCCL auspices. (f) Censorship and the Arts; and a number of lesser matters.

A study of the biographical details submitted by the candidates for election to the Executive Committee of NCCL in the last two years can to some extent provide a lead in determining the attitudes which NCCL adopts towards social and political problems; likewise affiliated bodies because, as an NCCL leaflet describing its work puts it, "as an affiliate your organisation contributes to the policy and financing of the movement and is seen to take a clear stand on civil liberties".

One of the senior members of the Executive Committee is *Mr Harry Francis*; the Assistant General Secretary of the Musicians Union, President of the Hounslow Trades Council, Secretary of the Confederation of Entertainment Unions and Treasurer of the Theatres Advisory Council. Apart from the year 1967 Mr Francis has served on the NCCL Executive for 21 years. He omits to mention other positions which he holds including: membership of six Labour party-banned Communist Front organisations – the British Peace Committee (General Council Member); the British-Rumanian Friendship Association (Vice Chairman); British Czechoslovak Friendship League (Treasurer); Society for Friendship with Bulgaria (Executive Member) and the pro-Moscow British-China Friendship Association (Vice Chairman). Mr Francis is a member of the Musicians Branch of the Communist Party.

Other successful candidates have included: *Miss Jocelyn Barrow*; General Secretary of Campaign Against Racial Discrimination (CARD) and member of the Community Relations Commission. *Mrs Grace Berger*, newly appointed chairman, who was the inspiration behind the *Draft Charter for Children's Rights*, published by the Advisory Centre for Education in association with NCCL. The Charter considers that "the trend towards sexual permissiveness is consistent with the growth of civil liberties" and it also advocates that children should be allowed to be excused religious instruction at the age of five if they so wish, and that where parents and children are in conflict an ombudsman should sort out their difficulties. Not surprisingly, NCCL lost no time in condemning the police seizure of *The Little Red School Book*. That was also an infringement of civil liberties! Mrs Berger was on the National Committee of the Anti-Apartheid Movement 1961-63 and was formerly

Administrative Secretary of the South African Freedom Association. Mrs Berger appeared as a Defence witness in the recent Oz trial at the Old Bailey. Her 16 year old son, Vivian, who produced the "Rupert Bear" cartoon in the Schoolkids issue, was called to give evidence for the prosecution. After the verdict Mrs Berger proclaimed: "Sadly there was no connection between the gay cheerful magazine and the vindictive, vicious legal process. I'm terribly concerned that the Obscenity Acts are being used to stifle mounting protest among young people". *Mr Benedict Birnberg*; a solicitor specialising in civil liberty law who is an executive council member of the Haldane Society, British affiliate of the Labour Party-proscribed Communist front body, the International Association of Democratic Lawyers. The Haldane Society was one of the multiplicity of organisations which placed an advertisement in the *Morning Star* on 1 May. *Mr Anthony Blond*, a publisher, author and broadcaster and Executive Member of the Defence of Literature and the Arts Society, an NCCL affiliate) which helped to ensure the appearance of *Last Exit to Brooklyn* on bookstalls in this country. Mr Blond, a vigorous campaigner against censorship, is, according to a recent issue of Oz, one of the Trustees and co-lessors of 43 King Street, London WC1 where the Gay Liberation Front hold some of their meetings. Mr Francis Deutsch; a lawyer and member of the Labour Party who is on the Central Board for Conscientious Objectors and who has submitted papers on Citizens Rights and Boy Soldiers, (a favourite NCCL theme) and Prisoners against the Bomb. *Professor John Griffith*; Professor of Public Law at the LSE. At the NCCL's 1971 AGM, Professor Griffith deplored the "unhealthy phenomenon" of university teachers "accepting the ridiculous titles and privileges (knighthoods, peerages and other honours) by which the State nobbles while it enobles its supporters". *Mr Sean Redmond*; the full-time General Secretary of the pro-Communist Connolly Association and an executive member of Liberation (formerly the Movement for Colonial Freedom). Mr Redmond is a member of the Communist Party and was consultative delegate to its biennial Congress in 1969. He was co-opted to the Executive Committee of NCCL in 1970 *Mr Brian Richardson*; an architect in Local Government ; Secretary of the Kent Gypsy Support Group, member of the working party on the Rights of children. "Wants to see more permissiveness and the privacy to enjoy it." *Dr Michael Schofield*; who has conducted

The author speaking at the Conservative Party Conference in Blackpool, October 1978

1942: My parents and siblings (from left to right) – Sarah-Anne, Penelope, my father Mark, myself, my mother Sybil, Graham, Pamela and Ruthie ...

... and in 2002 (60 years later) – Pamela, Penelope, Graham, Ruthie, the author and Sarah-Anne

If you want to help contact . . .

84

Conservative Central Committee Rooms,
16 Stamford Street,
Stalybridge,
Cheshire.

Tel: Stalybridge 2598

. . . where you will be put in touch with your local ward agent.

Thursday 28th February

SWERLING X

Polling 7 am. to 10 pm.

Sam Swerling

Conservative

Printed by Sovereign Press, Manchester
Published by H. Hibbert
16 Stamford Street, Stalybridge

My parliamentary candidature at Stalybridge and Hyde, February 1974

Come and hear
Sam Swerling

1. Wednesday, 2nd October.
   Mellers Primary School.
   7.30 p.m.

2. Friday, 4th October.
   Huntingdon Junior School.
   7.30 p.m.

3. EVE OF POLL RALLY
   Wednesday, 9th October.
   Manvers Pierrepont School.
   7.30 p.m.

POLLING DAY

Thursday 10th
October 1974
(7 a.m. — 10 p.m.)

A Polling Card telling you where to vote will be sent to you by the Returning Officer. Don't worry if you lose it. You can still vote providing you give your name and address to the person in charge at the Polling Booth.

If you want to help contact ...
Campaign Headquarters,
4 Oxford Street,
Nottingham.
Telephone Nottingham 43873

Printed by Pact Print Ltd., 14 Oxford Street, Nottingham.
Published by Brian Vinerd, 4 Oxford Street, Nottingham.

SAM SWERLING

Your Conservative Candidate

My parliamentary candidature at Nottingham East, October 1974

The author with Enoch Powell at a public meeting in East London, February 1972. Enoch and Peter Shore, former Labour Minister, were the first public speakers I heard *– see article at page 223*

The author with his loudspeaker campaigning against the Maastricht Treaty in Huntingdon, September 1992 – see article at page 296

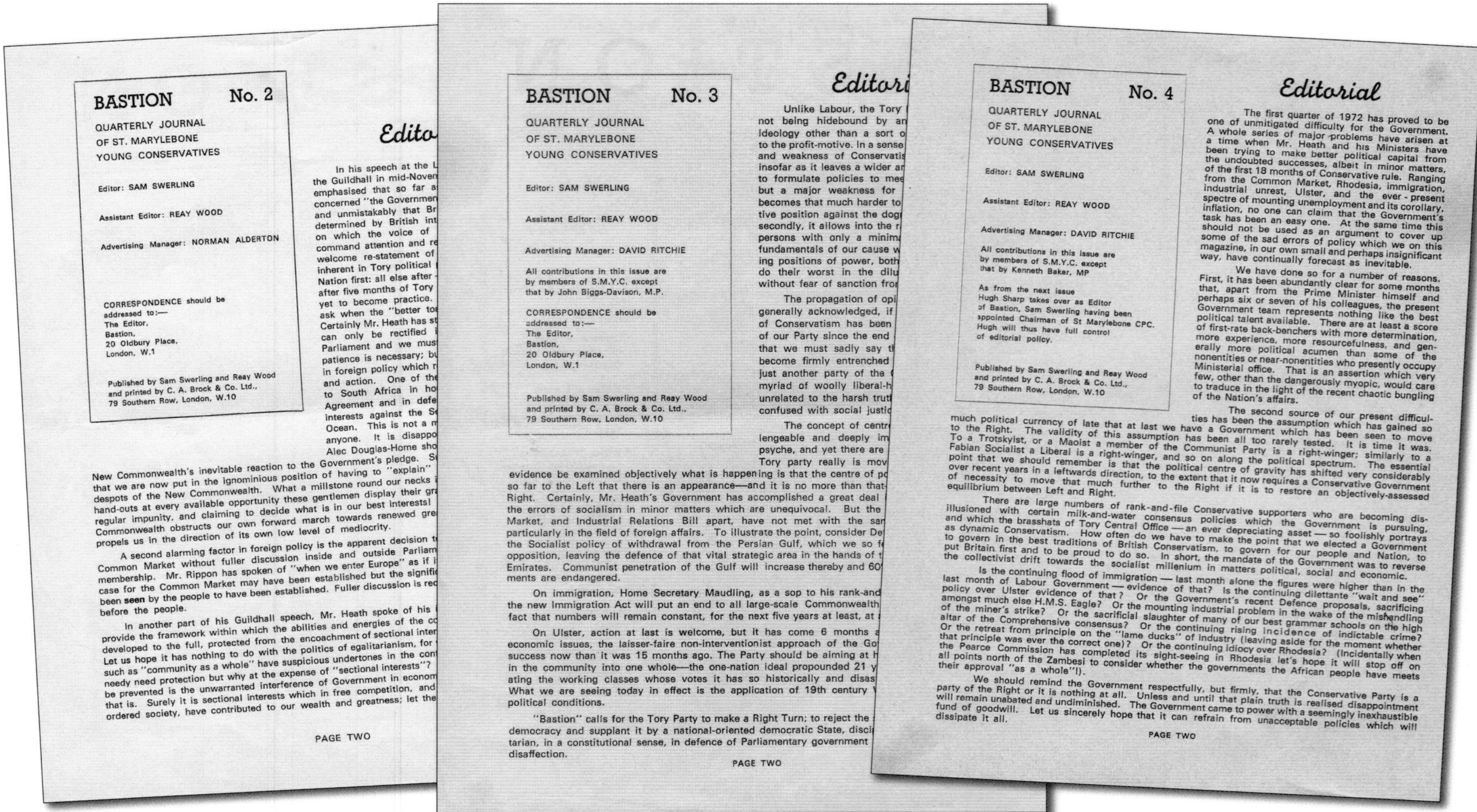

Some early editions of the Young Conservatives Magazine, Bastion

researches for the Home Office, University of London and Health Education Council. He is the author of *The Strange Case of Pot*, and was a member of the Wootton Committee.

The only candidate successful in election to the Executive Committee in 1970 who claimed membership of the Conservative Party was *Mr Gary Waller*, the former Chairman of Pressure for Economic and Social Toryism (PEST). Mr Waller's success seems due to the fact he is on the National Committee of the Anti-Apartheid Movement. An unsuccessful candidate from the Conservative Party in 1971 was *Mr Eric Chalker* who felt compelled to say of himself – "Active anti-establishment Tory for 15 years, five as an officer including Chairman of Greater London Young Conservatives. To a large extent responsible for leading GLYC's towards their present position of progressive Toryism."

Another successful candidate for election in 1971 was the *Rev Paul Oestreicher*, who has published two books on the relationship between Christianity and Marxism. Between 1961-1964 the Rev Oestreicher produced BBC religious broadcasts. Unsuccessful candidates included *Mr Des Wilson* and *Mr Tony Bunyan*, former National Organiser of the Young Liberals, who is presently executive assistant to Lord Beaumont and John Pardoe MP, and is a member of the National Peace Council. In *Time Out* magazine, which is printed at 374 Gray's Inn Road, formerly the Headquarters of the Connolly Association and the Movement for Colonial Freedom, Mr Bunyan is listed as their contributing editor on Agit-Prop.

In the face of such heavyweight competition the question remains whether any useful purpose is served by Greater London Young Conservatives remaining affiliated to NCCL. It is submitted that while it is always possible to co-operate with an organisation in a specific project – for instance, support for the NCCL's Computer Data Bank study and the related subject of privacy, and its attempts to bring consistency into the application of procedure relating to bail are cases in point – to affiliate is to identify oneself in broad measure with the principles, and the policies on which they are based, of an organisation. In the case of NCCL it seems there are too many factors present which make it a body unsuitable for affiliation, not the least of which is the almost complete absence of religious influence in the organisation and the disproportionately strong humanist, pacifist and internationalist representation.

It should be pointed out that other organisations are now in existence equally involved in civil liberties but from a more objective standpoint. It seems a fair criticism to make of NCCL, and one that characterises nearly all its campaigns, that for every civil liberty gained another is impaired. Peter Hain's right to organise the disruption of the South African Cricket tour (a spurious right if ever there was one) is not apparently outweighed by the rights of the majority to watch a game of cricket uninterrupted; the right of Rudi Dutschke to remain in this country (a major NCCL campaign) is not outweighed by a Nation's right, and duty, to exclude foreign nationals whom it considers undesirable; the right of Government to bring collective bargaining within the framework of industrial law and thereby protect both management and unions by more clearly defined legislation is elevated by NCCL into a civil liberty issue, and as an unwarranted infringement of a trade unionist's right to strike, which it manifestly is not. One could cite further examples.

In the final analysis a truly conservative approach to the question of civil liberty can only be realised through an acceptance of a synthesis between authority and liberty – a synthesis best reflected in the finest legal system in Europe; it cannot be achieved through the selective indignation of the National Council for Civil Liberties.

A more radical way forward

I wrote this piece for the Summer 1974 edition of *Monday World*, quarterly journal of the Monday Club and therefore designed essentially for internal consumption. It was also written for *The Spectator* in its 17 August 1974 edition where it reached a wider audience before the second of the two parliamentary elections of that year.

It reflects the pessimism and highly critical assessment made by right-of-centre Tories and others of the party as a whole. In particular, it challenges the myth that the Tories alone should be entitled to be regarded as the natural party of government by pursuing centrist policies. The issues are, I think, clearly stated and probably serve to show that lack of a distinctive ideology in the intervening years (1974 to 2016) has not been helpful; indeed more of a hindrance.

The Tory defeat at the last election has at least given the party time to step aside for the moment. The latest trendy idea to be put forward is that Conservatives and Liberals should combine to form a common front to keep the Socialists out. The damper has been put on this concept, however, by the Liberal rank-and-file's determination to have no truck with such a 'bedfellowship'. The very thought of it, though, does serve to illustrate the negative, uncritical aspects of Toryism which the radical right exists to fight against.

The last three months have offered the party the chance to reconsider some of its attitudes on essential policies, and the principles upon which those policies were conceived, and to commence the urgent task of restoring the morale of party workers and supporters throughout the country, inevitably at a low pitch after the disappointment and frustration of unexpected electoral eclipse.

The tasks that lie immediately ahead are perhaps made less daunting, paradoxically, by the knowledge that the Labour Party has embarked upon a programme more collectivist and ideologically-orientated in the direction of pure socialism than any of its predecessor administrations. This reflects not merely the leftwards drift in the Labour Party, but the perceptible shifting to the left of the centre of political gravity over the past few years – and the accompanying Tory shift with it. Sir Keith Joseph has frankly and openly characterised this as the pursuit of semi-socialism, a case of mistaken identity. One wishes that the Tories' new defence supreme, Peter Walker, felt the same; it was he who recently emphasised the paramount importance of Conservatives occupying the middle ground of politics – a pity Nye Bevan is not around to tell him about the dangers of getting run over while walking down the middle of the road!

As Chancellor Healey plans how best he can make the rich (£3,000 a year miners included) squeal by penal taxation to pay for his profligate expenditure, and Wedgwood Benn busies himself on ways of taking the productive capacity of large slices of industry into public ownership, the delineation of Labour policy unfolds in a way which should afford to the Tories a heaven-sent opportunity of formulating an election programme which can engage the enthusiasm of the people and provide an attractive, radical and genuinely authentic alternative to doctrinaire socialism.

In the *Swinton Journal* of Autumn 1971, Lord Butler declared that "it is perhaps the very generalised feeling that we are the national party that has given us our strongest claim on the affections and support of our fellow countrymen". In the climate of discontent and disaffection which pervades so much of our society and in the context of a raging inflation which threatens a social and economic upheaval, and for which the

Tories are widely, if unjustifiably, blamed it is positively dangerous to assume that this generalised feeling is prevalent; yet Tory spokesmen seem to feel that, come the crunch, the people will turn again to the party as being the only one capable of preaching and achieving national unity. They will only do so if a coherent, distinctive, almost fundamentalist approach to the nation's ailments is clearly discernible. The Labour Party machine appears to be working overtime in striving to represent *itself* as the natural party of government – the party capable of avoiding, as it sees it, the errors of Toryism, i.e. of confrontation with organised labour; of failure to curb the profits of big business; of callousness towards the weak and underprivileged; of inability to make manufacturing industry profitable; of presiding over poor export performance and low investment. Socialism is presented as the panacea and cure-all of our contagious diseases.

Much of this mythology has achieved a measure of acceptance in the country, moreover, because the Tories seem temporarily to have lost the battle of words in the propaganda war which counts for so much in politics today. For instance, there remains a persistent belief amongst the uncommitted that it was the Tories who sought a head-on collision with the unions, and that the Labour Party with its own unique arrangement with organised labour, its financial paymaster, can alone salvage the wreckage, whereas in principle there was little difference between the Industrial Relations Act and the Industrial Relations Bill of Barbara Castle, which ended so ignominiously on the scrapheap after the June 1969 surrender to the big battalions.

There is another persistent belief that Tory housing policy deliberately set out to force up rents to meet increased costs, whereas the system of rebates and allowances in the Housing Finance Act largely offset rent increases for those less well-off, and extended the system of protection to unfurnished tenancies provided by local authorities as well as to the private sector protection under Labour's 1965 Rent Act. Again, it is widely supposed that Labour is the party of compassion, and that its programme for the social services far outstripped in generosity anything which the Tories offered. This is palpably untrue. The provision of six new cash benefits and the pensions record of the last government was one of its most encouraging features. Nor can it be argued that social provision in this context was inconsistent with a right-wing, traditionalist view of the State having a limited role to play in protecting those less able to fend for themselves.

Despite this, in a mass democracy the power of communication is all-important and at the last election the Tories came out worst and the Liberals, whose policies on housing, industrial relations and social services are no clearer now than they were then, were able to cream off the vote of the apathetic and those contemptuous of the entire system.

The central question of the economy is now the subject of a pretty hectic, feverish debate in all areas of the party, from the Shadow Cabinet to the smallest CPC constituency committee. With the benefit of hindsight no-one can afford to assume a monopoly of wisdom in the matter. All the old conundrums need to be re-examined; whether a reduction in the rate of increase of money supply, with consequences of substantially increased unemployment and severe dislocation of business and industry, will dampen demand and set back hopes for a decent growth rate; whether this course will have only a marginal effect on inflation until the monopoly power of the larger unions such as AUEW, T&GWU and NUM is drastically curbed either (preferably) by voluntary action or enforcement; how best to cope with the possibility of slump and recession. All these problems are deserving of a most critical and detailed analysis, if only because if we get the wrong answers the democratic process may be incapable of repairing the damage and changing course. The probable consequence of such a calamity would be a Communist dictatorship.

Another highly disturbing feature about contemporary society is the way in which legal constraints are failing to deal with the aspirations, some legitimate others not, of powerful minorities.

Many Tories must feel bitterly disappointed at the acquiescence of the Shadow Cabinet in the repeal of the Industrial Relations Act. The determination of Mr Scanlon's engineering union in refusing to defend itself before the National Industrial Relations Court and the saga of the fines imposed upon it, the emotional sympathy for the five dockers imprisoned for contempt and the bizarre proceedings that bailed them out, and the concerted attack by the Left on the Act, its institutions and overall purpose have been rather ineffectually countered by the Tories. The image of the Act as a medium for 'union bashing' has simply not been dispelled. Neither has there been a sufficiently loud enough protest at the sordid attack on the integrity of the distinguished High Court judge, Sir John Donaldson (and the constitutional implications involved), by Michael Foot, one of the 'Three Left Feet' who have served the Labour Party in one capacity or another for the past thirty years or more.

Although the Trades Union and Labour Relations Bill re-enacts some of the Act, particularly the sections on unfair dismissal, there is much in the new Bill which needs to be vigorously opposed.

There are other aspects of our national life which are worrying an increasing number of ordinary people and which need to be tackled in determined fashion. Violence, truancy and indiscipline in schools, often caused by sheer boredom, could be reduced by lowering the school age to 15 for those who wish to leave at that age. The sinister growth of urban guerilla movements in Western Europe, with their international ramifications, and our own familiar example of the IRA, should be met by the return of the death penalty for sabotage and terrorist activities. Other developments might be an international agreement outlawing all "front" organisations which exist to support and succour terrorism, and an increased budget for the counter-intelligence service to meet the growing threat of internal subversion, so long discountenanced as a fantasy but now more readily acknowledged. The achievement of one nation, resourceful and independent, necessitates the effective elimination from political life of all those disparate groups which are parasitic on the body-politic and which render that ideal impossible.

Tories might also challenge more vigorously some fashionable beliefs, such as the hypocrisy of a socialism which can justify restrictions on freedom of choice and expression through race relations legislation yet regard increased legal controls over pornography as an unwarranted intervention of the State upon individual freedom. And in many other spheres we need to give greater emphasis to the values of service and obligation as a corollary to our basic rights and freedoms. Our trouble is that time may be running out on us.

Remedial action – not the "art of the possible"

I wrote this piece for *The Marylebone* quarterly journal of St Marylebone Conservative Association in October 1978. I was Vice-Chairman of the Association and was a Westminster City Councillor. It was to be the final year of the Labour government with James Callaghan as Prime Minister.

I set down the fundamental principles under which the Tories would win the ensuing election. Events showed that my opposition to a devolution programme to Welsh and Scottish assemblies was misplaced. It was an error made by many Tories at the time. Everything else I argued for then would have the same credibility today.

The description of politics as 'the art of the possible', attributed to Lord (then RA) Butler when Home Secretary in Harold MacMillan's government, has turned out with the benefit of hindsight to be most unfortunate, if not ill-advised.

No doubt when he thus described politics, Mr Butler was bearing in mind the limitations of what can be achieved by representative government; he was, perhaps, conscious of George

Bernard Shaw's cynical view that democracy consists of electing a government to govern and an opposition to obstruct that elected government from governing. Perhaps, also, Mr Butler could speak as he did in the knowledge that post-war Conservatism was not being met by a sustained Socialist challenge.

Instead of regarding politics as being the instrument of achieving possibilities the Conservative Party ought, it seems to me, to be steeling itself to the necessity of undertaking the most drastic remedial action in every sphere of our national life when, as surely will happen sooner or later, a Conservative government is returned to power with a thumping majority.

The objective expression will need to become: "Politics is the art of making possible what the collective will of the people demands to be made possible", notwithstanding any alleged constraints imposed by the system. For the unpalatable truth is that nothing short of a root-and-branch reversal of virtually every facet of government policy will suffice to satisfy the people's clamour for strong and good government. This will involve an irreversible shift away from socialism and marxism, and their handmaiden, liberalism, and the acceptance of a protracted course of unpleasant political medicine to bring about a truly patriotic, traditional and ethical society.

The drift to the left since the war has been a slow, almost imperceptible process to the extent that the people have been lulled into a false sense of security and a quite unjustified optimism that ultimately socialism will deliver the goods. Fed by a diet of propaganda from Socialist verbalisers and inspired by liberal intellectuals that 'big is best', that 'the State knows best', that individual freedom must give way to the community interest, and a hundred and one other dangerous nostrums and platitudes the reaction to these trends by opponents of socialism has been, until comparatively recently, muted, ineffective and lacking in conviction, if not downright spineless at times.

The opportunity to reverse this horrific collectivist drift has never been greater. The question therefore is: will the Conservative Party have the will and gumption necessary to avail itself of an unrivalled chance? The answer to this question will be in the affirmative if certain fundamental principles of Conservatism are adhered to in the art of policy-making.

The first such principle, above all else, is that the concept of the nation-state has always been viable, is still viable and will always remain viable for it represents the focal point of the individual's allegiance, an organic entity which encompasses a myriad of rights and duties without which life would become meaningless. That being so foreign policy considerations which fail to put the interest of Great Britain above the conflicting demands of other countries and certain international institutions (such as, for instance, that ineffable talking-shop of disunity called the United Nations) will be treated with deserved contempt by present and future generations of Britons.

What is being asserted, then, is that nationalism, as a political ideal, is perfectly capable of realisation by a strong Conservative government willing to stand some initial buffeting from dissident elements; nor is a programme of Tory nationalism inconsistent with our responsibilities to our EEC partners: indeed, the development of a right-wing European nationalism is the surest bulwark against the spread of international communism and the prospect of an increasingly isolationist and dispirited America.

The second principle which any Conservative government must adhere to if it is to succeed is that a proper equation between income and expenditure at national and local level must be maintained if inflation is to be brought under control. This is what Lord Hailsham has often referred to as a return to 'honest money'. A continuation of the present pattern of inflation will inevitably lead to collapse and total disintegration with unimaginable consequences, other than the certainty of some unspeakable tyranny.

The third principle which needs to be re-asserted is the primacy of parliamentary democracy – and within that principle the sub-principle that parliament must represent the people's will far more accurately – and the corollary to it, which is the overriding need to break the power and influence of unrepresentative institutions. I think there is great validity in the argument that minority protection has become minority privilege and the balance has slipped to a point where majority interest and majority viewpoints are merely regarded as the unsavoury expression of élitism.

The fourth principle, and in terms of immediate urgency the most important, is the restoration of the trade union movement to its traditional and acceptable role in society; that of bargaining agent between management and workforce. A

Conservative government will be faced with the necessity of reminding trade unions that they are not in business to discuss questions of economic management at national level; nor to interfere in matters which in no way affect questions of pay, employment conditions or living standards of trade unionists *quâ* trade unionists.

If the first of these four principles is to become a reality what needs to be done? The most pressing requirement is for the Conservative Party to abandon its misplaced commitment to devolution. The Declaration of Perth always was an error and, albeit belatedly, it is now coming to be seen as such. Devolved powers to Scottish and Welsh assemblies will mean more government, more expense, greater bureaucracy, and will lead inexorably to the break-up of the United Kingdom, which is what the SNP wants. Our national traditions need unity, not separation. Anyone who fails to see this self-evident truth in the Conservative Party has a degree of myopia beyond cure. Nothing short of a firm and unequivocal rejection of the whole concept of devolution will suffice. Such a move would strengthen, not weaken, the Conservative position in Scotland, and give renewed faith to such stalwart Scottish MPs as Edward Taylor and Iain Sproat. Because no compromise is practical on this issue Mrs Thatcher should pay less attention to the liberal wing as expressed in the opinions of Alick Buchanan-Smith, Malcolm Rifkind and Edward Heath.

Race relations is another vexed area of politics which has seen an indeterminate and ineffectual Conservative response. No one is denying that immigrant communities should be treated fairly and with consideration but very many Conservatives are proclaiming loudly from the constituencies that immigration should cease forthwith (instead it is in actual fact on the increase) and that immigrants should not be granted the status of a privileged minority, yet privileged status is exactly what the new Race Relations Act affords to immigrants. No longer will it be necessary to show intent to stir up racial hatred as a basis for prosecution; it will suffice to show that the natural consequence of words spoken or written, or material distributed is that racial hatred has been stirred up. This test of strict liability is quite unacceptable, objectionable in principle to this type of area of politics and gratuitously insulting to the host community.

Practical policies to implement the second principle will need the most careful research and scrutiny. The day of the trade union-inspired economic boycott or political strike must be brought to an end by the full sanction of the law. This is not designed to limit the importance or significance of trade unions but rather to recognise their legitimate status within an industrial framework, and to remind them that obligations and duties are the proper counterbalance to rights and privileges freely accorded them in an open Society.

Given the acceptance of a satisfactory trade union rôle it is not now suggested that any single remedy will extricate us from our self-contrived economic predicament; a combination of a number of remedies alone is what is required and a Conservative government is better placed to achieve this because it is not hidebound by any doctrinal relationship with vested powers, such as the Labour Party's historical link with the trade unions. Moreover, some of the difficulties which Labour claims would confront a Conservative administration are precisely the sort which the present Labour government, no less than past Labour governments, has been singularly unsuccessful in dealing with prices and incomes policies, bargaining rights (e.g. British Leyland), demarcation disputes, closed shops and much else. Wage-cost inflation produced by monopoly union power must be tackled, and can be tackled, by government providing the framework within which bargaining powers can be exercised. It will need much research and planning but it can be done, given the will to do it.

The manner in which it can be done together with the implementation of the third and fourth principles will be the subject of another article.

Conservative opportunity

I was invited to write this article in *The Marylebone* for that magazine's December 1978 issue. The Conservatives were in opposition and James Callaghan's premiership was in its later stages. I set down the issues which I believed would bring Margaret Thatcher to power and the manner in which they could be achieved.

If I were asked what were the three essential preconditions for good government my reply would be a stable economy; maintenance of the Rule of Law; an effective Defence policy. No one of these is more or less important than the other two; indeed, in a sense they are inextricably interwoven.

Doubtless most fair-minded people would have to concede that any modern government has difficult and sometimes insuperable problems to contend with: equally, they would have to conclude that in all three spheres Britain has suffered grievously under a socialist régime which, while boasting of its compassion, care and concern for the people, has implemented policies with exactly the opposite effect, creating in their wake squalor, defeatism, alienation and misery. Quite an achievement for the oligarchs of collectivism!

Yet not the least of the Conservatives' difficulties in capitalising on socialist incompetence is the realisation that Jim Callaghan, that avuncular and complacent operator, is not the easiest of political targets. 'A week in politics is a long time', was one of the less platitudinous incantations of Harold Wilson. So it is.

The more's the pity, because millions of electors, having short memories, will need constant reminding that very, very many weeks ago it was Callaghan, the disastrous Chancellor who devalued the pound; that it was Callaghan, the less than competent Home Secretary who stopped recruitment to the police force; that it was Callaghan, as the Queen's First Minister who has now presided over the massive mismanagement of the economy to the extent that 1½ million souls are out of work.

The burning question for Conservatives is how can we ensure victory at the next election now that the trends are not quite as propitious as they were a few months ago? Will it be sufficient merely to await the people's verdict on collectivism? In other words the malevolent effects of undiluted socialism?

My answer to this last question is in the negative. The time is ripe now for a full restatement of some of the fundamental tenets of conservatism and a clear exposition of the policies based upon those principles.

What is required of Mrs Thatcher and her colleagues in the Shadow Cabinet is a determination to protect tradition, patriotism, freedom, discipline and order in society and a commitment to reverse the collectivist drift of the past few years. It will involve, above all, a re-awakening of the popular will to action done in a great cause – the revival of our nation and our country.

This will involve sacrifice for all and several doses of unpleasant political medicine. In the economic sphere it will mean the liquidation of our overseas debt at the earliest opportunity, a proper equation between production and consumption so that we do not, as a nation, spend more than we earn – a proposition so unbelievably simple that only an addle-headed socialist dreamer could possibly gainsay the need for it. We shall also need to impress upon the huge monopoly unions, such as the Transport and General Workers Union and the Amalgamated Union of Engineering Workers, that their legitimate role in our national life is to secure the best pay and conditions of work for their members in an atmosphere of responsible collective bargaining – not the sort of pie-in-the-sky, irresponsible and unpatriotic behaviour currently manifest in the Ford workers' rejection of that company's 16 per cent pay offer.

Here, of course, lies the Conservative dilemma. Should the party embrace the concept of a voluntary incomes policy or leave market forces, through the law of supply and demand, to determine the size of the pay packet? There is a considerable weight of argument in favour of both solutions, and doubtless Mrs Thatcher will not be without advice at the appropriate time. I can only say, without fear of contradiction, that whatever effect wage increases in excess of production may have on the national economy in terms of inflation such increases undoubtedly cause unemployment by pricing workers out of jobs.

And here the Conservatives face the second of their economic dilemmas. What to do about the unemployment figures – the legacy of socialist mismanagement? Job creation programmes can be encouraged by relieving some of the company tax pressures on small and middle-sized businesses. This will enable companies to expand production, and invest in new plant and machinery.

Yet whatever the benefits brought to business through tax concessions and reductions it will not be to much avail unless the Conservatives repeal the unnecessary Employment Protection Act, which is a positive disincentive to expansion. No quibbling here. This Act must go, together with the industrial attitudes which have pervaded it.

Perhaps to a greater extent than ever before issues other than the economy will be brought before the people at the next election. Law and order is certainly at the forefront. The Conservative Party needs to put the punitive and deterrent aspects of punishment at the heart of its programme with the reformative aspect second. I make no apology for supporting capital punishment for certain types of murder and corporal punishment for violent crime against the person in the belief that protection of the public must be the primary consideration of government. No one can seriously deny that the abolition of the death penalty in 1965 was partially, if not wholly, responsible for the immense statistical increase in murder; nor can it be denied that the introduction of corporal punishment would diminish violent crime, the soaring figures of which are more than adequate testimony to the complete and total failure of the liberal, 'do-gooder' monopoly of virtue in this matter.

Mrs Thatcher must look to her grass-roots where popular instincts are more soundly based than the crackpot posturings of certain ivory-tower academics, far removed from the everyday realities of life.

Instinctive popular reaction to what has recently happened in Rhodesia suggests again that Parliament has got it wrong. Sanctions may conceivably have had a purpose (although I would personally deny it) when there was a chance to persuade the Rhodesian Government to change course. That is no longer the case now. The five principles agreed between Mr Smith and Lord Home in 1973 have been approved and are in the course of being implemented. Why, therefore, did the Conservative Party not vote against the sanctions order in November? Well, 114 patriotic Tories refused to assist Labour in its grand design to bolster up the Bolshevik-backed forces of Nkomo and Mugabe whose disgusting and vicious terrorism against innocent black and white citizens of Rhodesia causes any alleged misdeeds of South Africa to pale into insignificance.

Elsewhere in foreign policy matters, Mrs Thatcher has given a firm and courageous lead. Let us hope that Rhodesia is an aberration not to be repeated. One such area where her lead is thoroughly to be welcomed is the need for increased expenditure on defence. Naval and military defence must top the bill but full consideration must also be given to the very real prospect of urban terrorism in mainland Britain in the 1980s. Why should Britain, in this respect, regard herself any differently from Germany or Italy? At the very least this needs forward planning on a grand scale. It requires a strengthening of the Special Branch, Security Service (responsible for counter-intelligence) and the Secret Intelligence Service (responsible for overseas intelligence activity). None of this will please the National Council for Civil Liberties, Anti-Nazi League, CND, Ian Mikardo, Joan Maynard and other representatives of the protest industry. But it will have the backing of the great mass of public, which is what matters.

A little considered issue, in electoral terms, is that of housing. Yet as Sir Anthony Eden perceived in his call for a property-owning democracy, 'a well-housed nation is a happy nation'. Much needs to be done in increasing the building programme under the aegis of private enterprise.

Perhaps the Conservatives cannot go into an election promising rent decontrol but once in power they should take action. Two targets for repeal should be the Rent Act 1977 and the Housing (Homeless Persons) Act 1978, which imposes upon local authorities a statutory obligation to house all and sundry in their borough who allege homelessness. There are, of course, many genuine cases of homelessness; there are, equally, many idle spongers and layabouts using the machinery of the Act to acquire housing rights in front of those on the council waiting list.

It may sound banal to suggest that the coming election will be the most important ever. How often have we heard that before? Yet never has there been such a valuable opportunity to oppose the ideology of socialism with that of conservatism, with, ideally, its accent on patriotism, private enterprise, competition, initiative, stability, tradition and order; as against the former with its appeal to collectivism, state regulation, bureaucracy, mediocrity, liberalism, internationalism, permissiveness and national decline. The choice is that of the electorate, but the propaganda behind that ultimate choice can point to the higher virtues to which the nation ought to address its attention; the very survival of our country and people, rather weightier, perhaps, than the price of cod or the popularity of Coronation Street.

Zimbabwe – A pessimistic prediction

I wrote this piece for *The Marylebone* bi-monthly journal of St Marylebone Conservatives, for its June/July 1980 edition. Its content is, I think, clear reflecting an issue which caused deep divisions within the Conservative Party. Robert Mugabe hangs on as president amidst economic and financial chaos which has been all too predictable. Whites have been fleeing the country in their droves; farmers have been driven off their land and the country has suffered massive unemployment and hyper-inflation. Unfortunately, I and others predicted this would happen and it has.

I am grateful to Editor Richard Wassell for inviting me to contribute a piece in reply to his analysis of the Zimbabwe-Rhodesia constitutional settlement, which appeared in the last issue of *The Marylebone*. I have no doubt that my views do not represent a majority opinion in the Party – nevertheless, they do conform to that of a sizeable minority, which I think, as events unfold, will grow even larger.

Although a somewhat unrepentant, 'unreconstructed' imperialist, I warmly welcomed the internal settlement, being sufficiently realist to appreciate the need for accelerating the pace of African political advancement, in both economic and social terms, thereby thwarting any genuine cause for unrest. At the same time the internal settlement ensured the protection of the quarter million European population, without whose initiative, drive and resourcefulness the land of Rhodesia could never have reached its present stage of development.

Moreover, let it be remembered that Bishop Muzorewa's government, elected on a 64% majority of the electorate, had the support of the then Conservative opposition, untainted by Foreign Office dictation and interference. Harold Wilson himself had opted for recognition and the Boyd Commission, comprising Lord Boyd of Merton and other dignitaries, announced their satisfaction as to the essential fairness of the election, with one dissenting voice only, the Liberal peer, Lord Chitnis.

Why, then, was not this democratically-conducted election, in which the so-called Patriotic Front had been invited to participate but refused, the signal for the newly-elected Conservative Government of May 1979 to recognise the validity of those elections and bring Rhodesia into the universal family of independent nations under a pro-Western, anti-Soviet, private enterprise-based government?

The answer to that question lies in the dominating influence which the permanent officials of the Foreign Office have on the conduct of British foreign policy. It has been so, with inescapably disastrous consequences, ever since 1945. The thesis was that a settlement without the participation of the Patriotic Front leaders, Nkomo and Mugabe, would neither result in the cessation of hostilities nor international recognition.

Lord Carrington deferred to that craven, misguided and unchivalrous advice. Julian Amery MP, who would have made a marvellous Foreign Secretary, and other Tory stalwarts, were certainly not slow in their reaction. Perhaps the most pertinent questions to which Lord Carrington failed to give satisfactory answers were, first, why was the newly-elected Conservative Government unwilling to prosecute a vigorous counter-insurgency, anti-terrorist war in support of the Rhodesian armed forces, against the Marxist-inspired forces of Zanu and Zapu, using every available military measure to achieve that end together with sufficient economic reprisals against Zambia, Mozambique and Angola? Secondly, since when has the concept of 'international recognition' been the pre-condition for the grant of independence?

Has Britain so abased herself in the counsels of diplomacy that she is now required to defer to each and every squalid, abject one-party dictatorship, whether in Africa or elsewhere, in order to satisfy some unrealistic, indeed unlawful, political requirement, namely the abdication of British responsibility over her own colonial territory?

It is my firm contention that had the Government introduced a Bill conferring legislative independence upon Rhodesia, consistent with the six principles and in comformity with the internal settlement, every self-respecting sovereign state would have given its formal blessing to the new independent state.

Alas! We know what transpired – high jinks in Lusaka at the Commonwealth Conference, where Britain was twice threatened with expulsion from her own creation, and ultimately the Lancaster House agreements which the Tory Right regards as a shameful betrayal. Muzorewa's cause and that of his followers, to say nothing of the European destiny, were buried amidst the sordid appeasement of the repellent Nkomo and the even more repellent Mugabe, mass murderers, guilty of unspeakable crimes, largely against innocent Black tribespeople. Muzorewa's credibility was dissipated, while the massacre of British missionaries at the Elim Pentecostal Mission, the shocking murder by bayonet of little Natasha Glenny, aged 6½ months, the shooting-down of the Viscount aeroplane, etc., became forgotten nightmares as Nkomo and Mugabe, ex-terrorists, ex-guerillas, but now freedom fighters with the equivalent of diplomatic status, obtained virtually everything they bargained for.

Now we have the unseemly spectacle of Mugabe – exclaiming how much he loves Lord Soames (let it be said that the latter had a difficult task which he accomplished without blemish to his reputation) and the Reverend Banana dispensing earthly advice from his presidential seat.

It is true that Mugabe is preaching reconciliation and it is, of course, possible that the leopard has changed its spots; if so all to the good. But I fear the worst. I foresee a large scale exodus of Europeans. Indeed, already 35% of European civil servants have given in their notice and several thousand Muzorewa supporters are living in fear of harassment and intimidation. If Mugabe himself proves to be insufficiently resolute in the pursuit of collectivism he will, to be sure, be replaced by someone who will.

A great advance in industrial relations

I had become knowledgeable about industrial relations matters, and particularly their legal ramifications, during the late 1960s. Many of the preparatory government documents such as *In Place of Strife* and *Fair Deal at Work* will be remembered by older readers and, of course, industrial relations specialists. I wrote this article for *The Marylebone*, bi-monthly journal of St Marylebone Conservatives, for its May 1973 edition. The Industrial Relations Act 1971 was a major piece of legislation of the Conservative government under Edward Heath (1970-1974). Even if much of the content has been repealed the background to its introduction into the statute-book remains a compelling subject of study.

With the Industrial Relations Act 1971 now firmly operational, one is becoming increasingly accustomed to demands for its repeal. The Labour Party is already committed to this course of action and certain doubting Thomases amongst staid Tory voices are now adopting similar positions.

For instance, in the 23 December issue of *The Spectator*, the leading article casts grave doubts about the wisdom of the Act as a means of improving management – union relationships and providing a framework within which a fair system of industrial law might operate. "Sane heads within the Administration privately concede the follies enmeshed within the Act even when they decline to admit the profound misconception of the Act itself". *The Spectator*, perhaps with the benefit of hindsight, thus takes up the standpoint of every militant to the trade union movement seeking to ascribe the blame for poor performance in some industries to the fact of legislation rather than to place it where in all truth it really belongs, at the door of industrial wreckers, inefficient management and out-of-date negotiating procedures.

It is very doubtful whether any "sane heads" within the Administration have doubts about the Industrial Relations Act. It was never contended that legislation, of itself, could create good industrial relations but it was generally accepted both by the Government and by the Tory Party Annual Conference that within the framework of clearly defined legislation the processes of collective bargaining would be greatly simplified and the rights of the worker better protected.

Our economy has been confronted with difficulties in competing with other countries because increased wages have not been matched by increased productivity; much of this is the consequence of bad labour relations. Although by no means unfavourable compared with the record of some European countries in terms of time lost through strikes, Britain's strike record up to 1971 had been characterised uniquely by the fact that some 80% of stoppages were in breach of agreements with employers; much economic damage was being caused by the threat of sudden strikes and other forms of industrial action such as 'go slows', 'working to rule' and bans on overtime emanating from archaic wage structures, insistence upon over-manning and demarcation disputes. These were some of the features which bedevilled the industrial scene which needed correcting, and which formed the background to the passing of the Industrial Relations Act.

Nor were the misgivings about the state of industrial relations and the need for some legislation confined to the Conservative Party. The Labour Party itself set up a Royal Commission under Lord Donovan's chairmanship to examine trade unionism, having been compelled to pass the Trades Dispute Act 1965 in order to offset the loophole discovered (and thought never to have existed) in the Trades Disputes Act 1906 which has been exploited in the famous House of Lords decision in ***Rookes v Barnard 1964***. The Donovan Commission sat for three years. Its main conclusions were that although strikes per se were a contributory factor to our industrial malaise the real cause of the trouble was the breakdown of the system of collective bargaining. In particular, the Commission found that the existence of two systems of negotiating wage agreements, operating side by side, were the real bugbear. The one, a system of national, industry-wide agreements, and the other, more informal, system of shop floor bargaining tended to militate against industrial harmony and only served to promote unofficial strikes, payment-by-results schemes which were never properly structured, wage drifts and excessive increases in the amount of overtime worked.

It is a salutary exercise to examine the extent to which the Donovan proposals were reflected in the Labour Party's policy document ***In Place of Strife***, which, despite the beer and sandwiches at No 10, Mr Wilson and Barbara Castle were prevented from turning into legislation. ***In Place of Strife*** contained 25 proposals, 19 of which were recommended by Donovan. Companies employing more than 5,000 workers were to have to register procedure agreements with the Department of Employment: The Commission on Industrial Relations was to be set up; statutory machinery was to be inaugurated to protect employees against unfair dismissal; trade unions would be required to register and to observe certain standards in their rule books covering matters pertaining to discipline. These and many other proposals for reform of trade union law were thus accepted by the Labour Government and, *ipso facto*, a substantial section of the whole Labour Movement as providing a framework for looking ahead towards a better climate of management-union relationships. It cannot, therefore, be too clearly overstated that what has transpired since has not so much been an attack on the concept of industrial relations legislation as an attack on the complexion of Government which has introduced it. And Lord George-Brown is not far wide of the mark when he points to the growth of extremism and militancy which had spearheaded this attack and which has overtaken so many of our key industries.

The Conservative proposals for industrial law reform, so far from being misconceived and badly prepared, as *The Spectator* would have us think, were the product of meticulous research and analysis. As early as 1958 the Inns of Court Conservative and Unionist Society produced a policy document entitled ***A Giant's Strength*** which generated much interest and sparked off considerable debate within the Party. A decade later in April 1968 the Party's blueprint for industrial law reform ***Fair Deal at Work*** was published. Most of the proposals formulated found expression in the 1971 Act and it is surprising, in view of the alleged inconsistencies and hardships contained in the Act that ***Fair Deal at Work*** was never subjected to severer criticism at the time. The answer would of course be that public opinion had become so alienated by major industrial stoppages, such as the Girling Brake dispute (in which a strike of 22 workers resulted in 5,000 workers being laid off) and the Barbican and Horseferry Road disputes in the construction industry that it became politically unwise for the Labour Party to attack an idea which, in any case, it had itself first conceived. And certainly it can never be said that the Conservative Party failed to make its proposals known to the public at large. Indeed, a major plank of its election platform was fought on the issue.

Why is there such apparent hostility to the Industrial Relations Act? Vic Feather, General Secretary of the TUC, has accused the Government of wanting to "turn the clock back 100 years and curtailing the basic rights of workpeople and their unions". This sort of vague, generalised statement has typified the nature of the attack on the Government. Perhaps Mr Feather saw the role of the unions more clearly when he told the Annual Conference of the Clerical and Administrative Workers Union on 16 April 1972: "We are not only representatives of the public interest; we are the public interest". Another generalised statement is that the Act is "anti-Union" and will create more troubles than it is designed to cure. The Trades Union Congress has voted its overwhelming opposition to the Act (although it has relented on its former view that trades unions should not appear before the National Industrial Relations Court to defend themselves). On the other hand, some more accommodating noises have been heard. Roy Jenkins in a speech at Leicester on 24 June 1972, declared that the "mere slogan of repeal will not be enough". This would leave no framework of industrial law, and less protection than the unions have had since 1875. And the *New Statesman* of 23 June 1972 proclaimed that: "It is not enough for the Labour Party simply to give vent to ritual cries for the abolition of the Act". The whole Labour movement – and not just its top brass in secret conclave – should now be concentrating its collective mind on working out for the future a fair system of industrial law". On the Union side, Mr William Hogarth, General Secretary of the National Union of Seamen, in *The Guardian* on 5 May 1972, reflected the views of responsible leadership when he asked: "Do we want to bring ourselves down, as I say the Miners did, to the gutter to hold the whole country to ransom? I will be the last to want to take that action. I would rather resign first".

In the vanguard of the agitation against the Industrial Relations Act, need it be repeated, have been the Communists and the Trotskyists. Their influence, particularly the former, has been out of all proportion to their relatively small numbers, while their propensity for exacerbating difficulties has been infinite. Mr Wilson, to his credit, correctly appreciated the position at the time of the Seamen's strike in 1966 when he said that there was not a single industrial stoppage in this country in which the full weight of the Communist Party and its industrial apparatus was not brought to bear. Ray Gunter, a former Minister of Labour, has referred to the "Unholy Alliance" between the Communist Party and the Labour left in industrial affairs and Lord Robens has commented upon the "Communist conspiracy", in industry. During the 'Kill the Bill' marches and demonstrations before the Act became law, Communist involvement was very apparent. Huge amounts of literature from the left were devoted to highly subjective appraisals of the new law with the aim of mobilising the uncommitted. The intentions of the Communist Party and their cohorts are made abundantly clear for all who are prepared to read their literature. For instance, in "Carr's Bill – and how to kill it" by Bert Ramelson, the Communist Party's Industrial Organiser, under a section entitled 'The Death Warrant of Trade Unionism', it is stated: "Whatever else may be confusing in this conglomeration of legal double talk, what is clear is that workers will be robbed of this elemental and fundamental function of a trade union – the unfettered right to combine and use combined strength to compel the bosses to yield to what workers feel are their just demands". (Note the phrase 'compel the bosses'). At the 32nd Congress of the Communist Party in November 1971, Mr John

Gollan, the Party's General Secretary, in moving the resolution on 'Unity, the Communist Party and the struggle for socialism' declared: "Toryism is the traditional enemy of trade unionism. It is scared stiff of union strength being used in action. But we feel Mr Carr – the unions are not going to be brought to heel. The left and the Communist Party can look back with pride to the struggle against Carr's Bill, one of the finest in Labour history. It is because of that battle that the unions, with a few exceptions, are fighting Carr's Act and will make it inoperable". Statements like these have been quoted by Communist trades unionists in all the major conflicts to date.

Much of the animosity to the Industrial Relations Act has been directed towards the National Industrial Relations Court which came into being on 1 December 1971.

From its earliest decisions it became quite clear that the Court was not the 'bosses court' as it was so often described by its detractors. Nor was it 'politically' inspired. An examination of the judgments it has handed down reveals quite plainly that it is totally impartial. In two cases, which have been given scant publicity – ***Bloomfield v Springfield Hosiery Ltd*** and ***Clarke Chapman – John Thompson Ltd v Walters*** the court has created new precedents in holding that where a worker goes on strike and is subsequently reinstated by his employers his continuity of service for the purposes of claims to redundancy payment is uninterrupted. These decisions are clearly "pro-worker". In another case, ***Marshall v Harland & Wolff***, a shipyard fitter was dismissed from his employment after being absent sick for 18 months with no evidence at all as to when he might be able to return to work. Nevertheless he was allowed to claim redundancy payment, despite strong arguments that his contract of employment had been severed by long-term illness – hardly a "union-bashing" or "anti-worker" judgment.

The most vehement, and least informed, attacks against the Industrial Relations Act have centred on the concept of the "unfair industrial practice". The main categories of such practices include action discriminating against any worker on grounds of membership, or non-membership, of a union; action to force anyone not connected with a dispute to break a contract with an employer who is so connected; e.g. blacking of goods, sympathy strikes; action in breach of a legally enforceable collective agreement. In March 1972 the Industrial Court had to consider its first case on the question of an unfair industrial practice. The owner of a metal factory brought a complaint against four of his employees, all of whom had long records of service with the company (The Kaymet Company). Allegations were made that some workers had been encouraging their fellow workers to withdraw their labour. The way in which the proceedings were conducted is described by Gordon Scott, a law reporter in the NIRC, in an article in *New Law Journal* on 30 November. "The four respondents appeared in person and the writer recalls this case for its rather startling informality. The complainant employed was addressed as 'Mr Sydney' by the respondents. In his turn the complainant called the respondents by their Christian names. Sir John Donaldson demonstrated his ability as a conciliator, showing a clear grasp of the situation, coupled with charm and good humour. After an hour or so the parties were asked if they would care to discuss their differences privately and amongst themselves in the hope that matters might be settled without the court being required to make an order. The offer was accepted and in a short while the parties had returned to court with agreement reached". The informality thus described is by no means untypical of this court.

The first really major testing round for the NIRC were the docks disputes. On 23 March the court ordered an end to the 'blacking' of container goods by members of the Transport and General Workers Union at Liverpool and Hull Docks and on 29 March the TGWU was fined £5,000 for contempt of court as a result of a complaint of unfair industrial practice made by Heaton's Transport (St Helens) Ltd. On 20 April the court imposed a further fine, of £50,000 on the TGWU for confirmed contempt, and on 24 April the General Purposes Committee of the TUC finally decided to permit unions to defend themselves before the NIRC. The giant union was represented at the court for the first occasion on 3 May and on 9 May the TGWU requested, through counsel, the Court to review its orders on the question of contempt. Although both the ***Heaton*** case, and two other similar cases, were reversed on appeal, the Industrial Court's judgments were restored in the House of Lords, the principle being firmly established that a union could not escape the actions of its shop stewards even though the latter may have acted without the authority of the union. The vindication of the Industrial Court's judgments, and by necessary implication the

Industrial Relations Act itself is surely highly significant. The largest trade union in the country with a surfeit of monopoly bargaining power was obliged to recognise that the court could not be ignored and duly paid its fines, and secondly the TUC was obliged to stop boycotting the machinery of the Act. It is further arguable that the Act itself was not the immediate cause of the trouble in the docks. With containerisation, rundown of labour and numerous clashes between the varying interests of different groups of workers in the TGWU trouble already existed. As Mr Maurice MacMillan MP has said (28 June 1972) "What the Act was doing to these problems was to very properly focus attention on them; stop them being swept under the carpet; and to serve as a catalyst for a settlement". The subsequent, and undoubtedly bizarre, happenings involving the intervention of the Official Solicitor in the ***Midland Cold Storage*** case were never properly explained to the lay public and were used as a further means by opponents of the Act to discredit it. As the Jones-Aldington Committee had at that time just published its recommendations for enlarging the area of dock work the reasons for imprisoning the five dockers no longer held good, and it was this consideration which was paramount in the NIRC's decision to release the five men more than anything else.

The questions of the enforcement of judgments has been clarified further in the latest case on "blacking" – ***Howitt Transport Ltd v TGWU*** 10 November– by Sir John Donaldson, when he said, "in relation to organisations, we wish to make it abundantly clear that the penalties will, in all foreseeable circumstances, be financial, however onerous they may be; that they could range up to total sequestration of assets but that the liberty of the subject will not be involved". This highly important statement of principle has had little publicity. It takes away from the detractors of the Act their main source of grievance, namely that its machinery could be used to inflict judgments leading to imprisonment.

Whatever the economic consequences of the railwaymen's dispute in April 1973 the invocation of the Act's provisions only prevented a worse situation from developing. When the Secretary of State for Employment applied under S.138 for a "cooling off" order against ASLEF, NUR and TSSA in response to the work-to-rule orders issued by the Unions' Executives, the

Minister was doing no more than he was statutorily required to do in a situation which constituted "irregular industrial action short of a strike". It is noteworthy that Labour's ***In Place of Strife*** had envisaged similar procedures. The subsequent cooling-off period of 14 days was observed, and the Secretary of State's application for the three unions to take a ballot of their members was upheld, in the event justifying the unions' stated position. There can be no doubt at all that both the cooling-off period and the secret ballot greatly minimised public inconvenience and the hold-up of essential supplies. It is probable that but for the Act the consequences would have been more serious and it is certainly true that while the final inflationary settlement was being achieved through negotiation, the working of the Act averted worse industrial action.

The strange case of James Good has also helped to throw light on the way the Act operates. Good's determination to join the Amalgamated Union of Engineering Workers, the second biggest union in Britain and the most militant, brought him into stating his case before an Industrial Tribunal set up under the Act, notwithstanding the fact that his membership had lapsed on three separate occasions as a result of unpaid contributions. The AUEW, Sudbury Branch, kept out Good because of his support for the Tory Government and his record as a strike-breaker. In fact the Sudbury Branch under its Rule Book should have expelled at least a quarter of its members for arrears of payments, but failed to do so. The AUEW's blind obduracy landed them in difficulties which the Act was designed to save them from. Good sought to assert his right under Section 65 of the Act which states that no person shall be barred from membership, or members from attending meetings by any arbitrary or unreasonable discrimination. Had the AUEW, which is now alone among Trade Unions in its total boycott of the courts, presented its case at the Industrial Tribunal it might have secured the verdict and prevented the Industrial Court's fine of £50,000 plus costs being imposed. As it was the AUEW's case, which in this instance was not a weak one, was never heard. It can hardly blame anyone but itself.

One of the planks in Labour's platform to sabotage the Industrial Relations Act was that it would bring about an increase in strikes. In fact, so far the reverse is true. The total number of stoppages in the first six months of 1970 under the

Labour Government was 2,355, whereas the total in the first five months of 1971 was 1,004 compared to a total of 935 in the first five months of 1972, and the number of strikes in the engineering and motor industries, where wildcat strikes have traditionally been notorious, was halved between the first half of 1970 and the first half of 1971.

The Industrial Relations Act has had a number of other major successes; for instance, Industrial Tribunals received power to handle unfair industrial practices, breaches of contract of employment and compensation for unfair dismissal. 1,757 unfair dismissal claims and 148 other complaints were made in the first 13 weeks since the sanction relating to appeals to Industrial Tribunals became operative. Some 1,270 of these have been settled by Conciliation Officers and in 42% of cases tribunal hearings were averted; 221 voluntary settlements were achieved and 407 complaints withdrawn.

It is reasonable to assume that a fair number of these disputes would have been the cause of industrial action.

The importance to the government of the Industrial Relations Act should not be understated. It was a major plank in its industrial policy; it has by and large achieved its objectives and is seen as the great reforming measure it was conceived as. Above all it is essential for the Act to work and remain on the statute book because it is the product of comparative long term planning, the first modern attempt to bring about harmonious industrial relations through an orderly legal framework. The massive left-wing propaganda campaign to portray the Act as a betrayal of working class interests must be defeated by constant publicity demonstrating the very considerable number of provisions showing how, in fact, working class interests are protected and advanced by the Act. It will be a test of the Government's clamour for repeal with which it will be confronted in 1973.

Trade Unions: Further statutory progress

I wrote this piece for *Monday World*, quarterly journal of the Monday Club, in October 1980. It is an examination of the Employment Act 1980 and its impact on industrial relations. I am a supporter of collective bargaining, fair wage settlements and a constructive relationship between management and organised labour. Many of these issues and the background to them are addressed. My own experience within a trade union, NATFHE, has been of value. In more recent times, I have been more sympathetic to the closed shop concept in a way which I hadn't been when this piece was written.

There is no more disquieting political theme to Conservatives than that of untrammelled trade union power. The praiseworthy attempts to bring the unions within a framework of law, as embodied in the Industrial Relations Act 1971, came to nothing as that excellent piece of legislation became confused in the public mind with the counter-inflation policies, the world economic recession of 1972 and the miners' confrontation – and not vice-versa, note – with the Heath Government of 1973-74.

Much water has passed under the political bridge since those heady days and the Conservatives are again in a position to influence the proper relationship between organised labour and the rest of the community. Much of their preparatory work in opposition has become enshrined in the recently enacted Employment Act 1980.

Of course, there is still much that needs to be done to redress 75 years of unwarranted privileges granted to the labour movement but at least it is gratifying to see the government introducing measures on secret ballots and picketing that the Monday Club has been in favour of for some years – as outlined in previous publications, such as *Conservatism Regained* and *Signpost to Salvation*, and in particular, *Towards Industrial Sanity*. It is still, no doubt, galling to most that the new measures do not allow trade union funds to be sequestered in compensation for payment to strikers' families, and arguably, that sizeable quango ACAS, not dissimilar to the former Commission on Industrial Relations, could have had its wings clipped or been scrapped altogether.

Still, let us not be churlish. The reforms introduced are along the right lines. In this article, I shall seek to examine two specific areas of industrial relations in the context of the new law; both can be considered suitable cases for further treatment; the first is the whole vexed subject of immunities; the second is the closed shop.

In the knowledge that trade union immunities have existed largely unchecked since 1906, when the Trades Disputes Bill became law, the Conservative Government came to power in May 1979 with a clear-cut and popular mandate to redress the massive imbalance. The Employment Act 1980, sadly, is deficient over this issue although a Green Paper is promised in the Autumn with a view to examining the matter further.

Originally the Government did not contemplate tackling the question of immunities at all in the Employment Bill and it was only as a result of the House of Lords decisions in *Express Newspapers v McShane* (13 December 1979) and *Duport Steel v Sirs* that a working paper on 19 February 1980 was published as a basis for positive action. The effect of the House of Lords' judgments in the *Duport* case had been that there was not, in essence, two disputes as the Court of Appeal had held (one between the Iron & Steel Trades Confederation and the British

Steel Corporation, and the other between ISTC and the Government about financial assistance for BSC) but one dispute in which the private sector strike was manifestly designed to further the dispute with BSC and therefore "in contemplation of furtherance of a trade dispute" and subject to immunity.

The House of Lords decisions were evidently handed down with regret. Lord Diplock, for instance, in the *Duport* case pronounced:

> "given the existence of a trade dispute involves it granting to trade unions a power which has no other limits than their own self-restraint, to inflict by means which are contrary to the general law, untold harm to industrial enterprises unconcerned with the particular dispute, to the employees of such enterprises, to members of the public and to the nation itself" (*The Times*, 8 February 1980).

In his parliamentary statement introducing the new clause (now Section 17 Employment Act 1980) the Employment Secretary confirmed that ...

> "there is now virtually unlimited immunity for secondary industrial action. That is not a situation any responsible Government could allow to continue ... What the Government are therefore trying to do is to draw back immunity to a reasonable and sensible line" (2 April 1980).

The Tory Right would argue with some conviction that the Government's proposals do not, in fact "draw back immunity to a reasonable and sensible line" because they still permit secondary industrial action – that is, action taken against an employer who is not a party to the trade dispute – in circumstances where the action is taken by the employees of first suppliers of first customers of the employer in dispute and when the principal purpose, objectively judged, is directly to disrupt the supplies of goods or services to or from that employer. Moreover, primary action – that is action directed at the employer with whom the employees are in dispute – continues to retain a broad immunity.

So we face the prospect of an Autumn where the inadequacy of industrial law to restrain immunities will not be lost on the trade unions and their legal advisers in the impending struggles with the Government in the pay round. Unions will be able to stiffen their sinews laughing their way into Downing Street armed with the realisation that they can:

a) take secondary blacking action against major suppliers, such as the gas and electricity boards.

b) take secondary action preventing a customer from receiving his goods causing severe economic hardship, if not bankruptcy, to any small firm denied the goods for which it has paid.

c) instruct employees that they can still be allowed to picket their own workplace in support of a trade dispute even though they are not involved or concerned in any way.

Is this timid approach in the reform of a key feature of industrial relations really in accord with the aspirations of Tory voters and supporters? Does it redress the monstrous imbalance in power which has accelerated since 1906 and which the Tory Government pledged it would reverse? It is true that the promised Green Paper may take the matter further but the consultations associated with that particular activity will take an inordinate length of time and the Government's own economic difficulties will further encourage the argument that "this is not the most appropriate time to deal with the issue".

The other area of industrial relations where there is a considerable difference of opinion between the Government and a majority of its supporters is that of the closed shop. Only a closed shop (union membership agreement) emanating from agreement between employers and unions is covered by the legislation. It extends to the pre-entry closed shop agreement, which excludes individuals from a job unless they are already members of a specified union, as well as post-entry agreements whereby employees are required to join the union within an agreed period after commencing employment. It can also cover an agreement whereby all the workers in a particular section must either belong to a specified union or pay a contribution to the union equivalent to normal union dues. It is noteworthy that a closed shop agreement can be an unwritten 'arrangement' based on custom and practice, which itself can be criticised for lack of certainty and for investing too much power in the union in interpreting finer points of construction.

Under S.4 Employment Act 1980, where there is a closed shop a right is given to employees, and to those seeking employment, not to be unreasonably excluded from a trade union and to receive compensation when appropriate. And by S.58 Employment Protection (Consolidation) Act 1978 where a union membership agreement exists it is fair to dismiss an employee for refusing to join a specified union, except where he objects ... "on grounds of conscience or other deeply held personal conviction", or where he was not a member of one of the unions concerned at the time the agreement was made.

This so-called "conscience clause" has been widened from the original wording ("genuinely objects on grounds of religious belief to being a member of any trade union whatsoever"). Now, in the case of newly-established closed shops dismissal for non-union membership will be regarded as unfair if the union membership agreement was not approved in a ballot in which at least 80% of employees concerned voted in favour, the ballot being conducted in secret and giving all those entitled to vote the right to do so.

Government Ministers have repeatedly referred to the closed shop as a "tyranny" yet paradoxically the legislative measures taken to curb it deal not at root with the institution of the closed shop itself but merely with what are conceived as its worst excesses. This is certainly preferable to no remedial action at all but it is still cold comfort to the countless number of long-serving employees whose dedication and loyalty have resulted in monetary compensation and not job security, the object of the sacrifice made.

The Government has undoubtedly been influenced in its approach by the mellifluous tones of certain prominent industrialists and certainly some industries have made a powerful case for the retention of the closed shop principle; for instance, the acting profession has repeatedly emphasised that the theatre would die but for the retention of a closed shop and successfully identified the public interest with its maintenance. Arguably there are other professions equally at risk and whose extinction would be even more detrimental to the public interest.

Although the most cogent argument in favour of the closed shop is the familiar one that ... "he does not sow neither shall he reap", known as the "free-rider" syndrome, (on the grounds that the non-unionist enjoys the fruit of the union's negotiations with the employer yet makes no contribution to his share of the cost), the arguments against the whole concept of the union membership agreement are far more compelling: closed shops are an unacceptable infringement of a person's individual freedom and right of free association; the economic effects of the closed shop necessarily limit the number and quality of entrants to a union and thereby restrict the right to do skilled work.

The craft unions, for instance, use the closed shop to restrict entry to the craft. They require early entry through apprenticeship which causes shortages of skilled labour; moreover, production methods, job allocation and general conditions of work may be controlled by a workforce which is not necessarily the better equipped to make such decisions. A particularly significant example of this is in the newspaper and printing industry where the controversy over the freedom of journalists to belong or not to belong to the National Union of Journalists is a major, if not primary, cause of the beleaguered state of industrial relations in that industry.

Perhaps more significant than any of the aforementioned arguments, however, against the closed shop is the European experience. The Conservative Government has committed itself impliedly, through its membership of the European Economic Community, to the harmonisation and rationalisation of laws between member-states; yet in no other part of the EEC is there legislation in force specifically enabling a closed shop to be introduced. In France the closed shop was outlawed by a law of 27 April 1956 which inserted a prohibition into the *Code du Travail*; a similar situation pertains in Western Germany as a result of three decisions of the Federal Labour Court, and in Italy, under Article 15 of the *Statuto dei Lavoratori*, 1970. Any agreement which has the object of making the employment of a worker conditional upon his membership or non-union membership of a union is null and void. In the Republic of Ireland the Supreme Court has ruled that the imposition of a closed shop contravenes the constitutional rights of a worker. Additional to this, the European Convention on Human Rights asserts that freedom of conscience is a right and the Court of Strasbourg has recently ruled accordingly.

Again, the argument that good industrial relations are the invariable accompaniment of the closed shop is a demonstrable fallacy. Where closed shops are most widespread as for instance in the motor-manufacturing, ship-building, coal-mining and port industries, industrial disputes and stoppages account for a very considerable proportion of man-hours lost in industry.

In a climate where the economic recession shows no immediate signs of abating the Government's nerve is being tested as never before. Any departure from fundamental strategy will be treated contemptuously. Pressures will continue to mount, not least from the over-mighty TUC but should there be any weakening of resolve to do what still has to be done in the clear light of reality, as the Employment Act becomes increasingly tested in business, industry and commerce, then those who proclaimed from the outset that the new measures might prove inadequate will have seen their prophecy and insight borne out. The Government would do well to grasp the nettle at an early stage and strengthen the Act to meet the weaknesses outlined in this article.

Tackling crime – the way forward

This article of mine was written for the *Monday World* quarterly journal of the Monday Club in May 1972. The principles behind crime prevention, punishment and rehabilitation have not changed that much but what has changed is the huge increase in the volume of crime over the 44 years since this piece was written and with it the increase in the number of criminals in prison. It is incumbent upon government to improve conditions for prisoners, shorten sentences except with the most serious crimes, but above all, to build more prisons and prepare criminals for a life outside prison so that recidivism can be considerably reduced.

It will be recalled that the Conservative Shadow Cabinet, as it then was, convened a weekend conference a few months prior to the General Election of 1970 to determine an overall broad strategy for fighting the election, and adopting the political programme which would see it through the course of a five-year Parliament.

One of the central themes of this Conference was the high priority given to the issue of law and order and its corollary, crime and punishment. The prime instigator of this *bête-noire* of Tory ideologues was the St Marylebone Member, Rt Hon Quintin Hogg, QC, MP, who, as Shadow Home Secretary, was expected to hold that portfolio in a Conservative Government of the future. In the event Mr Hogg went to the Lords as Hailsham and much of the seemingly tougher approach to this troublesome issue departed with him.

For some reason the Prime Minister, while fully endorsing Hailsham's analysis of the need for a more realistic, pragmatic approach to law and order at Selsdon appointed as Home Secretary in Reginald Maudling, a man of considerable business and financial acumen but perhaps not altogether the ideal supremo for the challenging task of combating the mounting crime wave and civic disorder which characterised the whole period of Labour Government.

The alarming rise in crime statistics, as shown in the following Table, is surely indicative of the mistaken policies pursued by successive Governments in concentrating upon rehabilitation rather than punishment as the function and *raison d'être* of the criminal law.

CRIME STATISTICS 1961-1970

	Indictable Crime	Violence Against the Person
1961	806,900	17,601
1962	896,424	17,948
1963	978,076	20,083
1964	1,067,963	23,470
1965	1,133,882	25,549
1966	1,199,589	26,716
1967	1,207,354	29,049
1968	1,289,090	31,850
1969	1,488,638	37,818
1970	1,555,995	41,088

It is frequently asserted by the proponents of so-called liberal opinion that such figures can be misleading. The most specious arguments are usually advanced that in a tolerant, forward-looking, progressive climate of opinion (in other words, the cloud cuckooland which they alone inhabit) society should stiffen its sinews and be prepared, at whatever ultimate cost to the community, to integrate within itself all those disparate elements which reject the normal rules of behaviour and conduct which any civilised community requires for its self-preservation. Unfortunately, their unchallenged assumptions have generally impressed our legislators. Whereas disciplined, ordered societies would rather isolate lawbreakers, whilst always reserving to them the right to take their place again in the community after due process of law, the tendency under British democracy of recent years has been the reverse – to give to such lawbreakers another chance and to use the discretion which the criminal law often affords to make imprisonment a last-resort sanction.

This misconception of the notions of justice and tolerance are at root the explanation for society's failure to conquer crime, and thus are the public hoodwinked into believing against their better judgment that much of the penal legislation of recent years is the natural extension of society becoming more civilised and healthy? In fact the reverse is true for the so-called civilising influences of liberalism merely reflect the obsessional, almost paranoiac belief of the liberal mind that the criminal is a product of an unjust and illiberal society. The extremely low crime rate in an illiberal society, such as the Soviet Union, immediately disproves this thesis.

It is indeed sad that the wider implications of this absurdity have become so deeply implanted in the thinking of many sections of the Conservative Party. How often have we heard, for instance, that one of the most serious difficulties faced by those in the vanguard of the struggle against crime is overcrowding in prisons? A moment's reflection upon this obtuse proposition must lead to its rejection. Prison over-crowding has nothing remotely to do with the positive function of law enforcement; it may well be an administrative inconvenience for the prison service but that is all it can be. The answer to this particular problem lies in the construction of more and better prisons, a requirement made all the more pressing by the boom in the immediate post-war prison population of 1946 from 15,000 to the present figure of 40,000.

The last factor notwithstanding, and accepting that an increase in the number of prisons is necessary, the movement towards finding alternatives to prison seems unobjectionable, subject to the proviso that loss of liberty remains the central objective. But it does seem doubtful whether the experiment of the suspended sentence, pioneered by the Labour Government in 1967, is one worth continuing. The suspended sentence is derived from the Criminal Justice Act 1967, Section 39, the effect of which is that where a court passes sentence of imprisonment for not more than two years, it has power to order that the sentence shall not take effect unless during the period specified the offender commits another offence punishable with imprisonment, and a court then orders that the criminal sentence shall take effect. "The period specified", for the purposes of the Act known as the "operational period", must not be less than one year or more than three years. Moreover, the court upon passing a suspended sentence, must explain to the offender the meaning of such a sentence.

The deficiency of the suspended sentence as an instrument of policy is only too apparent. Apart from the fact that it embodies in the law the notion of "another chance", (which, however admirable on humanitarian grounds, is hardly likely to have deterrent value – indeed 55% of first offenders commit one or more further offences), it places an increasing burden on the probation services. In addition it is often advantageous, both to the prisoner and the community, if the prisoner serves a short spell in prison which may prove to have a salutary remedial effect upon him rather than serve a longer period later due to the failure of a suspended sentence. And yet despite the apparently self-explanatory benefits of such a sentencing policy, the Society of Conservative Lawyers, in its "Crisis in Crime and Punishment" is of the view that ... "most courts today regard prison as a sentence of last resort. But the courts all too often have no choice. Courts could be given a wider range of alternatives that do not involve any immediate loss of liberty".

Again it is sad to state that woolly thinking like this should inform such an important plank of party policy. Precisely what are these alternatives "that do not involve any immediate loss of liberty"? Is it now to be suggested seriously that the equation: criminal offence – loss of liberty: is to be replaced by some other equation which involves no such loss of liberty? Another interpretation might be that since it is proving extremely difficult to construct more prisons, even in this highly mechanised age, punishment should now be regarded as a very secondary criterion in the scale of things. Absent from the Society's assessment of the situation is the very alarming increase in the number of indictable offences already referred to and the resultant obligation, thus made more poignant, which the State owes to the community to ensure that a drastic reduction in crime of all sorts takes place. Is it not common sense to suppose that if the deprivation of liberty for a pampered few will help to secure the greater enjoyment of liberty for the law-abiding many then not merely justice, but good government as well, will be seen to have been done?

To return, however, to the question of the provision of alternatives in prison sentences, it may be recalled that Lady Wootton's Committee in its report on non-custodial and semi-custodial Penalties, published last Autumn, first broached this contentious issue with the disarming suggestion that it should be the prisoner, and not the courts, which should be given power to opt for the alternative. In other words, community service under strict supervision such as digging in hospital grounds, and road building (in itself an excellent concept) would only be an available measure of punishment if the criminal himself preferred it to imprisonment; the ostensible reason for permitting the criminal to dictate the punishment best suited to him is that the European Declaration of Human Rights bans any form of compulsory labour other than in a prison. It is, perhaps, an apt commentary on the decline of national sovereignty in the wake of increased internationalist sentimentalism that a Conservative Government, in its Criminal Justice Bill now before Parliament, is prepared to sacrifice its better judgment to the pressure of outside influences.

On the credit side, the Criminal Justice Bill has several good points. The Parole system, which has proved to be an unqualified success – the failure rate is a mere 5% – is to be extended to enable the Home Secretary, in certain less serious cases, to release people on licence on the recommendation of a local review committee. The Bill proposes the establishment of experimental centres providing for intensive supervision for certain types of offender as a condition of probation. Local Probation Committees, in addition to existing voluntary bodies, are to be given the power to set up and manage hostels for offenders and persons on bail who would otherwise be remanded in prison. The immediate advantage of this reform is that the cost of a man on probation is little more than £1 a week, whereas the cost of a man in prison is £25 per week plus the cost of Social Security for his dependants. Other specific advantages of the Bill are, first, that the maximum penalty for possessing firearms with intent to endanger life, and for using them in resisting arrest would be increased from 14 years to life imprisonment. Secondly, the courts will be empowered to make the criminal compensate the victim; particularly, Magistrates courts would have power to impose a compensation order on offenders to a sum not exceeding £400, while there will be no limitation on the power of higher courts to fix compensation. Thirdly, and in the long run perhaps most importantly, the concept of criminal bankruptcy is to be introduced into the penal system so that criminals should not be able to benefit from the proceeds of large-scale crime. Where the court is of the opinion that an offender has caused loss or damage to a property of more than £15,000 the criminal might be declared bankrupt, instead of merely being required to pay compensation. Running parallel is the notion of forfeiture of property; where an offender was convicted of a serious crime the courts would have the power to order the forfeiture of property used, or intended for use, in the commission of crime.

The question of the restoration of capital punishment for certain categories of murder continues to remain a thorn in the flesh of the Conservative body-politic. In 1965 the death penalty was completely abolished for a trial period of five years as a result of private members' legislation. Before the expiry of that period – in fact in December 1969 – the Labour Government, against strong Conservative protests, decided to shorten the trial period by tabling resolutions for total abolition. And in 1970 in both Houses of Parliament there was a free vote for abolition. Thus the Parliamentary consensus again conspired to defeat the known wishes of the vast majority of people on an issue of major national concern and at the 1971 Conservative Party Conference the Home Secretary declared that "Parliament is not likely to contemplate changing the law on capital punishment". Time and again opponents of capital punishment contend that statistics are inconclusive, and that the rise in indictable crime may not be referable to the abolition of the death penalty. Time and again they are proved wrong. How can they explain that during the second week of February 1972 nine murders were reported in six days at a time when Scotland Yard announced a staggering increase in crimes of murder and violence in London in 1971? How can they explain that the murder rate for England and Wales is worse now than at any time in history? Indeed, since 1965 convictions have nearly doubled in England, while in Scotland they have trebled. At the same time violence against the person has increased by 13.4 per cent in the last year. Throughout Britain assaults on policemen have risen to 8,000 and in the Metropolitan area alone 627 police officers were injured in 1970; in response to these trends the Police Federation recently voted overwhelmingly in favour of the restoration of capital punishment as a deterrent to murder and violent crime, and has stated moreover ... "We have been warning since 1964 that the violent crime spiral would continue unless there was a real deterrent. There is no capital punishment and there is no deterrent". It is incumbent upon the Government to take notice of such pronouncements if it is to retain the confidence of the people.

Other aspects of law and order which one would have liked to see the Government tackle in the Criminal Justice Bill are the whole range of common law and statutory offences involving public protest which badly need updating. The Public Meetings Act 1901, the Public Order Act 1936, and the various common law offences of riot, rout, breach of peace and unlawful assembly require to be codified. The nauseating series of demonstrations during 1967, 1968 and 1969 which resulted in serious confrontations between the police and student anarchists and riotous mobs in many ways were allowed to happen because of the imprecision of existing legislation. Any new reform should place greater emphasis in the importance of upholding public and civic order, while safeguarding the right of peaceful protest. It is all too apparent that many demonstrations, on this criterion, would be unlawful because their natural consequence is the attainment of objectives by other than peaceful means.

Perhaps the most important single pre-requisite to the conquest of crime and with it the maintenance of law and order, is the belief that crime can, in fact, be conquered. The psychological paralysis which inflicts upon society a belief in the inevitability of an increase in crime *ipso facto* impairs the prevention of it. So long as we are prepared to think only in terms of the containment of crime the problem will worsen. All the resources of a modern state should be utilised in achieving the ideals set out at Selsdon for unless some movement in the right direction becomes clearly discernible in the next year or so the problem may become well-nigh insoluble leading inexorably to the destruction of the national unity.

Book Review: Fellow Travellers of the Right

My book review, written for the *Monday World* quarterly journal of the Monday Club, April 1981 was chosen because it is both a fascinating subject in itself and one in which it is possible to draw a sharp distinction between ideological supporters of Nazi Germany and those who would claim that war, only 21 years after the end the previous one, was to be avoided at all costs.

The author established his literary reputation with the *Reactionary Revolution* ("an invaluable study of literary, historical and theological questions" – *British Book News*) and confirmed it with his major study, *Marshal Pétain,* widely considered to be the fairest and most objective appraisal of the French wartime leader.

It was no surprise, therefore, to the reviewer to find this 406-page survey of those personalities and organisations sympathetic towards, or at best not averse to, the aspirations of Nazi Germany, thoroughly absorbing, informative and compelling. Not least amongst Richard Griffiths's merits is his marshalling and presentation of much complex material drawn from countless sources, (as appears from the bibliography: pages 379-391), no doubt an asset consummately to be desired amongst all biographers but sadly so frequently deficient in most.

In many ways this study can be treated as a companion volume to Marxist author David Caute's[34] considerable work of a similar name. Both cover the whole syndrome of thought and action as it affected British political life during the relevant periods.

The opening chapter, *Weariness of Democracy and Admiration for Dictators,* reflects the emotive response to the 1918 Versailles peace terms felt by many well-placed people in Britain, taking their cue from the achievements, as it appeared to them, of Mussolini in Italy and the economic impoverishment and military disgrace of Germany now being rectified by the blandishments of Adolf Hitler in his early period as Chancellor of the Third Reich.

Typical amongst attitudes formulated in the 1920s and early 1930s were those of Francis Yeats-Brown, one-time assistant editor of *The Spectator* and a former soldier who had served with distinction in the Indian Army. As Yeats-Brown's biographer[35] put it: "the Parliamentary machine under Mr Baldwin, and even under Ramsay MacDonald, did not seem capable of mending matters. Just back from witnessing Signor Mussolini pulling down derelict areas in Rome, draining the Pontine marshes and establishing new and healthy colonies in the Campagna, he undoubtedly compared the achievements in Italy with the half-hearted methods at home – the new Europe already in being, in Italy and elsewhere, now became his chief preoccupation".

Again, George Bernard Shaw was warm in his praise of Mussolini's achievements, although he saw them as a reflection of his own predilection for socialism. Shaw's idiosyncratic brand of logic ("Democracy is a system of electing a government to govern and an opposition to obstruct that government from governing") countered some early revulsion for Mussolini because of the murder of the Italy Socialist Deputy, Matteotti, with the phrase: "....the murder of Matteotti is no more an argument against fascism than the murder of St Thomas a Becket is an argument against feudalism".[36]

---

34 *The Fellow Travellers,* Weidenfeld and Nicolson, 1973.

35 John Evelyn Wrench, *Francis Yeats-Brown,* 1886-1944, London 1948 pp 120-1.

36 Letter from G B Shaw to Frederich Adler, October 2, 1927, in *Bernard Shaw and Fascism* (1927).

The book skilfully traces the development of fascism in Britain through early movements such as Rotha Lintorn-Orman's *The British Fascists,* to Arnold Leese's rabidly anti-semitic *Imperial Fascist League* and finally to Oswald Mosley's *British Union of Fascists,* the largest of the three.

Much attention is given to the development of German contacts in the period 1933-35, the author contrasting pacifists, such as Philip Noel-Baker and Lord Allen, who found their way into the Anglo-German Fellowship, with those overtly sympathetic to Nazi Germany: amongst the latter were George Ward Price, political correspondent of *The Daily Mail,* whose numerous visits to Hitler and other Nazi leaders are recounted.

The part played by Joachim Von Ribbentrop, German ambassador to Britain until appointed Foreign Minister, in developing pro-German sympathy is underestimated, according to the author, although he concedes that Ribbentrop's obsession with the importance of London society – "two of London's great hostesses, Lady Cunard and Mrs Ronnie Greville, were bowled over by Nazism" (the former acting "like a twittering bejewelled bird" – p.311) – was a serious misjudgment in that it gave the Germans a totally false perspective of the strength of pro-German feeling in Britain at the time.

The best part of the book is Chapter 12, *The Extremists Isolated* insofar as it traces the rapid decline of pro-German sentiment occasioned by the invasion of Czechoslovakia, which most experts on the subject, the author included, considered had not a vestige of justification, less indeed than the invasion of Poland which precipitated the allies' declaration of war. Amongst the diehards in their support of Nazism to the last were George Robey, Edmund Blunden and Henry Williamson, while *The Link* retained its inveterate enthusiasm for all things Nazi, and Hitler in particular.

This splendid book, written with objectivity throughout deserves acclaim comparable to the author's earlier works.

My admission: an overstatement on local government election results

---

I wrote this piece for the journal *Monitor* in May 1973, just after a shocking set of local government elections results during a period of Conservative government (1970-1974). I accept that much of what I had written was overstated, although local government setbacks were not as commonplace, let alone inevitable, as they are now. One particular about-turn I now make is my reference to the sale of more than 9,000 council houses having been achieved. This has proved to be a bad mistake because successive Tory governments have refused to allow councils to use the receipts from sales in the building of new public sector housing stock, thereby contributing to ongoing shortages – a long-term bad error in policy.

The results of the local government elections are more than merely a defeat for the Conservatives and a triumph for Labour. They represent a crushing victory for apathy, and a stunning re-statement of a fundamental truth which has affected party politics in this country for many years: the total disenchantment of consensus politics, and with it a severe reproach to the bi-party system within which the consensus has flourished.

It is a saddening and chilling thought that many Conservative-controlled municipal authorities up and down the country have been swept from power, despite many sturdy achievements, by a minority of the electorate using the ballot box to register its protest against policies formulated by national government.

In this emphatic manner the whole basis of democracy is undermined and eroded. Take the Greater London Council under the wise and effective leadership of Sir Desmond Plummer during the past six years. A radical programme of reform – the sale of more than 9,000 council houses, a record house-building programme, a holding of the general Rate, the implementation of transport policies, more and improved recreational and leisure facilities – all this and more now to be sacrificed to a Labour administration hell-bent on spending £7,000 million in compulsorily acquiring all privately owned accommodation, handing out free fares – at ratepayers' expense mind you – and cancelling the Layfield Report recommendations on the ringways.

Yet we readily recognise many of the achievements of our Conservative Government in the fields of housing finance reform; in the radical reform of the tax structure; in the social service, particularly with pensions; in the industrial relations legislation. Nor do we underestimate the tremendous crisis of European if not world dimension, over inflation which this government is attempting to answer with its present prices and incomes policy.

Why then do I consider that apathy has conquered the nation? Could it not be that the Labour victory was a positive mandate from the people for the policies of socialism? Could it not be, alternatively, that any government in mid-term must expect electoral defeat locally? In both cases I think the answer is a negative one.

Apathy reigns supreme because we have moved into the age of a technocratic barbarism in which machines, not men, in which systems, not ideas, in which the commonplace, not the original, all dominate and envelop the hearts and minds of our people. In such an atmosphere inevitably the consensus, as expressed through the liberal-establishment, has found a temperate climate in which to improve its stranglehold while the mass-media, with one or two honourable exceptions, has been the means by which the opinion formers have secured their patronage. The local elections have merely been the full expression of this barbarism. And the good people of Britain have been rendered apathetic. Mass society with its contradictions and uncertainties, has contrived to blur the judgement of the individual and the consequences suggest catastrophe.

How can the slide towards the Orwellian prophecy be averted? It can only come through a massive regeneration of the British people, awoken from their slumber, to demand of a Conservative Government that other things are more precious than a 5½% growth rate, or a £600 million balance of payments surplus, or a gradual lifting of a credit squeeze.

All who love this country, who treasure its past and fear for its future, who observe the growing immigration problem, the mounting crisis of law and order, the increase in communist subversion, the decadence of the 'permissive society' as symptoms of national decline and weakness – all have a clear duty. It is to arouse the conscience of the people and to demand in the name of democracy that the gap between government and governed be reduced to insignificance by strong and effective action.

Unless the nettle is grasped soon a thousand years of patriotism, energy, inventiveness and thrift amongst other characteristic British virtues will lie smouldering in the ashes of a dying civilisation.

Letters with animus

(i) No good reason for change

This letter of mine in *The Daily Telegraph* published on 18 October 1977, is of limited and specific intent but it goes to a deeper purpose: should MPs moving from one party to another not be required to give detailed reasons for doing so?

Sir – Mr Reg Prentice's decision to join the Conservative Party should be accompanied by a few searching questions about his present political attitudes rather than by the unqualified welcome it has received in some party circles.

No one would question Mr Prentice's courage in disowning the Labour party at a time when he believes it has embarked upon an unremitting Marxist programme. But does this mean that he has genuinely acquired a taste for, and an acceptance of, Conservatism? His record as Secretary of State for Education, particularly as regards comprehensive and direct-grant schools, was diametrically opposed to that of the Conservative party. Mr Norman St John-Stevas, in March 1975, rightly described Mr Prentice's decision to abolish direct-grant schools as from September 1976, as "an unprecedented step of educational vandalism" (*Hansard*, 11 March 1975).

On 21 February 1977, speaking at the annual meeting of the Lincoln Democratic Labour Association, Mr Prentice suggested that he might stand as a "social democrat", adding that the label under which he ran was something still to be decided.

On Cup Final afternoon this May, at a conference of the Tory Reform group in Basingstoke at which I was invited to participate, Mr Prentice made some fairly scathing references about the Monday Club and Selsdon Group, and intimated that he was awaiting a political re-alignment of the centre of politics.

Mr Prentice should put the record straight. Has he undergone a fundamental change in his political thinking? Does he, for instance, still think that 0.7 per cent of the gross national product should be spent on overseas aid, a figure which the Conservatives always rejected? Does he now support private enterprise, a competitive society (rather than a "co-operative society"), choice in education, rejection of state monopoly? Or is he merely using the Conservative party as a vehicle for advancing his own political ambitions? If the former is the case, he is, indeed, a most welcome recruit, but if not then he isn't.

S M Swerling
Chairman, Political Committee
St Marylebone Conservative Association
London W1

(ii) A little local industrial difficulty

My letter to Fred Hardman, Conservative Trade Unionists National Chairman is clear. George Ward ran a printing company in North-West London, Grunwick, which became embroiled in a long-running industrial dispute. My view differed from other committee members. I append correspondence herewith.

Dear Mr Hardman – I have received the minutes of the CTU's National Committee Meeting held on Saturday 8 July. Unfortunately I was unable to attend this meeting, and my purpose in writing this letter is to express my profound disquiet at item 8, the Emergency Motion, which ... "deplores the action of the Standing Advisory Committee on Candidates in accepting George Ward for inclusion on the approved list of candidates for selection and calls for his name to be removed forthwith".

I understand this motion was passed unanimously. If I had been present there would certainly have been one dissentient voice; indeed, I would have argued forcibly against the motion. It is extremely difficult to understand why the National Committee has adopted this course. One may legitimately ask whether such a personalised motion is within the remit of the CTU. Our function, surely, is to advance the cause of Conservatism within the whole field of industrial relations and not to indulge in value judgements on the merits or demerits of any particular person. If, on the other hand, it is the view that George Ward's record should be subject to scrutiny by our Committee – which hardly has all the relevant and necessary information at its disposal in any event – then in my submission his achievement in building up a successful business and in withstanding overwhelming, unrepresentative (and in some cases unlawful) pressure from left-wing elements well qualified him at least to be considered for inclusion on the Parliamentary candidates list.

That being so the final decision as to whether or not he should be included has nothing whatever to do with our committee and rests with the properly constituted body for this purpose, namely the Standing Advisory Committee on Candidates.

I have heard it argued that George Ward's application should not have been accepted on the grounds, allegedly, that he has given insufficient service to the Conservative Party to warrant inclusion. That may or may not be the case. Again, whether or not it is the case is for the appropriate party organisation to decide and not our committee.

Moreover you will probably know of cases, as I do, where names have been included on the list (probably for very good reasons), despite a relatively short political record. Usually such persons have had successful diplomatic, business or professional or service careers behind them. In my view, George Ward falls into the category of someone with an outstandingly successful business career behind him.

In conclusion, I believe the CTU has departed somewhat ignominiously from its usually high standards in passing this motion and has brought upon itself a good deal of unnecessary opprobrium.

Yours sincerely

Signed – Sam Swerling

Greater London Area TU Representative on National Committee

Conservative Trade Unionists
32 Smith Square London SW1P 3HH
Tel. 01-222 9000

Sam Swerling, Esq.,
28 Charlbert Court,
Charlbert Street,
London NW8

1st August 1978

Dear Sam

Thank you for writing so fully and frankly to me regarding the CTU resolution on Mr Ward.

I shall draw the Committee's attention to the interesting points you raise and I hope you will be able to attend the next meeting.

The question was raised on 8th July because of the concern expressed by several branches and individual CTU members.

Yours sincerely,

Fred Hardman
CTU National Chairman

Response from Fred Hardman, National Chairman, Conservative Trade Unionists, dated 1 August 1978, to Sam Swerling's previous letter shown on pages 132 and 133

Conservative and Unionist Central Office

32 Smith Square Westminster SW1P 3HH Telephone 01-222 9000 Telegrams Constitute London SW1

Chairman of the Party: THE RT HON THE LORD THORNEYCROFT

Deputy Chairmen: ANGUS MAUDE TD MP, THE BARONESS YOUNG *Vice Chairmen:* REGINALD EYRE MP, GEOFFREY FINSBERG MBE JP MP, MARCUS FOX MBE MP, JOHN MOORE MP

14th August, 1978

Dear Sam,

May I congratulate you on the excellent letter you sent to Fred Hardman following the C.T.U. National Committee Meeting, on the 8th July.

Like you I was horrified at the motions that they passed. They have certainly stirred up a hornet's nest, perhaps they will before long realise the errors of their ways.

S——

Marcus

Marcus Fox
Vice Chairman

S. Swerling, Esq.,

Letter sent by Marcus Fox, Conservative Party Vice Chairman and MP for Shipley, in reference to Sam Swerling's letter to Fred Hardman, National Chairman, Conservative Trade Unionists, shown on pages 132 and 133

(iii) Currie's dilemma unanswered

Edwina Currie has always been something of a social liberal; she is entitled to be. In this letter of January 1994 I wanted to find out from her how she would resolve the potential conflict between the reduction of consent for homosexuals from 21 to 18 (now 16, since the Civil Partnerships Act 2004) and the maintenance of discipline and the observance of rules in schools. I am not sure that such conflict has been satisfactorily resolved. Her reply to me was inconclusive.

Dear Mrs Currie

Re: Criminal Justice Bill

I write in connection with the forthcoming parliamentary debate on the Criminal Justice Bill over the proposed reduction of the age of consent for homosexuals from 21 to 18, or, as you propose in your amendment to 16.

I am concerned about the opinions you hold on this contentious subject given your responsibilities as a governor of Repton School, where I was educated, where one of my sons is presently being educated, and where I gather you have a daughter in the sixth form. Your own personal views are, of course, a matter entirely for your own judgment but I am concerned about a possible conflict.

It seems to me that the nation is being subject to a veritable bombardment by those active in "gay" rights propaganda to a point where an attitude of benevolent neutrality, traditionally held by the vast majority of the population on homosexuality, is fast being superseded by one of considerable annoyance, if not downright hostility, at the antics of this egregious lobby, and deservedly so.

What has prompted my letter to you is to ascertain how you are able to reconcile your own predilection that the age of consent should be reduced to 16 with the natural expectation of every parent that their children should grow up normal, healthy boys and girls in a secure environment, where constraints against homosexual behaviour ought, if anything, to be strengthened, not weakened. Reduction of the age of consent, particularly to 16, will have a retrograde effect on boys (however minimal in numbers its impact) living in the relatively enclosed environment of a public school, because it may well encourage the belief that if such behaviour has the sanction of the law it must have some essential moral content by which it can be justified. I utterly reject that argument.

Would it be your advice, as a Repton Governor, that school rules and regulations should now be relaxed to allow consenting boys of 16 years and over to engage in homosexual practices if that were their transient inclination, or would you support a view that school discipline can only be effectively maintained by rigorous adherence to a code of moral behaviour which excludes the intrusion of domestic law into the life of a school such as Repton? If the latter, as I would expect, can you tell me whether the Bill contains any clause excluding schools from the operation of its provisions?

This issue has considerable significance. The Children Act 1989, which as you know became effective in October 1991, has already compelled schools to revise some of their rules, including 'fagging': some would argue this should be a matter for each school and not be the subject of diktat from government. By the same token would the State now be dictating to schools the manner in which moral behaviour is to be regulated?

In conclusion, in my last year at Repton, a music master was required to leave for improper behaviour with a sixth form boy which was reported by another boy. Would it be an unfair representation of your views – and I concede it may well be – to suggest that, in parallel circumstances today, you would be opposed to disciplinary action if that behaviour were consented to?

I am enclosing a copy of this letter to the Headmaster, and look forward to your response.

Yours sincerely
Sam Swerling

(iv) English village community denied by foreign power

My letter to John Gummer MP of 17 June 1996 is pretty self-explanatory. The villagers of Letchmore Heath in Hertfordshire were very badly treated. The facts are incontrovertible and Mr Gummer seems to have ignored them. Political correctness and foreign influence were more important to him.

Rt Hon John Gummer MP
House of Commons
London SW1

Dear Mr Gummer

Land at Bhaktivedanta Manor, Letchmore Heath

I have received a copy document from the government's Eastern Region Office in Bedford relating to your consideration of the report of the Inspector following the local inquiry.

As a resident of Bushey, living less than one mile from the Sandy Lane/Hillfield Road junction, I have a particular interest. I have set down other concerns in my letter to my MP, James Clappison, a copy of which I enclose.

I find your decision astonishing. It strikes at the very root of government Green Belt land policy and the effect of it is to subordinate the deeply-felt concerns of the community of Letchmore Heath and its surrounding area to the pressure of certain lobbies, including those long distances away from the area affected.

No person can reasonably object to the 1973 decision of the then Watford RDC to have upheld the use of the manor as a residential theological college for those wishing to partake of religious instruction in their professed faith. I defer to no one in my acceptance of the need for religious and racial tolerance. That, however, is not enough for the Krishna people. They want more. You must be fully cognisant of the several blatant instances of unauthorised use, leading to Hertsmere BC serving enforcement notices against ISKCON.

Unfortunately these lawbreaking activities appear to have influenced you not at all in your deliberations.

You acknowledge that there is a general presumption against inappropriate development in the Green Belt and that such development should not be approved except in very special circumstances (para 12). Given that to be the position it appears that the informed views of several Conservative and Liberal Councillors, opposed to the development for clearly-stated reasons, as well as the many residents who expressed their views, counts for little in your judgment. Be reminded of *para365* listing the organisations opposed to the development.

Aldenham Parish Council,
Letchmore Heath Village,
Elstree and Borehamwood Green Belt Society,
Hertsmere Conservation Society,
Patchetts Green,
Roundbush and Aldenham Conservation Society,
Radlett Society and Green Belt Association,
Aldenham School,
Roundcroft Kennels,
Elstree Forge.

These organisations, surely, are the very essence and backbone of rural life – pillars of the community which Conservative policy ought to be sustaining, not alienating. You have preferred, evidently, (for that is the right word) to pay more regard to groups such as: Confederation of Indian Organisations (UK), Institute of Indian Culture, National Congress of Gujarati Organisations (NCGO), Sign on to Krishna (sic), Vishnu Hindu Parishad (UK).

I do not argue that these organisations' opinions do not merit some consideration but I contend that they are absolutely peripheral when weighed against the feelings of the local English community of Letchmore Heath and its surrounding areas.

If you feel the interests of multiculturalism (not, let me hasten to add, multi-racialism) should be enhanced may I refer you to the very scholarly assault on multiculturalism, its de-educating objectives and all its other absurd nonsenses, made by George Walden MP in *The Sunday Telegraph*, 8 September 1992.

The truth behind the dreadful decision you have taken is that you knew the eyes of the Hindu world were upon you and that a politically-correct verdict was expected. Both you and the Prime Minister received strongly-worded letters from Vishna Hindu Parishad (VHP) in India and the President of the Bharatiya Janata Party (BJP). Further in December 1995, a meeting of VHP trustees in Delhi passed a resolution that you should uphold the (so-called) devotees' appeal.

It is a sad day indeed when a Conservative Minister cannot recognise the strength of feeling of his own people and prefers the demands of a foreign power and the propaganda of an alien culture.

I have voted Conservative at every election, national and local, since 1964. This is the sort of issue which leads me to question the virtue of continuing to support the party. I may abstain at the next General Election.

Yours sincerely
S M Swerling

(v) False premises, wrong conclusions

This letter to Lord Parkinson, with copies to named persons, was written in October 1997. The Labour Party had been in power for six months under Blair's premiership. I had become critical about the way the Conservative Party was moving. I set down my misgivings covering some of the important subjects in politics. I received cordial responses from most of the recipients.

Dear Lord Parkinson

Conservative Party

I write as someone who was a constituent of yours when you were MP for Hertsmere and who has worked unremittingly in one capacity or another for the Conservative Party over thirty years, as a former parliamentary candidate, Westminster City Councillor, Hertsmere Borough Councillor, Chairman of the Monday Club and party worker at every election since 1966, local and parliamentary. I can fairly claim that the Conservative Party is as much 'My Party' as it is William Hague's.

The main burden of my letter is to express very deep reservations about the direction in which the Party is moving, something which has been severely aggravated by the deliberations of the Party Conference. I suspect that a fair proportion of the party feels the same way. Of course, the Tories are bound to face an uphill task after their crushing electoral defeat and inevitably certain internal reforms of the party are overdue and needed, but the scale of recrimination, backbiting and indulgence in '*mea culpa*' politics is precisely not what is needed. There has been a huge amount of it.

The party is already coming to wrong conclusions based on false premises. The reasons for our defeat are that 18 years is a very long time for any political party to govern – you yourself have made this point forcibly; secondly, the events of 16 September 1992, which forced us out of the Exchange Rate Mechanism (ERM), portrayed the party leadership as being grossly incompetent in the management of the sterling crisis. Despite the then Government's overall strong performance in managing the economy, the image of failure never left the peoples' consciousness. The element of 'sleaze' may have been a factor but I think its impact has been overstated. If this analysis is correct, as I believe it to be, it is surely ridiculous that the voluntary party should so resoundingly take it out on Conservative MPs, particularly those who spoke out against the Maastricht Treaty, and blame them for our defeat. Defeat probably became inevitable in 1992.

I thought that Lord Archer made a particularly silly speech suggesting that the voluntary party should effectively constitute 50% of any electoral college. Party workers should acknowledge that their function is to support, not to arrogate to themselves the power of decision-making over important issues for which the majority are singularly ill-equipped, having neither the knowledge, vocation nor aptitude to make other than a minimal contribution. I suspect that for some if you put an elephant on the platform with a blue rosette pinned on its trunk it would get a standing ovation for making an appropriately suitable noise.

I would give the voluntary party 10% of the vote. The party needs less internal democracy, not more. It is sound policies and responsible parliamentary opposition based on clear conservatism that will bring about a revival of Conservative fortunes and restore membership in large numbers.

I found the attacks on Lord Tebbit and Alan Clark wholly uncalled for and symptomatic of the jittery state the party is in. In more robust times allegedly controversial comments would have been debated and analysed in good spirits; but now, it seems, an insidious political correctness is raising its ugly head whereby party functionaries feel compelled to inform the media how outraged they are and that so and so is just a maverick whose opinions can be discounted.

Unlike most, I actually read Lord Tebbit's speech on multiculturalism, printed in full in *The Daily Mail*. I agree with every word of it: so evidently did 500 others at Blackpool and probably millions of others elsewhere.

Multiculturalism is being badly confused with multiracialism. Multiracialism, in most urban communities, is a political fact. It is the consequence of large-scale immigration over decades, demonstrably against the wishes of the indigenous population. This is indisputable. Whole areas of Britain have been transformed unrecognisably by this process. That is not to suggest, of course, that substantial numbers of immigrants are not individually well integrated, or do other than make a valuable contribution, one way or another, to the nation. Those that have done so, many of them most usefully in the Conservative Party, no doubt see themselves as British and in law are so. Nevertheless, I share the views of Enoch Powell and some of his foremost supporters in the 1960s, like Sir Ronald Bell, Sir Cyril Osborne (even earlier), Harold Gurden and Norman Pannell, all of whom warned that the whole debate really concerned numbers. Numbers were of the essence because if you had four or five million immigrants living in an overcrowded island like Britain, you would get the sort of strains and tensions that you could avoid if there were, say, a fifth or a tenth of that number.

Amazingly enough, a fortnight ago I heard Michael Howard state on *Newsnight* (when of course it was important for him to say how much he disagreed with Lord Tebbit) that immigration controls were very strict. A senior immigration officer, Peter Thompson, is on record as stating that, putting together bogus asylum seekers (94% of all asylum seekers, most of whom are economic migrants rather than migrants with a well-founded fear of persecution, for whom there should always be a refuge), illegal immigrants and overstayers from a temporary permit, the true level of immigration is running at about 90,000 a year, the highest figure for two decades and that these numbers are likely to get bigger, not smaller. I understand that there are now 44,000 unprocessed asylum applications in Britain. What a sad commentary on the Conservative government's conduct of this area of Home Affairs, given that it is known that 19 out of every 20 of these people are involved in criminal deception. Maybe these bogus asylum seekers and illegals are destined to become part of the great new inclusive society of compassionate conservatism.

As Conservatives, we should surely promote integration and encourage the maximum degree of conformity to achieve the nearest we can get to a homogeneous society. I thought Munoh Chopra, the 15 year old boy, made a particularly good speech, on the opening day of the Conference, exemplifying the best traditional family values about which he spoke feelingly, in stark contrast to the 26-year old brassy woman from Slough who felt she needed to tell us, no doubt with Central Office prompting, how typical she was of younger Conservatives in her love of multiculture, pop music and all things modern. I understand Master Chopra attends King Edward VII School, Birmingham, the *alma mater* of Enoch, and one of the best academic schools in England, where all the best virtues are instilled.

Lord Tebbit, of course, was not discoursing on multiracialism, immigration controls or race relations. His speech was on multiculturalism, a particularly pernicious left-wing importation from America which, amongst other things, attempts to politicise multiracial communities away from integration by de-educating them in the culture, conventions and traditions of the host nation.

William Hague, for his part, has said he attended the Notting Hill Gate carnival in August with his fiancée because he saw it as an expression of multicultural values. He seems to think this is certainly the 'biggest cultural event in England'. It attracts about a million visitors but its value in terms of true British and European culture is negative when compared, for example, with the beautiful music which can be heard for two months at the Henry Wood Promenade concerts which have been running for over 100 years and which are broadcast to over 18 countries attracting much bigger audiences. Maybe Mr Hague and his new wife will next summer be attending a promenade concert at The Royal Albert Hall, where the music of Elgar, Vaughan Williams, Beethoven or Mozart can be heard, in their baseball caps and iced lollies!

I enclose for your attention a salutary article on multiculturalism by former Conservative MP, George Walden, which appeared in *The Sunday Telegraph* on 8 September 1991. Mr Walden, scholarly and intellectual certainly, is hardly a repository of right-wing opinion so his piece is particularly interesting. Multi-culturalism promotes nihilism and rejection. Lord Tebbit is absolutely right that it could lead to the 'balkanisation' of Britain.

I dread to imagine what would have happened if Lord Tebbit, and not George Walden, had written exactly the same piece in September 1997, a week or so before the Conference? Attacks on Norman Tebbit are even more inappropriate because of the immense contribution he has made to the Party's success over a very long period of time during his period in office as a Minister and Party Chairman. For some years I served on the Greater London Area CPC as well as the Trades Union National Advisory Committee (TUNAC). I used to write papers on industrial relations law reform as a university law lecturer. TUNAC members remember his support and contributions to the GLA with gratitude. It ill-behoves William Hague to make, quite frankly, nasty, cheap remarks about ' ... leaving the cricket field'. Mr Hague would do better to read Lord Tebbit's autobiography, *Upwardly Mobile* (1988), one of the most readable political autobiographies of recent years, which has many valuable insights. He might learn something useful.

Criticism of Alan Clark's remarks is just as incomprehensible to me. Quite evidently he did not mean what he said to be taken literally and afterwards indicated as much, but intended to make the point, as I heard it, that too soft an approach to IRA/Sinn Fein would get us nowhere. Even if Alan Clark's remarks were to be interpreted literally, I would have thought that 600 off the premises would pale into insignificance compared to the 3,400 murdered since 1969. Of course, in policy terms, the 'peace process' cannot lead to a long-term solution (although as a short-term expedient it may have some value) because the antagonists have irreconcilable objectives. There are only two possible solutions to what is a conflict of identity: one is the incorporation of Northern Ireland into the Republic by Treaty of Cession; the other is the integration of Northern Ireland into the United Kingdom on a permanent basis. Everything else is moonshine. The latter solution should be established as Tory policy and without deference to President

Clinton, the United Nations or any other internationalist interference. It does, of course, mean taking out the IRA, something which could be achieved if there was the will, which I doubt there is. Tories should heed the opinions on this subject of the late, great journalist of *The Daily Telegraph*, T E Utley.

And so to intolerance, homosexuality and William Hague. Mr Hague seems to want to elevate tolerance into a political virtue, as opposed to a civic value. He is hopelessly confused. Let him consult every tract in Conservative philosophy, from Burke to Disraeli; through Oakeshott to Scruton; from modern Catholic social teaching to the wisdom of Lord Jakobovits and Jewish tradition. Tory precept is against him and so are the vast majority of people. Homosexualists in fact constitute less than 2% of the population. All surveys establish this. Civic tolerance has its expression in political action through policies which protect the sick, the elderly, the disabled. The Conservative record here has been a very good one. I am in favour of the maximum degree of State help and private provision for those unable to fend for themselves. But that does not mean we should prop up anti-social, degenerate behaviour in the name of tolerance.

Isn't some clear thinking needed? When I was a schoolboy I remember reading *Against the Law*, Peter Wildeblood's moving account of his feelings as a homosexual man being branded a criminal for private acts with adults. He was prosecuted with one Major Pitt-Rivers and Lord Montagu of Beaulieu. It led to the Wolfenden Report, the passing of the Sexual Offences Act 1967 and the de-criminalisation of homosexuality between consenting adults in private. That will all be known to you. Surely that reflected a common ground of acceptance for Tories, although it wouldn't have saved the Tory Armed Forces Minister under MacMillan, Ian Harvey, caught with his trousers down in Hyde Park examining the credentials of a young Guards Officer. I remember this rather sad man who used to attend Paddington Conservative functions where more often than not he was the worse for drink.

The Tory position became a rather sensible one. No doubt substantial numbers, as far as one could judge it, of homosexuals were active in the Party. They didn't go on proselytising about their 'rights' or how glad they were to be 'gay'. I doubt any of them quite matched that promiscuous 'cottager' from the Labour Party, Tom Driberg, although, like him, some may have got on the Church of England Synod. They accepted their condition and people accepted them. I remember a splendid old queen in the Greater London Area, also from Paddington, who had started his political career after the war on the far left and had moved to the radical right. Everyone knew he was as queer as a coot but he didn't bang on about his condition. When he attended meetings we used to call out 'backs to the wall, lads'. He loved every moment of this sort of banter. That was what true tolerance meant.

William Hague's attitude to homosexuality is entirely different. It is not one of benevolent neutrality. He's deadly earnest. He wouldn't otherwise have sent a letter to the TORCHE people, one of whose nefarious activities on their recent parade was to blow up a giant condom and place it on the head of an effigy of the Pope. On what basis does Mr Hague think this sort of lowlife can make a useful contribution to the Conservative Party? The real debate that needs to take place in the Conservative Party in the weeks and months ahead concerns not form but substance. The Party did not lose the last election because it was too hard and needs to become softer. Michael Portillo really is talking arrant nonsense. I read in one newspaper that he has arrived at his new 'thinking' after discussions with a 27-year old poet and Miss Koo Stark. What has come over him? The party needs to move to a principled, nationalist political perspective, embracing a doctrine of national preference. Britain must start to come first again. Nation, tradition, hierarchy, charity and order should be the new watchwords of Conservatism – not the spineless, soft sentimentalism of a bogus compassion and 'inclusiveness' about which we heard rather too much at Blackpool.

William Hague has every opportunity in front of him. A fine orator and excellent brain, he will start recouping popular support when he comes to recognise that the Conservatives' way forward is not consensus and soppiness, but a principled approach to the political issues of the day. I am sending a copy of this letter to a number of political associates in the party as well as the persons named.

Yours sincerely
Sam Swerling

Copy to: Rt Hon Lord Tebbit CH, Rt Hon Alan Clark MP,
James Clappison MP, Rt Hon Michael Howard MP,
Rt Hon William Hague MP, Michael Portillo Esq

(vi) Head-on with David Davis MP

The following letter was written by me on 24 October 2001 to the Conservative Party chairman, at that time David Davis MP. Mr Davis replied in an unsatisfactory manner for the reasons I have given in my attached comments.

Dear Mr Davis

I write in connection with the suspension of the Monday Club from the Conservative Party – a decision I find to be unconscionable, undeserved and thoroughly undemocratic, which brings no credit whatsoever on the Party or its leadership, and which has indubitably given rise to seething bitterness and resentment.

I would like to have a copy of the Party's rules whereby this decision has purportedly been taken (if there is a cost for this I shall be happy to send a cheque).

I have a certain interest in these matters, having been a Club member since 1965 – one year later than my membership of the Conservative Party itself. I became Chairman of the Monday Club following Major Patrick Wall, MC, VRD, your predecessor as Conservative MP for Haltemprice. I knew Pat Wall well. Like me he was also a Conservative city councillor at Westminster. In my case I served for four years (1978-1982) after which I became unqualified having moved residence to Hertfordshire. He would have turned in his grave at this decision. So would his great friend and colleague, John Biggs-Davison, another Monday Club stalwart.

The Club has had a long and pervasive influence on the Conservative Party. During Mr Heath's premiership (1970-1974) the Club had five government ministers – Julian Amery, Geoffrey Rippon, Teddy Taylor, John Peyton and Robert Boscawen (whip). There were 32 MPs in the Club in 1973 and 38 peers. Ted Heath got on well with the Club and saw it as having a distinctive voice of value. The Club was allowed a free hand to voice some fairly radical views. Did this do any harm to the Party? Not at all. Why should it now?

Yes, there is an answer to that last question. It is that a group of self-important publicists in the Party, whose self-esteem is exceeded only by their shameless arrogance, have decided they want to kill off groups like the Club. Its very existence offends their liberal views. Step forward Stephen Norris, John Bercow and the peripatetic Lord Taylor of Warwick, an unreconstructed loudmouth who holds the dubious distinction of being the only failed Conservative parliamentary candidate to be elevated to the House of Lords on a first electoral failure. Some years ago I remember talking to Nirj Deva, the very capable Indian-born Tory MP and now, of course, an MEP. He told me how strange he found this.

I fear you and Iain Duncan Smith have been taken in by malevolent influences. The sanction brought to bear against the Club is to be challenged by a number of individual members in the courts. Whatever the Party rules may declare they are subject to an equitable individual requirement of transparency, openness and fairness in the application of procedures.

Manifestly, these requirements have been ignored. Indeed, what has happened has been the arbitrary exercise of power in a wholly illegitimate fashion. Have you or IDS ever seen or read a Monday Club pamphlet, publication or newsletter? I doubt it. If you had, you would notice a total absence of racism or ignoble behaviour towards anyone on account of their race or national origin. I know of no-one in the Club who would not deplore openly discriminatory behaviour. That should not, however, prevent a proper, considered discussion of immigration, one of the major issues of our times, which is currently being ignored by politicians and yet which is deserving of very serious analysis and debate.

The likes of Enoch Powell, Ronald Bell, Harold Gurden, Cyril Osborne, Norman Pannell, Peter Griffiths and others are no longer to be found in the Conservative parliamentary party. The Party is diminished by this lacuna. The Monday Club is perfectly entitled to hold views on immigration and to express them without fear or favour and without being shut up by the leadership. Is it or is it not the case that in January 2001 a national opinion poll showed that 67% of the public thought there was too much immigration and that it should be substantially reduced? Under the new Bercow/Norris-induced dispensation is this something now to be quietly forgotten about? Is Lady Thatcher a racist because she talked about being 'swamped' by immigration?

As to the last question, apparently yes, because now what counts is not whether you are a racist but whether you are perceived by others to be so. Utterly undemocratic and unfair.

This matter can be successfully compromised by the Club agreeing to refrain from references to voluntary repatriation (which seems to so offend the leadership, notwithstanding that it was part of the Tory manifesto in the 1970 general election and, indeed, part of the Immigration Act 1971 and is still on the statute book), but retaining full rights to be able to comment freely on immigration.

Yours sincerely
Sam Swerling

David Davis's reply:

Thank you for your letter of 24 October concerning the Monday Club and I do appreciate that you feel strongly about this matter given your involvement with the Club.

There is, however, concern about some of the views which have been expressed in the publications of the Monday Club, particularly on its website and the offence which they have caused. It was, therefore, decided that certain assurances should be obtained from the Club before its association with the Party could continue.

I am aware that many long-standing, committed supporters of the Party also belong to the Monday Club, and I hope the situation can be resolved.

Sam Swerling's comments:

The procedure adopted to suspend the Monday Club are hardly in the best traditions of the Conservative Party. The meeting with the Club's officers was not a negotiation; it was a *fait accompli*. It is highly questionable whether the Party has any lawful authority to act in the way it has done. The Club is an unincorporated association. It does not have an existence separate from that of its members, all of whom have to be members of the Conservative Party. There is nothing in the Conservative Party's relationship with a body which has never had any formal standing in the Party – any more than the Bow Group or the Tory Reform Group have ever done.

(vii) Enforced removal of true Tory

During the mid-2000s, the Conservative Party was in something of a panic. They badly wanted to become the governing party again after many years of New Labour under Blair. The Tory leadership was becoming more and more autocratic and nervous. My piece here, a letter published in the *West Sussex Gazette* in April 2005, ... shows the extent to which Central Office sought to assert control over what was said and done, even to the point of dismissing MPs and candidates.

Sir

The enforced resignation of Howard Flight is one of the most disgraceful events I can recall since I joined the Conservative Party in the mid 1960s.

Arundel and South Downs is not the only association to have fallen victim to the dictatorial behaviour of Tory campaign headquarters which at much the same time succeeded in getting rid of an excellent young candidate, Adrian Hilton, for making wholly justified comments about the nature of the Maastricht Treaty. Well done to the Slough Conservative for resolutely refusing to accept the new candidate foisted upon them.

Arundel Tories should have done the same.

In truth, the association officers showed a lack of moral courage. When they were presented with the ten candidates on 4 April (at which time Howard Flight was determinedly standing his ground) they should have refused to interview any of them, making it clear that they already had in place a unanimously-endorsed adopted candidate.

Whatever Mr Flight's indiscretions may have been he did not deserve to be de-selected as a candidate. Moreover, since he had already been adopted any procedures set in train before he had been re-adopted were breaches of due process and almost certainly unlawful. I understand from a friend who was at the meeting on 6 April of the whole association, that Dr Fox, who had appeared in the constituency two days earlier to give the officers their orders, appeared to address the assembled gathering. What right had he to be there? I am also reliably informed that Nick Herbert, the successful candidate on the night, was allowed to speak for seven minutes longer than the first candidate and that he made no mention of his personal status which, with some courage certainly, he did at the time the candidates were reduced to three. This may or may not have affected the final decision.

The sad consequence of what has happened is that constituency associations, historically sovereign entities within the traditions of the Conservative Party, are no longer so. Democracy is the worse for it and Arundel has lost a very fine MP and Slough an excellent, young, aspiring candidate.

Yours faithfully
S Swerling

(viii) Howard's acclamation of Cameron – My response

This letter written to Michael Howard on 12 September 2006 is quite clear in its content and runs parallel to my article about David Cameron in *Right Now* journal – see page 284.

Dear Mr Howard,

I saw the comments you made in *The Times* yesterday about how "brilliantly" David Cameron was performing as Conservative leader and how everyone in the party should embrace the changes of direction in which he was taking the party – although you didn't indicate what the final destination might be: Nirvana, or oblivion?

I joined the Conservative Party in October 1963 on leaving university and remained a member until May of this year. During that time I played some part – as a Conservative councillor, parliamentary candidate (both in the 1970s) and part-time researcher and occasional speech-writer for Julian Amery and John Biggs-Davison. I was also Chairman of the Monday Club (1980-1982). Certainly, I never called for, nor anticipated, the wider body of the party to support my own distinctive Tory nationalist opinions but what has now happened to this once great party is an appalling example of political cowardice. The Tory Party cannot win under Call me Dave (CMD). It is as simple as that. He has none of the substantive qualities to bring success and it amazes me that so many party members are unable to see it. All fluff and no detail.

I resigned my membership and wrote to the party chairman, Francis Maude, explaining why. Unsurprisingly, I didn't receive a reply, let alone an acknowledgement, from this lugubrious personage, who, I have no doubt is responsible for some of the newspeak balderdash emanating from Central Office.

My letter to Maude set down eight specific reasons and was posted off just at the time CMD invited us all to be nice to "hoodies" and understand their predicament:-

i) The refusal to recognise tax cuts as a precondition of economic stability, rather than the reverse. (I have read in *The Times* today Osborne's opinions about tax cutting, confirming his economic illiteracy).

ii) The pronouncement by Letwin that the party now believes in "the redistribution of wealth" – an essentially marxist conception of economics which should have no place in Conservative thinking.

iii) The rejection of the re-introduction of grammar schools and, *ergo*, the notion of competition at all levels of education (you certainly cannot have supported this – I recall your parliamentary ovation, first-rate, in which you slammed Blair as an Old Fettesian for having criticised "this grammar school boy").

iv) The disgraceful acceptance of positive discrimination in the selection of parliamentary candidates.

v) The plan to introduce tax breaks for homosexualist couples, thereby challenging the institution of marriage as the primary social unit of society and its essential uniqueness.

vi) Notwithstanding the public's very clear dislike of continuing mass-immigration (60,000 a year – "There will be no further large-scale immigration" – Ted Heath, March 1971), the Tory Party has remained mysteriously silent on the matter.

vii) The weak and unsatisfactory approach to Britain's continued involuntary absorption in the European Union and the refusal to encourage even a debate about the merits and demerits of our continuing membership.

viii) The wholly unjustified support by the Conservative leadership of the Iraq War in which 107 (then) British soldiers have been killed for no good reason, in clear defence of the well-established principle of international relations – non-intervention in the internal affairs of a sovereign state.

Why do you suppose the Tories did so appallingly badly in Dunfermline and then Bromley? Answer: because the core vote is deserting it. Opinion polls are hardly favourable. A 7% lead is nothing. The electorate doesn't want another Anthony Charles Lynton Blair. The cap will fall off CMD's head I'm afraid. Some of the Conservative election results at the council votes in May were truly dreadful – (look at the analysis of the Rowntree Institute) – particularly in Northern towns, where they have gone backwards. In 124 of 286 council seats they were defeated by the British National Party.

I share Matthew Parris's opinion in *The Times* today – the lack of substance is destroying the party and so it will continue to do, so Edward Leigh's opinion about the core vote is wholly correct.

I will rejoin the Party when Cameron goes and not a day before not that this will concern you in the least although in truth it is replicated a million times and more by others.

Yours sincerely
Sam Swerling

cc: Edward Leigh MP, Mark Field MP, James Clappison MP

1) I would not have written this letter to you if I did not have enormous respect for your excellence as Home Secretary and how sad it is to me that a senior party figure can move from being a Tory traditionalist to a social liberal.

2) The Tory 'A' List is a complete farce. Good for Jacob Rees-Mogg on getting selected.

3) George Osborne should get lessons from John Major – the best Financial Secretary to the Treasury we ever had.

(ix) Wretched wrongheadedness

Mrs Spelman's behaviour towards people whom she dislikes is well known in political circles. My letter to her reflects my view of her wretched bullying, amongst other matters referred to her. If the content may seem overheated she deserves some aggro in the same proportion as she likes to dish it out on those less powerful than herself.

Mrs C Spelman MP
House of Commons
London SW1

26 July 2010

Dear Mrs Spelman

The Burkha

I have read your comments concerning this garment.

I am appalled by your unnecessary intervention. Unlike the turban which is a religious obligation for Sikhs, the burkha is a superfluous piece of apparel which can be threatening for those who have to confront it and totally alien to our customs and liberties. Very few people agree with you. It can also be used to conceal weapons and bombs – see for instance Pontecorvo's film *Battle of Algiers* depicting events in the Algerian War of Independence (1954-1962).

You are, of course, no stranger to controversy. Apart from the fact you are widely seen as an expenses racketeer (notwithstanding any special pleading you may raise for yourself) for which you should have been required to resign or have been expelled from the Conservative Party.

Many people will remember your wretched bullying of Nigel Hastilow, an excellent Tory candidate, when as Party Chairman you put him in a position that he had to resign for daring to speak well of Enoch Powell.

Whereas you are something of a political nonentity Enoch was one of the great politicians of the last century whose name will live on for decades while yours will be cast into oblivion in the dustbin of history.

The coalition may not last its full term. If so you will be out of a job. You will have deserved it.

Yours sincerely

S Swerling

(x) Persuasion, not perception

I wrote this published letter to *The Evening Standard* on 29 July 2010 which is self-evident as to its content. Politics is about substantive policies and the need to persuade through reasoned argument. Nicholas Boles MP needs to undergo a re-education.

Sir,

As a Conservative Party member for four decades, I read Nicholas Boles's piece (Evening Standard, 24 May) with mounting incredulity. He constructs the argument that politics is a matter of perception and that policies should reflect that. I find this a counsel of despair. He even advances the suggestion that the Tories would be better to have a traditionalist leader to implement 'radical change' – code, presumably, for social liberalism. This oxymoronic thesis will get the party nowhere.

It is not perception that the Tories need to address but rather the need for persuasion: to persuade the electorate that they have policies worth voting for. The starting point needs to be a frank admission that the election result was very poor. Michael Howard , as leader, got a great deal wrong, including the disgraceful decision to compel Howard Flight's resignation. The Tories should never have supported Blair's illegal adventure in Iraq. What happened to the essentially Tory principle of non-intervention in the internal affairs of sovereign states? Far too much timidity surrounded the campaign. Too little was devoted to environmental issues, nothing of note was heard about European policy – and here we should embark upon a wide-ranging debate on our continuing membership of the EU – and the tone towards tax cuts was apologetic. The immigration and asylum policy deserved more hard detail attached to it. Interestingly, Mr Boles thinks that only someone like Mr Adam Afriyie, MP, is qualified to deliver the message – otherwise (perception again) people apparently may think: 'same old Tories' (Mr Boles's words). Very curious!

The Conservative aspiration should be to develop substantive policies across the board which will engage the electorate's enthusiasm, not to hover about in a vacuum of meaningless platitudes fuelled by the highly transient notion of perception.

Yours faithfully
Sam Swerling
Past Chairman
The Monday Club (1980-1982)

Political fear and paranoia – my detailed study

The events of a six-month period within the life of the Monday Club (March-August 1973) may not appear to readers to be a matter worthy of other than purely peripheral consideration. Why should it be of any concern to the outside world? Should it not remain as an 'in-house' problem? Apart from the value which historical political researchers might find I conclude that dissemination of facts is better than concealment of the truth.

In this fairly lengthy piece, which I wrote for the benefit of club members attending a crucial meeting at London's Caxton Hall on 20 August 1973, I have set down the background to the many disturbing occurrences which threatened to destroy the Monday Club altogether. Given its large membership at the time and its not inconsiderable influence within constituencies on the Conservative cause it seemed to me that I was justified in trying to right the many wrongs which were taking place at the time.

It has to be remembered that there were wide divisions within the Conservative Party on both economic policy and the European question. In his third year of government Edward Heath was hardly universally popular.

The public interest in the internal problems of the club were giving rise to an incessant and damaging media publicity of a type which dominated the broadsheet press and television. This showed that what the Monday Club said and did was, indeed, something of national interest going well beyond the confines of the club's own distinctive agenda.

---

1. Introduction

At a time when the Conservative Party needs a strong, unified and effective right-wing it is impoverished by the absence of one. Why? Because the Monday Club has sadly declined in influence and been rendered a largely ineffectual organisation, torn by internal divisions and public rancour. This sad state of affairs we urgently seek to correct.

This document seeks to establish objectively the facts of what has happened, why it has happened and to give the membership for the first time reasons as to why the decline has set in.

Let it be firmly stated at the outset that no personal animosity is intended towards Mr Guinness nor are we attempting to suggest he has not played a valuable part in the development of the club by his writings and his five years membership of it. What we find incontestable is that under his leadership the Monday Club has become a largely discredited organisation; for that reason we seek his displacement in order to once again rebuild our club before it is too late.

2. The Lincoln By-Election

In the normal course of events the recent Lincoln by-election would call for little comment. The fact that the Conservative candidate was the Monday Club chairman was evidently a matter of some interest, particularly as this was a by-election and the public gaze was thus focussed on our standard-bearer more than would have otherwise been the case. The result is immaterial. It seems unlikely that any Conservative candidate would have secured a higher poll. From a right-wing standpoint, however, members have expressed deep dissatisfaction that:

a) The Chairman's view on capital punishment, while not intended to be absurd, undoubtedly seemed absurd in the context in which his words were spoken.

b) The Chairman, having invited Mr Enoch Powell to speak on his behalf, withdrew the invitation. Such a distinguished person as Mr Powell is surely deserving of better treatment.

c) Some Monday Club members, having gone to Lincoln to canvass for their Chairman, were upset at being told to play down their membership of the Club, as if to suggest membership was in some way inimical to the Conservative Party.

3. The Monday Club Elections

a) The Preliminaries to the Monday Club 1973 election

Two candidates offered their services as Chairman; Jonathan Guinness and George Young, the latter reluctantly and only in the absence of any other candidate. Since the club election was shortly after the Lincoln by-election it is not surprising that there should have been a contest for this important position.

From the outset of the announcement of candidates seeking positions a public examination of the club's internal affairs took place. The press of late March and April is full of letters and press statements which should never have been disclosed. The sum effect of this publicity has been catastrophic; yet not a single attempt was made to stop it.

b) Allegations of National Front Influence

The first public suggestion of National Front interest in the Monday Club, at least in the context of these elections, was a report by Peter Gladstone Smith in *The Sunday Telegraph* on Sunday 25 March. Under a headline "Monday Club in new rift", Mr Gladstone Smith claimed that "the resignation of all but six of its 22 Conservative MPs is imminent". He claimed that "a powerful group of newcomers plans to convert the club to a 'populist movement' ". The group, he said, was drawn mainly from the "6,000 members in branches" (a grossly inflated figure in any case). Mr Gladstone Smith then managed to enlarge upon this piece of fiction with the allegation that there were plans for this group to abolish loyalty to the Conservative Party, lower the subscriptions and seek to attract "about 3,000 members of the extreme right-wing National Front who would resign from the Front to form a rejuvenated Monday Club".

A report of National Front infiltration also accompanied the club elections of 1971 in the *Peterborough* column in *The Daily Telegraph*.

Mr Gladstone Smith's sources of information about the Monday Club never were very good. He was responsible for an earlier report, incorrect and unsubstantiated, to the effect that the Special Branch thought that Monday Club members might be gun-running in Ulster!

A further report concerning the National Front and the Monday Club appeared in *The Daily Telegraph* on 27 March. It was written by James Allan and headed "Monday Club fear of extremists"; paragraph 2 of this report stated:

- "Mr Jonathan Guinness ... said yesterday that if his opponent ... wins next month 'it could be considered a move in the National Front direction'."

Paragraph 4 stated:

- "Mr Guinness is not alone in fearing that many of those urging the election of Mr Young are doing so in the hope that with him as chairman they could move the group more in line with National Front thinking."

On 31 March an article by Patrick Cosgrave appeared in *The Spectator* entitled 'Who are the right?' This set out to analyse the various fragmentations of the Tory Right and repeated what had been said in *The Sunday Telegraph* ...

- "And there is a rumour that the rumour that 3,000 National Front members are to be invited to join the club is in fact a scare engendered by the supporters either of Mr Guinness or Mr Young as a ploy in the election to the chairmanship."

If the National Front were seeking to acquire a control over the Monday Club it is surprising that it has not been more forthcoming in admitting as much. In an interesting article in a spring issue of the journal *Spearhead* "Who is trying to sell the Monday Club and why?", the Activities Organiser of the National Front, Mr Martin Webster, firmly denies attempted infiltration of the Club by his party. On the question of the source of the scare stories Mr Webster says:

- "At the end of March Mr Gladstone Smith of *The Sunday Telegraph* telephoned me and stated that he had information to the effect that the NF Chairman, John Tyndall, had attended a Monday Club anti-immigration rally in Shoreditch, London, on 13 March, and that after the rally he and Mr G K Young, one of the contenders for the Chairmanship of the Monday Club, had had an informal discussion in a nearby public house, during which discussion Mr Young was said to have promised Mr Tyndall the following: that if he (Mr Young) were elected Chairman of the Club he would reduce the national members' subscription, abandon the Club policy of insisting that Club members support the Tory Party, allow the induction into the club of 3,000 NF members and ultimately break the Club away from the Tory Party in order to establish a populist political party."

Mr Webster goes on –

- "I was able to prove to Mr Gladstone Smith that his information was utter rubbish, as on the night in question Mr Tyndall was in Nottingham addressing the local branch of the NF – which meeting was reported in the following day's *Nottingham Guardian* Journal (I was later to discover, as no doubt was Mr Gladstone Smith, that Mr Young was likewise not in Shoreditch on the night in question). However, this did not prevent Mr Gladstone Smith from publishing in *The Sunday Telegraph* the above-mentioned 'proposals' which were the alleged outcome of a discussion which had never taken place, and which he knew had never taken place."

On 1 April, in a letter to *The Sunday Telegraph*, Mr Webster made it clear beyond doubt that the differences between the National Front and Monday Club were fundamental:

- "The National Front, in terms of its membership and its steadily growing electoral support, is largely a working-class movement. While we are able to absorb

> ex-Monday Club members who come to accept our policies on economics and finance, we have no wish to endanger the unity of our movement by taking in people whose 19th century views on free enterprise oblige them to condone 20th century monopoly capitalism and international usury."

It might further be questioned how Mr Young could have been seeking a rapprochement with the National Front when he is a pro-marketeer, a merchant banker and an advocate of a free market economy, all of which the Front is opposed to."

Comment

The importance attached to claims of National Front involvement, which are proved to be totally unfounded, should not be under-estimated, at a time when the Club was buzzing with stories of spies, forged circulars, burglaries and the rest it was convenient that this myth should be allowed publicity without being affirmatively rebutted by the Club's leadership.

c) The Circulars

No sooner had the nomination papers of the candidates for the various positions been received than a series of strange circulars began appearing. Much talk about the origins of these circulars has been heard. So far as we are concerned we shall confine ourselves to the facts. The first circular to appear was from a group describing itself as *'The Conservative Underground Press'* with a fictitious address. The Club's addressograph plate was used but there is no evidence whatever that a club member was responsible. Nearly all members appear to have received this disgraceful circular which was hostile to the Chairman and favourable to his opponent.

While the *'Conservative Underground Press'* document was being received an authentic circular from Market Bosworth in Leicestershire was being despatched to members. This was an electioneering stunt on behalf of the Chairman, sent out by his father-in-law, Mr Dennis Lisney, under an illegible signature) and leaning heavily on the dangers of

National Front infiltration so cleverly inculcated into the minds of the membership at that time. The Chairman first of all claimed that this circular was a response to the *'Conservative Underground Press'* circular and that it was a form of protection. When it was conclusively proved to him that it could not, from the timing of it, have been in response he agreed that it went out because he had 'come to hear' that dirty work was afoot against him, although quite what he then understood this dirty work to be is not at all clear. The Market Bosworth circular repeated *The Daily Telegraph* (27 March) story of James Allan; suggested that certain candidates would be 'loyal' while presumably others would not and had the effrontery to leave out such a distinguished club member as Mr Ronald Bell QC, MP. The effect this circular had on the membership's judgement is quite evident. Only Mr Bell, Mr Swerling, Mrs Carthew and Mr Day managed to defy its prognostications while to all intents and purposes the many other excellent candidates who stood for election might in the prevailing climate of uncertainty as to who was 'loyal' and who was 'not loyal' just as well have never put their names forward.

In the meantime the Monday Club's director circulated the membership informing it that the *'Conservative Underground Press'* was a forgery and that no such organisation was known of.

On 9 April a circular, again with a Market Bosworth imprint, was received at the Club office, claiming to be a letter from the Chairman and expressing his views in as unattractive light as possible. This circular, a forgery, was in fact received by very few people indeed. Yet the 10 April edition of *The Guardian* carried an article by Malcolm Stuart entitled 'Monday Club Suspects Spies', saying that "the club's 3,000 national members yesterday received a letter purporting to come from Mr Guinness". This is not correct as the Club office has subsequently fully admitted. A similar story appeared on 10 April in the daily paper of the Trotskyist Socialist Labour League, *The Workers' Press*, under the heading "Monday Club election becomes more bizarre". Likewise, in *The Daily Telegraph* under the heading "Guinness letter forged" and *The Economist* under the heading "You takes your choice" (14 April). It is appalling that no attempt has been made to offset this deception and more appalling still that anyone should have sought to ingratiate the Press with this type of damaging story.

The circular became the occasion for the Chairman to circulate the whole membership to the effect that a forgery from Market Bosworth had been sent to them; the letter contained a PS which stated 'future forgers should note my signature' which emphasised that the Chairman clearly assumed that it was the work of a club member, despite the lack of any credible evidence for this assumption. Many members thus assumed that it was the first Market Bosworth circular which was forged since that was the only circular from Market Bosworth they had received. We know of a number of members who have said this.

Here again, Mr Martin Webster provides a useful lead in establishing the authorship of the forgeries. The Club's leadership has quite unabashedly assumed (see letters 14 April – *The Daily Telegraph*) that the forgeries were the work of person or persons unknown who were Club members and supporters of Mr Young's candidature for the Chair. Mr Webster in his letter to *The Sunday Telegraph* (see earlier) says "if the Monday Club leadership and Scotland Yard are seeking those who issued forged circulars to club members before the recent club elections, they should look in the direction of the same group who published the anonymous smear booklet – *'Monday Club – a Danger to British Democracy'*; the same group that raided the homes of leading Club members last year. This same sinister organisation raided the head office of the National Front in 1970, stole files, then flooded our membership with forged circulars purporting to have been issued from our governing body".

Comment 1

If it be asked what is the relevance of recalling the story of the forgeries it is that some of it has never been known to the membership, some of it has been kept from the membership's knowledge and it was substantially the reason why Mr Jim Bourlet, the Club's ballot officer at the election felt compelled to state his dissatisfaction at the nature of the subsequent enquiry into the conduct of the club elections. Furthermore, it helps to explain why so many members felt so bitter; and to explain why it is now felt imperative to have the Electoral Reform Society supervise the next elections.

Notwithstanding all this it is utterly untrue to suppose that these events alone constitute sufficient basis for challenging the results of the elections: It is what has happened since the elections which is the cause of the two Special General Meetings which have been convened. This categorically gives the lie to those few members who contend that the Special General Meetings are a deliberate attempt to overturn the results of the AGM. They most emphatically are not.

Comment 2

The period preceding the elections was notable for its press publicity; it must have been hoped that this would cease completely and give way to responsible comment on political issues. Not a bit of it. During May, June, July and August the situation in relation to the media became worse. The membership was discovering what was happening to the club, insofar as it was discovering anything at all, not from the Club leadership but from the columns of *The Times, The Daily Telegraph, The Financial Times, The Guardian* (very objectively), *The Economist* and the provincial press. The Chairman's repeated promises of purges which he usually told the Press about before his own Executive Council (see for instance *The Daily Telegraph* 2 May, 'Guinness to expel rebels from Monday Club'; 'Guinness confident of Monday Club backing' – *The Times*, 1 May; and *The Daily Telegraph*, 21 May) was a constant feature of the publicity; it was as if the Press was the recipient of information which had to be disclosed to the world in order to satisfy some external source. It was certainly an omen of what was to come, and personalities were as dominating a factor as policies.

Comment 3

The Press during the Club election campaign was never disabused of the idea that in some mysterious way the battle for the Chairmanship between Mr Guinness and Mr

Young was one between moderates and extremists respectively. The fact is that in this content many members did not so much vote for but rather against one or the other. Some who supported Mr Young certainly did not share his views on immigration. Others supported him while not sharing his European views, while yet others did so because they could not contemplate a further year under Mr Guinness's chairmanship. The attempt to categorise members according to their electoral preference has had an extremely unfortunate effect on the Club's standing and reputation, and been grossly misleading into the bargain.

4. Expulsions and Resignations

While it is unquestionably true that there has been a certain degree of internal bickering and unpleasantness in the past, it has always been contained, never been allowed to dominate the Club and certainly not adversely affected the Club's reputation as a responsible right-wing pressure group.

It is important that these events should be explained to the membership since the only source of knowledge has been through the indirect, and often inaccurate, source of the press.

a) Mrs G Goold and the West Middlesex Branch

On 4 December 1972, it was noted by the Club's Executive Council that Mrs Goold and some members of the West Middlesex Branch had publicly announced their intention of supporting a National Front candidate at the Uxbridge by-election. Accordingly, it was resolved to disband the West Middlesex Branch, request the resignation of Mrs Goold and review the membership of individuals in the branch. This requires no comment. Clear, decisive action was taken, justified in all the circumstances.

b) Mr Len Lambert and the Essex Branch

On 8 January it was decided that the Essex Branch should be required to give a general account of its activities through its chairman, Len Lambert, because of adverse press reports of its activities, so it was claimed.

On 26 February, Mr Lambert appeared before the Executive Council and explained at length the structure, workings and policies of his branch. It was resolved that the Chairman with two other members of the Executive Council should hold an informal meeting with members of the Essex Branch Committee.

On 16 March the Essex Branch was addressed by the Chairman of the National Front at Chelmsford. Mr Guinness, campaigning at Lincoln, had requested Mr Lambert to cancel this meeting on the grounds that it was likely to associate the Monday Club in the public mind with the National Front, or at least seem to be in a context which did not sufficiently dissociate the Club from the Front. Mr Lambert has said that he discussed the Chairman's request with his committee but decided to proceed with the meeting on the grounds that extremist Left elements and members of the Young Liberals were demanding that he should cancel the meeting and that any retreat would be seen as a sop to left-wing pressure. Mr Lambert, for his part, explained the position in a letter to *The Daily Telegraph* of 16 April, entitled 'Open Forum tradition in the Monday Club' –

- "The Monday Club branch mentioned by Mr Jonathan Guinness (4 April) as 'allowing National Front members to speak' was the Essex Monday Club. Perhaps I may be allowed to correct some of the gross distortions of this event which have been hysterically paraded as a justification to re-elect Mr Guinness as Chairman.

  The Essex Club has a tradition for the 'open forum' type of meeting and our decision to invite a National Front speaker arose following the surprising results of recent by-elections. If the National Front was emerging as a political force, we felt it necessary to know more about it.

  The meeting was not 'advertised' and with the exception of the local Press the public were not admitted. It was a normal meeting and followed similar events at which we have argued and debated with political speakers ranging from Communists to Common Market and including Mr Guinness himself ... Why is it that our Chairman did not raise a similar objection when we had a Communist speaker to an Essex Club

> meeting? Or for that matter when Mr Vic Feather was invited to address the national club in London?

On 16 April the Executive Council resolved to call for the resignation of Len Lambert but that the matter should not be discussed in the Press. Mr Guinness informed Mr Peter Thornton of *The Daily Telegraph* (article *The Daily Telegraph* also 16 April) that the Essex branch of the Monday Club had refused to meet an executive council deputation seeking to enquire into alleged links between the National Front and the Monday Club, claiming that the branch's decision had been aimed at him personally by Mr Lambert. Mr Guinness said: "If I am re-elected to the Chair I think I will be taking a harder attitude than I have done so far". Mr Lambert claimed that he had not refused to see the Chairman. "We would accept him down here but there would be some pretty hard talking", he said. A further reason for Mr Lambert's expulsion was his refusal to surrender the membership lists of his branch in accordance with a request from the Director on instructions of the executive council. Such a request was sent to all branches and so far many branches have not complied. Mr Lambert said that he was not opposed in principle but that office security was so appalling that he would not be able to guarantee to members that their names could not be divulged.

Mr Lambert claims that the reason he failed to appeal was that part of the substance of the complaint against him was wholly untrue; namely that the Essex branch had convened a meeting in support of the National Front whereas, in fact, the meeting was one of a series in which minority party speakers of all persuasions were given a hearing. On 15 May Mr Lambert's expulsion was confirmed.

c) Harvey Proctor and the Economics Policy Group

During February the then Editor of the Newsletter, Mr Sam Swerling, invited Mr Proctor, then Chairman of the Economics Policy Group, to contribute an article to *Monday News*, not in his capacity as Chairman of the Group, but as an individual, in order to counterbalance one already submitted by Michael Orme, then a member of the Executive Council. Mr Orme's article broadly advocated the Government's economic policy while Mr Proctor's argued against any form of incomes policy at all. Mr Proctor's article also criticised Mr Guinness's views, as expressed, at Lincoln on economic policy.

Mr Guinness dismissed Mr Proctor from the Chair of the EPG as a consequence. Much ill-feeling was caused among its members. Mr Guinness claimed that he was dismissing Mr Proctor, not because of the *Monday News* article, nor because of Mr Proctor's own personal views but because his political philosophy ruled out any consideration of incomes policy at all. On 24 March an article appeared in *The Daily Telegraph* by Godfrey Barker in which both Mr Guinness's views and Mr Proctor's views were set out. Mr Guinness said:

- "For the Government to act without some kind of prices and incomes policy is like thinking one can become chess champion while excluding the use of one's queen's rook."

Mr Proctor claimed that Mr Guinness had 'quite clearly' betrayed the doctrines contained in "Aims of the Monday Club", and that Mr Guinness was committed to all forms of 'state interference' in the economy.

Although Mr Guinness's views are certainly accepted by many club members as regards economic doctrine, it is equally true to assert that conservative governments have not always had resort to wage and price restraints and therefore reference to 'chess champions' and 'queen's rooks' is singularly inapt.

On 15 March the Economics Policy Group committee met where the matter was discussed. Mr Proctor received letters in support from Mr Bourlet and Mr Victor Montagu and a letter from Mr Edward Taylor MP (which 'regrets the decision'), and one from Mr Orme who 'can see no cause for removing you', (Mr Orme can probably now see good cause why he came to be left off Mr Lisney's 'loyal' list). The general consensus was that the EPG had been opposed to an incomes policy for over two years and could not now change its mind just because the government had introduced one. It was further observed that the Club's

Executive Council had already approved as a club pamphlet from the Group *The State and the Economy* which argues the 'non-intervention' economic case.

On 16 March a letter was sent by eight members of the EPG to Mr Guinness conveying their disquiet at the manner in which Mr Proctor was removed as Chairman. It concluded by saying –

- "We feel that any attempt to reverse policy at this late stage can only lead to grave dissension within the Club, and weaken the credibility of our public pronouncements, something we would all deplore. It is also difficult to see how the Economics Policy Group could hope to operate effectively with a Chairman forced unwillingly upon its members and trying to pursue a policy to which many of us are opposed on grounds of principle."

At a meeting convened on 29 March by members of the EPG a discussion on the Club Chairman's actions took place. It was noted that; first, not all the members of the Group had been informed that the Group had been dissolved; secondly, the Group's original letter to the Chairman protesting at Mr Proctor's dismissal which was taken by Mr Guinness as a resignation could not possibly be so construed; thirdly, only the Executive has the power to disband a group which at this point in time it had not taken. One member of the group, Mr Beverley Antrobus, one of the earliest members of the club, said that he felt intellectually insulted by the Chairman of the club presuming to teach him economics.

Fresh attempts to re-constitute the Economics Policy Group have not been successful. The Chairman was hoping that a former executive council member, who had been left off Mr Lisney's 'loyal' list (see earlier) and was not re-elected, would fill the breach. He declined to do so.

5. Expulsions and Resignations from the Executive Council

a) The months of May and June were somewhat less turbulent. Despite the strange circumstances surrounding the elections in the club there was a general disposition to get the club back in working order. It was generally anticipated that a full enquiry into the leaks of the club's election results would reveal the source. This was not to be, however. It was also hoped that damaging headlines in newspaper articles concerning the club (see for instance "Senior Tory MPs' fears over future of Monday Club" – *The Financial Times* – 13 April; and "Monday Club MPs' plan to do their own thing" – *The Observer*, 29 April) would be a thing of the past, soon forgotten in a new climate of unity. Two days after his election victory, the Chairman announced to the membership via *The Daily Telegraph* (2 May – Guinness to expel rebels from Monday Club) that he was going to expel the rebels, but who the rebels were and how they came to be rebels he was clearly not too certain about!

- "I am certain that the disruption was too systematic not to have been planned – I'm not saying by members. But it was coldly calculated to disrupt the club. If you look at the pattern of the disruption it was very systematic but in whose interest I would not like to say."

Such breathtaking lack of clarity and such impartially assessed evidence no doubt came to be the criteria upon which later portentous events were to unfold. All those who dared question the Chairman's autocratic powers were presumably to be adjudged "rebels" and dealt with accordingly.

On 21 May a *Daily Telegraph* report carried the headline "Leadership inquiry demanded in Monday Club". This call came from the club's Provincial Council which Mr Guinness himself had been instrumental in setting up two years earlier, although by its own admission it was never more than an *ad hoc* body. The Council was reported as asking Lord Carrington, the Conservative Party Chairman, to conduct the inquiry as members were –

- "suspicious at the cloak and dagger atmosphere surrounding the club's affairs".

Mr Guinness, in the same report, claimed that the club was now in serious danger because of 'violent personal bitterness' among some members (quite right but hardly the thing to tell the newspapers). He said he had no comment to make on the inquiry demand but he believed his "opponents" were conducting "a silly, clever, smear campaign".

Although Mr Lambert's expulsion was confirmed on 15 May, his branch did not suffer a similar fate until 19 June when the Executive Council met again. Despite assurances that the matter would not be revealed to the Press *The Guardian*, on 20 June carried a headline "Monday Club split" by Jackie Leishman, the first paragraph of which read –

- "The Monday Club has voted to disband its Essex branch because of disobedience. Mr Guinness said after a meeting at the House of Commons last night that the expulsion would go into effect immediately but that under the club's rules the branch had the right of appeal within 28 days."

A similar headline appeared in *The Times* of 20 June– "Branch is expelled by Monday Club", with roughly the same content.

On 9 July a letter appeared in *The Daily Telegraph* from Richard Devonald-Lewis, Sir Ian MacTaggart, Bee Carthew, Victor Montagu, Roy Painter, Jim Bourlet, Audrey O'Reilly and Adrian Day, dissociating themselves from a criticism made by Mr Guinness of Mr Enoch Powell's widely misinterpreted Stockport speech. They made the point that Mr Guinness's article in *The Monday News*, in which he took Mr Powell to task ...

- ... "may have given the impression that he spoke for the entire Club and Executive Council; we wish to assure you that this is not the case."

Mr Guinness defended his criticism in *The Daily Telegraph* on 12 July–

- "My statement was designed to clarify the thoughts of members of the club in case Mr Powell had confused them; and to pinpoint the fact that Mr Powell's conditional advice to abandon the party would not in present circumstances even have the effect desired."

This brought a further response from Roy Bramwell, Ian MacTaggart and Roy Painter, and yet a further response from the Chairman on 21 July under a headline "Monday Club seeks to influence policies", which contained a somewhat quixotic and ironical last paragraph congratulating Mr Painter for having "exercised the faculty of logical thought" by joining the National Front!

b) Bee Carthew expelled; – Ronald Bell, Professor Ford, Geoffrey Baber resign; Sam Swerling resigns, Adrian Day and Valerie Harkess expelled.

The events which followed the Executive Council's meeting on Monday, 9 July represent the blackest day in the Club's history, an utter denial of the principles of natural justice and democratic procedure and, without question, are the immediate cause of the special general meetings. True to form, the membership has been informed via the newspapers since the document sent out from the Club office, entitled "After Trouble – Opportunity", is a travesty of what happened.

Mrs Bee Carthew was re-elected as Meetings Secretary at the April elections, a post which made her one of the seven Club Officers. More than halfway through the executive council meeting a motion of no confidence in her was put and carried by 9 votes to 3 (EC complement 24). Some executive members had left the room believing that no more important business remained to be done. Mrs Carthew asked the reasons for this action and was told there were no specific reasons but a number of general reasons. There was no advance notice that such a drastic step was to be taken, no item was placed on the agenda, and no preliminary warning even given to Mrs Carthew. She refused to resign, whereupon a further motion was put and carried expelling her from the club, subject to a 28-day appeal. This miserable, shabby action led to the immediate resignation of Mr Bell, Professor Hugh Ford and Geoffrey Baber. In "After Trouble – Opportunity" these three distinguished members of the club were not mentioned by name. Club members who do not read the daily papers or who only read the so-called "popular" press can have had no knowledge of what happened. In his letter of resignation, made public, Mr Bell refers amongst other things to the high level of "personal recrimination".

Amongst some of the general reasons advanced for the decision to expel Mrs Carthew were the fact she was a signatory to *The Daily Telegraph* letter of 9 July (albeit in an individual capacity and not as a club officer), and the fact that there had been an unpleasant disagreement between herself and the Club's Director over arrangements for Mr Enoch Powell's address to the Club on the subject of Ulster in the House of Commons on 26 June.

Neither reason seems remotely justified. Her appeal was dismissed after she had been denied the right to appear before the Council with her legal adviser in August.

The members heard what was happening via *The Guardian*, 14 July – "Monday Club loses three members in procedural row"; "Mr Ronald Bell resigns from the Monday Club" – *The Times*, 14 July; *The Financial Times*, 16 July – "Rally behind party, Guinness urges Monday Club".

In the latter article Mr Guinness's statement in "After Trouble – Opportunity" about subversion is recalled:

- "For at least three years there had been a group who were sufficiently dissatisfied with the present leadership to be prepared to use almost any method to 'capture' the club."

This sort of nonsense, unsubstantiated by any evidence at all, has already caused at least one political commentator, who has been following the club's difficulties closely, to remark that if the club should fold up it will be a "sad case of political paranoia in early middle life" – Tony Geraghty, *Sunday Times*, 22 April.

6. The Requisitions

a) The first requisition

News of the expulsion of Mrs Carthew and the resignations of Mr Bell, Professor Ford and Geoffrey Baber greatly disturbed very many people in the club. A requisition called for under Rule 17 was submitted by 50 members which called for the Chairman to resign and the Executive Council to be suspended and the club's affairs, furthermore, to be suspended until the next Annual General Meeting.

At the Club's next exclusive council meeting on 24 July the question of the legal validity of the requisition was discussed. At that meeting Mr Day was expelled for doing the unheard of thing in the Monday Club – speaking to the Press, and moreover *The Guardian*, about his intention of moving a vote of censure against Mr Guinness, and the Women's representative, Valerie Harkess, was expelled for not expressing her confidence in the Chairman and for being a requisitionist. The next event in what a senior club member has not inaptly described as the British version of the 'night of the long knives' was the successful moving of a motion to expel the 50 requisitionists; this, in effect, for doing precisely what the Club Rules permitted them to do!

The Chairman's argument was that the requisitionists' expulsion was due to their call for a cessation of club activities rather than their call for his resignation. This he thought was very damaging to the club whereas they contended that the damage had already been done and a breathing space was required to repair the damage. What is undeniable is that whether the requisition was damaging or not was a purely subjective judgment depending upon attribution of the blame.

The day after this meeting Mr Swerling resigned from the Executive Council saying he thought the Monday Club had ceased to be a valuable influence on the Conservative Party, and on 27 July Mr Victor Montagu, the former Lord Hinchingbrooke, author of the Club's outstanding pamphlet *The Conservative Dilemma*, and for many years a valued member of the Club's Executive Council, contributed an important letter to *The Daily Telegraph* in which he decried the lack of unanimity in the club and accused Mr Guinness of indulgence in "bogey-man politics, eliminating his opponents and charging them with Marxist orientations". The latter remark was a reference to Mr Guinness' conversion to the view that it wasn't really the National Front who were the trouble but Trotskyists.

In the meantime the Chairman and the club's executive council, or what remained of it, was forced to concede the right of the requisitionists to hold the Special General Meeting under threat of High Court injunction. This appeared in headlines in *The Guardian*, 28 July as "Monday Club executive backs down" and "Monday Club's 50 sacked members win right to vote" – *The Daily Telegraph*, 28 July and "Roll on Friday" – *The Economist*.

Mr Guinness asked his supporters to boycott the meeting called for on 20 August to discuss the motion contained in the requisition. His argument was that the motion was legal but would have no legal effect. One of his supporters Judge Gerald Sparrow, a former Judge of the International Court, in a letter to *The Daily Telegraph* on 29 August after the result said he thought the motion was legal but that Mr Guinness need not comply with it, a strange invocation of the legal maxim: "no man is above the law".

In the meantime some attempts were made at seeking a reconciliation – see later.

At the meeting on 20 August held in Caxton Hall the motion was passed by the substantial majority of 236 votes to 54, but Mr Guinness thought this was just "a silly season stunt". Soon the members were to hear via *The Daily Telegraph* how at least 100 people walked out before the vote was counted! – an independent observer at the door has said the true figure was between 10 and 20. The meeting over, a second requisition was then put in hand to tie up necessarily the loose ends.

b) The second requisition

In a leading article in *The Daily Telegraph* called "Monday Blues" on 17 August it was observed that –

> "At a time when the Government is either drifting in a socialist direction or responding to mainly bureaucratic pressures, there is an obvious need for an intelligent Right-wing group to provide countervailing pressures."

This ideally is the role of the club, but split by the internal schisms of the past nine months, bad leadership and the little attention given to politics this role has become that much harder to fulfil.

After the outcome of the first special general meeting over a hundred people immediately requisitioned a second meeting with the intention of implementing the content of what was decided at the first meeting. In the meantime the second batch of 50 requisitionists were receiving their marching orders. Whereas the Executive Council had decided that the motion at the first meeting "is purely destructive of the Club and is advised that it is incompetent in law", for some strange reason the second meeting, which arose out of it, was not apparently "incompetent in law". Mr Guinness and the rump of his executive although feeling it is "against the grain to ask you to attend this meeting" (such a nasty thing to have to do in the height of the silly season) evidently wish to put up a slightly better show than last time. Perhaps this was because several of Mr Guinness's own committee members had not thought it the wisest thing to do to boycott the first meeting. And so the stage is set for the second, decisive meeting.

In regard to Press reports about the Tuesday Club it should be emphasised that this ridiculous idea was firmly rejected by the overwhelming majority of those who had supported the motion on 20 August. *The Times* report of 21 August – "Monday Club rebels reject split" is an accurate summary of events. Mr Hugh Simmonds put the matter in perspective –

> "We have captured the heart and the mind of the Monday Club and nothing that we do at this meeting can reduce the pressure on Jonathan Guinness to recognise that fact."

7. Attempts at Reconciliation

Attempts to reconcile the differences in attitudes, policies and general outlook among club members should have been a major priority undertaken by the club leadership. Very little, if anything, was done. A feeling of utter despair and hopelessness pervaded the club from the end of June onwards. Three constructive attempts were made to resolve differences. Mr John de Vere Walker and Mr David Pilleau, of the Ulster Group, and Mr Sam Swerling, who had resigned from the executive in late July and who at that time had taken up a neutral position, all held meetings with senior members of the club. Mr Walker and Mr Pilleau did a great deal of hard work seeking to find common ground while Mr Swerling, who was not a requisitionist of the first meeting but was for the second meeting, produced a 12-page document in early August, which found approval amongst many neutral club members, as the basis of a compromise. It provided for –

a) Confirmation of Mr Guinness as Chairman.

b) Unconditional re-instatement of all expelled members.

c) Reconstruction of disciplinary rules which had been the cause of so much difficulty, reformation of the branch system, and a code of practice relating to press media.

These proposals were submitted to the founders of the club, an equal number of the requisitionists and the Director. The Director expressed "great interest and hope" in them. The founders were not, however, hopeful and indeed on the very evening when an undertaking was given (13 August) that the proposals would be given due consideration the executive council went on to confirm further expulsion notices. When in due course Mr Swerling explained his proposals to Mr Guinness, Mr Guinness replied that any basis for a settlement would have to include what amounted to a public confession of wrongdoing by the requisitionists and even then no general amnesty could be contemplated, although many of the requisitionists' cases would be favourably considered. So while a general amnesty can be granted in the Greece of Papadopoulos with all the tensions there a general amnesty cannot be granted, as part of a compromise, in the Monday Club of Guinness! Mr Swerling has said that it was at this point that he felt the requisitionists had justice on their side and that he would henceforth fully support their cause.

Mr de Vere Walker, in the meantime, still remained fully willing to meet anyone who felt a solution was possible but as the bitter personal vituperation and recrimination continued prospects receded and became negligible.

8. Common Market – Free Market

One of the canards of their whole sorry business has been the myth that Mr Guinness's opponents have been motivated by extraneous considerations of turning the Monday Club into an anti-Common Market forum and a vehicle for the propagation of Mr Enoch Powell's economic views.

This is complete nonsense. The feeling against the present Guinness regime embraces many members who not only support our entry into the EEC but who, like Mr Guinness, support an incomes policy. Furthermore, it embraces many who either supported Mr Guinness for the Chair in 1972, or 1973, and in some cases on both occasions.

A fair statement of the Common Market issue is contained in a letter of 9 July which appeared in *The Daily Telegraph* –

> Sir
>
> As members of the Monday Club we wish to dissociate ourselves from the criticism of Mr Powell's Stockport speech expressed by the Club Chairman, Mr Jonathan Guinness, and reported in the national Press.
>
> The official position of the Monday Club on the issue of the Common Market has been one of neutrality, but on the three occasions when the case for British entry was discussed it was heavily defeated.
>
> By using the first person plural in his statement Mr Guinness may have given the impression that he spoke for the entire Club and Executive Council; we wish to assure you that this is not the case.
>
> (Signed) Richard Devonald-Lewis, prospective Parliamentary Candidate, Islington Central, Chairman North London Monday Club; Sir Ian MacTaggart; Bee Carthew; Victor Montagu; Roy Painter, prospective Conservative Parliamentary Candidate, Tottenham; Jim Bourlet; Audrey O'Reilly, Vice-Chairman South West London Monday Club; Adrian Day, Executive Council, Young Members Representative, N7.

In his letter of resignation from the Executive Council Mr Swerling argued that –

> ... two possible solutions were open if these two vital matters of policy had ever been seriously discussed at length by the Executive Council. The first was to accept the difference of opinion and permit the existence of both an

Economic Policy (Interventionist) Study Group together with two study groups likewise co-existing and doing research on the benefits and disadvantages of the Common Market. This would have satisfied all parties in the sense that it would not have deflected from the Club's essential purpose, that is, to offer research for the benefit of the Party. At the same time it would not have deflected from the accepted view that we do not purport to have a corporate viewpoint on any political subject. In the prevailing division in the Club I feel that that would have been, and indeed still is, the best solution. Secondly, it would have been possible to come down firmly in favour of the course now being adopted by the Government on both issues. In the event I can see that no clear decision of principle has been taken but a rather strange procedure adopted instead – that is the appointment of Chairman of study groups by the Chairman of the Executive Council, whoever he may be at any time, with the composition of the personnel of the study group being determined at the discretion, and to the satisfaction, of the Chairman of it. This is what has led to inevitable divisions in one particular study group and seemingly caused its dissolution.

9. Club Reconstruction

The chaos which exists in the Monday Club cannot be allowed to continue. What has undoubtedly contributed to difficulties is the archaic and thoroughly unsuitable system of elections, rules for press releases and branch structure.

When the motion of 24 September is passed it is to be hoped that those who have charge of the club's destinies will make a full examination of these defects. Already valuable work was done by a sub-committee under the leadership of David Storey, but many of the proposals first enunciated last year are no longer suitable. It is respectfully suggested that reconstruction along the lines set out below may help to avoid some of the pitfalls of the past year.

Comment

The present structure of the governing body of the club and the system by which it is elected each year seems far from satisfactory. The full complement of the Council, as at present constituted, is 24 and each position (apart from that of Director and the co-options) is contested every year, which is taking the democratic process to an absurdity and in a direction unsuited to a club of our type; it is also probably a unique practice among political organisations, providing for uncertainty. It is also unsettling.

Proposals

a) Effective as from the Annual General Meeting 1974, the following would constitute the officers of the club.

1. Chairman
2. Deputy Chairman
3. Vice-Chairman
4. Vice-Chairman (under 30)
5. Treasurer
6. *Monday World* Editor
7. *Monday News* Editor

The major changes here are the formal recognition of the position of a Deputy Chairman and two Vice-Chairmen, one of whom would be the representative of the Young Members of the Club, elected by the Young Members at their own Annual General Meeting. This would accord with the practice observed in every Conservative constituency association in the country which has a Young Conservative Movement. It reflects the importance which the Club should attach to attracting more Young Conservatives into the Monday Club and playing their part in national revival.

The other six officers would be elected in Annual General Meeting to serve for a period of two years. In the event of the Chairman, for instance, becoming indisposed, retiring, or resigning, the Deputy Chairman would assume the position. In the event of the other officers likewise, casual vacancies would be appointed by the other officers acting jointly until the next Annual General Meeting when in addition to one third of the Executive Council (selected by ballot) re-submitting itself for election or retiring the person taking on the casual vacancy would also re-submit himself/herself for re-election or retire.

The positions of Meetings Secretary and Membership Secretary would cease to carry the status of officer. In the case of membership, some of this work is already done by the Director and the question of acceptance or rejection of new members is surely best carried out by a membership sub-committee. In the case of meetings, it is suggested that a meetings sub-committee would fulfil the purpose better than one person. In addition such a committee would have the function of initiating rallies, demonstrations, etc. One of the Vice-Chairmen, or the Deputy Chairman, would have overall responsibility on the Executive Council for these matters.

b) Nine ordinary members of the Executive Council to be elected by postal ballot at Annual General Meeting from the membership, three of whom shall re-submit themselves (selection by ballot) for re-election after one year; a further three at the end of two years, and the final three at the end of the third year. In the event of a casual vacancy arising a co-option, as at present, shall take place and in the event of an ordinary member not seeking to serve a second or third year at the end of any year an election shall take place for a replacement in the same manner and in addition to the one third.

c) i. A women's representative to be selected as at present.

ii. A universities representative to be selected by Club university students.

iii. Two branch representatives to be selected: for method of selection, see *infra*. Categories c(i), c(ii) and c(iii), would submit themselves for re-election annually.

d) Co-option of –

(i) Director of the Action Fund.

(ii) One member of the Club on majority vote of Executive Council.

The full complement of the Executive Council would then be reduced from 24 persons to 22, and the present jamboree each year with its seemingly inevitable press publicity would be greatly lessened. The above proposals also accord, or are similar to, with the constitutions of many other political clubs and organisations.

Establishment of Disciplinary Committee

Comment

The immediate cause of the requisitions have been the discontent with the way in which the club's disciplinary procedures at present operate. These procedures are clearly unsatisfactory and fail to distinguish between officers, other elected executive council members, and ordinary members. Furthermore, they omit reference to a number of elementary safeguards granted to a person under threat of expulsion which even an alleged criminal facing prosecution would be entitled to; namely, a full statement of its breach of rule in question, advance notice of intention to move a resolution of expulsion, the matter being placed on the agenda, etc.

The following proposals we believe are fair, and will be seen to be fair.

a) The establishment of a Disciplinary Committee, effective as from the Annual General Meeting 1974, comprising six persons, as follows: the Director, (Chairman) one Club Officer, (to be selected from among their members), one other Executive Council Member, (to be selected from among their number), one member of the Branches Council (to be selected from among their number), two ordinary members of the club of at least three years standing immediately preceding an Annual General Meeting (to be nominated and selected by ballot yearly). This makes a total of six persons.

b) Where it is alleged that a member of the club has broken a rule of the club notification of same shall be given to the Director in writing stating the nature of the breach. The Director shall then consider whether a *prima-facie* breach of the rules has taken place: if it has, he shall then consider whether the breach is sufficiently serious to warrant the convening of the Disciplinary Committee to hear the charge. If the matter can be settled amicably and an undertaking received that such breach will not be repeated no further action need be contemplated. If, however, the Director forms the opinion that it is a serious breach he will then convene a full meeting of the Disciplinary Committee, constituted as above.

c) The member will be given one week's advance notice giving details of the alleged breach and invited to present his case before the Committee, either orally or in writing. He may invite one person to act as a witness or assist him in presenting his case.

d) When the allegations have been heard the Disciplinary Committee may then either dismiss them or confirm them. In either case any operative decision must be taken by a two-thirds majority (that is four persons). If the decision goes against the member he may appeal within 28 days on the merits of the decision. If he does not appeal his expulsion takes effect from the expiry of 28 days from the decision of the Disciplinary Committee.

e) In the case of an appeal, a written report of the submissions and arguments (agreed beforehand by the Disciplinary Committee), shall be presented by the Director to every member of the Executive Council at least three days before the Council next meets. The Council at their meeting, after examining the evidence and after hearing any such representations as in c) will then by a two-thirds majority vote of at least 15 persons present, decide whether to allow the appeal or dismiss it. In the former case the member retains full rights of membership; in the latter the member ceases forthwith to be a member of the club.

f) The above procedures will be dependent upon the Rules being fully known to, and understood by, the members.

It is envisaged and hoped that the disciplinary procedure in the new climate of unity will rarely need to be invoked.

Branches Council

At present branch representation in the national affairs of the Monday Club is not very satisfactory. There are two possible viewpoints. One is the winding-up of the branch structure in the club; the other is to establish a proper working relationship between the National Club and the network of branches. The first possibility is ruled out on the simple grounds that there are many excellent branches doing good work. What is lacking at present is mutual respect and understanding and a proper framework within which branch matters can be discussed amicably and sensibly with the National Club leadership.

Proposals

a) Effective as from the Annual General Meeting 1974, a Branch Council be established to replace the *ad hoc* Provincial Council of Branches which was never officially constituted.

b) The Branch Council would comprise the Chairman and Secretary of every established Monday Club branch. Its essential purpose would be to meet at appointed times at least four times a year for the purpose of consultation and exchange of ideas. It would on inception elect from amongst its own members a Chairman and a Secretary and its first business would be to accept nominations from amongst its number for election to the Club's Executive Council.

c) The main function, it is envisaged, of such a Branch Council would be to make suggestions and offer ideas for the improvement of Club organisation and politics in any respect.

d) As new Club branches come into existence, so would the Branch Council expand accordingly.

e) The Branch Council would liaise with the Director and comply with the Executive Council request for a list of all branch members to be held at the offices of the National Club.

f) It is suggested that the officers of the Club meet the Branch Council at least three times a year.

These proposals are designed to induce the maximum confidence in the procedures and decisions of everyone holding responsible office in the club.

Press and Publicity

The recent spate of publicity concerning the internal affairs of the Club has badly damaged the Club's immediate future.

It is suggested that all matters concerning the internal affairs of the club should not be discussed in the Press, on radio or television. When confronted with requests for information on such matters members should not give it. This is already a policy decision of the club in principle (Executive Council minute, June 1972).

Further rules could be established in a code of practice to be drawn up by a sub-committee early next year.

10. Conclusion

We consider that the above survey provides irrefutable evidence of the justice of the case of those who seek an end to the present nonsense in the Monday Club and the club's re-establishment as an effective, responsible and constructive pressure group of the Tory Right. We would only add that Mr Guinness's letter to members of 14 September in which he seeks to accredit responsibility for "leaks", "Anonymous publications", and "Resignations" is in direct contradiction of our evidence; study this evidence and the correct version will be immediately apparent. Furthermore, and finally, if Mr Guinness seeks to suggest that most Monday Club MPs are behind him we could produce abundant evidence that at least six of our MPs firmly believe the contrary including one who refused to serve on the club's Executive Council for the same reasons which brought about another's resignation.

Monday Club decline

This letter to then Chairman of the Monday Club, David Storey, in February 1990, marked the point at which I came to the conclusion that the Monday Club was beyond redemption. It would muddle on for another three years under ineffective leadership but would cease to have any continuing impact as a pressure group. I express my views as someone who retained most of the key positions in the club. Most good things come to an end and for me this was it, although it nominally still exists but no pamphlets are published and no study groups are in place.

Dear David

Recently I received my annual subscription notice. For some years my wife and I have paid a joint subscription. This year my wife told me she could see no point in remaining a member of the club as she was not able to attend meetings and there was nothing else that the club did which warranted her remaining a member. Anything that was worthwhile involved a further expenditure of money.

This gave me food for thought. She is, of course, quite right. I suspect discontent amongst ordinary members (unless apathy has replaced it) is stronger than it has ever been. As a membership organisation it has to be said the Monday Club appeals probably to less than 10 per cent of its already meagre numbers – I believe now under 700.

In terms of effectiveness in its primary purpose as a pressure group within the Conservative Party it really has ceased to have any essentially distinctive voice: it has lost virtually all the important political debates it has engaged in (or been overtaken by them) in the past fifteen years and is regarded by many aspiring Conservatives at best as an anachronism and at worst as a poisoned chalice which will damage any prospect of political advancement. This relates back, of course, to some extent, to "the troubles" of the 1972/73 period. I would except from this criticism the work of the Foreign Affairs Committee which functions very effectively.

I regard all this as very sad indeed because much of the active membership comprises good quality people whose voluntary activity ought to be leading to affirmation of the club's stature rather than witnessing its continuing decline.

One certainly accepts that a pressure group is bound to suffer during a period of sustained Conservative government but the extent to which the Monday Club has been diminished in the public mind, and within the ranks of its own membership, is alarming, salutary and wholly avoidable.

Issues of leadership are at the centre of the problem. Controversial though you may think this to be, I cannot think Lord Massereene's presidency is an asset. He is now a fairly elderly man whose best political years are clearly past. He should make way for a more dynamic figure or, better still, the club should function without a president and simply word the fact that Lord Salisbury was its first patron. Is that not esteem enough?

The function and purpose of so many Vice-Presidents is also curious and obscure. I notice that two gentlemen, called Jepson and Murray, have been added to the list. I know neither of them but I do know that at no time has any information been given to the membership explaining why it has been thought a worthwhile exercise having their names added. Maybe they are thoroughly deserving. I recently read Murray's pamphlet: *Recall to Greatness*. Priced at £1, containing unnumbered pages, without a publisher's address and replete with several typographical errors, it is precisely the sort of generalist production which makes me shudder. Devoid of content and substance, and making not a single recommendation for political action how can it have passed scrutiny? Maybe it wasn't scrutinised. It reminds me of the ramblings of a final year political philosophy student – well written, certainly, but having no core at all. It stands most uneasily amongst other well-researched and documented papers produced.

What image are these Vice-Presidents supposed to convey for the Monday Club? If it is 'respectability' the more 'respectable' the club seeks to become the less dynamic will be its political message. I see no place for them: people are not deceived that easily. This leads me to raise the issue of the club's relationship with, and somewhat sycophantic view of, the Prime Minister herself.

Throughout the period of your Chairmanship Mrs Thatcher's standing has been viewed as unassailable and unassailed within the counsels of the club: an extraordinary reverence which her record, seen from the standpoint of the radical right, she simply does not deserve. Hardly a murmur of rebuke or criticism, even constructive criticism, has been levelled at her door. It has always been the fault of some junior minister, some underling or 'presentation failings' when some profoundly anti-traditionalist ideas have been taken on as party policy.

Obviously, views as to Mrs Thatcher's contribution over the past ten years to Conservative resurgence (or, in reality, the lack of it) will be at variance; many regard her as the best thing since sliced bread, a sort of redeemer. Personally, I see her as a most over-rated Prime Minister who has benefited hugely from an incoherent and ineffective Labour Party. My own view is unimportant. What is important is that judged by any measure of objectivity the Monday Club comes off very badly in terms of implementation of policy on the 'gut' issues which concern so many of us, whether it be immigration, race-relations, Northern Ireland, Rhodesia/Zimbabwe, law and order, and others. The consequences of government policies have been little less than disastrous (whether or not she has personally embraced them).

There is a certain reciprocity in the matter too. Mrs Thatcher has never thought much of the Monday Club, something readily discernible from the fact that while she has found time on several occasions to address functions of the Bow Group and

Tory Reform Group, I cannot recall a single occasion when she has been able to find time to address the Monday Club or to speak favourably of it, as has Enoch Powell.

Consistently, and predictably, Mrs Thatcher has promoted ministers of moderate ability, such as Viscount Whitelaw, to important posts where others ought to have found preferment. How is it that Julian Amery and John Biggs-Davison, two outstanding figures of the traditional Right, were never offered ministerial rank in her governments?

You may well say: but how does this affect the Monday Club? I believe it does insofar as the club's general outlook, its political standing and success are so often represented as inextricably linked with the good fortunes of Mrs Thatcher and her continuing dominance of British political life.

I think this attitude, so commonplace within the club, is dreadfully misconceived. She does undoubtedly deserve credit for her steadfastness over the Falklands; her determination to defeat inflation; her nullifying of trade union power, and her championing of British influence in Europe. These are undoubtedly substantial achievements, none of which the club would fail to acknowledge readily and handsomely. It is also true, I think, that she effects right-wing attitudes in public pronouncements: the sadness is that, in her, the difference between rhetoric and action is truly remarkable: it is very pronounced indeed. It is this very lack of principled action which convinces me that Mrs Thatcher is not really 'of the right'. The following examples cannot be gainsaid:

a) her indifference towards sanctions against Rhodesia.

b) her willingness to compromise Northern Ireland's territorial integrity through the Anglo-Irish Agreement.

c) her refusal to stand firm against further permanent immigration.

d) her unwillingness to dismantle the race-relations industry which, more than any other quango, is a slug on the cabbage of political life, encouraging in the process the cultural decay of our kingdom.

e) her refusal to countenance the re-introduction of grammar schools in the scheme of secondary education.

So my view is that the Prime Minister, admirable though many of her qualities may be, does not adhere to the beliefs and tenets of the national, traditional Right. She is, in essence, an old fashioned Whig, deriving her thinking from 19th century liberalism, much of which is alien to the Tory tradition. As Britain enters the 1990s amidst mounting lawlessness, environmental pollution (with litter and filth everywhere to be seen), Muslim fanaticism, rampant and unchecked multi-culturalism ingrained in the national psyche to our enormous detriment – the question needs to be asked: Whither the Monday Club?

Chairman, your own contributions to the club are not in question: your hard work is recognised and not in doubt. Yet I hope it is not ungenerous of me to ask whether a great deal of such effort is, in fact, misdirected? The national membership cannot be aware of what is happening because it is not being informed: there is no *Monday News* or *Monday World* and activities which do take place go unreported. Further, I believe, Chairman, that your own apparent unwillingness to write letters to the press or issue press statements (which I understand you consider to be the function of study group chairmen) can only add to the impression that the club has either lost its collective voice or is unwilling to take part in any form of political controversy: if the latter were true shouldn't we all pack up and go home? At present, the only occasion when the club seems to come into its own, in terms of publicity, is the Annual Party Conference.

The obsession with a national referendum on capital punishment again seems to me to be a complete waste of time and effort and largely unproductive. Does the Monday Club think that capital punishment is the key law and order issue? Maybe it is, but I doubt it. What about the countless other law and order issues where this government's ineptitude and weakness have reduced the public to a sense of hopelessness and pessimism, particularly in inner-city and urban areas?

Of course, there are severe limitations upon what any pressure group like the Monday Club can reasonably achieve, accepting the constraints of the voluntary principle and the lack of the urgent funding which we have unsuccessfully sought for so many years. Nevertheless, I believe that a number of administrative and structural arrangements should be made, at no cost, if the club is to be restored to some semblance of efficacy and become responsive to its national membership. I outline some of them here:

1. The club could, and should, produce a members' bulletin, perhaps quarterly, which would be a detailed report on all facets of club work: reports of meetings, Branch activities, young members' activities, etc. The whole point of this would be the dissemination of information. Members could then see that perhaps their subscriptions were encouraging worthwhile activity.

2. An informal discussion circle should be instituted whereby members would be encouraged to produce an 'occasional paper', leading to constructive debate. I remember attending many worthwhile sessions in the days when Adrian Fitzgerald, David Levy and Ian Crowther were prominent in the club. Generating political thought is a very important accompaniment to political action. These discussion circles could perhaps be regionalised and their deliberations recorded in the members' bulletin.

3. A heightened awareness of the importance of debate among the young membership. Some years ago I offered to sponsor a YMG debating competition leading to a trophy of some sort, provided that not less than 12 debaters took part. I never received a response. I repeat the offer.

4. The restoration to the political agenda of the club of four national conferences a year. When Pat Wall was chairman, between 1978-80, a period during which I had the privilege to be Deputy Chairman, these events took place with great success: they were invariably well attended. During my own period as chairman (1980-82), the conferences continued at the same rate in my first year but did tail off in the second. I am to blame for that. The club appears to have fewer conferences these days, certainly national conferences. Can they not be restored?

5. The restoration of big public meetings when urgent issues arise. The threatened influx of hundreds of thousands of Hong Kong Chinese ought to be such an occasion. I share the sentiments of Tim Janman MP entirely. How these people, however worthy, can claim

a right of abode in Britain completely defeats me. As the late Sir Ronald Bell once said so cogently: ".... Who looks at his passport and thinks twice about it unless to travel abroad for a temporary purpose?" (Public meeting, Westminster Central Hall, 6 September 1972).

6. The inauguration of formal and informal links with other like-minded, domestic groups, essentially Conservative, to promote common political purpose. The same ideal should extend to European political organisations working to promote a more national content to domestic policies. Examples of parties where I believe informal links would be appropriate are: Fuerza Nueva, in Spain; Front National, in France, and Movimento Sociale Italiano, in Italy. These are resurgent nationalist groupings of the radical right standing, very broadly, for much the same sort of ideals as the Monday Club, even though they are not linked, as the club is here, with a Conservative party of their own. The important point is that in much the same way as movements of national self-consciousness have re-awoken the will to independence in Eastern Europe, so should the new decade usher in a similar spirit of political idealism to throw off the shackles of decadence and unprincipled modernism which pervades so much of our European continent. The Monday Club could become the constructive catalyst of such a development, certainly within the Conservative Party in Britain.

Chairman, like you, I am entering my 25th year of membership of the Monday Club. I am convinced that the club needs a serious renewal of purpose and vitality. I am sure you, Cedric and other members of the council have the ability to provide it; but will you do so? Many of us perceive the club is dying on its feet. I challenge you and members of the Executive Council to recognise the problems and use your very best endeavours to correct them and prove me wrong.

With best wishes.

Yours sincerely

Sam Swerling
Chairman, Monday Club, 1980-82, Deputy Chairman, 1978-80

cc: All Executive Council members, Other relevant parties

Monday Club – further evidence of decline

This piece written by me and published by the Monday Club Restoration Committee in May 1993 effectively marks the end of the club as a Conservative Party pressure group. For 23 years, while it has trundled on, it has done virtually nothing and its membership has dwindled to very small numbers.

The Monday Club has become an impoverished, discredited and somewhat useless political movement in the past 12 months. Why should this have happened so inexorably, so rapidly?

The answer to that question is simple: leadership of very poor quality; the personal vainglory of Dr Mayall; and an executive council of minimal ability. Political activity has been negligible. The club has remained ominously silent over Maastricht, the ERM, the Matrix Churchill arms issue; the Heseltine pits fiasco; the crisis of law and order; incipient chaos in South Africa; the Criminal Justice Act 1991 disaster; Major's feeble leadership and much else besides.

Has Dr Mayall written a single letter to the Press? Has he found the energy to issue even one press statement about any of these vital issues? Has he once put his head above the political parapet to advance the cause of the Monday Club? The answer is a resounding NO.

Added to all this has been a petty, vindictive spitefulness which has led to recrimination against several of the Club's most active and effective members.

i) Mayall and his executive council in April 1992, against the Club rules, refuse the nominations to executive council posts of several club members.

ii) Mayall, at the 1992 Annual General Meeting, agrees to "consider" the co-option at the next executive council meeting of those whose nominations were refused – such "consideration" (as will be explained) never took place.

iii) Mayall publishes and presents, in the name of the Monday Club, a pamphlet on the Maastricht Treaty, in breach of executive council procedures before which such pamphlet was never discussed or considered. It is of poor quality and could have been written under Central Office guidance. It is wholly against Monday Club policy.

iv) Mayall, at the same AGM, presents a truncated version of a paper on agriculture written by Marguerite Boyd-Howell, after such pamphlet has been carefully put together, annotated and approved in accordance with club rules. The author was so disgusted with what had been put out in her name that she demanded its withdrawal and later resigned from the Club in complete disgust.

v) In mid-June 1992 Mayall announces the cancellation of the Dinner, organised by Gregory Lauder Frost, on behalf of the Club, in honour of Enoch Powell, to celebrate his 80th birthday. This would have been a prestigious event, giving good publicity to the Club apart from being something which very many people were looking forward to.

   Mayall tried to suggest that Mr Powell had himself cancelled the dinner. This is completely untrue. Mayall himself cancelled it. Why? On the ridiculous pretext that a number of alleged extreme right wingers wanted to wreck the event – a truly absurd proposition. Why, then, was this important event cancelled? Only Mayall himself knows.

Could it have been that Enoch Powell might have said something uncomfortable about Maastricht which Central Office would not have approved of and which Mayall, conscious of his own parliamentary ambitions, would have been closely identified with? To this day the cancellation of the dinner has not been explained to anyone.

vi) At an executive council meeting in June 1992 Stuart Millson, Sam Swerling, Brian Rathbone and Michael Smith, with more than 75 years' membership of the Club between them, were "expelled" under procedures which owed more to Star Chamber methods than a proper democratic hearing. The consequence of these "expulsions" is that they are being contested in the courts; all indications are that the four plaintiffs will win their action and that Mayall and his co-defendents will have to pay substantial costs and damages.

vii) And so the Monday Club trundles on – without effective leadership; without political vision; incapable of even putting out a decent pamphlet or newsletter and, most significantly, on the sidelines while the Conservative Party, under weak leadership, deserves a constructive and effective critique from the Tory Right. The Monday Club cannot provide that critique under the present collection of low grade individuals who control its destiny.

Sam Swerling

Published by the Monday Club Restoration Committee
12 May 1993

FN into the mainstream

I started to follow the progress of the Front National in France during the early 1990s having come to the view that this party had many similarities with the Monday Club of which I had been a member for over 25 years, although, of course, whereas the FN was an established political party in its own right the MC was a pressure group within a party, the Conservative Party. Both the FN and MC were traditionalist, patriotic movements although the former's key doctrines had elements of left-nationalism as well as right-nationalism in them.

The media in this country, which has not always been respectful of the truth, especially if it should get in the way of a good story, characterises the FN as a party of the extreme-right without ever attempting to explain what this means and why it is an appropriate, let alone fair, way to describe the principles and policies of the movement.

I have spent a fair amount of time involved with the FN, attending their congresses and conferences in Paris as an overseas guest and getting to know their leading figures, including both Jean-Marie Le Pen and his daughter Marine Le Pen.

I have also organised visits to London of leading figures in the party and introduced them to MPs and other dignitaries. At no time have I witnessed the alleged racism of which there have been accusations, falsely and at times maliciously made.

My visit to Paris in the spring of that year confirmed what I saw – that the FN had entered the political mainstream. I hope the unconvinced will feel able to take a more measured view, both from this article, written for the September 1995 quarterly journal *Right Now*, and other pieces written.

In the week before the French presidential election on 23 April 1995 I was on vacation in Paris. It was a marvellous opportunity to witness the contrasting styles and opposed political programmes of some of the contenders for the Elysee Palace. I went to the final campaign meetings of Lionel Jospin, Edouard Balladur and Jean-Marie Le Pen. The first two gave fairly predictable, solid but somewhat uninspiring, accounts of why they were best equipped to run France for the next seven years. Each meeting attracted about 1,500 people, largely party faithful.

Le Pen's meeting, on the Thursday, took place in a huge, specially constructed marquee at the Pelouse de Saint Cloud, in the Bois de Boulogne, just opposite Longchamp racecourse. Under the glare of floodlights some 12,500 (official figure) Lepénistes, seemingly drawn from all classes of the community, and from all quarters of France, from countless hundreds of young men and women from the Front National de la Jeunesse to the *anciens combatants* of France's many colonial wars and Second World War, prepared to greet their hero. "Can-can" dancers entertained the crowd in the pre-meeting warm up. And then to the strains of Verdi's *Nabucco*, Le Pen mounted the stage to tumultuous applause. His two and a quarter hour speech, delivered without a note, was remarkable for its wide ranging content, clarity and calm delivery. He is, without question, the finest political orator in France.

The doctrine of national preference, the pivotal ideology upon which the FN's programme has been constructed with a compelling coherence, was explained in detail. France would come first; French people would have priority and French traditions and institutions would be preserved above all else. And not a word of racist rhetoric, of which Le Pen is so often and so falsely accused, was to be heard. A resounding rendering of the *Marseillaise* concluded the proceedings as the crowd departed into the still spring night with optimistic expectations of Sunday's result. In the event, Le Pen obtained exactly 15% of the vote: 4.7 million adherents. This level of support, and the FN's recent municipal election successes, serve to confirm that the FN has entered the mainstream, much to the chagrin of the *classe politique*.

What is evident too is the impressively high quality of those who work for the FN. The *curricula vitarum* of the 650-strong National Support Committee for Le Pen's presidential campaign give an insight into people of distinction and eminence in their various walks of life, ranging from numerous academics at universities, including a number of emeritus professors, lawyers, doctors, holders of various awards for service and bravery, escapees from Nazi concentration camps, businessmen and women and industrialists. One name on the list is that of Robert Hemmerdinger, a longtime friend of Le Pen, a captain in the Free French forces, vice-president of the national committee of French Jews, resistance medallist and a regional councillor for the Ile de France. The list represents a microcosm of what the FN actually is – a conservative-based, nationalist political movement but one which is entirely democratic in its structures and intentions. Yet rarely has a politician been so vilified as has Jean-Marie Le Pen.

Respected French journalist and prize-winning novelist and film-maker Roger Mauge has written an informative biography entitled *La Vérité sur Jean-Marie Le Pen* (France-Empire, 1988). Mauge first met Le Pen in 1956. Le Pen, at 27 the youngest deputy in France, had just resigned his seat to fight for the cause of French Algeria. Of particular interest is how Le Pen led a number of his fellow law students on a mission to stop the breach of dams causing flooding endangering Amsterdam in 1953. Le Pen's military career is recounted in detail; how he fought with distinction and bravery in Indo-China and Algeria and taken part with the French forces in the Suez operation of 1956 alongside Israeli and British soldiers, and how he had always taken a pro-Israeli line in the Middle East conflicts. Le Pen has indeed consistently supported Israel and, in February

1987, met with representatives of 24 American-Jewish organisations with whom he had "positive and cordial" exchanges (interview, *Jerusalem Report*, 27 February 1992). Before the meeting I engaged in conversation with a young Jewish French doctor from Amiens, a member of the FN since 1988. He was fiercely proud to tell me of his huge admiration for Le Pen and that, whatever the FN's detractors may claim, it is not a racist but a nationalist party and one with hundreds of active Jewish members; likewise black and brown members and supporters both in Metropolitan France and in the DOM-TOM (French overseas possessions), particularly Martinique, Guadeloupe and New Caledonia. What better evidence can there be to nail the lie of Le Pen's alleged racism and anti-semitism?

An illustration of anti-Lepéniste hysteria whipped up by the Left and the media was the aftermath of the dreadful desecration of the Jewish cemetery at Carpentras in southern France on 9 May 1990, where 34 graves were opened, tombstones overturned and the body of a recently buried 81-year old man laid on a neighbouring grave and impaled upon a parasol stick. "Anti-racist" demonstrations were organised at an instant, in Paris and elsewhere. "FN to blame", "Le Pen responsible" shrieked the hate-merchants. Yet not a shred of evidence could be found to link the FN with this atrocity. In his fortnightly internal communiqué, Le Pen wrote: "The abominable violation of the Jewish cemetery at Carpentras has shamed and revolted me as all men of heart. I have said so. I say so again. But since the beginning of this affair I have sensed that one was going to exploit it against the Front National and myself ..."

Amongst countless others to speak out against the mischievous lies were Fernand Teboul and Bernard Antony. Teboul, an FN municipal councillor in Vaucluse (where Carpentras is situated), and significantly recently re-elected with an increased vote, declared: "I am Jewish and one hundred percent French. I have come to the gathering organised at the cemetery for I am protesting against the desecration of the tombs. But I do not associate myself at all with MRAP (Movement Against Racism and Friendship Among People) and LICRA (International League Against Racism and Anti-Semitism)". Antony, European Deputy, regional councillor for Mid-Pyrenees, president of Chrétienté-Solidarité and founder-editor of the daily newspaper, *Présent*, urged French people not to fall for the incredible provocation which is trying to make people believe that the FN resembles the Hitler régime". For a supposedly racist party it is curious too how many supporters the FN has among France's Muslims. Prominent among these is Sid-Ahmed Yahiaoui, a regional councillor for the FN in the Ile de France, and fifteenth on the party's European list. Interviewed by *Le Figaro* on 16 February 1995, Yahiaoui declared that Le Pen was in no way racist, adding: "I am, like him, a war orphan and many things bring us together. My commitment at his side gives me a feeling of the sacrifice of my own father, a senator from Oran, brought up and assassinated in Algeria after independence, for his attachment to and love of France".

Although the British media is little better than the French, ostracism of the FN has not been absolute. The Ulster Unionist MP, John Taylor, also an MEP, was a member of the FN grouping in the Euro-Parliament (called the Technical Group of the European Right) which he considered a perfectly acceptable thing to do. At the time of joining, he described the FN as " ... not at all extreme" and said that he agreed with the party's strong support for NATO (uniquely among French political parties) and their strong opposition to terrorism. (Editor's note: The FN is also one of only two French political parties opposed to Maastricht.) And Lord Plumb, then leader of the Conservative Group in the European Parliament, has been guest of honour of the FN at one of their European Right conferences. Overseas, Le Pen has met ex-President Reagan on a European delegation visit, as he has Omar Bongo, President of Gabon, President Nakasone of Japan, then-President Felix Houphouet-Boigny of the Ivory Coast and other heads of state.

The municipal elections in June 1995 have seen the implantation of the FN at local level in most areas of France. In 1989 the FN put up 15,106 candidates from whom it secured the election of 239 members of the provincial assemblies; 54 mayors of smaller towns, 1,191 councillors of municipalities and 3 members of the *Conseils Généraux* (counties). The advance has been spectacular, for this time it put up 25,680 candidates in 477 towns of more than 5,000 inhabitants, and in 193 towns of more than 30,000 inhabitants. The FN has more than doubled its number of councillors and has taken control of three municipalities – Toulon, Orange and Marignane, adjacent to Marseilles. Mayor of Toulon is Jean-Marie le Chevallier, European deputy, regional councillor for Provence-Alpes Cote d'Azur (PACA) and formerly head of Le Pen's private office, a highly cultured man whose mayoral tenure is likely to solidify FN support in the region. Certainly the FN election manifesto, which featured immigration least among its concerns, took opponents by surprise.

In his book, *The Dark Side of Europe* [Edinburgh University Press, 1990], Geoffrey Harris, a senior European Parliament official, has written "Whilst his [Le Pen's] policies are often far from detailed, they are not very different in substance from those of, for example, some of the right-wing candidates for the Republican nomination for the Presidency of the USA, not to mention Ronald Reagan himself". FN strategists favour unity with the Gaullist right whenever feasible. The theme of "unity of the right" has been the guiding principle behind many leading intellectuals joining the party. One such is Yvan Blot, very close to Le Pen, and formerly head of the academic think-tank, Club d'Horloge, who joined in 1989. In an article in *Le Monde* in April of that year, Blot stressed the urgent need for a coming together of the right-wing parties, a thesis he had developed when one of Jacques Chirac's closest associates. For much the same reason were the adhesions to the FN of Jean-Yves Le Gallou, leader of the party in the Ile de France, and Jean-Claude Martinez, European Deputy, Professor of Public Law and Political Science at the University of Paris, and the FN's principal spokesman on fiscal matters. However, the differences between the Gaullist parties on European and economic questions now make unity less likely and certainly the mutual antipathy between Chirac and Le Pen suggests the FN will continue to draw support exclusively under its own banner.

What approach, if any, should the British Conservative Party adopt towards the FN? Much can, and should, be done. Reciprocal visits to congresses and conferences at both senior level and between the parties' youth wings could be instructive. The climate of opinion may be changing. It will need to if our nation is to be preserved. In this regard we have much to learn from the example of the FN in France.

(i) Blue, White and Red – Late summer festivities in Paris

My article in *Right Now* journal, December 1997.

Tens of thousands of patriots from all over France descended upon the Pelouse de Reuilly on the edges of the Bois de Vincennes, eastern Paris, on the weekend of the 27/28 September for the 17th renewal of the Front National's annual festival, the Bleu, Blanc, Rouge. They were rewarded with two days of fine, warm weather.

Already larger than the Gaullist UDF, and fast approaching the size of the RPR, the FN has had a highly successful year. The BBR was just the sort of jamboree to celebrate it. With support levels in some regions of France (particularly in the south and the industrial north east) running at over 35%, and with national opinion poll ratings at 16%, the FN's progress seems irreversible. Its proven record of competent local government, in Toulon, Marignane, Orange and, more recently, Vitrolles, has led to its enhanced political stature and credibility, and encouraged increasing numbers of French men and women to embrace its core nationalist values.

The festival is a key event in the FN calendar – a three-line whip for party activists. All the national and regional leadership attend. The party's 93 branches proudly set forth their colours and achievements, while the 18 various associative organisations, covering economic, social, cultural and intellectual endeavours, of one sort or another, display to the enthusiastic masses their work and their linkage to the FN in the political process.

The Pelouse de Reuilly, in fact, is an ideal setting. Once a royal hunting ground the land was given to the City of Paris by Napoleon III as a park for public use. The festival events are meticulously organised and laid out by the FN's manifestations committee on a grand scale. Two avenues of marquees and smaller tents, about 400 yards in length, meet at a central point in the form of a cross. All the party's regional branches reserve their places. Oysters, charcuterie, armagnac and cider are consumed ravenously as if there were no tomorrow.

On the periphery, pony rides, dodgem cars and coconut shies (with effigies of the failed politicians of the Fifth Republic inviting targets) all do brisk business. Fathers in sports jackets and ties, mothers and elderly matrons in sparkling summer dresses rub shoulders with a sprinkling of skinheads. Army veterans, wearing the red or black berets of the paratroops or marine infantry, mingle freely with people dressed in a variety of country costumes. Everyone feels at ease at what the FN describes as "this grand festival of unity and nationhood".

I was attending my third successive BBR. It was an ideal opportunity to renew friendships and sample again the atmosphere that the festival uniquely generates. The first stand I visited on the Saturday morning was manned by Professor Jean-Claude Martinez, an FN Euro MP and one of the party's foremost intellects. A taxation expert at the University of Paris II (Assas), he is the author of eleven books; one a 300-page account of how France would be run in Le Pen's first hundred days in the Elysée Palace. Martinez, who has recently been placed in charge of the FN's "shadow government", is a rapporteur of the agricultural committee of the European Parliament. We chatted for a few minutes before I moved on to see Bruno Gollnisch, also a Euro MP, the FN Secretary-General, who succeeded Carl Lung (the party's social affairs expert, and also a Euro MP) two years ago. Gollnisch, another formidable intellect, was the youngest ever Dean of Law School at Lyon III University. He expressed unqualified optimism for the future development of the party and was particularly gratified by its huge expansion in universities and colleges.

At mid-day the first of a series of political discussions and debates, lasting in all four hours, began in the central arena marquee. Each discussion period was led by a party expert, on subjects as diverse as the economy, industry, immigration, security, taxation, local government and defence. The audience seemed to be particularly knowledgeable.

On the Saturday evening I was invited by the Paris region federation (Ile de France) to their dinner party. After a splendid four-course meal, the guests settled down to a one-hour rendering of patriotic songs performed by former members of the parachute regiment in the presence of Jean-Marie Le Pen – no slouch himself when it comes to lusty singing.

The Sunday events at the BBR got into full swing in mid-morning after celebration of open air Mass, a traditional feature of FN gatherings. The crowds were bigger than on the Saturday. My first visit was to the tent of the catholic nationalist newspaper, *Présent*, displaying its books and pamphlets. I spoke with Georges-Paul Wagner, Le Pen's advocate in numerous lawsuits, now retired from practice but a leader writer with the paper. With him was Caroline Parmentier, a young campaigning journalist with a big following, whose new book, simply entitled "Journaliste", chronicling her 10-year career with the paper, was worth every franc of the hundred I paid for it, on account of its insights into the lies and mis-representations that the national movement faces from the French media, an observation equally applicable to the weekly National papers, *Hebdo* and *Rivarol*, both of which are in the FN camp.

I was then particularly pleased to meet the distinguished Jewish journalist, Jean-Pierre Cohen, former editor of the weekly *Minute* and current member of the FN's Central Committee. With Bernard Antony (Euro MP and leader of the FN satellite grouping, Chrétienté-Solidarité) Cohen has written a formidably documented booklet: "Ni raciste, ni antisémite", a compelling rebuttal of allegations of racism and anti-semitism levelled against the national movement by the left, liberals and politically correct. It should be compulsory reading for the uninformed.

After taking in further debates at the central marquee I looked forward to the principal event of the festival, the closing address of FN President, Jean-Marie Le Pen. 70,000 were now in the pelouse. Preceded by a contingent of "Anciens Combattants" acting as an honour guard, led by veteran Master of Ceremonies and much-decorated war hero, Roger Holeindre, Le Pen purposefully strode through the massed ranks of his supporters towards the platform to a rendering, first of Christophe Colomb's "Conquest of Paradise" and then the "Chorus of the Hebrew Slaves" from Verdi's *Nabucco* – immensely evocative music.

In a wide-ranging address lasting just under two hours, Le Pen spoke about the party's year, its achievements and its aspirations. He strongly emphasised the democratic and republican outlook of the FN and that no one would have cause to fear its inexorable advance unless they themselves rejected the democratic process. I left the BBR with an instinctive feeling that the party's ultimate triumph against all the odds, may not be that far away.

(ii) Truth trumps distortion

In this letter to *The Spectator* published in its edition of 25 April 1998, once again I have sought to establish the truth about the Front National and its leader rather than allow the media's constant distortions to hold sway in the public consciousness.

Sir: One reason for the increase in the Front National's vote at the regional elections in France, to which Douglas Johnson refers in his piece, 'From Papon to Le Pen' (11 April), may be that the electorate simply does not find the FN to be the party it is widely portrayed to be by the media. One person in six now votes FN.

In *Le Monde* on 15 April, Jean-Marie Le Pen wrote a letter emphasising that his party was democratic, republican and '... a declared adversary of all forms of totalitarianism'. In the same paper, in its 29-30 March edition, Pierre Descaves, a chartered accountant and a member of the FN's political bureau (governing body) and the party's senior councillor for the Picardy region, was reported as saying, 'For us, all citizens have the same rights and duties without distinction of colour, race or religion', a comment which led the Gaullist (UDF) regional president, Charles Baur, to remark, 'I look to what men say, not what it is suggested they will say'.

Elsewhere, increasing numbers of Gaullist politicians are asking themselves the pertinent question: why should it be so awful to co-operate with the FN in regional government when the Socialists are combining in national government with the Communists?

The FN has within its ranks some very high-quality people: intellectuals in abundance, university professors, lawyers, doctors, architects, businessmen and women, as well as war heroes and escapees from Nazi concentration camps. Maybe Vichy supporters are there as well, but the other political parties have their fair share too. Further, for a party that is allegedly racist it is surprising to find the FN has the backing of a fair number of French Jews, Muslims and Arabs, as well as black French men and women, many of them holding responsible positions in the party.

(iii) Some more truth

This letter to *The Spectator*, published in its edition of 4 May 2002 was supportive of journalist John Laughland's earlier piece. At a *Spectator* drinks event a week afterwards Boris Johnson, then editor, expressed amazement at my letter's content, saying he had known nothing of what I had revealed.

Sir: Congratulations to John Laughland for his superb piece on Jean-Marie Le Pen ('Why does everybody hate me?' 27 April). I've known J-M.L.P for 15 years – and many of his nearest associates, too, including Bruno Gollnisch and Jean-Claude Martinez, both MEPs and both university law professors of distinction.

Jean-Marie Le Pen's success is partly attributable to the fact that the French electorate do not believe that he is the ogre he is made out to be by the mass media; nor is he. For instance, his clumsy remark that the Holocaust was 'a point of detail of the history of the Second World War' is never qualified by its context. In fact, less than 60 seconds after these words were uttered (in an interview with two journalists on the television programme, *Grand Jury RTL-Le Monde*, on 13 September 1987, when he was repeatedly asked what he thought of the revisionist theses of MM. Faurisson and Roques), Le Pen went on to state, 'There were many deaths, hundreds of thousands, perhaps millions of Jewish deaths and also of people who were not Jews'.

In October 1997, the Front National published a pamphlet, *'Ni raciste, ni antisémite'* ('Neither racist, nor anti-Semitic') by Bernard Antony, an FN MEP, and Jean-Pierre Cohen, a Jewish journalist member of the FN, a devastating rebuttal of the allegations of racism levelled against the party.

If Le Pen and his party are thought to be beyond the pale, an examination of the *Comité de Soutien* (National Support Committee) for Le Pen's candidature would indicate very much the reverse; it makes salutary reading. It comprises university professors in abundance, lawyers, doctors, scientists, businessmen and women, and others who have made their mark in French life, including, interestingly, several internees of Nazi concentration camps and a number of black FN members in leading positions – among them Huguette Fatna, Farid Smahi and Stéphane Durbec (the youngest FN regional councillor in France in 1998).

(iv) The March 2004 regional elections – further progress

I wrote this piece for *Right Now* in June/July 2004, showing the FN's advance in the March regional elections despite certain internal conflicts and questions as to who should ultimately succeed Jean-Marie Le Pen, as party president.

In the maelstrom of burgeoning corruption which increasingly is the daily diet of political life in France's Fifth Republic, the Front National emerged from the country's regional assembly elections, held on the 21 and 28 March, with its reputation for integrity and probity firmly intact. Well does it deserve its motto – *Têtes haut, mains propres* ('heads high, hands clean').

The FN did extremely well in the 1998 regionals, when 237 councillors were elected. But then it suffered the highly damaging split in January/February 1999, when Bruno Mégret, former deputy to Jean-Marie Le Pen, led a breakaway faction to found the Mouvement National Republicaine (MNR). The MNR has been virtually obliterated from the political scene, scoring a derisory 0.87% share of the national vote compared with the FN's 15.7%.

Buoyed by Jean-Marie Le Pen's signal achievement in reaching the second round of the presidential election in 2002, thousands of French patriots, from all walks of life – doctors, lawyers, university professors, businessmen, students and artisans – rallied to the FN's standard as candidates in every one of France's 22 regions for the first round of voting. They did commendably well to consolidate the party's standing as the third largest political formation and the only one untainted by a major scandal.

The FN was able to stand candidates in 17 of the 22 regions for the second round, having failed to reach the first round threshold of 10% in just five regions – Auvergne, Bretagne, Limousin, Corsica and the Loire – and then by less than 1.5% in four of these regions.

Le Pen himself was disqualified from standing in Provence Alpes Côte d'Azur (PACA) in the most bizarre circumstances. His residence in Nice had been accepted in the previous 16 years as an acceptable abode but this time the authorities saw to it that he would not be allowed to stand. He was replaced by Guy Macary, a distinguished advocate, as head of the PACA list. Nevertheless, Le Pen played a prominent part, visiting all regions in his capacity of FN president.

Outstanding results were achieved in the Vaucluse, Var, Alsace, Picardy (where the FN secured 26.94% of the vote) and Nord-Pas-de-Calais (where the party list, led by the party's secretary-general, Carl Lang, obtained 24.1% of the vote). By contrast, the party did much less well in the Ile-de-France, encompassing Paris and its environs, where the lists were led by Marine Le Pen, younger daughter of Jean-Marie, who replaced Martine Lehideux, (one of the *grandes dames* of the movement, amidst some controversy).

The full number of candidates elected by region was: Alsace, eight councillors; Aquitaine, seven; Basse Normandie, five; Bourgogne, six; Centre Val de Loire, nine; Champagne-Ardenne, six; Franche-Comté, five; Haute-Normandie, six; Ile-de-France, five; Languedoc-Rousillon, eight; Lorraine, nine; Mid-Pyrénées, eight; Nord-Pas-de-Calais, 16; Picardie, eight, Poitou-Charentes, three; Provence-Alpes-Côte d'Azur, 19; Rhône-Alpes, 18 – a total of 146.

Within the structures of the FN itself, the rise of Marine Le Pen has not been without its internal conflicts. Bernard Antony, former MEP, who leads the party's fundamentalist Catholic wing, Chrétiénte Solidarité, has resigned his positions within the political bureau and central committee because of it, on the grounds of nepotism. It is salutary that Le Pen's son-in-law, Samuel Maréchal, has resumed political activity and is head of list in the Loire region for the forthcoming European elections. Already much debate is taking place within the inner councils of the party as to who will succeed Le Pen when he retires, probably in 2007. Grassroots favourite is the current deputy and delegate-general, Bruno Gollnisch, who has been an MEP since 1986. Outstanding public speaker, professor of Japanese at the

University of Lyons, and stalwart supporter of Le Pen, Gollnisch is not the only strong candidate. Another is Jean-Claude Martinez, also an MEP, expert on budgetary and fiscal matters and widely regarded as the best brain in the European Parliament, with 11 scholarly books to his credit. An outsider would be Carl Lang, who would be seen as a consolidator, while Marine Le Pen would have to improve her standing within the party's central committee, where she presently only manages 34th place in the party's rankings. (Gollnisch was top by more than 80 votes).

Meanwhile, Le Pen's vigour and political acumen remain undiminished. For a man of 75, his oratorical prowess is remarkable. At the May Day celebration to commemorate Joan of Arc in the Place de l'Opera, in a speech lasting an hour and 20 minutes, he exhorted his 10,000 strong audience to renewed efforts to maximise the vote for the party's candidates in the forthcoming European elections. Only a vote for the FN, he told them – and who could disagree? – could prevent the headlong charge towards the new European Constitution, federalism and betrayal.

(v) Internal strains and disputes

I wrote this article for *Right Now* in its March/April 2005 edition. It records certain internal problems at the FN and how they might be resolved. While it seemed at the time that Marine Le Pen would be unlikely to succeed her father that has been proved not to be the case. I was wrong, therefore, to believe that the party would implode.

Political leaders rarely retire in good time and after plentiful deliberation. By failing to nominate or recommend a successor (thereby ensuring some degree of continuity and a smooth transition) they contribute to their own party's later decline in fortunes.

In France, this problem is asserting itself, albeit in wholly different conditions, within the Front National (FN). The party president, Jean-Marie Le Pen, 77 next year, who founded the

FN with four comrades-in-arms, has been its chief motivator and guiding spirit for the 32 years of the party's existence. Until 1988, his power was uncontested. There was then the damaging split with the Paris deputy, Bruno Mégret, when one third of the members left to join Mégret's Movement National Populaire. But at least that was a clear split, and the FN was very soon able to re-establish itself as France's leading nationalist movement, with Le Pen's position totally secure.

That has remained the position until the last six months. Persistent rumblings are now being heard throughout the FN. Is not the great man showing a certain physical tiredness? Is he not guilty of a certain nepotism by constantly promoting his youngest daughter, Marine – she became a vice –president of the party in 2003, a prestigious post in the FN – as well as his son-in-law, Samuel Maréchal (married to Le Pen's second daughter, Yann) whose ambitions, it is widely thought, far exceed his abilities? In fairness to Maréchal, he was a highly successful national organiser of the Front National de la Jeunesse, the party's youth section, in the period 1994-2000.

A further source of strain is the growing belief among many senior members that the internal structures of the FN concentrate far too much power at the party's centre at Saint-Cloud, just outside Paris. This, it is said, is to the detriment of the 92 federations (regional branches) and impeding national activism.

It was to give vent to these developing concerns that Jacques Bompard and Bernard Antony, two of the FN's most popular and respected figures, convened a 'University of the Summer' in Orange (in Vaucluse, Southern France) at the same time that the party organisation had convened its own summer university at Enghien, 12 miles north of Paris. Both conventions took place in late August over a period of three days. The party leadership felt the Orange event was a deliberate provocation, designed to siphon off many of the party's activists who would otherwise have been at Enghien. It certainly did have that effect, with 486 signing up for Enghien and 392 for Orange.

Bompard is mayor of Orange, where he has transformed the town hall dramatically. Even his opponents acknowledge his successes. He has been mayor for nine years and has been re-elected on a first ballot, getting over 60% of the vote. He represents one of the FN's real successes in practical terms. A dental surgeon by profession, Bompard's political career is prototypical of many French nationalists of his generation. A staunch defender of *Algérie Francaise*, he joined the youth movement Occident in 1964 (where Gaullist ministers Alain Madelin and Gérard Longuet cut their political teeth) before helping to set up Ordre Nouveau in 1968, with Francois Brigneau and other patriotic polemicists. He later became a deputy in the French parliament, representing Vaucluse for the FN between 1986 and 1988. The extent of Bompard's popularity can be gauged from the fact that, at the elections for the party's central committee at the last congress held in Nice in April 2003, he came fifth with 722 votes. Bernard Antony obtained 715 votes, while Marine Le Pen languished in 34th place, with 453 votes.

Antony, Bompard's friend and collaborator, heads the party's fundamentalist Catholic wing, Chrétienté Solidarité, which is deeply implanted within the FN. Antony is a former MEP for the FN, where he spoke with eloquence on many occasions for Europe to re-assert its Christian heritage against the onset of liberal decadence and Islamic fundamentalism. Recently, he savagely criticised Samuel Maréchal for having proposed the concept of a 'French Islam', saying this was an "intellectual monstrosity".

Bompard and Antony are formidable influences in the direction of the debate now enveloping the FN. Bompard addressed the three alternate strategies which lie at the heart of the FN's problems. Should the party remain a populist protest movement, but not much more than that? Or should it embody a radical alternative political philosophy, that of French nationalism under a doctrine of national preference? Or should it become (as both he and Antony believe is the strategy of Marine Le Pen) a force for compromise with the governing UMP party?

The participants at Orange were virtually unanimous. The second of these three alternatives was the only way forward to the FN. Bompard was particularly critical of Marine's social liberalism, especially her loudly proclaimed support for *in vitro* fertilisation and abortion, while Antony noted that Marine's sub-group, Genérations Le Pen, designed to attract new members between the ages of 25 and 40, had been singularly unsuccessful – notably in the Paris region, where Marine is the party leader and *chef-de-file*, having replaced longstanding party stalwart, Martine Lehideux. In his closing speech at Orange, Bompard delivered the main thrust of the intellectual argument for FN reform. The days of the *chef* holding authoritarian power over the membership should come to an end. What the party needed, he said, was not one leader, but a hundred leaders in every canton, municipality and region to achieve real implantation. Wide-ranging debate needed to take place at all levels of the party. Regional branches would also have control of the party's funding on an agreed basis instead of being starved of funds from the centre.

It could hardly be thought that revolutionary ideas – within the FN, that is – would not elicit a savage response from Jean-Marie Le Pen himself, the Bureau Executif, the nine-strong principal decision-making body (comprising Le Pen himself, Dominique Chaboche, Roger Holeindre, Jean-Claude Martinez MEP, delegate general Bruno Gollnisch MEP, national secretary Carl Lang MEP, Marine Le Pen MEP, Martine Lehideux and party treasurer Jean-Pierre Réveau) and the 50-strong consultative body, the Bureau Politique.

Bompard would have to face sanctions for his indiscretions and so would Marie-France Stirbois, an authentic heroine of the FN, widow of Jean-Pierre Stirbois, the party's first general secretary, who died in a car crash in 1988 and herself a former deputy for Dreux and MEP for over ten years. Marie-France found herself removed as *chef-de-file* in Nice by an altogether less able figure in mysterious circumstances, but thought to relate to criticism of the rapid advance of Marine Le Pen.

In late September, the Bureau Executif suspended Jacques Bompard from the Bureau Politique for six months for acts of indiscipline within the party, and Marie-France Stirbois for three months. Bompard immediately announced his intention to contest the suspension. He described it to the press as "a refusal of the high authorities of the Front to open a debate on the proper functioning of the movement". It appears that Le Pen himself wanted a more severe sanction, but that Gollnisch, Lang, Lehideux and Réveau were strongly opposed.

On the same day as the Bureau Executif's meeting, Bompard reacted strongly to a hostile interview given by Jean-Marie Le Pen to *Minute*, a Right-Wing weekly journal sympathetic to the Front, in which he described Bompard and his associates as being "of the extreme Right". Bompard retorted: "Who are these people of the 'extreme Right' – are they the tens of thousands of Catholic militants, nationalists, royalists and traditionalists, those whose political aspiration centres round the theme of identity and who for 30 years have stuck posters on buildings, distributed party pamphlets, been available 24 hours a day, been physically attacked and even lost their employment so that he, M Le Pen, may be elected?"

When the Bureau Politique met to confirm the BE's decision, one of the doyens of the party, Pierre Descaves, a regional counsellor for Noyon (Oises) who has consistently topped the poll in elections for his region, circulated a paper to BP members which was highly critical of the party leadership. He considered that there was "a deep malaise at the heart of the FN". He was particularly critical of Marine Le Pen, whom he considered to be unsound on many political issues, including her apparent wish to make common cause with the Gaullist majority. He concluded his paper by stating that "there is a thought-police (*police de la pensée*) outside the FN; it is not necessary to inaugurate one at the heart of the FN's counsels. M Bompard has committed no serious error and the sanction taken against Mme Stirbois is both inopportune illegal". Descaves is a highly respected personage within the FN, and his work will have a resonance throughout the party membership.

How might these issues be satisfactorily resolved? For a start, by a much wider internal debate sanctioned by the party leadership; that will help allay concerns. But it will not be enough. Jean-Marie Le Pen's massive contribution to the success of the FN so that it is a permanent part of the French political landscape and, indeed, the only honest and uncorrupted party in France, is unquestionable. He now needs to make a deeply significant and salutary further contribution: to announce that he will designate Bruno Gollnisch, delegate-general of the party, university professor at Lyon III, MEP and regional counsellor for Rhone-Alpes, as his rightful successor, and that the succession will take place at an agreed date within the next two years. If that happens, the future success of the FN will be assured. If, on the other hand, he favours his daughter, the party is likely to implode.

(vi) William Hague, MP, gets it wrong again

I wrote this letter to William Hague MP on 10 April 2006 because much of what he said in his interview was variously pessimistic, inaccurate or critical of people to whom he should have shown much more respect. I regard him as one of the worst foreign secretaries for decades and a supporter of warmongering as he showed demonstrably at the time of the so-called African spring, which has been nothing less than an utter disaster and predictably so.

Dear Mr Hague

I read the Face to Face interview of yourself in Monday's *Daily Telegraph* by Rachel Sylvester and Alice Thomson.

I was a Tory Party member from the early-1960s until very recently, when I resigned my membership because I profoundly disagree with David Cameron's make-over of the party so that it is, in many areas, indistinguishable from New Labour. Your own change of views depresses me.

I share entirely the opinions of Lord Tebbit and Anne Widdecombe on the new Tory dispensation; the party cannot win from the centre/left or centre ground. Already by-election and council election results of recent weeks are showing how poorly the Tories are doing: - viz, Dunfermline, and at the local level Heanor in Derbyshire (-17%) and Keighley (an area you well know: -14%).

None of my Tory friends agree with what is happening. Some may put up with it but without much conviction.

I note your comments about Jean-Marie Le Pen (about whom I have written at some length) and Alessandra Mussolini (granddaughter of Il Duce Benito Mussolini). As it happens I know Alessandra Mussolini. She is extremely bright and not at all extreme. She has made many useful contributions, particularly on social policy, in the European Parliament. Of course, I understand the Tories would not join up with the Droites Européennes but you cannot, in fairness, deny the calibre of some of its elected members, e.g. Professor

Jean-Claude Martinez, of the FN (one of the finest brains in the Parliament and budgetary committee expert), and Bruno Gollnisch also of FN, multi-linguist and Professor of Japanese Civilisation at Lyons III University. In truth, there are more intellectuals of the right lined up with DE than are to be found in the Tory MEP contingent!

I cannot see the Tories winning the next election – they have become too de-natured and I'm afraid the electorate will punish them for it.

Yours sincerely

Sam Swerling

(vii) Adieu, Marie-France

I wrote this piece, in commemoration of the untimely death of Marie-France Stirbois. It appeared in *The Clarion* in its June 2006 edition. I was saddened by the passing but comforted to some extent by the knowledge that she will long be remembered and admired for what she did and stood for.

One of the authentic heroines of French nationalism is no longer with us. Marie-France Stirbois, widow of the first secretary-general of the Front National, Jean-Pierre Stirbois, died on Easter Sunday this year. I had the privilege of knowing this remarkable woman for over 15 years and regularly met up with her at the Bleu, Blanc, Rouge festivals in Paris, and on other occasions.

She was, in effect, one of the *grandes dames* of the party, a close associate of Jean-Marie Le Pen, and long-time member of the party's Central Committee and Political Bureau. Apart from being a very fine public speaker, Marie-France will be remembered for her energy and dynamism, particularly in the early years of the FN's development from splinter group to party of influence (1977-1985).

Marie-France's particular legacy was her ability to turn a hopeless cause into a political success. She cut her teeth in the town of Dreux, a sort of French Orpington, a dormitory town with substantial overspill population from the Paris suburbs. When she and her husband started their political work, in what was a hostile and unpropitious environment with less than 1% of opinion in support of the Front, most people would have given up in despair. Yet over a period of 18 months, Marie-France managed to establish a substantial power-base in the town, through hundreds of hours of canvassing, leafleting and poster-sticking, often amidst violent hostility. She was an immensely brave woman, on one occasion being punched to the ground and hospitalised for four days.

In 1986, Marie-France's political opponents realised they couldn't beat her on their own, so they set up a Republican Front coalition to no avail, however, for she won the seat in the second round of voting with 61% of the vote. She became a European Deputy for the FN in 1994 and remained so for eight years, making many valuable contributions on diverse matters, from the environment to social security. In 1998 Marie-France became party leader in Nice and was elected regional councillor for Provence-Alpes-Côte-d'Azur (PACA). She remained faithful to the FN after the damaging internal split with Bruno Mégret in 1999, but in the last phase of her life, she was critical of some of the FN's orientations and suffered a three-month suspension from the party's governing council. In his tribute to her in the FN's monthly journal *Français d'Abord*, Jean-Marie Le Pen described her as a woman of dynamism and devotion, without whose presence the FN would never have got off the ground.

The legacy of Marie-France Stirbois's life and work has, I believe, a particular resonance. It is that dedication, belief in a noble cause – the triumph of the national ideal, hard work and resilience, all of which qualities will be rewarded with ultimate success.

Adieu, Marie-France Stirbois, patriot and French nationalist of the first order.

(viii) Regional elections – Good news for Marine

I wrote this analysis for Allan Robertson's Swinton Circle journal in February 2016. It demonstrated that if French elections were based on a single electoral vote the FN would in all likelihood form the government of France. The results were dramatically good, presaging a strong vote for Marine Le Pen in the May 2017 presidential election.

The French regional elections, which took place over two Sundays in December 2015, the 6th and the 13th, offered a realistic opportunity for the Front National (FN) to measure the extent of its continuing progression in French politics under the dynamic leadership of Jean-Marie's youngest daughter, Marine Le Pen.

The internal ructions within the party had already produced seriously damaging publicity leading ultimately to the old man's expulsion from the party and his removal as *président d'honneur* of its leadership.

As an augury of future successes, including Marine's challenge for the French presidency in May 2017, the FN had already done formidably well in the European parliamentary elections in May 2015, coming top of the pile with 24 elected MEPs, the largest among French parties. The names include the great scholar and intellectual, Bruno Gollnisch (first elected in 1989); youngest ever Dean of Lyon University law school, and Jean-Marie's right-hand man for over 20 years. Others included Jean-François Jalkh, the party expert on immigration statistics, a French MP (1986-1988) (one of 36) during the years of proportional representation, whose knowledge is encyclopaedic; and Florian Philippot, deputy party leader, ex-civil servant and multiple academic prize winner and Marine's closest associate.

In the event, the FN outdid all its own expectations and those of the commentariat of the political class. It arrived top in six of the 13 regions gathering 28.42% of all the votes, defeating the centre-right parties, reconstituted as LR, UDI and MoDem, which obtained 27.08% and the Socialist party of President Hollande who, despite his firm stance in handling the terrorist atrocities, appears to be more than ever a busted flush.

The FN figures in the six regions in which they were successful show a very clear breakthrough into the political mainstream.

In *Alsace – Champagne – Ardenne – Lorraine* Florian Philippot's list pulverised the other candidates into submission:

Party	List Leader	Votes Obtained	Percentage
FN	Florian Philippot	641,122	36.06%
LR/UDI/MoDem	Philippe Rickert	459,138	25.83%
PS	Jean-Pierre Masseret	286,438	16.11%

The remaining 22% of votes were split between six smaller lists.

In *Centre – Val de Loire* Philippe Loiseau, the FN *chef de file*, led his party to victory in five of the six departments as follows:

Party	List Leader	Votes Obtained	Percentage
FN	Philippe Loiseau	262,154	30.49%
LR/UDI/MoDem	Philippe Vigier	225,776	26.25%
PS	François Bonneaux	209,022	24.31%

The remaining 19% of votes were split between five smaller lists.

In *Bourgogne – Franche-Comté* the FN list was led by Sophie Montel, a party member of over 30 years standing. It triumphed in seven out of the eight departments.

Party	List Leader	Votes Obtained	Percentage
FN	Sophie Montel	303,128	31.48%
LR/UDI	François Sauvadet	231,053	24.00%
PS	Marie-Guite Dufay	221,357	22.99%

(The MoDem component candidate of the centre-right ran separately, gaining 31,429 votes – 3.26%). The remaining 17% of votes were split between six smaller lists, all of whom failed to qualify for the second round.

In *Languedoc – Roussillon – Midi-Pyrénées*, the FN list was led by Louis Aliott, Marine Le Pen's companion and the party's secretary-general. The FN achieved here an historic score for the region.

Party	List Leader	Votes Obtained	Percentage
FN	Louis Aliott	653,543	31.83%
LR/UDI/MoDem	Carole Delga	501,287	26.07%
PS	Dominique Reynié	386,977	18.84%
EELV-FG	Gérard Onesta	210,602	10.26%

The remaining 13% of votes were split between six smaller lists which failed to qualify for the second round.

In *Nord – Pas De Calais – Picardie,* the northern-most region of France, the FN list was led by Marine Le Pen to triumphant success, doubling its vote from the previous poll in 2010.

Party	List Leader	Votes Obtained	Percentage
FN	Marie Le Pen	908,989	40.64%
LR/UDI/MoDem	Xavier Bertrand	558,360	24.96%
PS	Pierre de Saintignon	405,189	18.12%

The remaining 16% of votes were shared between six other smaller lists which failed to qualify for the second round.

In *Provence – Alpes – Côte d'Azur,* the southern-most region of France, the FN list was led by Marion Maréchal-Le Pen, niece of Marine, and rising star of the party.

Party	List Leader	Votes Obtained	Percentage
FN	Marion Maréchal-Le Pen	719,706	40.55%
LR/UDI/MoDem	Christian Estrasi	469,881	26.48%
PS	Christophe Castaner	294,395	16.59%

The remaining 17% of votes were shared between six other smaller lists which failed to qualify for the second round.

A little about Marion herself. She is the adopted daughter of Samuel Maréchal, whose first marriage was to Yann, Jean-Marie's middle daughter. Maréchal was a former director of the *Front National de la Jeunesse* (FNJ), the Front's youth wing. Maréchal's second wife is a grand-niece of ex-president Félix Houphouët-Boigny of the *Côte d'Ivoire* (Ivory Coast) who was a close friend of Jean-Marie Le Pen for many years. Enemies of the FN would not wish to know this.

Marion has made a rapid advance in nationalist politics, winning a parliamentary seat at Carpentras in southern France (Vaucluse). Very early on she made her mark in parliamentary debates with her *sotto voce* measured arguments. In a recent prime-time television debate with Alain Juppé, 72 year old Sarkozyist Mayor of Bordeaux, Juppé was trounced on every polemical issue, to the amazement of those watching.

In an article in *The Sunday Telegraph* on 5 December 2015, French journalist, Anne-Elisabeth Moutet described Marion as "the new girl wonder of the far right, a glamorous 25 year old poised to break down many conservatives' qualms."

The big question would now become: following their excellent first-round results (almost certainly proving that on a once-only voting system, the FN would become the government of France), could there be a translation of that vote into the second-round results? If, for instance, Marine Le Pen became a regional president she would control a region the size of Denmark and a budget of £3.6 billion. In the case of Marion being voted into the presidency of PACA the budget would be upwards of £4.2 billion. As the boffins would say: 'there's everything to play for'.

Alas, history of French second-round elections and the sheer cussedness of the centrist and left parties would continue to exclude the FN from regional power by instructing their rank-and-file to vote for the centre-right. By dint of such self-loathing and undemocratic manipulation are French elections won and lost. Yet the final results display a substantial movement of opinion towards the FN. The party is on the march; its long overdue success may not be far off, especially if there should be constitutional revision of the voting system.

Hereunder, therefore, are the second round results in the six regions where the FN finished on top in the first round.

Alsace – Champagne – Ardenne – Lorraine

Party	List Leader	Votes Obtained	Percentage	Seats
LR/UDI/MoDem	Philippe Rickert	1,060,029	48.40%	104
FN	Florian Philippot	790,141	36.08%	46
Drivers Gauche	Jean-Pierre Masseret	339,749	15.51%	19

Bourgogne – Franche-Comté

Party	List Leader	Votes Obtained	Percentage	Seats
PS	Marie-Guite Dufay	402,941	34.68%	51
LR/UDI/MoDem	François Sauvadet	382,177	32.89%	25
FN	Sophie Montel	376,902	32.44%	24

Centre – Val de Loire

Party	List Leader	Votes Obtained	Percentage	Seats
PS	François Bonneaux	364,211	35.43%	40
LR/UDI/MoDem	Philippe Vigier	355,475	34.58%	20
FN	Philippe Loiseau	308,422	30.00%	17

Languedoc – Roussillon – Midi-Pyrénées

Party	List Leader	Votes Obtained	Percentage	Seats
PS	Carole Delga	1,092,969	44.81%	93
FN	Louis Aliott	826,023	33.87%	40
LR/UDI/MoDem	Dominique Reynié	520,011	21.32%	25

Nord – Pas De Calais – Picardie

Party	List Leader	Votes Obtained	Percentage	Seats
LR/UDI/MoDem	Xavier Bertrand	1,389,315	57.77%	116
FN	Marine Le Pen	1,015,649	42.23%	54

Provence – Alpes – Côte d'Azur

Party	List Leader	Votes Obtained	Percentage	Seats
LR/UDI/MoDem	Christian Estrasi	1,073,485	54.78%	81
FN	Marion Maréchal-Le Pen	886,147	45.22%	42

Enoch Powell, Tribune of the people

This article, with its title: *Enoch Powell, Tribune of the people, prophet unfulfilled*, was written by me for the book *Standardbearers* published by the Bloomsbury Forum in April 1999. I was fortunate to have known Enoch and his wife Pam for over 20 years.

If it is an indisputable fact that Enoch Powell was the most intellectually gifted politician of his generation – arguably of the 20th Century – it is equally true that for many who saw him as the standard bearer of British nationalism, his career achievements in politics never matched their most optimistic aspirations. Powell himself had no illusions: "all politicians ultimately end up as failures" he once famously remarked with a good dose of cynicism.

Born in June 1912 and educated at King Edward VII School, Birmingham, and Trinity College, Cambridge, Powell became Professor of Greek at Sydney University, Australia in 1937 but returned to England at the outbreak of war in 1939 to join the Royal Warwickshire regiment as a private soldier. Within the course of five years, he had risen through the ranks to become a brigadier, the youngest in the British Army.

Classical scholar, particularly renowned as an expert on the works of Herodotus, published poet, speaker of nine languages (including Welsh and Urdu), Powell's early life marked him out as a man of unusual brilliance with an extraordinary breadth of knowledge destined for the highest honours. Yet it was only in 1950, at the age of 38, that he secured a safe seat at Wolverhampton South-West, representing that seat, and later South Down, for a Parliamentary career spanning 37 years.

In his autobiography, *Memoirs* (Sidgwick & Jackson, 1978) Reginald Maudling, whose own political career was conspicuously unmemorable, both as Home Secretary and as Edward Heath's right-hand man during a phase of colourless, shapeless Conservative government (1970-74), wrote admiringly:

> "I shared a room with Enoch Powell at the Conservative research department for two years ... I do not recall meeting anyone else who had a mind with such power for acquiring knowledge. At one stage, Enoch was determined to become the expert in town and country planning. He acquired the standard textbook, and read it from page to page as an ordinary mortal would read a novel. Within a matter of weeks he had fully grasped the principles of the problem and the details of the legal situation. Within a matter of a few months, he was writing to the author of the textbook, pointing out the errors that he had made."

Maudling's specific tribute was echoed in more general terms a hundred times at his death. Norman Lamont, Chancellor of the Exchequer, 1990-93, a man currently suffering obloquy from the Conservative hierarchy for alleged disloyalty, in much the same way as Powell had suffered, described him as the "greatest politician of my lifetime".

This observation could be acute and significant insofar as Lamont may see a role for himself in incipient crisis (sparked off by a world economic recession and civil unrest in Europe as a result of EMU and the drive towards federalism) as nationalist-leader around whom the people will rally when the Blair dream turns into nightmare and Hague's vacuity fails to recapture Tory support in the country.

Part of the greatness which Lamont saw in Powell was his intellectual fearlessness, his moral courage and his impeccably high standard of political speechmaking and debate. It may be argued that Powell's unwillingness to compromise would inevitably lead to failure within a political system in which give and take are perceived as necessary preconditions to success. Powell would argue that there is a clear distinction to be drawn between matters of detail and issues of principle. Detail can be refined, modified and improved upon; principle is immutable, and cannot be sacrificed for expediency, least of all political expediency.

Two principles informed the active period of Powell's political thinking. First was the primacy of nationhood; the second was the role of Parliament as the protector of the nation's democracy.

An unanswered question, where Powell is concerned, is whether he ever envisaged in his earlier years in Parliament the possibility of the 'nation' being anything other than a composite of the peoples of the United Kingdom, as Oswald Mosley had done after the war with the development of his 'Europe a Nation' thesis. Whereas in the 1970s and beyond, Powell's vehemence against the Treaty of Rome and the political dimensions of the Common Market was unsurpassed by any other politician, during his two-year period as a minister in MacMillan's government (between 1957-59) and for five years thereafter he was remarkably muted on the subject. Indeed, at one stage he is on record as stating that if the balance of economic advantage favoured Britain's entry into the EEC (as it was then titled) he would not be opposed to it. The assumption must be that he cannot have supposed at that time that nationhood would be compromised.

Powell's love of country was reflected in the value he placed on continuity and tradition, and the place therein of the armed forces and the church. Even if he had been an atheist, he would still have seen the church as a stabilising influence of permanence. Interestingly, this is a position common to many atheists or agnostics of conservative disposition.

Yet Powell was remarkably liberal, paradoxically, when it came to social reform on matters affecting personal conduct. He was always opposed to capital punishment and voted in favour of its abolition in 1965. In this regard, he had much in common with other imperial Tories of that era, such as Julian Amery and John Biggs-Davison. Although a firm believer in the institution of marriage, he supported divorce reform legislation, both in 1957 and 1973 on the Benthamite principle that the state has no vested interest in refusing to release unhappy people from their state of unhappiness. Powell also favoured the Wolfenden proposals for homosexual law reform which led to the Sexual Offences Act 1967 and probably would have supported the reduction in the age of consent to 16. Moreover, Powell was not opposed to abortion law reform.

What these attitudes on social reform demonstrate is that Powell's logic told him that the state's function, no less than with economic management, is that non-intervention, or perhaps more accurately non-interference, is a guiding principle of almost universal application. Powell believed that on matters of personal behaviour, individuals can only be answerable to their conscience. Political commentators opposed to Powell's opinions on immigration, Europe and other issues, sacrifice objectivity for emotion when labelling him as a man of the extreme right. One characteristic, amongst others, of someone of the extreme right within a political spectrum is a reasoned belief in the value of authoritarian ideals added to a healthy suspicion of democratic practices as a mechanism for getting things done. By those criteria, Powell falls well short of the crypto-fascist status to which he has been elevated by the liberal-left.

The principle of nationhood was essentially the background to all major debates in which Powell became involved, both in Parliament and outside: immigration, Europe, Northern Ireland and defence. What marked out Powell from his contemporaries was his unrivalled mastery of detail, the impeccable quality of his research, the conviction of the rightness of his analysis, the deep respect which he commanded from millions of people and the sense in which he came to see himself as a man of destiny who had come to save the nation from treacherous policies which would inevitably lead to disaster.

Immigration is undoubtedly the subject most commonly associated with Powell. During the 1960s, Conservative politicians such as Cyril Osborne, Norman Pannell, Harold Gurden and Ronald Bell made frequent incursions into the dangers of foisting a multiracial society upon an unwilling population through a wholly false interpretation of citizenship rights allegedly owed to foreign passport holders. Powell shared these concerns, but didn't enter the fray until the late 1960s. His so-called 'Rivers of Blood' speech, made on 20 April 1968, made a dramatic impact. It struck an emphatic chord with much of the population, but of course it was politically incorrect to utter the truth on such a sensitive issue, let alone in the graphic language that Powell used. The technocrat Heath dismissed Powell from his shadow cabinet, engendering thereby an unrelenting enmity between the two men.

On account of his deep, abiding faith in Parliamentary procedures and institutions, Powell declined to do what many were urging him to do: to build an extra-parliamentary mass movement which would propel him into the Conservative leadership on the back of popular resentment. Entreaties made to him in the summer of 1968 by a number of influential backers in the party to hold a dozen large-scale rallies throughout Britain, culminating in a million-strong rally in September, never came to fruition despite at one point fairly advanced plans being formulated. Powell never quite saw himself as a latter-day Mussolini marching on London with nationalist legions in his wake.

Powell's aversion during this period to the notion of rallying the people in direct action against manifest political wrongheadedness rested on the quaint belief that the British people would eventually react through the ballot box against the treachery of the political class. But the truth is that an effective response can only be shown through plebiscite or referendum, constitutional mechanisms to which Powell as an avowed Parliamentarian was opposed. It can never be achieved in the ordinary way through elections, since single issues, however vital and significant in themselves, become swallowed up in other issues, many of them peripheral and transient.

History shows that Powell, and with him the majority view in the country, lost the immigration debate with the disastrous consequences he predicted, and on a far worse scale at that. We now have the phenomenon of bogus asylum seeking, which is now costing the taxpayer £2.1 billion per annum, equivalent to 1p in the pound for every taxpayer. Voluntary repatriation, once part of the Conservative election manifesto, is now a forbidden subject. An anaesthetised people is now forced to accept what is being served up before them without a murmur, while the burgeoning race relations industry is waxing ever fatter on mounting public subsidy.

Powell came to see the Common Market as serious a threat to national identity as large-scale immigration. For him they were two sides of the same coin, neither less important than the other. Hindsight can only be a reflective tool when assessing crucial events, but suppose that Iain McLeod and Powell had not refused to serve in Alec Douglas-Home's government upon MacMillan's retirement in October 1963, but instead participated in it. The Conservatives would probably have won the 1964 election – Labour won it by a majority of four seats – Home would have stayed in office and Heath would never have become Prime Minister with the disastrous consequences on the European issue that ensued. Powell used to counter that sort of argument by emphasising that he was not blessed with any divine degree of prescience; many of his ardent supporters would claim otherwise!

From the late 1960s, Powell was adamant that, despite its name, the European Economic Community, and Britain's participation in it, was a political and not an economic question – one which could not be obliterated by a deluge of figures and economic propositions. Estimates of Britain's balance of payments; the differing components of Britain's imports and exports; whether the food prices within the community would be higher than the world prices – all of these might be of importance if the argument was between conflicting economic priorities, but they could not be used to detract from the essence of the debate, which was whether the 'economic community' would strengthen or weaken the sovereignty of people and Parliament. Powell concluded that the EEC would gravely damage parliamentary institutions and that, for that reason alone, it should be firmly opposed. Along with (especially) Peter Shore, Michael Foot and Tony Benn, Powell was the most formidable advocate of withdrawal from the EEC in the referendum campaign of May 1975, which produced a 2:1 majority in favour of staying in. This at a time when Powell had left the Conservative Party and called upon people to vote Labour at the February 1974 election (at which the writer was a Conservative candidate) because it was only with Labour that Powell envisaged any prospect, however remote, of British withdrawal from the EEC, which was essential to recovery of national self-government.

Powell's influence on the Maastricht Treaty debate with its federalising tendencies was minimal due to the onset of his final illness. Experience may have told him that *ex post facto* referendums, while no doubt inviting and raising optimism, are fraught with dangers of unfulfilled expectation as the process of 'historic inevitability' begins to assert itself. The promised referendum on the single currency with the Euro up and running is likely to be lost. The people will come to conclude under a barrage of misleading propaganda that Britain's rightful place is within EMU because there is no alternative. Yet again the hideous 'TINA' will have triumphed. Within five years, Britain will be a province of the new state, Europe, such powers of self-government retained only with the permission of the new European government. That is precisely the apocalyptic vision that Powell had. One cannot assume that in such conditions he would have continued to advocate the constitutional path to bring about national recovery.

Powell's contribution to defence debates in parliament rested on his deduction that since Britain had liquidated its Empire and given freedom to its former colonial subjects, it should stop the pretence that it had some role to play as a universal policeman. He regarded the Commonwealth as a farcical institution and the United Nations as a vehicle for American aggrandisement and sabre rattling.

Powell was determined to challenge conventional strategic thinking whereby one of the justifications of European union was defence and Western solidarity. He poured scorn on NATO's nuclear strategy and was particularly critical of government policy that British contractors providing armaments to our armed forces should share the work with firms situated on the mainland of the European continent.

Whereas Margaret Thatcher always regarded the NATO alliance as of primary importance, Powell believed it to be destructive of Britain's self-confidence and national interest. Powell was always distrustful of American strategic policy, partly because of his unusually favourable attitude towards the Soviet Union, but also because he thought the Suez adventure of 1956 a profound mistake. The 'special relationship' between Britain and America was one that he regarded as placing Britain in a subservient position.

On the other hand, the major defence operation involving British forces in the last twenty years, the recovery of the Falkland Islands from Argentina in 1982, met with Powell's total endorsement. At the end of the Falklands War, Powell was adulatory of Margaret Thatcher's part. He asked the following question in Parliament: "Is the Right Honourable Lady aware that the report has now been received from the public analyst on a certain substance (i.e. iron) recently subjected to analysis and that I have obtained a copy of the report? It shows the substance under test consisted of ferrous matter of the highest quality, that is of exceptional tensile strength, is highly resistant to wear and tear and to stress, and may be used with advantage for all national purposes?" (*Hansard*, 17 June 1982, c. 1082)

This little encomium must rank as one of the greatest compliments ever paid to a Prime Minister by a serving Parliamentarian.

Powell's attitude to Ulster was essentially one of simplicity in what is, in political terms, and historically, a matter of great complexity. Ulster should be treated in relation to the United Kingdom no differently from, say, Colchester. The people of Colchester are part of the United Kingdom; so are the people of Ulster – period. That position should pertain until there was irrefutable evidence that the people of Ulster no longer wanted to remain subjects of the Crown. Powell was particularly unimpressed by the argument that Ulster deserved different treatment on account of the fact that one-third of its population felt allegiance to a foreign power. He condemned the duplicity of successive British governments in asserting the indissolubility of Ulster's union with the UK while doing, as he argued, all in their power to undermine it.

Powell's major policy disagreement with Margaret Thatcher was the Anglo-Irish Agreement of November 1985, which gave to Ireland influence over the governance of the province. He saw that as a shocking betrayal. No doubt the Iron Lady had begun to shed her ferrous qualities. The intellectual logic of Powell's position was unassailable; the integration of Ulster on a permanent basis into the fabric of the UK would deprive the IRA of the prospect of detaching it by force and therefore lead the IRA to abandon 'the armed struggle'. At one point, Powell argued that cession of the province would be a more honourable outcome than the inchoate, uncertain constitutional future which Ulster had and now faces as a result of 'the peace process'.

Enoch Powell's contribution to the life of the nation has been immense. Enough has been written to fill an encyclopaedia. To many in the formative years of their political careers he was both prophet and inspiration. Sir Alfred Sherman, founder of the Centre for Policy Studies, and one of the Conservative Party's most eminent political thinkers since 1945, has written elsewhere of the distinguishing role between priests and prophets. In the conservative journal, *Right Now*, Issue No 19, he wrote: "The prophet indicates new directions while the priest organises and implements the prophet's visions. It is given to few enough to be either, and fewer still to be both. Enoch never quite made up his mind. His natural penchant was for the prophet. But this never worked in Britain. Here the prophet must be his own priest, turning objectives into strategy and tactics, campaigning, mobilising supporters, nationally and locally."

Man of action in wartime of proven organisational competence, what might have been if Enoch Powell had used that dynamism to mobilise the millions who would have responded by carrying him to power at the head of a Conservative government dedicated to the implementation of nationalist principles and policies?

Tory Party leaving me, not vice-versa

This piece was written for *The Clarion* magazine in June 2003. The Conservatives had been out of office for six years and seemed unable to do much to land any decisive blows on Labour's government, which would continue to rule for a further seven years. If I appear to have been overcritical of the Tory performance and some of their leading figures my argument is that it reflected the Tory mood at the time and that it was no more than what was deserved.

After watching on television hundreds of idols, or exhibitionists, according to your viewpoint, competing for the no doubt prestigious and eponymous title 'Elvis Presley Lookalike 2002' to commemorate the 25th anniversary of the famous singer's death, the thought came to me; what is the connection between Presley and the Conservative Party? I came up with the immediate answer. The Tories have donned his mantle, a-rocking and a-rolling all over the place; thrashing about for solutions, rudderless and shapeless, like a sailing craft trapped in the teeth of a force-eight gale.

Will the Conservative Party ever become the party of government again? If the answer to that question is 'no', then it only has itself to blame for its lack of character and wholly mistaken analysis of the problems confronting contemporary Britain.

Forty years ago things might have been different. The Conservative philosopher, Michael Oakeshott, in his celebrated work *Rationalism in politics and other essays* (*Methuen* 1962) wrote that the distinguishing features of Toryism were a regard for the lessons of experience, a respect for tradition and posterity, a reluctance to destroy established beliefs without replacing them with something manifestly better and a sceptical attitude towards what is loosely termed 'progress'. Roger Scruton and Maurice Cowling, other Conservative sages, have expressed themselves in similar vein, but to formulate a set of beliefs and attitudes is not nearly enough. What was so apparent then, as much as it is apparent now, is the dismal failure to appreciate the importance of a coherent political ideology within which these cherished ideals could be expressed. The only ideology that could possibly encompass the true aspirations of a populace with any degree of patriotic sentiment is nationalism, the highest expression of the human spirit, the idea that the nation is placed first and that all policy – economic, social, and that covering foreign relations – should be dictated by the needs of the British people.

Yet no significant politician of the post-war period with the exception of Enoch Powell (and in his case ten years too late) ever sought to articulate the need for such an ideology with the consequences that are all too evident today – imperial scuttle, mass immigration, the rise of the European Union and betrayal in Ulster. This seemingly irreversible litany of self-destruction, and much else besides, will have caused many nationalists to give up hope. I write 'seemingly irreversible' because a great act of will, resolution and dedication can still effect a swing of the political pendulum; indeed, some hopeful signs are beginning to emerge as we have witnessed in the results of elections in certain European countries.

Whether such a transformation can be achieved through the agency of the Conservative Party or by one or other of the, as yet, smaller political parties remains to be seen. Many will contend that the Tories are already beyond redemption. Two factors, at least, support this view – the first is the arrival of Iain Duncan Smith as party leader and the second is the emergence of a pseudo-philosophy best described as 'perception politics'.

Duncan Smith has been in charge for 12 months. Proclaimed by some as a right-winger (although there is little in the historical record to have ever justified such a label) he was presented as the new white knight in shining armour who would lead the Tories back to the sunlit uplands of power. Some aspiration! His performance so far has been dismal. Regularly worsted at the dispatch box in Parliament by Blair, lacking oratorical skill and surrounded by mediocre, uninspiring colleagues with negligible focus on policy issues, Duncan Smith exhibits minimal leadership qualities. Worst of all he has enmeshed himself in political correctness to such a degree as to suggest he is incapable of independent thought. Not content with disowning the Monday Club, he has insulted the Carlton Club by declining to join until it admits women members (which it has every right to refuse as a private members club); closed down Eurosceptic pressure groups like Campaign Against a Federal Europe (CAFE); and seen to it that no serious debate takes place within the Conservative Party on immigration or Europe when such debates are most urgently demanded by events. Moreover, IDS implicitly defers to every trendy idea put before him by the Portilloite fringe, hellbent on destroying not only every semblance of nationalist feeling but the very foundations of moral order.

So a weak and vacillating leader is persuaded that what counts in politics in 2002 is perception. The construction of politics must be determined not by what is right and sound but by the likely response they will elicit from the 'don't knows' and minorities. The last few weeks have witnessed some extraordinary public pronouncements deliberately aimed at ingratiating the Conservative Party with the least rewarding and most pernicious elements of our fractured society. Alan Duncan for instance decided to unburden his liberal conscience by pronouncing himself to be 'gay', as if one didn't suspect this to be the case. This apparently earth-shattering revelation by Duncan (the author, incidentally, of *Saturn's Children* which advocates the legalisation of drugs distribution) was considered to be so significant that party workers at Central Office assembled for a 'photo-call' at which several other uncloseted 'gays' revealed how proud they were to have 'come out'.

This disgusting spectacle, in the manner of a Faustian burlesque almost, was contrived by people who seriously imagine that it may have some effect in making the Conservatives more electable. In truth, it will have disproportionately alienated thousands more than it could conceivably attract. Still, Tory Party Chairman Theresa May was impressed; she congratulated Duncan for being 'so upfront'. May, of course, is the very embodiment of perception politics. She owes her elevated status entirely to her gender and nothing else. In parliament, as Shadow Secretary for Education and Employment (1999-2001), and subsequently as Shadow to John Prescott, at Local Government and the Regions, May has proved herself to be a mediocre debater and has otherwise made little impact.

More recently, the press reported a 'highly placed Tory insider', commenting about May and Caroline Spelman, Shadow International Development Minister, that 'the best thing about them is that they look and sound like Liberal Democrats'. This sort of negativism and self-loathing, bordering on the schizoid, just about epitomises the way in which the Tories are plumbing the depths. But there is more. On 11 August, *The Sunday Telegraph* reported that Tory candidates of the future would be required to undergo a 'check-out girl test' (no, this is not a mid-summer prank) to see whether they can speak to 'ordinary people'. Apparently Gillian Shephard, a party vice-chairman whom I had always regarded as one of the saner elements at Central Office, insists that candidates will benefit from talking to shop workers. Two other vice-chairmen (don't worry, it won't be long before they're vice-chairwomen) Patricia (call me 'Trish') Morris and Angela Browning will be visiting every constituency without a sitting MP to lecture constituency parties before the selection process.

> Let readers join me on an imaginary conversation as Ms Annabel Winthrop-Murgatroyd, an aspiring Tory candidate, with all the credentials that the Tory Reform Group can offer, aged 31 and ambitious to a degree as a public relations consultant, presents herself at the check-out till at Tesco's supermarket, Nottingham City Centre, one Thursday afternoon. 'Trish' Morris accompanies her. The target of her conversation is Mrs Connie Smith, housewife, aged 53 and check-out assistant at till 14. It goes like this:
>
> **A W-M** I will only be a few minutes. May I ask you some questions for our focus group?

CS Certainly m'duc (the three people in the queue nodding pleasingly).

A W-M Let me start with the economy. What's your view of the money supply and the M1/M3 basis of it?

CS Money supply? Mine runs out on Tuesdays, m'duc. Hubby subs me. I never go on M1. Too many snarl ups. M3? Wouldn't know – where is it?

A W-M Thank you. Most informative. Now a question about Bush. What's your view?

CS Well, my late father used to say: "Never beat about the bush – get straight to the point". That's my view, m'duc.

A W-M Quite, so with Saddam Hussein – would you take him out?

CS (Looking puzzled) Nasser Hussain, what a ….

A W-M No, no, I mean ...

CS Don't interrupt m'duc. Lovely cricketer. What a captain. And that Michael Vaughan. What a smasher! 197 at Trent Bridge, m'duc. Only round the corner. He can take me out whenever he wants!

A W-M (Sheepishly) I love cricket too. Three more questions. First, the Tories want to introduce a new blood transfusion system into the health service. What's your view about haemophilia?

CS (Reddening with age) String 'em up. That's what I'd do with them – string 'em up, m'duc.

A W-M No, I don't think you quite understood me.

CS Oh yes I did. String 'em up was my answer (massive endorsement from queue of 27).

A W-M Secondly, do you have a view about our increasingly multicultural society? (One or two Sikhs in queue shuffle uneasily).

CS That's easy, m'duc. Enoch Powell had it right (loud applause). He came from these parts, well Birmingham anyway.

A W-M	Ah, but things have moved on.
CS	Not round here they haven't, m'duc.
A W-M	(Getting irritated) But Mr Powell is dead.
CS	Not round here he isn't, m'duc. (CS bursts into uncontrollable laughter).
A W-M	And finally, Mrs Smith, do you have a view about Dame Shirley Porter, your employer and former Tory leader on Westminster City Council?
CS	(Looking furtively around her and fidgeting in her check-out seat). Dame Shirley Porter? Well I do have an opinion, m'duc, but I want to hold on to my job! (Spontaneous bursts of applause all round Tesco; check-out queue now numbers 59).
A W-M	Thank you so much, Mrs Smith. That was most enlightening. Your views will now be analysed by our think-tank and I will personally pass them on to Mr Duncan ....
CS	(Quick as a flash) I'd string him up too. Disgusting nancy boy parading all his dirty linen in public.
A W-M	(Bemused) Mr Duncan Smith, I was about to say, not Mr Duncan. Anyway, thank you very much. (A W-M departs from Tesco's, placing tape recorder in smart briefcase, with a beaming 'Trish' Morris, confident of having acquired hundreds of new supporters to the Tory cause).

And so we return to reality. The leading figure behind the perception politics strategy is Francis Maude. The son of Angus Maude, a genuine right-winger and traditionalist minister in Heath's government (1970-1974), Maude junior cut his political teeth on Westminster City Council (1978-1984). He became a Member of Parliament for Warwickshire North (1983-1992) and later for Horsham (1994 to present). At various times he was Under-Secretary of State at the Department of Trade and Industry, and Minister of State at the Foreign and Commonwealth Office. With the Conservatives in opposition he served as shadow chancellor and shadow foreign secretary before retiring to the back benches.

Maude's adventure in opportunism and careerism with willing accomplices, John Bercow, Steven Norris, Archie Norman and others is to set up a new 'think-tank' called Conservatives for Change – C Change in short. He wanted to make change in itself a political virtue, but everything he has done so far amounts to spin with no substance. Some of Maude's vaporous posturings have been set out in two articles; the first appeared in *The Spectator* of 23 March 2002 under the caption 'A Phoenix – Not a Dodo – It is five to midnight for the Tories'. The second appeared in *The Times* of 24 June 2002 under the heading 'Male, white, straight – and doomed to extinction if we don't change'.

Both articles are worthy of some analysis. Taking the second piece first, Maude advances the ridiculous theory that what is at the root of current Conservative failure is the fact that it is too male dominated and that females should receive the benefit of positive discrimination in selection contests for party positions; likewise that there are too many whites and too few blacks and Asians, and too many heterosexuals and too few homosexuals. Unless these imbalances are corrected, he argues, the party will never get back into government. Well it may not get back into government but not for the reasons he gives for, in truth, Maude's opinions are arrant nonsense, born of political ignorance and a total lack of awareness as to why people vote as they do.

At one point he writes: "Society's more relaxed approach to gay people makes many Conservatives uncomfortable and some still feel uneasy with the assertive multiculturalism of younger Britain". There is little evidence that multiculturalism has greater appeal among younger people than it has among older people. It is thoroughly unpopular everywhere. Maude's use of the word 'still' in the passage just quoted is particularly cunning. He wants to raise the perception of widespread endorsement of multiculturalism yet most people have sufficient intelligence to appreciate that multiculturalism – the insidious process of de-educating the white, indigenous people of these islands in their own history, conventions, traditions and more – is the surest route to decline and oblivion.

Towards the end of his *The Times* article, Maude shamefully re-opens the class war rhetoric of the left on schooling. 'No amount of insisting that I went to a thoroughly meritocratic direct grant school (yes, but actually a public school, Abingdon School, in Oxfordshire) will displace the assumption that I must have been to Eton. I remember being irritated in a radio discussion when one of the participants said: "But you come from a moneyed family, your father was a Conservative MP" '. Maude is ashamed that anyone could possibly suppose that his parents might send him to Eton, one of the finest and certainly most famous public school in England. Henry Cooper, Britain's greatest heavyweight boxing champion, can stand proud to declare his son was educated at Eton but perish the thought that Francis Maude might ever have been within its hallowed precincts, or muddied his knees on the playing fields of Agar's Plough. None of which is to suggest that state schools, direct grant schools or grammar schools (what is left of them) cannot provide an equally challenging and rewarding education. But Maude doesn't want to make this argument; he wants his C Change movement to be in the vanguard of overturning what he considers, entirely falsely in my opinion, people's perceptions of the structure of secondary education.

Turning to consider Maude's first piece, in *The Spectator*, the central thesis is much the same but at least he gets off to a good start. 'We must again become a genuine national party, as Disraeli insisted'. But then 'We must show real respect for all, male and female, rich and poor, black and white, gay and straight'. Just like that! Such profundity of thought. The notion that respect should not be earned, as opposed to arbitrarily given, is at variance with every tenet of human nature and sensibility. As for Disraeli, it is worth recalling that in his novels, *Coningsby* and *Sybil* he writes at length of the need to elevate the condition of the poor and it may reasonably be claimed by Conservatives that their social policies on poverty over a 100-year period, including those developed out of the better features of the welfare state, have been more beneficial to the genuinely poor than the policies of either the Labour or Liberal Party. It is therefore specious of Maude to imply that helping the poor (or the vulnerable as he would prefer it, to embrace, in reality, feckless and antisocial people) is some great invention emanating from his 'think-thank'.

Maude then attempts to define what characterises modern conservatism and he concludes his piece with this remarkable (for a Conservative, that is) observation:

> 'We should not have to take a Trappist vow of silence on the great European issues. We must have an outlook that

> is so unmistakably internationalist that it could never occur to anyone to depict us as narrow, "xenophobic", "Little Englanders".'

He is not here talking about international co-operation between sovereign independent nations. He doesn't mean that at all in what he has written. Nor is he suggesting a higher level of participation in some of the more beneficent activities – and there aren't many of them – of United Nations agencies such as UNICEF and UNWRA. No, he is clearly exalting the true meaning of internationalism, which is that of a global ideology which subordinates the nation to the demands of the 'world community' and the machinations of the New World Order. Indeed, internationalism is the mechanism for collectivised social control and the reduction of the nation state to an entity without power, influence or authority in defence of the liberties of its own people. Maude is hardly an apprentice in these matters. It was he, let us remember, together with Douglas Hurd, as Foreign Secretary of the time, who signed the Maastricht Treaty, the natural successor of the Rome Treaty and a treachery later to be compounded by the treaties of Amsterdam and Nice, the culmination of the Euro-internationalist grand project to reduce the nations of Europe to the status, effectively, of regional councils.

Nationalists within the Conservative Party know the score. Many will feel, with me, that the party has left them rather than they have left the party. It amounts to much the same thing – a long, arduous mountain to climb to reach the promised land.

David Cameron's official portrait from the 10 Downing Street website – see article at page 284

Marie-France Stirbois with her sash of member of European Parliament, at the Front National's march in honour of Joan of Arc, 1 May 2004 in Paris, France – *see article at page 216*

Penny Mordaunt MP – see article at page 295

Infamous photograph of a Muslim soldier displaying the severed head of Blagoje Blagojevic, a Serb from the village of Jasenove near Teslic. The photograph was seized from Saudi Arabian fighters captured in Crni Vrh near Teslic, Bosnia & Herzegovina – *see article at page 256*

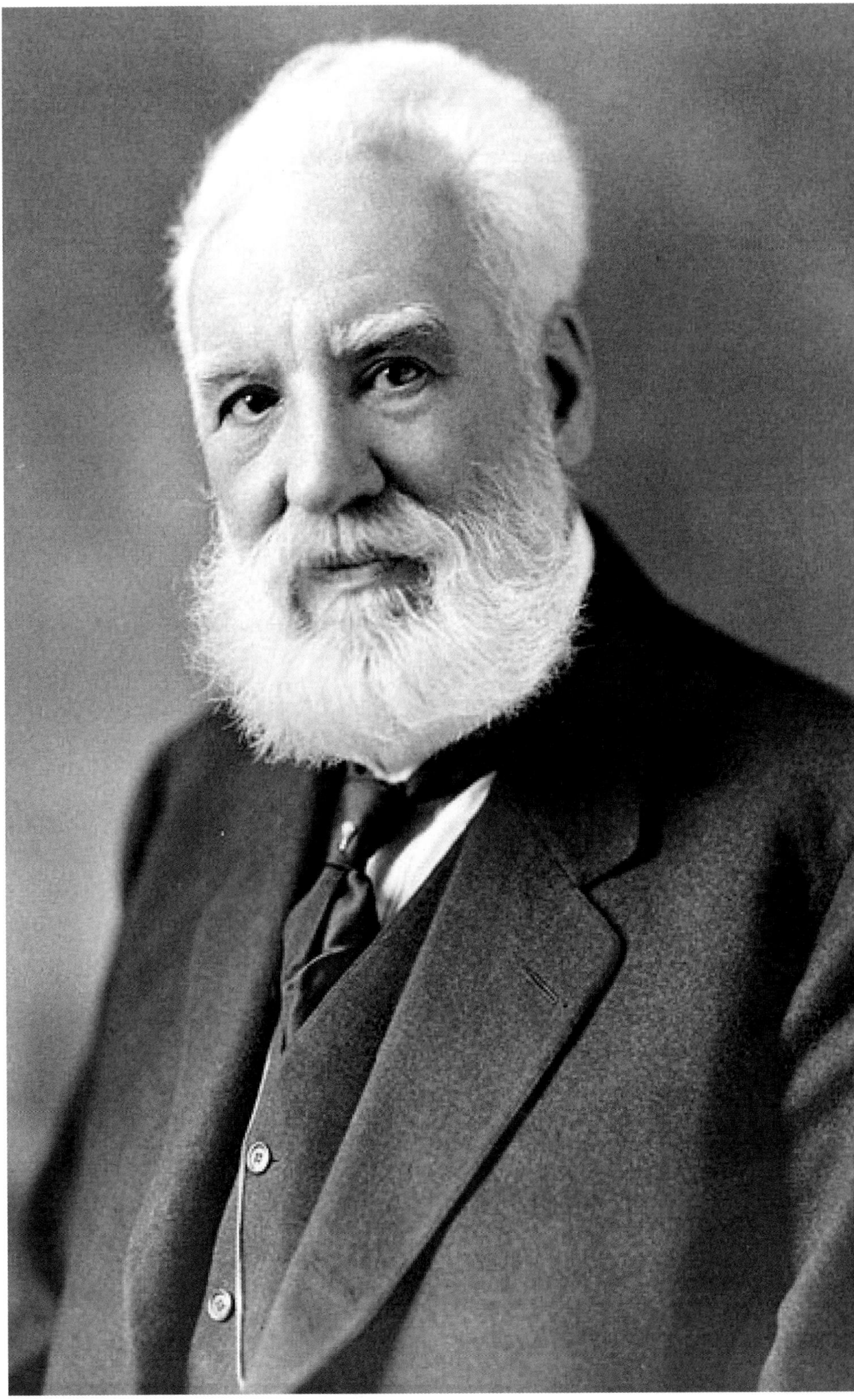

Portrait of Alexander Graham Bell – see article at page 241

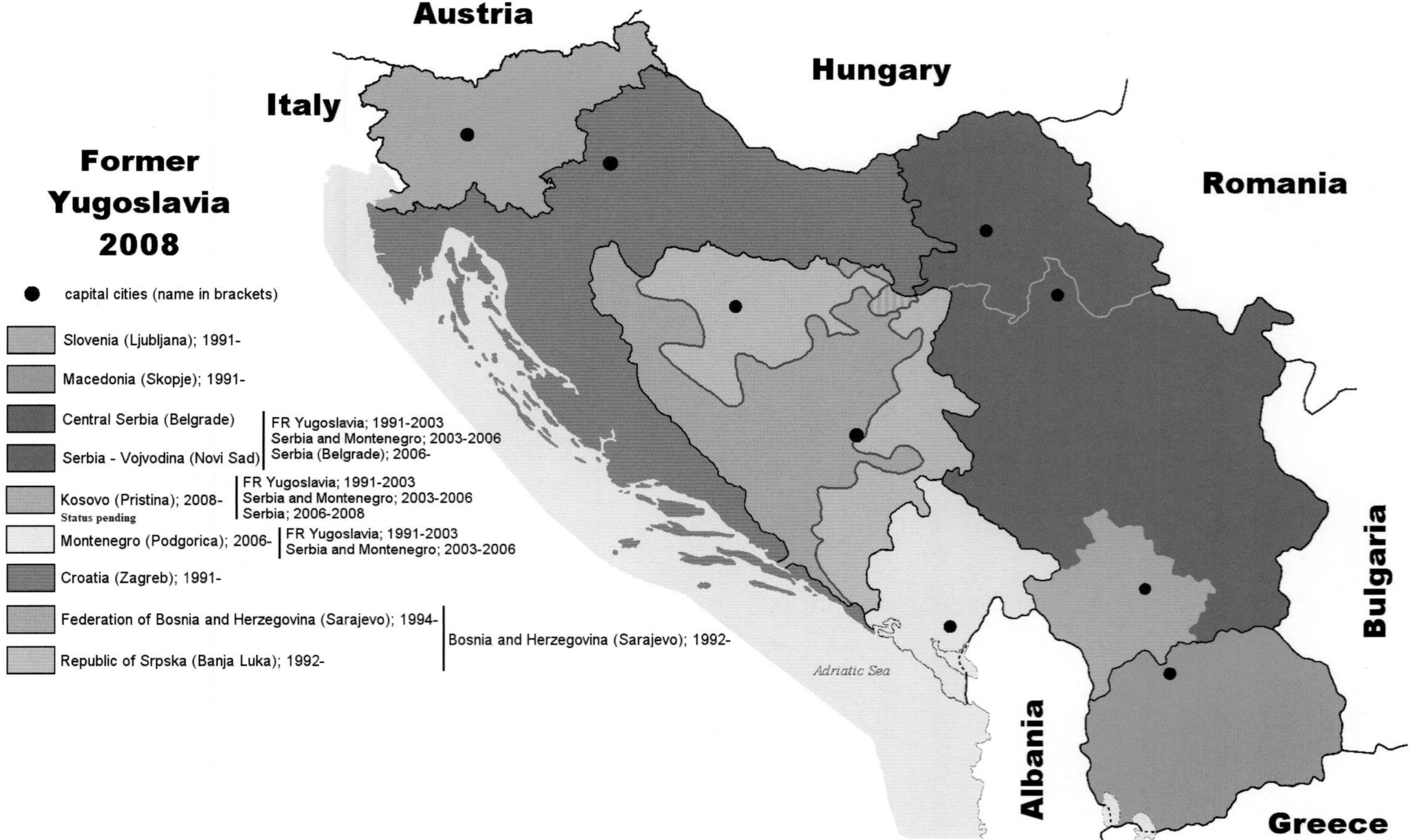
Former
Yugoslavia
2008
capital cities (name in brackets)
Slovenia (Ljubljana); 1991-
Macedonia (Skopje); 1991-
Central Serbia (Belgrade)
Serbia - Vojvodina (Novi Sad)
FR Yugoslavia; 1991-2003
Serbia and Montenegro; 2003-2006
Serbia (Belgrade); 2006-
Kosovo (Pristina); 2008-
Status pending
FR Yugoslavia; 1991-2003
Serbia and Montenegro; 2003-2006
Serbia; 2006-2008
Montenegro (Podgorica); 2006-
FR Yugoslavia; 1991-2003
Serbia and Montenegro; 2003-2006
Croatia (Zagreb); 1991-
Federation of Bosnia and Herzegovina (Sarajevo); 1994-
Republic of Srpska (Banja Luka); 1992-
Bosnia and Herzegovina (Sarajevo); 1992-
Austria
Italy
Hungary
Romania
Bulgaria
Albania
Greece
Adriatic Sea

Map of former Yugoslavia including Kosovo independence

Angela Merkel at the EPP Summit in Brussels, March 2016 – see article at page 295

Former Watford FC manager and chairman Graham Taylor, pictured at a football match on 9 May 2010. I think he would have approved of most of the article at page 271

Dumbing down: Pre-eminence of knowledge and memory

A decline in educational standards at every level is, in my opinion, beyond serious dispute even if performance at public examinations might throw some doubt on this assertion. I wrote the accompanying article for *The Clarion* bi-monthly journal in September 2004 and have no reason to alter anything I have written.

A recent survey conducted by *Encyclopaedia Britannica* reveals an astonishing (but in no sense surprising) ignorance of significant historical events in Britain. Christine Hodgson, Marketing Manager of EB, recently told *The Times*: "As a nation where history has shaped the face of the world it seems incredible that the younger generation has decided to dismiss it. Britain is envied for its rich history. I think it's time for all of us, not just young people, to hit the books again."

Such lack of knowledge of landmark events as revealed by the survey – for instance, D-Day; the names of Henry VIII's wives; the length of Queen Victoria's reign; the significance of the

Battle of Hastings; that Alexander Graham Bell invented the telephone, or that Galileo invented the microscope – is less a commentary on young people and their priorities than testimony to the pervasive influence of the liberal educational establishment, from primary school level to secondary schools, to local education authorities right through to university vice-chancellors, which collectively have wrought such disastrous decline in standards over the past 40 years or so.

The *Encyclopaedia Britannica* survey has been replicated a hundred times by other surveys. According to research by Professor Loreto Todd at the University of Ulster, echoing statistics produced by the National Skills Task Force, seven million adults are functionally illiterate. They cannot speak properly; they cannot construct sentences which are comprehensible; they cannot write letters and their listening attention span is less than two minutes.

Is it any wonder, then, that these deficiencies are so sharply reflected in our national life – particularly in television. The most challenging and interesting programmes that one can view invariably commence at times when most people have to retire to bed. A good instance of the general point made is that of the evening news bulletin. The process of reading it is thought to be such an intellectually demanding exercise that it requires two persons to perform it – no one item lasting more than a minute before the other reader takes over so as not to lose the viewer's attention.

I have no doubt at all that the principal cause of decline has been the downgrading, if not displacement, in the scale of priorities of knowledge, listening and memory, three interdependent faculties. This has occurred either as a deliberate policy stratagem or through appalling negligence in the devising of syllabuses at all levels of the curriculum.

Alexander Pope, the 18th century poet, novelist and literary master, author of *The Rape of the Lock* and verse translator of Homer's Iliad is noted for the famous aphorism: 'A little learning is a dangerous thing'. It was as axiomatic then as it is today that peripheral or incomplete knowledge is as dangerous as total ignorance, especially where it is used as a basis for the construction of policy, because it is destined to lead to a blinkered, obsessive approach which denies the possibility of rational and wholly visible alternatives.

Whether opinion-formers and policymakers are sincere, ideologically-motivated or just plain misguided cannot conceal the essential truth which is that their influence, the product of inadequate knowledge allied to disingenuity, has been nothing short of a catastrophe for British education.

Traditionally, even in the most specific activity at vocational or professional level, competence has been determined by knowledge: its acquisition, absorption and distillation. Take, for example, the technical exercise of will drafting. In the case Banks v Goodfellow (1870) Chief Justice Cockburn stated the requirement of testamentary capacity to be an appreciation of the nature of the exercise, a full recollection of the extent of one's property and a recognition of the claims to which the testator should give effect. The Chief Justice went on to include the need for 'a sound mind, memory and understanding' English case law is full of examples of the invalidity of wills in consequence of a failure to satisfy these rigorous tests.

The rationale of the above illustration is that knowledge and memory should be ineradicable values at the centre of any scheme of learning endeavour. For many of us what we learnt in our earliest schooling had a pattern and a clear purpose to it: for those of the younger generation that may not have been their good fortune. Four instances will exemplify what was, but no longer is, part of the curriculum, the loss of which in each case has been thoroughly retrograde: (1) dictation in English classes which had immense benefits. It taught the pupil to listen carefully, to transfer what he heard into writing and to learn how to spell accurately. For generations of pupils dictation would form a very useful preparation for note-taking at lectures, something at which too many students today are totally deficient: (2) in geography lessons, identifying the countries of the world and learning their capitals was never questioned as being of enduring value: (3) placing historical events in date order in history lessons was always the first question in the common entrance examination to independent schools, an exercise in developing memory skills and of clear usefulness: (4) learning two verses of a poem and making a recitation in front of the class, an activity promoting accuracy and self confidence. Apart from developing an interest in poetry it also enhanced the faculty of memory.

Although it should not be supposed that the development of a retentive memory is necessarily or inevitably an indication of basic intelligence it is a generally accepted truth that a person with innate intelligence usually carries with that asset a good if not capacious memory.

The traditional attributes and educational customs, incorporating so many undeniably valuable qualities are loathed by modernists who regard them as relics of the old world with no place in the new educational agenda. The modernist perception is that the acquisition of knowledge is not an absolute value in itself at all but something which is inherently useful only when placed in a social context. So the Norman Conquest or the Battle of Agincourt should not be taught purely as momentous events in history but as a source for examining how, for example, the French treated prisoners of war in 11th century Britain or 15th century France, or how women were deployed as auxiliaries on the battlefield. Such matters may of course be genuine subjects of research in a university course devoted to social history but they remain subsidiary, relatively unimportant issues; at the primary and secondary education phases they have nothing whatever to do with the exposition of knowledge. Nor do they have any educational value for schoolchildren.

When Tony Blair intones the ridiculous mantra 'education, education, education' he is, of course, echoing the modernist view. He utters these words with vigour, usually in front of susceptible, uncritical audiences. But what does he mean? Assuredly not that people should become genuinely more knowledgeable or better educated in some useful discipline; or that they should become more literate or less philistine in their tastes in the arts, particularly music. What he wants is that greater numbers should fall in line with politically correct liberal dogma in keeping with the brave new world order of multicultural, internationalist ideology. Objections to such a creed have to be snuffed out and people 'educated' into a state of total receptiveness.

Labour party higher education policy, from which neither the Liberals nor the Tories have uttered one word of dissension, is that university numbers should be increased from 30% to 50% of school leavers. This utter folly confirms the prevailing orthodoxy which dictates that the more students you put through higher education the better equipped they will turn out to be to face life's challenges, embark on a useful career and become conscious of their civic responsibilities.

The truth is, of course, the reverse. More means worse – not that this unduly bothers the collegiate of university vice-chancellors. For them what counts is the need, to use the modern idiom, 'to put bums on seats' so as to sustain their own jobs, maintain the government subsidy through the block grant and satisfy the Higher Education Funding Council which sets the targets and fixes the quotas. The idea is to invent ever more ridiculous useless honours courses to add to 'media studies', 'multiculturalism in 21st Century Britain', 'dance in contemporary society', and heaven knows what else! Such programmes of alleged study accommodate the need to 'celebrate diversity' and 'widen access' (i.e. lower standards), the buzz phrases of education's political correctness.

The end product is indisputably familiar – the bending of regulations to allow manifestly unfitted people, many from 'disadvantaged communities' to partake of a university education, however poor their entry qualifications may be, when their time would be better spent getting work experience in a trade or pursuing a business activity.

It is in the field of professional education that modernist theory has most recently done untold damage. Nowhere is this better illustrated than in the solicitors' qualifying examination course. The public has a strong vested interest in wanting the very highest professional standards from its lawyers. It is the public who pay the bills, often inflated fees for mediocre advice. It is not surprising that complaints of professional incompetence and inadequate service are today running at very high levels and in many cases in respect of solicitors who qualified in the last five years.

It was in 1992 that the General Council of the Law Society, the solicitors' governing body, decided to ditch the qualifying examination known as the Law Society Finals (LSF) and replace it with a course untried in concept, virtually experimental and fiercely opposed from within the profession by those who saw in it, quite rightly, the likelihood of a much easier course and a frontal assault on knowledge as the basis of legal learning.

The year long LSF course had been in place since 1979 and was generally regarded as rigorous, academically testing and demanding of very hard work and effort. It had the clear virtues of disciplined learning, the absorption of large amounts of detail and preparation for regular written tests in eight core subjects leading to eight tough examination papers spread over 11 days.

All the papers were unseen and the pass mark was set at 50% subject to the usual adjustments in cases where students dropped below that standard in two papers but where they had compensating strength elsewhere to take the average over the requirements for a pass.

Now none of this may seem at all remarkable. To many readers knowledge acquired through digestion of expensive legal texts accompanied by practical skills, such as will drafting, negotiating a divorce settlement or drafting a deed of conveyance, would probably reflect what would be expected of a candidate hoping to become a trainee solicitor. The main practical learning skills would be acquired during articles of clerkship.

The method of teaching was one of proven excellence and durability. The lecture, which would usually last for one and a half hours, would consist of the lecturer giving notes, the student transcribing the notes and suitable explanations being shown on the blackboard/whiteboard. A good, clear authoritative voice was part of the lecturer's craft. The educational theory behind this didactic method was that students learn best 'through the pen', that is, the diligence required to take notes accurately would in itself improve concentration and promote a desire for wider reading and preparation for the weekly seminar or tutorial session.

Generations of students went through this syndrome of learning with no evident educational disadvantage associated with it. Surprise, surprise: the most intelligent, dedicated and hard working prospered and came out top, while the least intelligent, least hard working, most complaining and feckless would end up failing. The proportion of pass to fail was approximately 68% to 32%. Most students studied at the well known law training centre, the College of Law, a highly respected institution founded in 1962 and affectionately dubbed 'the College of Knowledge' because of its long-held conviction of the need to inculcate into students knowledge as the indispensable precondition for success in the examination and a sound background for entry into articles.

The same enemies of knowledge would become the driving force behind the destruction of the LSF and the introduction of the new course, pompously called the Legal Practice Course, in September 1994. The central thesis of these knowledge-haters is that what really counts in the world of legal education is not reading, learning and absorption of detail but that students should become sufficiently canny to know what to look up in the books and where to look it up. They shouldn't be required to burden themselves with too much in their head. From the outset of the new course content would be reduced by 40%, formalised, structured learning would disappear; the three-hour unseen examination would be replaced by 'open-book' examinations; tutorials would be replaced by 'workshops'; the central examining authority would be replaced by individual institutions setting their own papers, with variable standards.

After seven years of this ideologically-driven leftist social engineering, the results have been disastrous. Candidates of very moderate ability in many cases are now entering the profession and standards are declining every year. The rigour and toughness of the old course have been obliterated. Fairly recently some of the top firms in London made known their objections to the Law Society very firmly. Their trainees did not know enough law and the LPC was a deficient foundation. Modest changes for the better have been introduced but the net effect remains unchanged, the course has failed and has been seen to have failed, except, that is, by the ideologists of the education committee of the Law Society and their hangers-on.

Tinkering with the present structures will not even begin to address the national education malaise at all levels that besets Britain. What is required is a revolution of insight and action by the best brains enthused by a truly nationalist ideology. I hope to be able to set out such a programme in a future article.

The Times reports on 1 December 2016 that bright state pupils are now able to benefit from "lessons in private school rigour". Apparently, a group of state school teachers are now embracing much more reliance on knowledge and higher academic expectations in examinations. The teachers spent two years observing and teaching lessons in four independent schools, prompted by concerns that their own state schools were not sufficiently stretching their most able pupils at GCSE and A Level.

Their report is highly significant. Experience is telling them that encouraging self-learning by pupils is not a didactic method which can possibly be compared with knowledge-driven instruction. My article highlights at every level how true this is.

The principal of Christ the King, a sixth form college with 3,000 students on three sites in Lewisham, London, is reported as saying: "... knowledge is key, students having facts at their fingertips". It was noticed how lessons in private schools went beyond the syllabus, with pupils being expected to work hard at homework, and how groups of bright teenagers encouraged each other.

Could we be moving to a new dawn in secondary education?

Tories: A loss of identity

I wrote this piece for *The Clarion* magazine in April 2005. It was not far away from an upcoming election. Michael Howard was Tory leader. I maintain here, as I continued to do, that lack of clear ideological positioning was a handicap and not an asset. It is still true in 2016. It would not be long before I resigned my membership of the Conservative Party. My reasons are made clear.

Old habits die hard, especially if they are bad ones. I should know. I've been a paid-up member of the Conservative Party for nearly 35 years. Throughout this time I freely admit I've been labouring under the delusion that if I, and others who share my opinions, campaigned hard enough we would reach the promised land and herald the dawn of a new political awakening. Such achievements as I personally may be able to claim – four years as a city councillor and four as a borough councillor – have had absolutely no effect, of course, on the direction of party policy.

Others with right-wing nationalist credentials no less ardent than my own have trod the same path. At the highest level one thinks of the likes of Enoch Powell, Ronald Bell and Richard Body. At local level the irony is that those of nationalist persuasion abound in their several thousands. They resolutely refuse to leave the Conservative Party. Certainly, constraints on leaving, all of them artificially imposed, exist in many forms: tradition, custom, family membership ties, even social standing, but strongest of all perhaps, is the deeply ingrained feeling that the Tories alone offer a brake against national decline and the triumph of socialism.

These sentiments are highly irrational and are readily countered by two entirely reverse propositions. The first is that the Tories are as much to blame, if not more to blame, for the advanced state of decadence that characterises so much of our national life as any other political party; the second is that New Labour has disowned socialism as a philosophy of government and embraced, in an opportunistic way, a form of social utility which allows it to rely on buoyant economic conditions, low unemployment and generous social welfare provision to keep the natives happy.

There may be some recent movement as people begin to see through Blair's political chicanery. The Tories should have been able to take advantage of this but they are unable to move away from their obsession with the need to occupy the 'centre ground' of politics, as they see it. I constantly remind myself of an aphorism frequently employed by the late Sir John Biggs-Davison MP (one of the best Tory MPs, Ulster loyalist, brilliant writer and scholarly exponent of the values of nationhood). "He who walks down the middle of the road soon gets run over". JB-D was a revered figure on the Tory Right. He hated a lack of ideological commitment – he described the middle ground as the 'triumph of nothingness' and 'a wonderful opportunity for the mediocre'.

By its failure to articulate a clear ideological position, which ought to be that of Tory nationalism, the Conservatives are proving to be the most uninspired opposition party since the war. The next few weeks will be revelatory because nothing is more calculated to sharpen the political reflexes than the imminence of a general election. The self-loathing condition of the Tory parliamentary party in opposition may fairly be compared with an aspiration towards a right-wing government, basing itself on clearly defined nationalist principles., which is shared by me and, as I have already indicated, thousands of other natural Tory supporters. At any rate, it allows for an analysis in some detail of the deeply rooted differences which exist within the party between the leadership and many among the grass roots.

A good starting point is Iraq. Michael Howard, following the ineffectual Duncan Smith, has chosen to position the Tories as the faithful vassals of Tony Blair, who, in turn, has proved to be no better than the obedient poodle of George W Bush. In terms of principle, Howard's posturing is badly misconceived. Apart from alienating hundreds of thousands, or even millions, of potential supporters, it is folly because it takes no account of the doctrine of non-intervention in the affairs of a sovereign independent state (which is essentially a Conservative doctrine), as well as being in breach of international law which, for a declaration of war, requires the concurring votes of the permanent members of the Security Council of the United Nations. This was never obtained to legitimise the invasion of Iraq.

Legalities aside, as has often been asserted in the columns of *The Clarion*, no country should embark upon war without a very good reason for doing so and only where there is a distinct and proven threat to that country's own safety. There may have been an argument in favour of 'hot pursuit' at the end of the first Gulf War but none whatever existed two years ago. Howard's equivocations have demonstrated his lack of leadership quality. Over 80 British soldiers have been needlessly killed in the Iraq conflict and 250 have been injured. By his humiliating subservience to Blair on this issue Howard has betrayed the ideal of parliamentary opposition in debate. In truth, he should have been calling for Blair to be brought before the International Criminal Court at The Hague for waging aggressive war.

Saddam Hussein may have been a harsh dictator but was his rule over Iraq any more severe than that of, say, Bokassa, Mengistu or Mugabe? The end product of this meddlesome venture is the likelihood that there will be inaugurated a Shia hegemony which will lead to a strengthening of Islamic fundamentalism in that region. Now *that* could be a threat to the safety of Britain.

No less humiliating to this country has been the Tory failure to digest the effect of the various treaties of the European Union: Rome, Maastricht, Amsterdam and Nice. It is a political contradiction to have given support to these anti-national measures (better described, perhaps, as nation-breaking measures) while proclaiming the iniquities of the Constitutional Treaty. All have as their central purpose the same objective; the transformation of our nation into part of a Federal Union, with the European Commission as the central government of that Union state. Britain will have only such reserved powers as are accorded to it by Brussels. Yet Conservative policy proposals are failing to grasp this reality. Shadow Ministers, particularly John Redwood, who ought to know better, talk and write about the repatriation of powers from Brussels, appearing to believe that within the existing framework of institutions this would be possible. Clearly, the effect of the treaty obligations are not understood. Have they not heard of the *acquis communautaire*, empowering the Council of Ministers to veto unilateral rejection of specific measures? This doctrine was introduced into the Treaty of Amsterdam.

Further, the onset of qualified majority voting in decision-making diminishes any serious prospect of unilateral rejections. On top of this, the law of treaties is absolutely clear. *Pacta sunt servanda* – treaties are to be observed in their entirety. The European Court of Justice would rule that further British 'opt-outs' could not take place without a substantial majority vote (80 per cent) of member states. Such a vote is exceptionally unlikely.

Does Mr Howard realise or appreciate any of this? He is either ignorant of the details of the European Union or just plain devious. I do not offer an opinion as to which, but if he does have a true love of Britain (which he is incessantly proclaiming from the rooftops) I would expect him to make a seminal pronouncement: that when the British people reject the Constitutional Treaty in early 2006, as assuredly they will, he will campaign vigorously for Britain to leave the European Union at the earliest opportunity. In practical terms he may not be able to lead in this direction before the referendum but with weight of popular opinion likely to be in favour of leaving the EU his mind should be firmly set on this target. He should speak the truth, which is that the entire European political construct is the product of a massive fraud and confidence trick played out on the British people with a shamelessness which defies adequate description. Every accretion of power since 1975 by the European centre has been represented as something fundamentally different from what it is.

However, I do not think Howard exhibits the necessary mettle to make the pronouncement I have described, which would need to be made before the election campaign starts. Of course, it would generate a split; but that is precisely what is needed. Indeed, it is against the background of just such a determination to keep the avowed wishes of our people in check that Howard's recent policy proposals on immigration and asylum should be judged. They have been met with some acclaim by the popular press and have, therefore, opened up something of a debate which is all to the good. But the reality is that they are much too little and far too late to have any usefulness, and have been delivered almost apologetically.

Howard constantly trumpets the contribution of immigrants in their various spheres of life. Well, certainly, doctors, nurses, transport workers and others, as individuals, many of whom have been settled here for decades, work hard and in the main are law-abiding people. Yet none of this has the least relevance to the central issue, which is whether Britain has a continuing vocation to become an increasingly multi-racial and multi-cultural society. That is a decision which our own people are entitled to make in a referendum. The politicians cannot be trusted to make it on their behalf.

In making that decision the people should weigh up the social consequences of mass immigration in terms of the resources expended on social housing, welfare benefits, educational budgets and the breakdown of law and order in urban communities, I have not the slightest doubt that the balance of advantage is set firmly against all but minimal immigration into the United Kingdom.

It is salutary to recount from the pages of the *London Evening Standard* of 16 February four reports (and there were only four altogether) relating to the commission of criminal offences. One concerned a 16 year old white girl who was snatched off the street in South Norwood and gang-raped by three men "all said to be black". The girl managed to escape after a terrible ordeal lasting over an hour. A second concerned a young black man, Rafik Alleyne, sentenced at the Old Bailey to life imprisonment for the murder of one Andrew Sams, also black, in a drugs feud. Sams had been shot in the head in West Norwood in April 2003. A third report concerned a Harley Street doctor, Fayez Mahfouz, who was struck off by the General Medical Council for having severely burned two women and injuring 60 others, all of whom claimed to have been "badly disfigured". The fourth report involved a science teacher at a Newham comprehensive school,

Dr Junaid Sheikh, who was jailed at Snaresbrook Crown Court for helping to run one of Britain's biggest counterfeit telephone accessory operations, described as a "family criminal enterprise".

I should emphasise that my recitation of these reports is in no sense intended to suggest that immigrants in general have propensities for criminality (which would be untrue and unfair) but that in proportion to their numbers, immigrants and immigrant-descended communities commit crime *disproportionately*. This is empirically found to be incontrovertible by several scholarly sociological and criminological surveys. It is an entirely legitimate matter to raise for open debate, yet these uncomfortable truths have as little appeal for Howard as they do for Blair. Indeed, the mere mention of them is calculated to raise the stereotypical cry of 'racism', such is the extent to which intellectual terrorism now overshadows rational debate.

The very minimum policy proposals that the Tories should be presenting to the electorate are: a complete moratorium on all further immigration for five years, after which a review should take place following a national referendum; the abolition of the Commission for Racial Equality and Equal Opportunities Commission, both of which are in favour of positive discrimination against whites; the repeal of the Race Relations Act 1976 and Human Rights Act 1998; and the refinement of welfare benefits so that invalidity benefit would be retained but housing benefit, family credit, income supplement, access to the social fund and unemployment benefit would be reduced by 50 per cent. This would be applied uniformly. Inevitably it would lead to substantial voluntary re-emigration in many urban communities.

So far as asylum is concerned, better in reality in the majority of cases described as illegal immigration, the Geneva Convention of 1951 should be abrogated. The rationale of this measure was the protection from persecution of those living under communist régimes. These circumstances no longer pertain. No appeals should be allowed against asylum decisions, and those allowed in should be strictly limited to a minimal number. I would suggest 500 (Howard has indicated he would allow in 15,000). Such persons would need to obtain from the appropriate British Consulate a certificate verifying their *bona-fide* status procured by affidavit and based upon clear-cut evidence of actual or threatened persecution.

One further issue which falls outside the theme of identity (to which I have addressed myself in this article) is the thoroughly unconservative drift towards social liberalism. Howard himself is at the forefront of this development. It is appalling that the shadow cabinet failed to accept the Tory backbench amendment to the Civil Partnership Bill (now an Act), which would have accorded similar rights to those co-habiting in non-sexual relationships, such as brothers and sisters or other family arrangements. Homosexual rights were attained under the Sexual Offences Act 1967, following the recommendations of the Wolfenden Committee. Acts between consenting adults in private would be legalised. That should have been the end of it. Yet by supporting a whole range of liberalising measures the Tories are implicitly attacking marriage because it is the very uniqueness of marriage that makes it the proper institution from which social rights and obligations flow.

Similarly, the Tories' defensive posture on extending drinking hours and opening up more casinos reflects confused thinking. They suppose it enhances 'freedom', whereas it encourages social delinquency, irresponsibility and fecklessness, which are the negation of freedom. It may be added here, following the revelation that vice in London is now almost entirely under the control of the Albanian mafia, that a forthright political position would be to close down this entire racket within 48 hours, round up those operating it and put them behind bars before deportation. Do I think the Tories would ever advocate such measures? No I do not.

Given my antipathy to so much of what today's Conservative Party stands for, should I and others tear up our membership cards? Mine expires in September. For some time I have justified my own continued membership on the impractical argument that the Tories have left me rather than I them. The issue came into sharper focus for me last Sunday – in church of all places! The vicar announced the opening hymn: "Awake my soul and with the sun ..." a beautiful, rousing hymn the second verse of which runs: "Redeem thy misspent time that's past and utter with a glorious voice ..." Yes, our time has indeed been misspent, but whither now? The 'glorious voice' referred to in the hymn can only be heard within the massed ranks of nationalist idealism.

The Balkans: A badly flawed approach

The countries of the Balkans can be described as having had largely unhappy histories. Their peoples have diverse customs and beliefs. The First World War originated ostensibly because of the murder of Archduke Franz Ferdinand in 1914 at Sarajevo and the Second World War saw deep divisions of loyalty between Serbs and Muslims.

In this article I express my wholehearted support for Serbia and the Serbs, victims of 25 years of misconceived policies aimed at denigrating them and in defiance of the wise and well-established principle of non-intervention in the internal affairs of sovereign states.

The break-up of the former Yugoslavia can effectively be dated from June 1991. The Serbs, the dominant ethnic and religious group, were fundamentally opposed to the break-up. This is hardly surprising. The Serb-controlled army fought a 10-day battle to stop Slovenia from unilaterally leaving the union before a ceasefire was declared.

Fighting with Croatia lasted until January 1992 when the Yugoslav army withdrew although divisions of its troops remained in major Serb areas of Croatia.

In June 1991 Croatia followed Slovenia in declaring its intention to become an independent state. The Serbs in Croatia who had never forgotten their kin, so many of whom had been murdered by the country's pro-German régime in World War II, duly rebelled. Between July and August 1991 full-scale war broke out between Belgrade and Zagreb over the Serbian areas of Croatia. By late August the Croatian town of Vukovar had fallen to the Serbs after an 86-day siege with heavy casualties on both sides.

The European Community, fearful of violence on the borders of Western Europe, considered that holding Yugoslavia together as a unitary state offered the best chance of establishing peace but by September 1989 the national parliament of Slovenia had already approved constitutional amendments giving rights to secede from the Yugoslav Federation.

By December 1991 it had become apparent that the EC members (12), under heavy German influence, wanted to recognise Croatia's independence. Hans Dietrich Genscher, German foreign minister, claimed that delay in recognition "would encourage the Serbs to continue the war", a gross overstatement of the actual circumstances. Eventually, EC foreign ministers adopted the German position and agreed to recognise an independent Croatia. Unsurprisingly, this enraged many because Serb and Croat leaders had secretly agreed to divide Bosnia between them.

Thus the German geopolitical strategy prevailed. Almost certainly Britain agreed because it wanted German support over the negotiation of the Maastricht Treaty (1992) so that in effect we had a 'quid pro quo', a wholly disreputable foreign policy carve-up. If this reading of events is not to be seen as accurate why is Genscher on record as stating: "We helped you on Maastricht, please listen to us on this one".

Croatia and Slovenia having become independent states in December 1991 in early April 1992 the European Community formally recognised the independence of Bosnia-Herzegovina under President Izetbegović whereupon fighting escalated, with the Federal Air Force assisting the Serb forces, culminating in the bombing of Sarajevo.

Serbian opinion was justifiably outraged at the denial of the creation of a Serbian national state. Lord Peter Carrington at least was clear. By recognising other Yugoslav republics, but not theirs, Serb resentment at manifest unfairness and inequality would lead potentially to unrelenting warfare.

Bosnia could have remained within the rump federation to its profit but taking the course it did only served to heighten the disparities and ancient hatreds existing between different peoples and opposed ideologies, proving the utter failures and impracticalities of state-sponsored multiculturalism.

In the event, Radovan Karadzic, the Bosnian Serb leader, responded to Izetbegović's decision by declaring a Serb state within Bosnia called 'Republika Srpska', with Sarajevo as the capital described by Karadzic at the time as being "currently under enemy occupation". Throughout the summer months of 1992 fighting broke out mainly in Eastern Bosnia. The Bosnian Serbs with aid from the Yugoslav National Army had taken control of 70% of Bosnia. Terrible atrocities took place without doubt but somehow while opprobrium was levelled against the Christian Serbs, the Muslims of Bosnia and their leader Izetbegović in particular avoided any critique of their own atrocities.

The United Nations imposed sanctions against Serbia and established six safe havens for Muslims in Bosnia. The UN lamentably failed to protect these areas and substantial numbers of Muslims were unlawfully killed at Srebrenica in July 1995. What happened there was shocking although many observers, not all pro-Serb, hotly dispute the numbers. NATO proceeded to bomb Serb positions leading Serbia to agree a peace treaty with Bosnia dividing the region between Serb and Muslim/Croat states.

The decision that Britain should play a part within NATO in Bosnia in waging aggressive war against the predominantly Serb control of Yugoslavia was a predictably catastrophic folly. Participation in foreign wars where no essential British interest is involved is a recipe for disaster and has been seen to be so in many theatres of war.

The principal reason for the ongoing crisis in the former Yugoslavia has been because most Western leaders and decision makers, abetted by the media, are ignorant of historical and geopolitical factors in the Balkan regions.

Finding a solution to the entrenched communal differences in the Serbian Province of Kosovo would almost certainly prove to be beyond those, fundamentally ill-equipped through lack of knowledge and understanding, to discharge their responsibilities efficaciously. Despite propaganda to the contrary, it is far from the case that it is mainly Albanians who have been the victims of the civil war in Kosovo. Serbs and Montenegrins have been ethnically cleansed from Kosovo throughout the century. In the early 20th century the Serb/Albania population of Kosovo was in the proportion 3:1. During the Second World War, 10,000 Serbs and Montenegrins were murdered by Albanian extremists and a further 17,000 were expelled. After the war when Tito's communist government opened the border between Kosovo and Albania an estimated 320,000 Albanians came from Albania and settled in Kosovo.

The Yugoslav government tried over a period of time to find a peaceful and enduring solution for Kosovo. Months before negotiations in Rambouillet the government sent delegations to Kosovo's capital, Pristina, no less than 56 times to begin meaningful talks with the ethnic Albanians who were already receiving financial support from their diaspora in Germany and the United States. The proposals in Rambouillet were presented to the Yugoslav delegation as a "take it or leave it" package, with most parts being non-negotiable. Former American Secretary of State, Dr Henry Kissinger, commented: "The terms negotiated in Rambouillet guaranteed huge bloodshed even before it started. These demands could not have been met even by a more reasonable Serbian régime" (reference to Slobodan Milošević's leadership). Had the terms been accepted it would have taken away sovereignty from Yugoslavia. Indeed, the degree of autonomy offered in Rambouillet by the West would have meant that, after three years and a plebiscite, Kosovo would become a separate state.

It is fact that since NATO entered Kosovo in June 1999 the border between Kosovo and Albania was not properly guarded. Large numbers of Albanians, believed to be as many as 70,000, illegally entered Kosovo. Some of them were involved in criminal activities and drug trafficking.

American intelligence sources have now admitted that they helped to train the terrorist Kosovo Liberation Army (KLA) before NATO bombed Yugoslavia. William Walker, former American ambassador in El Salvador, who once organised the shipment of arms to Nicaraguan 'contra' rebels under cover of humanitarian aid and who was implicated in the process against Oliver North[37]. wrote a letter to the Serbian Unity Congress on 24 February as chief of the OSCE Mission in Kosovo:

---

37 Lieutenant-Colonel Oliver North was dismissed from the American National Security Council in November 1986 after the revelation that money from arms sales was channelled to 'contra' rebels in Central America.

> "I do have great respect for the men and women who serve in the United States intelligence community. It, like other governments' intelligence services, has a rôle in development of a government's foreign policy. Events prior to the bombing of Yugoslavia, in particular the alleged massacre in Racak, have shown that the American government from the beginning of the civil war in Yugoslavia had its own agenda to destabilise the country and get a foothold into the Balkans".

Indeed, the United States now have in Kosovo one of their biggest military bases in Europe. For many months they trained former KLA activists at Bondsteei, near Urosevic. Only a fraction of what was happening has ever reached the public.

A memorandum submitted by the Serbian Unity Congress to the Foreign Affairs Select Committee of the House of Commons on 23 May 2000 makes salutary and compelling reading, not only as regards the historical record but also the other side of the argument to the prevailing orthodoxy: Muslims good, Christians/Serbs bad, being presented to the Committee.

> "The main reason for the continuing crisis in the former Yugoslavia is because a great number of the leaders and decision makers in the West, including the media, are ill-informed and ignorant of historical and geopolitical factors concerning the Balkans region.
>
> It is not only the ethnic Albanians who have suffered in the recent civil war in Kosovo. The Serbs and Montenegrins have been ethnically cleansed from Kosovo throughout the century. At the beginning of the 1990s the demographic ratio was 3:1 in favour of Serbs. Between 1880 and 1905 the Austro-Hungarian empire encouraged Albanians to uproot the Serbs and over 150,000 Serbs and Montenegrins were expelled from the region of Kosovo. A census in 1921 revealed that the ratio of Serbs to Albanians was nearly equality of numbers: 52:48. This figure became unbalanced during the Second World War when, under Italian occupation, some 10,000 Serbs were murdered by Albanian pro-Nazis and a further 17,000 expelled. When Tito's communist dictatorship opened the border between Kosovo and Albania an estimated 320,000 Albanians came from Albania to settle in Kosovo.

Albanian extremists had separatist aims well before 1989 when autonomous status was taken away from Kosovo. The ethnic Albanians ominously refused to take part in any census after 1971 as they wanted the world to think that there were more of them than is the case. During demonstrations in Pristina (Kosovo's capital city) between 1972-1974 Kosovan separatists demanded the creation of a "Kosovo Republic" amid great hostility, declaring that they would take Kosovo from Serbia by any means possible, including outpopulating the Serbs on account of their higher birth-rate. In fact, the Albanian birth-rate in the 1970s was the highest in Europe.

Before the civil war in the former Yugoslavia started in 1971, 24 different nationalities lived there. That situation pertains today. While NATO bombs were falling on Serbia some 55,000 Albanians were living amicably alongside Serbs in Belgrade. It is, therefore, absurd to maintain that the Serbian government and the Serbs as a people planned and executed ethnic cleansing on a grand scale whether in Kosovo or elsewhere. It was a civil war and as with all civil wars, apportioning blame is usually too simplistic an action.

UN Security Council Resolution 1160 sanctioned the supply of weapons to all sides in this conflict, yet the embargo was not applied to Albania whose diaspora were sending arms and substantial funds to the terrorists in Kosovo, some being proceeds of drug trafficking with the full knowledge of the American government. Carl Bildt, the former peace mediator in Bosnia Herzegovina, said in January 1999: 'One of the main preconditions to stabilise the situation in Kosovo is to establish complete control of the Yugoslav-Albanian border where the bases of Albanian separatists are'. This was never properly achieved".

Having made my own personal study of the Balkans conflicts I began to make my own contribution, writing several published letters to national newspapers defending the Serbs against their denigrators. One such letter appeared in my local newspaper, *The Watford Observer*, on 4 June 1999.

Sir

Claire Ward's (Labour MP for Watford) defence of the bombardment of Yugoslavia cannot disguise a number of indisputable facts surrounding the Balkans conflict.

1. The exodus from Kosovo accelerated massively immediately NATO began its operations on 24 March, both in Kosovo and Serbia. Although atrocities have taken place which are inexcusable and to be condemned most of those fleeing have done so to avoid the bombing and so as not to be directly caught up in the civil war between the terrorist Kosovo Liberation Army and the Yugoslav National Army and security forces defending its national territory.

2. Mr Gamble's description of a "low level conflict" (letters 21 May) before 24 March is wholly accurate. If Miss Ward thinks otherwise let her be reminded of the ethnic cleansing in the Krajina region of Croatia in October 1995, when 260,000 Serbs were forcibly removed in 18 days, or Vukovar in February 1996, when the same fate befell 60,000 Serbs; or the more recent terrible events in Rwanda, Sierra Leone and Chechnya when no one, least of all NATO, lifted a finger – all massively worse in scale.

3. The Rambouillet terms were presented to President Milošević as a "take it or leave it" ultimatum. No Head of State could have accepted what was demanded, despite the propaganda of Dr James Shea of NATO (so comfortingly re-invented for public consumption as "Jamie").

4. NATO's punitive action against Yugoslavia is in total breach of international law and the rules of war. Apart from the non-reference to the United Nations because NATO knew the matter would not pass the Security Council or the General Assembly under the 'uniting for peace' procedure) the bombing is in breach of the *Hague and Geneva Conventions*; in breach of the *Vienna Convention* on the Law of the Treaties (1980) and the *Helsinki Final Accords* (1975). Further, the absence of a declaration of war alone makes the bombing illegal, while NATO itself under the Atlantic Council Charter 1949 pledged itself as a defensive force to uphold the UN Charter. It has lamentably failed to do so.

5. The merciless, unrelenting and illegal devastation of a sovereign, independent nation which threatens no other

> state is an act of barbarism of which Hitler would have been proud. I am ashamed of the Conservative Party (of which I have been a member for 35 years) lending its support to New Labour's cultural imperialism. The true international war criminals are those planning and waging this terrible conflict against Yugoslavia.

NATO should stop its illegal bombing; an international peace presence under UN authority rapidly deployed in Kosovo; the KLA disarmed; a general amnesty declared; the refugees returned to their homes and the institution of a pan-Balkans Conference under the chairmanship of a respected statesman, such as Lord Carrington or Lord Healey. A permanent peace settlement for the whole Balkans region, on the basis of mutual respect and reciprocity, can then become an achievable objective, given goodwill.

Yours faithfully
S M Swerling

In early October 1999 *The Times* published a letter from myself which elicited 22 responses directly to me, only one of which was critical.

NATO's 'criminal' action

From Mr S M Swerling

Sir

In his letter (September 30th) the Secretary of State for Defence contends that NATO acted in accordance with international law in its bombing of Serbia. Lord Robertson of Port Ellen is wrong.

NATO never sought to obtain the affirmative vote of the UN Security Council that the UN Charter requires. The North Atlantic Treaty of 1949 by its own constitution pledges to uphold the charter yet NATO has clearly breached it.

Further, the British Government and NATO countries were in violation of (i) the 1980 *Vienna Convention* on the Law of the Treaties, particularly Articles 51 and 52, forbidding coercion and force to compel a state to sign a treaty and (ii) *The Helsinki Accords* Final Act 1975, which guarantees the territorial borders of the states of Europe.

> No account of special pleading from apologists of NATO's criminal and cowardly campaign against a sovereign independent state can justify its behaviour.

One of the most erudite protagonists of Serb interests has been Radomir Putnikovic, a Bucks-based author and Balkans specialist. For many years he was Vice-President of the Serbian Unity Congress. In a letter to him of 13 July 2000, Edward Leigh MP asked whether Kosovo had been effectively partitioned and whether there was a safe area for Serbs. Mr Putnikovic's response was emphatic:

> "You have asked whether Kosovo is now effectively partitioned. The answer is that it isn't. As a result of intensive ethnic cleansing of non-Albanians there are now a number of enclaves, some larger than others, holding thousands of Serbs and some smaller holding a couple of hundred. The safest area for Serbs now is north of Kosovo, either side of the River Ibar down to Kosovska Mitrovica, close to the Serbian border. Serbs and Albanians as well live there. Both are attacked and abused there on a daily basis by the Albanian extremists. In other places in Kosovo, Serbs, Turks, Christian Albanians and others live under the protection of KFOR in numbers of a thousand or so in enclaves: Obilic, Gracania, Orahovac Vucitrn Prizren and Podujevo. There are also villages and places where some Serbs live in enclaves and ghettos.
>
> In Pristina, the capital of Kosovo, controlled by the British before NATO intervention, some 46,000 Serbs lived. Now just a few hundred remain. You will now understand the scale of ethnic cleansing which has taken place over the last 12 months.
>
> The population of Pristina alone has doubled over the last year. There are now between 400,000-500,000 Albanians, a great number of whom are not Albanians from Kosovo but from Albania proper. We asked Keith Vaz MP how the border between Kosovo and Macedonia and Albania is guarded, and how it is that so many Albanians have entered Kosovo illegally. We have never had a straight reply. Our information is that about 350,000 Albanians are now living in Kosovo without any right to do so.

> The British Government is using the same spin-doctoring technique in Kosovo as they do with other issues concerning matters in this country. They are suppressing information which is not favourable and exaggerating such minor successes as they claim to have had. I am only sorry that the Conservatives, as the opposition party, do not challenge them about Kosovo in the way they do on other issues.
>
> Lord Robertson said a few days ago on a recent visit to Kosovo that he was "pleased with the situation, in general". How can he make such a misleading and inaccurate statement? The Serbs are not allowed to go to church on a Sunday without a KFOR escort or visit their loved ones' graves. Apart from 106 destroyed churches, thousands of Christian gravestones have been upturned and wrecked. After the arrival of international forces last year into Kosovo Albanian extremists committed vile atrocities, brutally murdering, for instance, 14 villagers who were gathering in the harvest in the village of Gracko. A few days ago some families under the protection of KFOR gathered for a commemorative service in the cemetery to find that a considerable number of the graves had been destroyed. Is it these events about which Lord Robertson feels able to declare that he is "pleased with the situation in general"? How utterly contemptible."

In answer to a letter from Clive Soley MP on 31 January 2000, in which Soley had sought to place the entire blame on President Slobodan Milošević for events in Kosovo – in itself an ignorant and untrue assertion, Mr Putnikovic responded with devastating effect:

> Some politicians like yourself go to Pristina, the British-controlled part of Kosovo and come back making statements that all is well in the Serbian Province of Kosovo and that the non-Albanian population is protected by KFOR. That is absolutely not true. You know full well that many Serbs either used to or still remain in Pristina. An instance is Pristina hospital where their presence would continue to be essential but all the Serbian doctors have been pushed out by intimidation and brutalisation in the presence of British troops. Are you aware of what is going on in the other parts

of Kosovo under the control of the Americans, French and Germans? Albanian extremists carry on their murderous policy towards everybody who favours co-existence and reconciliation in Kosovo, whether Serbs, Turks or Albanians.

On 12 January, Albanian terrorists in the suburbs of Prizren butchered four Slavic Muslims, the Skenderi family. The following day they went back and killed twin sisters, also members of that family. It is evident from your last letter, as it is from previous letters, that you continue to blame Milošević and the Serbs as a nation for the civil war in Yugoslavia in order to cover up the failure of the British government to keep control of the situation in Kosovo and to justify the genocide being committed upon Serbs.

The British government is under an obligation to protect all the people of Kosovo under the terms of Security Council Resolution 1244. It is also to promote the spirit of reconciliation and not give credence to terrorist acts as you appear to do. This can only encourage the Albanian extremists in Kosovo.

APPENDICES

From RP to BBC Radio 2 News London – 21 March 2004

The latest information we have from Kosovo is that in 72 hours 26 churches and monasteries have been destroyed by Albanian muslims, some dating back to the fourth century. More than 200 Serb homes have been torched, many fields of crops burned and 37 people killed with several hundred injured, including some peacekeepers. Even livestock, especially pigs, have been burnt alive. Admiral Gregory Johnson, the US Commander of NATO forces for Southern Europe said that riots and torchings constituted 'ethnic cleansing'.

From RP to Prime Minister, Tony Blair – 28 May 2007

From 12 June 1999 when British and NATO troops entered Kosovo more than 250,000 Serbs and other minorities have been ethnically cleansed. 151 churches and cultural monuments have been destroyed or desecrated by Albanian muslims. Over the last eight years, 7,583 recorded acts of violence have been committed on the minorities, mainly Serbs. 1,248 non-Albanians have been killed with a further 1,369 kidnapped and missing, now presumed dead, with many others injured and disabled. Out of 158,000 Serbs officially recognised as 'ethnically cleansed' by UN organisations, less than 5,800 have returned to their homes in Kosovo. Albanians in Kosovo have been wiping out the names of regions, towns and villages and any images of the past, including books and libraries. The purpose behind that is to eradicate everything associated with Christianity and Serbian heritage. By contrast, over the last 7 years 213 mosques have been built in Kosovo with funding from Saudi Arabia. All this terrible destruction , acts of violence and intimidation of non-Albanians has been taking place in the presence of British and NATO troops in contravention of UN Resolution 1244.

Most appalling is how your government never presented the true picture of what was taking place in Kosovo. You must be aware that American intelligence agents helped to train and arm the terrorist Kosovo Liberation Army before NATO bombed Yugoslavia. You personally and your ministers have covered up the crimes committed on a regular basis by Albanians over the past eight years. For political reasons you have presented, to Parliament and the public, intervention into Yugoslavia as a 'success story' (whereas it has been nothing of the sort) in order to get credibility for further intervention in Afghanistan and Iraq.

Under your premiership 33,000 tonnes of bombs were dropped on Serbia, resulting in the killing and maiming of several thousand innocent people and damage to the country in excess of 97 billion dollars.

Most Serbs and myself have no alternative other than to regard you, Mr Blair, as an international war criminal who should face justice at the Hague Court.

From RP to Jim Murphy MP, Minister for Europe
– 13 September 2007

I have just come back from Belgrade, where I had a meeting with a Serbian Government Minister. The plan for Kosovo is dead, as far as the Serbs are concerned as it disregards with impunity the territorial integrity of Serbia. In the event of a unilateral declaration of independence by the Albanians without a UN resolution the Serbian government proposes to reject such a treacherous plan. Perhaps you can explain upon what basis and according to what provisions of international law the current British government intends to allow 15% of Serbian territory to be taken from Serbia to facilitate the "independence" of Kosovo.

Kosovo has been mismanaged by the UN. The main responsibility lies with the governments of the USA and Great Britain, both of whom instigated intervention and the bombing of Yugoslavia. You evidently support proposals about so-called "supervised independence" of the Serbian provinces of Kosovo and Metohija which means nothing less than establishing a NATO state to satisfy the strategic areas of the United States in setting up a permanent NATO military base in Southern Europe.

From RP to William Hague MP at Conservative Party Central Office – 18 April 2015

British foreign policy on Serbia and Kosovo has been misconceived and disastrously executed. Out of 156,000 Serbs 'ethnically cleansed' from Kosovo only 6.5% have returned to their rightful homes. In most parts of Kosovo, the Serbs still do not have freedom of movement, whether to go to church or visit the graves of their loved ones. The destruction of spiritual and cultural monuments is still taking place. 70% of Christian graves have been destroyed or desecrated and NATO cluster bombs have contaminated 6 million square metres of land in Serbia. 14.5 tonnes of radio active material were dropped on Serbia and Kosovo during the bombing of Yugoslavia, the result of which is now a huge increase in cancer-related illnesses.

The events which have taken place is hardly a surprise to anyone who has followed your policies on the Balkans, given that as Foreign Secretary you had an "adviser", one Arminca Helic, a Bosnian muslim, a refugee from Bosnia. Do we have to believe that she has a fair and even-handed view of events in the Balkans countries, coming to this country, as she does, after the civil war in the former Yugoslavia? I note that after working for you for four years she has been promoted to the House of Lords.

From RP to Rt Hon Philip Hammond MP, Foreign Secretary – 14 October 2015

I write on behalf of many Serbs in the diaspora and our homeland to express great disappointment and disapproval about Srebrenica where the British Government tried to get their resolution passed at the United Nations on 8 July 2015. The resolution was ill-prepared, drafted without the Serbian Government being part of the process or even consulted. In the first draft of the resolution, there was no consideration whatsoever about what happened prior to the tragic events in July 1995. Srebrenica was supposed to have been a de-militarised zone, which, despite a UN Resolution, was not, for which the British Government was responsible as well. It was guarded by a small Dutch military contingent of 200 peacekeepers, who did nothing to stop the Bosnian Muslim extremists coming out of the enclave of Srebrenica and slaughtering the Serbian population in the surrounding towns and villages of Protočari, Skelane, Kravica and Bratunac, the result of which was 3,412 Serbs were killed, some of whom were children shot with their hands tied with wire. British, American and French Intelligence services knew very well what was going on in the enclave. Muslims from this country, as well as from Iran and Saudi Arabia, were going to Bosnia to fight for the Bosnian Muslims "to kill the Serbs". So inevitably, tension had been rising between the warring sides and reached boiling point, prior to the onslaught in Srebrenica, yet the British Government did nothing to prevent it.

The Resolution in question was amended seven times. In one of the first drafts the British Government made the outrageous claim that "tens of thousands of women, men and children were raped by Serbian soldiers", later to be amended to several thousand. Where is the proof of that? Give the Serbs evidence that thousands of women and children were raped! Also give us the exact number, not a round figure, of Bosnian Muslims, massacred in Srebrenica by the Serbian army. The figures have varied in the past from 4,970, the number stated at the trial in the Hague of General Tolemir to 6,000, up to a figure of 8,000, the dictate by Paddy Ashdown when he was Governor of Bosnia Herzegovina.

In a letter to Baroness Williams of 19 February 1993, I asked where her information came from that Serbs had raped 50,000 Bosnian women which she widely publicised in the USA and this country. Baroness Williams replied in a letter to me dated

25 February 1993, that her source of information was *The New York Times*, *Newsweek* and the Austrian Ministry for Interior Affairs, all of whom got their information in 1992 from the Bosnian Information Centre in Sarajevo. Even the most exaggerated statements made by Paddy Ashdown never stated that Serbs raped children. We are informed that instrumental for the Resolution of Genocide by the British Government were Paddy Ashdown and Arminka Helic, the latter, until recently adviser and chief of staff in the office of your predecessor, Mr William Hague. The reward for her work has been a seat in the House of Lords. Ms Arminka Helic, is a Bosnian Muslim refugee known to the Serbs for her "discreet work" and someone who detests everything to do with and coming from Serbia.

You said, Mr Hammond, that the aim of the Resolution brought to the United Nations was to bring reconciliation between the warring parties in the civil war in Bosnia Herzegovina, Bosnians and Serbs. What was the result of that? On the 14 July 2015, Mr Aleksandar Vučić, the Prime Minister of Serbia, as a gesture of goodwill and reconciliation went to the memorial at Potočari, Bosnia, and was stoned. It is no surprise to anybody what happened having in mind that the British Government's Resolution in the UN was one-sided, presented with extreme bias and animosity, politically motivated with the sole purpose to humiliate and accuse one side only, the Serbs, for the events in the civil war in Bosnia and Herzegovina.

I had the pleasure of knowing and working with, amongst other British politicians, Tony Benn, a great parliamentarian. Once I provided him, on behalf of the Serbian Union Congress, with a statement which he asked for about Serbian refugees from Croatia, and said, I hope that now the British will be fair to the Serbs. He replied: "Don't count on it". The Resolution about Srebrenica is an example of how the British have treated the Serbs many times throughout history with ignorance and arrogance, even with contempt. The examples are many, and revealing indeed. Many people in Serbia feel nothing good will come to them from this country. The efforts of a few people with integrity and a fair mind for good relations between two countries, such as Sir John Randall, Tam Dalyell, Lord Carrington (letter dated 18 May 2004: "You well know that I feel the Serbs have been unjustly treated"), Lord Tebbit, Alice Mahon, to mention only a few, seem to be lost for ever.

Football at the crossroads

My love of Association Football is second to none. I have been a season ticket holder at Watford Football Club for four decades and was watching matches there many years before that. Yet something is very wrong with the professional game, particularly the premier league. In this article, published in the bi-monthly journal *Identity* in November 2007, with additional material added, as indicated, I set down my criticisms and proposals for reform.

Public revulsion at the greed and graft involved in English soccer has never been more acute than it is to-day: multi-millionaire foreign tycoons with no real interest in the game other than lining their pockets buying out famous clubs; massive salaries being paid to highly overrated players; the decline of decent English boys coming out of the football academies; spiralling increases in ticket pricing. All these things are unmistakable indications of decline in our national game and, in many ways, a microcosm of so much of our national life.

In particular, the supposed showpiece of the game, the premiership, exhibits all that is worst in professional sportsmanship – diving is now commonplace, celebrity excesses at night clubs are rampant and managerial recriminations against referees and other managers are played out every week on television and in the newspapers. Who cannot be other than totally disgusted at the spectacle of Rio Ferdinand of Manchester United and England haggling through his agent about whether his *weekly* salary should be £110,000 or £115,000 – three times more than the average *annual* wage.

Equally appalling was the retention of the Swede, Sven-Goran Eriksson as English national manager despite his poor record and his much publicised personal misconduct, unbecoming to a man who should have been setting an example.

Yes, English football in 2007 is far from being at peace with itself. How different it was forty years ago. Saturday 30 July 1966 was a memorable day for the whole nation. It was a beautiful midsummer's afternoon. The streets were deserted, the beaches empty. Bobby Moore (truly the type of heroic figure the need for which was admirably alluded to in the *Identity* editorial of January) the inspirational England defender and captain, mounted the 39 steps at Wembley to receive the Jules Rimet trophy from the Queen. The World Cup was ours. I had the good fortune to be there as I had for all England's matches. The entire nation was riveted to television screens absorbing a thrilling match against West Germany, culminating in hat-trick hero, Geoff Hurst, banging in the fourth goal in the dying seconds of the game as spectators started spilling over the barriers to acclaim the players just as commentator, Kenneth Wolstenholme, memorably articulated the most apt of phrases: "they think it's all over, it is now."

Association football in England had reached its apotheosis. Players like Moore, Bobby Charlton, Jimmy Greaves, Gordon Banks and Alan Ball were mobbed wherever they went. There was a real spirit of patriotic feeling and adulation which lasted for months. Technical excellence, physical fitness and wonderful sportsmanship were dominant and had won through.

To be a professional footballer in that period meant limited wages but a generalised sense of purpose that money was subordinate to the achievement of self-improvement and the attainment of the highest standards. Much of Sir Alf Ramsay's dedication to the game as England's manager rubbed off on the massed ranks of English footballers. Ramsay once said that the best game he had ever seen was that in which the combined Oxford and Cambridge University side Pegasus defeated Bishop Auckland in the amateur cup final in the early 1950s. He wanted the Corinthian spirit of high-minded love of the game for its own sake to be translated into the professional arena. At least his aspirations in that direction were not encumbered by foreign managers, as there are to-day in abundance, or large numbers of foreign players or parasitical agents skulking in corners plotting how best to induce the next breach of a player's contract for a more lucrative "deal" elsewhere.

The grim reality of English soccer now is that it has become a battleground for mega-rich businessmen to plot boardroom take-overs and buy-outs with little or no regard for the overall welfare of the club itself, its players or its supporters. Firm remedial action needs to be taken and I will be setting out how I think it can be achieved given the necessary will.

Managed decline is, perhaps, the best expression to describe what has befallen soccer. The governing bodies in England, the Football Association, the Football League and, specifically, the Premier League have a lot to answer for. Their collective weaknesses are endemic in the game's current travails. Football's response needs to be drastic and thorough–going in every facet of the game. It is often stated that sport and politics shouldn't mix but reform and renewal cannot be undertaken unless clear nationalist principles inform the necessary changes that English soccer needs to embrace, combined with a commitment and co-operation from the local communities in which a club is based: in short, the ideal can be realised through the national and the local working in harmony.

Chelsea Football Club is the most celebrated instance of foreign domination but there are others: effectively Chelsea is owned by Roman Abramovich (Russian); Aston Villa by Randy Lerner (American); Fulham by Muhammad Fayed (Egyptian): Manchester United by Malcolm Glazer (American) and Portsmouth by Alexandre Gaydamak (Israeli). The most recent entrant to the ownership stakes of a premiership club is Eggert Magnusson, an Icelandic biscuit manufacturer and a former president of Iceland's Football Association. Magnusson's club is West Ham. He owns 5% of W H Holding, the corporate entity that purchased West Ham for £85 million with the remainder (95%) owned by Bjorgolfur Gudmundson, the Icelandic Landsbanki chairman and so Magnusson's financial backer W H Holding has, in effect, funded the deal with equity and loan capital in equal measure. The take-over earned Terence Brown, the former West Ham chairman, £30 million for his 37% shareholding in the club. In an early public statement Magnusson proclaimed a policy of continuity, yet within only four matches manager, Alan Pardew's services were dispensed with. Not that Pardew should have been surprised because on 4 December the egregious Magnusson told the press that "Pardew's throat will be cut if he cannot steer well clear of relegation." The West Ham faithful should be under no illusions. If the club is relegated, Magnusson and Gudmundson, notwithstanding their protestations to the contrary, will be off the Upton Park premises in double-quick time, disinvesting and precipitating a financial crisis for the club. They will tell the media loudly no doubt that they are not getting an adequate return on their investment.

One of the more mysterious features of the West Ham foreign take-over has been how two Argentine internationals, Carlos Tevez and Javier Mascherano, came to join West Ham on the earlier of the two transfer deadline dates. Both came from Brazilian club Corinthians for no transfer fee, so was it that the spirit of Corinth had re-entered our capital city? Far from it. Instead, a considerable sum was paid to their personal agent and manager, one Kia Joorabchiam, an Iranian businessman, for arranging the deal in return for which West Ham were given first refusal, strictly in law a right of pre-emption, to sign the player permanently if another side came in for them but they would then have to meet the asking price of more than £50 million for the pair. If they were sold the profits would be split with Joorabchiam, the backers and the club. This disgraceful, and possibly illegal, arrangement is certainly against all notions of transparency and symbolises the sort of wheeler-dealing that is going on at club level; it also displays the pernicious influence football agents are having on the game, a matter I address later on.

Another club beset by the influence of foreign ownership is Liverpool F C, one of the most successful clubs in England over many years. Here it was Dubai International Capital, the private equity investment arm of the Arab state and its banker, J P Morgan, which made the early running. The Maktoum family, of which Sheikh Mohammed is the head, owns Dubai International Capital. What connection, one might ask, have the rulers of Dubai with the English city of Liverpool, or is that the sort of politically incorrect and uncomfortable question one shouldn't be asking? Highly significantly *The Daily Telegraph* reported that a confidential document had come into its possession showing that Dubai International Capital were planning to borrow £300 million to finance their £450 million purchase of the club and that it was seen purely as a business deal associated with the new stadium.and that D.I.C. planned to sell in 7 years and make a very fat profit, providing for them a return of around 25% on their investment for every year of ownership. There were no plans at all to invest in new players.

Mysteriously, D.I.C. pulled out of the Liverpool venture although one can surmise that the bad publicity had something to do with it. That became the opportunity for American tycoons, George Gillett and Tom Hicks, to step in. Gillett owns the Montreal Canadians ice-hockey team and Hicks is the owner of the Dallas Stars hockey team and the Texas Rangers baseball side. Neither has the remotest connection with Liverpool. Together they have bought up more than 62 per cent of Liverpool's shareholding and are apparently confident in acquiring a 100 per cent takeover. £175 million is being spent on acquiring Liverpool's shares, £80 million of debts are being underwritten and £215 million is to be expended on the club's new stadium. Nothing has yet been declared to the club's supporters about the anticipated substantial rise in ticket prices in consequence of this mega-finance expenditure.

Newcastle United F C are also poised to go foreign. Here the present club chairman is Freddy Shepherd with connections to the Belgravia Group, a Jersey-based (tax haven naturally) investment company. Shepherd is keen to sell. There is a stock market value of £107 million (again very over-valued) and debts of £80 million. Shepherd owns 26.7% of Newcastle and the club's most recent annual report discloses that he and Douglas Hall's family (which has a 41.5% shareholding) would be entitled to two years' salary of more than £900,000 and £800,000 respectively if a takeover proceeded on top of their overpriced capital. Do the supporters of the club have a view about all this? They certainly wouldn't formally be able to express it – the annual meeting is held 300 miles away from Newcastle and 50% of the shares are held outside the North-East. One of the prospective purchasers was Polygon, an American financial consortium, but they have recently pulled out, having informed the Stock Exchange that following talks they no longer intended to make an offer. Other foreign consortia will assuredly take their place. Shepherd's priorities are clear. He was reported in *The Times* (12th December) as stating: "It's getting to the point now where multi-millionaires are not enough. You need to be a billionaire. Of course, I would like that here."

Perhaps Shepherd had Chelsea's Roman Abramovich in mind. He is the king of the football barons. He made his £10.8 billion fortune from the oil industry when Russia's public utilities were privatised in the 1990s. He has already spent £450 million writing off Chelsea's debts. The club's utterly spendthrift policies include expenditure of £276 million on player transfers in less than four years. Abramovich has distorted the transfer market by lavishing tens of millions of pounds on overpriced players who, because of the "large squad" policy, then languish in Chelsea's reserves. Such players' market value then becomes unassessable, adding to the distortion.

Seemingly, Chelsea will go to any lengths to secure their objective of being top dog in England and Europe, as witness the "tapping up" of Ashley Cole after Chelsea representatives met the left-back without Arsenal's permission (at the time his employer) at a London hotel; or the £30 million signing of Andriy Shevchenko who has been a complete flop at the club but is a personal friend of Abramovich and therefore has a protective ring encircling him.

How, one might ask, did Abramovich amass his billions, even in the comfy environments of post-Perestroika Russian capitalism? How has he retained the patronage of President Putin while other businessmen, profiteers from privatisation, have either been jailed or exiled? Chelsea's faithful should not be over-confident. Abramovich's obsessions tend to be fairly short-lived. He got out of oil, he retired from the governorship of Chukotka, a province of North-West Russia, after six years and it is unlikely he will be hanging about at Chelsea if the club's fortunes should decline which, at the time of writing, is beginning to happen: Chelsea would then have an appointment with the Knacker's Yard.

The above analysis demonstrates the disastrous effect on the game of foreign ownership which necessarily extends through to foreign management and the uncontrolled number of foreign players in the English game, however good their individual talents may be. Tied in with this is the incontrovertible truth that there is a serious lack of home-grown English talent at the highest levels of the game.

Only the policies of a government structured on soundly based principles giving firm leadership can be certain of redressing these endemic fault lines. Sir Trevor Brooking, arguably the most respected figure in the game, is on record as stating that 60 per cent of 11 year olds leaving primary school are "physically illiterate", that is, that they do not possess the basics of physical movement, agility, balance and co-ordination.

Instead of acquiring land to house the massive rise in immigration, government should engage in land reclamation and requisition schemes in nationwide policies to give opportunities to the millions of young people in England to play soccer regularly. This should be associated with a national physical education policy for all schoolchildren to produce fitness. Compulsory games under teachers and qualified instructors for at least one hour every day would go some of the way towards achieving a healthier nation through a more balanced curriculum.

Such policies would help to reverse the current drift towards closure of many youth football academies attached to professional clubs because of the lack of talent being developed. If the academies close, the supply line of English players will dry up. Given that each academy receives a £2 million annual investment, some club chief executives consider that more immediate results would accrue if it was ploughed into the transfer market. This short-term and greed-driven attitude will inexorably hasten the total globalisation of the football market and eliminate altogether scope in English players for improvement. In to-day's climate a great player, but late developer to achieve that status, such as Kevin Keegan, would still be plying his trade in Scunthorpe United reserves as Keegan in fact did for two years in the early part of his career.

What, then, is an effective nationalist response? One response is the imposition of a statutory maximum number of non-British players playing in any of the four major leagues. I suggest that no club should be allowed more than one foreign player, and then only for a short fixed-term contract, and no foreign manager should be permitted to manage an English club. This is not "xenophobic" or antiquated. It is the realistic application of very well-defined principles of national preference at a time of reconstruction. Another is that foreign ownership of English football clubs should be brought to an end. Richard Scudamore, chief executive of the Premier League, is the last person to be put in charge of this project. In an interview with *The Times* on 11 December he had this to say: "The switch to foreign ownership is inevitable and neither good, nor bad, like our airports being brought by foreign investors or British companies buying firms abroad."

I regard this as a total capitulation: a sell out of British or, more particularly, English soccer interests. The likes of Scudamore are unfitted to executive posts in the game. Presumably he colludes in Abramovich's funding of Chelsea F C which is tantamount to a mini-state subsidising its nationalised industry. The appropriate response is the invocation of English laws against unfair competition. One of Europe's football authorities, UEFA, is at least thinking on similar lines. At a recent plenary meeting it decided that Chelsea's multi-million pound recruitment policy of the likes of Shevchenko, Michael Ballack and Didier Drogba, subsidised by Abramovich's billions, is against European laws governing unfair competition. Here, at least, English law and European law speaks with one voice.

Support for reform has come from an unexpected source. Arsène Wenger (*The Times*, Wednesday 13 December) Arsenal's manager expressed concern about the uncompetitiveness of the premiership claiming that once the financial potential of clubs goes beyond their natural resources there emerges a recipe for bankruptcy. Mind you, Wenger has been the foremost practitioner of foreigner preference in his team selections in recent years.

Moreover, Lars-Christer Olsson, chief executive of UEFA, in a speech at the State of the Game, 2006 Report, by Birkbeck College, University of London emphasised that the problems experienced in the English game do not arise in other countries. "You have a system which allows speculation in football clubs ... listing clubs on the Stock Exchange is what is giving the opportunity for short-term investment in football clubs ... it would never be possible in Barcelona or Real Madrid because they are owned by their fans."

Olsson is right. The Spanish model with suitable adjustments to meet the conditions of the English game needs to be introduced here. The only effective way is through government action after legislation and tightly-knit regulation.

I would support the setting up of an English National Football Corporation, funded from national taxation passed into the sport and recreation budget. The E.N.F.C. would be given powers of compulsory purchase of foreign-owned English football club assets and then offer back 49% of ownership rights to private subscription within the body of genuine supporters in the locality of the particular club.

To those fainthearts who might complain that this is expropriation my answer is that the honour and integrity of the national game demands it. In any case, compulsory purchase is hardly a novel phenomenon. The Acquisition of Land (Authorisation Procedure) Act 1946 has been on the statute book for 60 years giving local authorities powers to acquire land in the essential national interest; by the same principle is it that the E.N.F.C. should be invested with the necessary powers. Foreign consortia and individuals would be bought out at realistic prices reflecting a club's actual worth and not the grossly inflated alleged market value, based as it is on imponderables such as anticipated values placed on players, endorsements and future expectations. Probably 50% of current value would represent an optimum figure. To illustrate my point the Watford player Ashley Young was valued at £5 million on 10th January 2007 but by 22 January, after competition for his services from West Ham, Tottenham Hotspur and Aston Villa, he was finally sold to Villa for £9.6 million; an interesting mark-up in less than a fortnight!

Each club would have the legal title in their assets vested in four trustees who would be drawn from the local community. Four is the maximum permitted by law and one would envisage prominent business people or professionals taking on this role, charging reasonable fees confined to their administrative duties. Additionally, each club would appoint facilitators who would be responsible for the allocation of a wider share ownership scheme and work in co-operation with the club's trustees in the dispensations of the club finances. The E.N.F.C. would retain an overall advisory and regulatory function and would keep ownership of 51% of each club's assets which might be used for the wider interests of the game and not necessarily be ploughed back into the club itself. A three-sided relationship between E.N.F.C., the trustees and facilitators would combine the best of the national and the local.

To achieve this mechanism all clubs would cease to be public companies and become unincorporated associations. From the appointed day under appropriate legislation clubs would be de-listed and decorporatised, that is have their company status abrogated. No dealings with individual shareholdings would take place without the sanction of the trustees and facilitators. The net beneficiary would be football itself and the football-loving public, not the greasy palms of finance-capitalists and short-term speculators. Football club leadership would be taken out of the hands of chairmen and profiteering shareholders and vested in responsible football club members, locally based.

Football managers would get on with the job of football management and their task would be simplified because those rapacious middlemen, football agents, would be prevented from functioning. Each professional player would be required to sign two contracts; one with the E.N.F.C. in which they would promise to uphold the ethics and best interests of the game as a sport with very heavy sanctions for breach and the second contract with the club for whom they play. Here I would advocate 12 month periods of contract with an option to renew, available to club and player for a further 12 months. Further extended periods could be negotiated. A player would not be permitted in any circumstances to breach his contract. A player would then become a free agent at the end of the contract – known in the game as the Bosman ruling, and it would mean the player could then pass to a new club without any transfer fee.

The elimination of transfer fees and the pernicious influence, as it is to-day, of agents is crucial to the well-being of the game. I would also advocate a ceiling on players' wages. The present nonsense has to end. A responsible formula would be that a limit is placed based on a correlation between the club's capital assets and its gross annual income. The practice of loaning players from one club to another would also come to an end and fall outside the terms of the player contract.

The elimination, or the near elimination, of transfer fees will render football agents obsolete. At present agents are creaming off massive fees which should be going back into the game. As a matter of public policy their true function needs to be identified. To whom are they accountable? An agent has to have a principal. Is it the player or the club? Lord Stevens' enquiry's recommendations have made some tentative proposals but they have no teeth. The drastic but necessary solution is that all players' concerns should be dealt with through their clubs. They are not selling a product but a service. Clubs under my reforms will be accountable to their trustees and the E.N.F.C. Agents will disappear from the game. The influence on the game of Abramovich's friend, the Israeli agent Pini Zahavi, is truly salutary. Here is a man involved in countless hundreds of transfer deals from which he has made millions of pounds in commissions. He helped to set up the Russian's Chelsea purchase, brokered a meeting between Abramovich and Eriksson, then England manager on a salary of £5 million a year, and was present at the illegal Ashley Cole 'tapping up' meeting. He also introduced Kia Joorabchiam to the West Ham board and is thought to have played a part in Alexandre Gaydamak's Portsmouth take-over. Zahavi is also an adviser to the Hero Football Fund, an investment vehicle that will buy stakes in promising players' transfer rights. Most recently Zahavi negotiated a £3 million payment for himself from Middlesborough when he arranged that club's £7.5 million purchase of his client player, Yakubu Aiyegbeni, from Portsmouth in July 2005.

The likes of Zahavi will have no place in the game if the new dispensation is introduced. It would then be up to the World football bodies, especially FIFA and UEFA to act in similar fashion.

English football is at the crossroads. Unless radical reforms are introduced within a relatively short timeframe I fear for the future of the game in this country. At present the likes of Stanley Matthews, Billy Wright and Alf Ramsay must be turning in their graves, appalled at the transformation of a great sport into corrupt business-dominated chicanery. Only the advent of a realistic government to power will bring about the will to institute the necessary radical reforms.

Other developments since I wrote this piece seven years ago have centred around a number of clubs, notably Leeds United, Everton and the club-collecting activities of Jordanian billionaire, Hasan Abdullah Ismaik. Ismaik, who owns a majority (60 per cent) stake in the German Second Division club, 1860 Munich, but not a voting control in the club (since only 49 per cent of the voting rights is permitted) has set his sights on buying into English football. He told *The Daily Mail*'s Sportsmail section in December 2015:

> "The difficulties we are facing in Germany mean we are ... regretting not coming to the UK, and we think we should now come and buy a club."

Just like that. No affinity with our country over a period of time. Simply being a fat cat serves the necessary purpose.

Leeds United have recently been the subject of a proposed buy-out from Massimo Cellino. On behalf of Leeds United Fans Ltd (LUF), of which he is the chief executive, Dylan Thwaites, an internet entrepreneur, made just under £60 million from selling his firm, Latitude. He now wants the latitude to front up a fan-based consortium. Half a million pounds has been raised but given that Leeds do not own their ground, are millions of pounds in debt and have a pretty average team in the Championship to boot, the prospects of acquisition are bleak – indeed, virtually unrealisable.

Meanwhile, an American consortium is allegedly seeking a £200 million take-over of Everton Football Club and an Asian-based consortium is also knocking at the door of Goodison Park.

So where do premiership club owners now come from in 2016?

England (7)	
Crystal Palace	(Steve Parish)
Everton	(Bill Kenwright)
Newcastle	(Mike Ashley)
Norwich	(Delia Smith & Michael Wynn-Jones – England/Wales)
Stoke	(Coates Family)
Tottenham	(Joe Lewis)
West Brom	(Jeremy Peace)
USA (5)	
Arsenal	(Stan Kroenke)
Aston Villa	(Randy Lerner)
Liverpool	(John W Henry)
Man Utd	(Glazer Family)
Sunderland	(Ellis Short)
Russia (2)	
Bournemouth	(Maxim Demin)
Chelsea	(Roman Abramovich)

Wales (2)	
Swansea	(Morgan Family)
West Ham	(David Sullivan & David Gold – Wales/England)
Italy (1)	
Watford	(Gino Pozzo)
Switzerland (1)	
Southampton	(Srivaddhanaprabha Family)
Thailand (1)	
Leicester	(Srivaddhanaprabha Family)
UAE (1)	
Man City	(Sheik Mansour)

The content of my original piece regarding football agents has effectively been endorsed by the distinguished sporting journalist of *The Times*, Matthew Syed.

In an article of 9 November 2015, he wrote:

> "There is a caricature of the average football agent as slimy, dodgy and treacherous. I have met probably over 30 or 40 over my time as a journalist, and do you know what? The caricature is wrong in only one crucial respect. It greatly under-estimates just how disreputable these parasites really are."

Explaining that the agent's role should be to nurture the development of players and to smooth the path into retirement at the appropriate time, Mr Syed went on to state:

> "Their incentive structure is to orchestrate a few high profile transfers and to bring in as much commission as possible ... the tragedy, of course, is that few agents have any conception of a fiduciary duty, and would not give a damn about it even if they did."

Cameron – How much Toryism?

This article appeared in *Right Now* magazine, January/February 2007 edition. It is my own assessment of David Cameron as Conservative Party leader before he became Prime Minister in 2010 when he won the general election of that year and formed a coalition with the Lib/Dems in government. Cameron was a competent parliamentarian but he did very little of Conservative traditional substance to mark him out as distinctively Tory. Having lost the referendum and handed over the reins to Theresa May his reputation has, as a consequence, been in decline. In my view, he only has himself to blame.

Although David Cameron is entitled to a short breathing space to settle in as Conservative leader, early signs are far from propitious. In fact, they are decidedly unfavourable, viewed from the standpoint of the traditional Right. Everything about Cameron suggests that he is predisposed to political, economic and social liberalism, and is determined to move the party in that direction.

I profoundly hope he fails. Compared with his leadership rivals – Clarke, Rifkind, Fox and Davis – I rate Cameron a clear fifth in ability and aptitude but then we are living in times when image, perception and shallowness dominate over substance, knowledge and experience. Cameron's CV is desperately thin for a party political leader. Bag carrier to Norman Lamont when Britain was catapulted out of the Exchange Rate Mechanism in 1992, public relations boffin with Carlton Communications PLC for several years (in a quasi-political capacity) and author of the party's election manifesto in May 2005, which was wholly devoid of seriously distinctive Tory substance, his record hardly represents the empirical test of achievement.

Against these factors, Cameron's educational background (Eton and Oxford) should stand in his favour, although privately he claims to be embarrassed by it. One does, however, wonder how much study Cameron has made of Tory antecedents. Does he appreciate or have any cognisance of Britain as our ancestral homeland; of the great Tory philosophers, scholars or writers who have contributed so much to conservative thought down the years – of Burke, Disraeli, Joseph Chamberlain and T S Elliot; of conservatism in an age of social revolution; of the idea of a spontaneous order, or the myth of a 'middle ground'? Cameron could usefully study the late Lord Coleraine's (Richard Law, son of Andrew Bonar Law) 1970 volume, *For Conservatives Only*, of which (Lord) Robert Blake, esteemed Tory historian, wrote, "It is, I believe, a very shrewd assessment of what has gone wrong with the Conservative Party and a notable blow against guff, humbug, hypocrisy and double-talk". What resonance these words have in the context of the Cameronian Conservative Party of 2006!

I suspect the foregoing passes Cameron by, for he travels with the lightest intellectual baggage of any Conservative leader, whatever his scholastic achievements may have been. This may explain why he appears consciously to avoid detailed debate, tending to rely on platitudes and generalism. There was no better illustration of this than during the recent fiasco of the EU budget debate, in which Blair agreed to sign up to the new £583bn EU budget for 2007-2013 without securing any commitment to slash large subsidies to French farmers and where, at the same time, Britain's contribution to Brussels was raised from £3.5bn to nearly £6bn in order to accommodate the new members from eastern Europe. Cameron's response should have been immediate and uncompromising in its tone, but it was neither. It was left to William Hague as foreign affairs spokesman to make the first Tory utterance, which was fairly bland and certainly not condemnatory. Cameron himself put in an average performance in his PMQ responses in parliament, which reinforces one's sense that he sees the EU as an issue to be avoided if at all possible. His approach is minimalist, as seen in his pledge to withdraw Tory MEPs from the European People's Party, when what is needed is a serious debate within all sections of the Conservative Party (those that still function, that is) of the merits of withdrawing altogether from the EU, given the obvious benefits of so doing.

I had a useful insight into the shape of things to come when I attended the Tory hustings meeting for Davis and Cameron in London in late November. Less than halfway into the meeting, half the audience appeared to be nodding off. At least Davis offered a view on substantially cutting immigration levels, whereas Cameron had nothing to say about this – although more recently he has declared what a wonderful thing mass immigration has been for our country and therefore implicitly how we should all be truly thankful for the colonisation of our country by foreigners.

On Iraq, in response to a question on what essential British national interest was at stake and how many more British soldiers are needlessly to be killed (present count, 98), Cameron boringly trotted out the tired old cliché of how we should stand by our American allies. Not for him any consideration of the possibility of non-intervention in the affairs of a sovereign, independent state, a wholly principled, and true Tory, position.

Behind the Cameron project of "challenge and change", on which he repeatedly pronounced with relish, lie some pretty unappealing figures, including the party chairman, the lugubrious Francis Maude, ex-party chairman Theresa May, who insulted every party worker at the annual conference in 2002 with her disgraceful comments about the Tories being 'the nasty party', the peripatetic propagandaist Nicholas Boles and millionairess businesswoman Margot James (see Editor's note below). It is to such figures that Cameron will be looking constantly for approval. He has already pleased them hugely. In a speech in Leeds in mid-December, Cameron made this foreboding declaration: "I'm today appealing to every woman in Britain, and everyone from a black or minority ethnic background who shares my passion to change Britain for the better, who shares our values, sitting in the room, or watching at home, to stand for parliament in the Conservative cause".

Aspiring Tory parliamentary candidates of traditionalist disposition should be under no illusions about the new Cameronian social order. The likes of Boles and James, the clones of (Lord) John Taylor of Warwick (see Editor's notes below), will be well to the fore in the 'priority list' of 140 target seats which the Tories will need to win to secure a majority in the House of Commons, while more conventionally Conservative candidates – e.g. white, middle-class, married, churchgoing, rugby-playing investment bankers – will no longer be in favour. An exaggeration? Perhaps, but that is indubitably the way in which the party is moving. Apart from any moral considerations, such positive discrimination runs the risk of rebounding on the Tories, by lumbering the party with all kinds of hopeless candidates who will make asses of themselves, just as 'Blair's Babes' have done.

If the Cameron project does succeed (which I doubt), it will be much more to do with economic downturn than 'middle ground' positioning. If such economic downturn fails to materialise, the party will be marooned in a mire of nothingness.

In conclusion, I note that the Cameronians have further groundbreaking ideas. Oliver Letwin, the policy supremo, has pronounced the party to be in favour of the redistribution of wealth, a doctrine marxist in conception and further to the left even than Old Labour countenanced when it introduced capital gains tax in 1965. At the same time, Bob Geldof has been appointed an adviser on global poverty to Iain Duncan Smith's Social Justice Commission, due to report in mid-2007. Geldof's long-held views are that 'racism' and a shortage of international aid are the Third World's major deficiencies, whereas most of us, I would suspect, consider that lack of bilateral trade agreements and bad governance are the main causes of the problem.

All this, and much more, leads me to believe that the Conservative Party has decided effectively to abolish itself.

Editor's Notes:

Nicholas Boles is a former Westminster Conservative councillor, and a prominent member of the so-called 'Notting Hill Tories'. He was co-editor (with Michael Gove and Ed Vaizey) of the 2001 work, *A Blue Tomorrow – New Visions for Modern Conservatives*. He came to public prominence during the general election of May 2005 by being an openly homosexual

Conservative candidate for what had been thought a winnable seat (Hove; he lost by a narrow margin). He is now the Director of the think-tank Policy Exchange.

Margot James co-founded The Shire Health Group in 1986, a public relations company in the healthcare sector now owned by Ogilvy & Mather (by whom she is now employed). She stood as the Conservative candidate in Holborn & St Pancras in the 2005 general election – the party's first openly lesbian candidate – and has recently been appointed a Conservative Party Vice Chairman, with responsibility for women.

John Taylor, a black barrister who unsuccessfully stood for the Conservatives in Cheltenham in the general election of 1992, was subsequently ennobled by John Major, a move widely (if privately) regarded at the time as tokenism. Much of Lord Taylor's energy since ennoblement has been consumed in criticising 'Tory racism', real or imagined – an activity which inevitably attracts accusations of ingratitude from some Tories.

Coalition government: Something of a damp squib

The advent of a coalition government filled me with foreboding. I assumed this would rule out any prospect of distinctive Toryism. My piece written for *The Clarion* magazine in July 2010 sets out my fairly low expectations and what would be needed in the national interest however low its likelihood of fulfilment. The catastrophe of the Iraq invasion and my view as to what should happen to Tony Blair are made clear. I hoped Cameron would offer something better in foreign policy. I also set out my reasons for extolling the benefits of economic nationalism, not as a replacement of free trade liberalism but as a corollary to it, for the reasons given with a number of beneficial examples.

The coalition has, of course, been replaced by a Tory administration. It is in its early stages and Cameron has resigned, replaced by Theresa May, his promise in January 2013 to hold a referendum on the European Union having now taken place with an outcome which, sadly for him, will haunt him for the rest of his days.

Elections come and go but nothing very much ever changes. The politics of liberal-internationalism remain dominant. This time, however, the people got what they didn't vote for – a coalition government of a distinctly pinkish hue. 'Call me Dave' Cameron is installed as Prime Minister and Nick Clegg is sucking up as his deputy.

Cameron's politics are very far removed from the nationalist tendency which once influenced Tory party thinking through the likes of Edmund Burke, Benjamin Disraeli, Joseph Chamberlain, Percy Wyndham Lewis, T S Eliot, John Biggs-Davison, Ronald Bell and Enoch Powell, to name but a few.

I doubt whether Cameron, who travels with the lightest intellectual baggage and who has never had a job outside the political milieu, sees himself as having anything in common with those scholars and luminaries. If he had been living in the 1840s, unlike them, he would have supported the Whig line and voted for the repeal of the Corn Laws which subjected British farmers to bankruptcy and ruin by allowing the importation of foreign wheat instead of protecting our own agricultural production.

Cameron is a liberal through and through. Certainly, he has a difficult immediate task with the massive budget deficit of £172 billion, the product almost entirely of international finance–capitalism, and I wouldn't lay long odds on his succeeding in reducing the deficit: the last thing he should be doing is crowing about having earmarked £6.2 billion in early cuts – no more than 3.7% of the grand total.

The practical imperative is to continue to get through to as large a number of people how different Tory nationalists are from others. To that end we need to emphasise that in two key areas, foreign policy and the economy, we have already been proved correct in our analysis and wholly justified in our propaganda. If we take the former first, we argue forcibly that the primary principle of international relations is that of non-intervention in the internal affairs of sovereign independent states. Iraq is a litmus test. Britain's intervention in that unhappy land has been the biggest foreign disaster since the second world war – worse even than Suez. It has been a wholly avoidable catastrophe. Blair was determined to risk the lives of our brave soldiers by obstinately refusing to give Hans Blix, the UN weapons inspector, the extra four weeks he had requested to put the non-existence of weapons of mass destruction beyond all reasonable doubt.

Moreover, Sir John Scarlett, director-general of the Secret Intelligence Service, MI6, had warned Blair and his associates that he (Blair) was inviting a Muslim backlash of potentially disastrous proportions and so it has turned out to be with the London bombings in July 2005 and the consequential constant high/severe terrorist threat warnings which MI5 has been compelled to issue ever since.

Blair may now be so-called Middle East peace envoy (fat lot of use he has been so far) although most of his time seems to be spent on a worldwide lecture tour boosting his already hyper-inflated ego to the tune of millions of pounds of fees from those stupid enough to listen to him. A more appropriate destination for this warmonger would be facing an indictment at the International Court of Justice at the Hague for waging aggressive war against a sovereign state. Over two hundred of our soldiers have had their young lives taken away in an illegal war – which manifestly it was because of the absence of an affirmative vote of the Security Council of the United Nations.

This veritable folly of invading Iraq, with whom we had no quarrel whatever given that the first Gulf war conflict had been concluded 12 years earlier, has proved our position to have been unimpeachable. So it is with Afghanistan. It may be a NATO operation but we are heavily involved and the death count of our soldiers already sadly exceeds that in Iraq.

Cameron's first words at the dispatch box after the Queen's speech were a spurious incantation and nauseating salutation to the latest victims of this avoidable war which is only attractive to the political class which no doubt sees a resource opportunity (oil pipeline construction contracts).

Cameron should have followed Labour Prime Minister, Harold Wilson's example in the mid-1960s when he refused to commit British troops to American President Lyndon Johnson's Vietnam war effort. That, too, as it proved to be, was an unwinnable war with a very heavy toll on lives. There was always an alternative to sending our young men on foot patrols only to be blown up by hidden bombs by snipers who fall back into the hills.

A Tory nationalist approach is decisive. It is to recall our troops immediately because of the indisputable reality that Britain's terrorists are bred and trained, not among the Taleban masses of Afghanistan in that backward, untameable land, but on the streets of our own towns and cities of England, as events have already demonstrated.

The second area of sound policy is to extol the benefits of economic nationalism. As Alastair Harper, in the last issue of *Identity* (Issue No 103) recently perceptively wrote: "the grand paradox of globalisation is that whilst on the surface it promises the unity of the world its effect is already bringing about the world's destruction." A timely truism which accentuates the need to argue why our alternative deserves proper scrutiny. Our difficulty is that the political class will not even debate the merits of protection, selective import controls and the primacy of manufacturing as a resource maximising profitability and full employment. In the hands of our opponents "British jobs for British workers" is a meaningless mantra for them and they know it. For us, it is the very lifeblood of the nation's well-being.

Economic nationalism, indeed, is a wholly relevant and appropriate doctrine. We should embrace it with fervour. At various times and under differing conditions, it has been endorsed by Disraeli, Joseph Chamberlain, John Maynard Keynes, J K Galbraith and (Lord) Robert Skidelsky (Keynes's biographer), all of whom have made out strong cases for the politics of protecting the home market against free trade liberalism.

Just as we used to adopt Imperial Preference beneficially towards the countries of our empire and later Commonwealth Preference so now we should engage in the idealism of National Preference supported by 'most-favoured nation' clauses in commercial contracts, where necessary, with foreign countries most favourable to our economic ideology.

Trading on world markets should be seen as complementary to, rather than as a replacement for, building an economy in which our objective is to strive for a high degree of self-sufficiency and autarky. Specifically, tariff barriers should not be seen as obstacles to efficiency but rather as the necessary means for bringing about full employment and higher productivity achieved under maximum employer/worker co-operation.

Nothing better illustrates the negation of the above than the present European economic system of enforced dumping of surplus agricultural production. Our policy should be (outside the constraints of the European Union which we would leave) to direct surpluses as we thought fit including, if necessary, alleviating genuine suffering and poverty. Such a policy is in antithesis to the disaster of free-trade globalism which only profits the very wealthy while impoverishing the rest of us. There has been no better illustration of this than how the abrogation of the Commonwealth Sugar Agreement in the late 1940s and early 1950s in which the collapse of the sugar market in Jamaica and Trinidad, because we could secure marginally better prices elsewhere, brought about increased unemployment in the West Indies and led to the precipitate migration of West Indian labour to the United Kingdom.

Some parallel consequence is seen in the Cadbury-Kraft take-over. Here, we had an iconic, household name; a profitable chocolate manufacturing company, founded in 1824 by Quaker brothers, employing 48,000 people worldwide with more than 9,000 at eight sites in Britain. Cadbury's shareholders were offered 840p for each share (probably a fair market price) plus a 10p share dividend, as against an original offer of 761p.

As usual in these sort of take-overs, the British workforce and its welfare seems to be the last thing to be considered. More than 10,000 job cuts world-wide is considered likely by analysts in order to slash costs to repay the cash Kraft requires to borrow for the deal. Somerdale, the Cadbury factory near Bristol, is already under closure and Kraft's record doesn't exactly exude confidence. In 1993 it bought chocolate manufacturer, Terry, and within two years it had closed its York factory having promised not to do so. The factory was sold to developers with production shifted to low-cost Eastern Europe. Kraft's poor reputation in the food industry is long established. It is shocking that a quintessentially philanthropic brand such as Cadbury, with its long history and overall excellence, has sold out to a plastic cheese company.

The precedents for Cadbury employees are unfavourable. For instance, when York-based Rowntree were taken over by Nestlé of Switzerland, within two decades the British company's workforce had been reduced from 33,000 to 3,250; a 90% shake-out.

Further take-overs of British industry are likely because of the fall in sterling, which makes companies cheaper for foreign buyers. A major target is Smith and Nephew, a leading developer of medical devices such as artificial hips. P & O suffered the full treatment. It was acquired by D P World of Dubai for £3 billion in 2006. Its shares have fallen by two-thirds, valuing its 52 ports, including Tilbury and Southampton, at only £4.5 billion. Corus, formed from the merger of British Steel with the Dutch group Hoogovens, was bought by the Indian conglomerate Tata in 2007. Corus announced just over a year ago that it would end steel-making in Teesside with over 2,000 jobs lost. Just about the only companies off-limits for take-over would seem to be Rolls Royce and BAE Systems, both major defence suppliers in which government retains substantial shares.

The wholesale decimation of British manufacturing industry by foreign companies and conglomerates has to be arrested. One step would be to cancel all 'most-favoured nation' status government contracts for reciprocal trading rights which we already have in place unless economic regulation is introduced to prevent the take-over/merger of industries in pursuit of free-trade liberalism.

Further than that, we should introduce compulsory purchase measures to make it unlawful for foreign companies to acquire anything more than a fractional stake in our businesses and industries. This can be achieved through pre-emption, a process authorising government to vest assets in a holding company, a national economic corporation, which would then re-distribute them on sale among prospering economic interests in Britain. Such a programme could have prevented the electricity and gas industries from falling into foreign hands over a period of 10 years.

Pre-emption is not a novel idea. It has operated for many years in a number of other countries, notably Switzerland, Austria, Greece and Japan, where it was instrumental in assisting that country's economic recovery in the mid-1990s.

Tory nationalists need to sweat blood and tears to bring about the necessary transformation.

The European Union: from despotism to national sovereignty

The European Union has passed through a number of phases, from the Treaty of Rome 1957, the Single European Act 1986, the Treaty of Maastricht 1992, the Treaty of Amsterdam 1998, the Treaty of Nice 2000 and, finally, the Treaty of Lisbon 2007. The Referendum Act 2015 paved the way for a national plebiscite to which the people gave a resounding affirmation of a desire to leave the European Union. I have written three separate articles.

The first was for my local newspaper *The Watford Observer* published on 21 January 1993, in response to Hertfordshire MEP, Derek Prag's piece a fortnight earlier. My opposition to the Maastricht Treaty is set out. The European Union came into being on ratification replacing the European Community which in turn had replaced the European Economic Community. The second article I wrote for *Identity* magazine which was published in September 2007. I set down the background to the Lisbon Treaty and developed my arguments, as have others, that it was nothing less than a political construct designed to remove the last vestiges of national sovereignty from the British people. My third article is a chronological account, between April and June, of how the protagonists, the Remain and Leave campaigns, developed their polemics with not a little ferocity, culminating in the result I had sought for over forty years. The mechanics of its implementation will not be fully known until after publication of this book.

(i) Maastricht Treaty disaster

Is Britain about to lose its essential identity: its very nationhood? If the Maastricht Treaty is ratified by all 12 countries there can be no doubt, the answer is "Yes". This concerns me greatly; it appears to concern Euro-MP, Derek Prag, not at all to judge by his article in *The Watford Free Observer* on 7 January 1993. Or perhaps Mr Prag has a different conception of what is at stake.

When Britain entered the EEC in 1973 I was an enthusiast as I saw an economic free trade area to be something of estimable value. I supported the "Yes" campaign in the 1975 referendum. Had anyone suggested at that time (Ted Heath, perhaps) that 18 years on Britain would be pointed irrevocably in the direction of a European super-state, of federal dimensions, against the popular will and with massive loss of national sovereignty I would not have believed it. Yet that is the prospect that now faces our British people, under the management of a highly Europhile government.

Derek Prag is a relentless Euro-enthusiast. He is entitled to be, but his piece gives a false perspective of how British interests are going to be satisfactorily preserved in an increasingly federal and bureaucratic state. A national opinion poll, taken in October 1992, showed that 75 per cent of the British people wanted a referendum on whether Britain should ratify the Maastricht Treaty. This is significant and hardly surprising given the shameful way our national politicians have avoided debate on the treaty's content and sought refuge behind meaningless jargon of the type that concludes Derek Prag's article: "They (the British) would choose to be with John Major, at the heart of Europe, with a full say in everything that goes on".

What a pity, then, that choice is to be denied our people if Major has his way on this most constitutional of issues. Could it be that Major knows full well that if he sanctioned a referendum he would lose resoundingly? The new European state, envisaged by Maastricht, confers new European citizenship to which all of us will be subject. A British national will now owe allegiance, as a citizen of Great Britain and Northern Ireland, not only to that national entity (and the Queen as its embodiment) but to the new super-nation of Europe. Allegiance is a very personal quality; historically, dual allegiance has led to disloyalty and opprobrium, and in some cases has brought with it cruel persecution. When, in a recent letter, I asked the Foreign Office what steps I would be able to take to renounce my new "European citizenship" (for which I feel repugnance and contempt) I was told there was no mechanism by which this could be achieved.

So there we have it. I, and millions like me, face the prospect of a compulsorily-imposed split loyalty. God Save the Queen! Hail Jacques Delors! Derek Prag misinforms his readers about "subsidiarity". Its meaning is far from "simple". How come that a recent convocation of constitutional lawyers was unable to place any objective meaning on the word? He then proceeds to quote five lines from Clause 3(b) of the Treaty but omits the key phrase of the clause – "in areas which do not fall within its exclusive competence"; and so the real question becomes: who determines which matters are within, or outside, this "exclusive competence"? The European institutions or the national parliaments? Almost certainly the former; why else Title 1, Article F(3) of th Treaty: "The Union shall provide itself with the means necessary to attain its objectives and carry through its policies".

No architect of General Powers enabling legislation could have done better. Both Mr Prag and Mr Major contend that subsidiarity moves power away from the European centre to the national parliaments. This is complete fiction. It does the reverse – it enhances the authority of the Commission and diminishes the status of national parliaments and nothing that was discussed at the Edinburgh Summit in December alters that position. Derek Prag thinks some of us are being a bit beastly about the Commission – "it is time we stopped being paranoid about the Commission", he declares. Really? The Commission, through its directives, imposes ever more rules, regulations and restrictions on our daily lives. Anyone who has read "Gulliver's Travels" must wonder if the EC Commissioners and their hordes of civil servants are a real life enactment of the "Academy of Projectors" at Lagado, so ridiculous are the majority of these directives. Who else would order the destruction of banana plantations in Madeira because the bananas grown there were "the wrong size"? Who else would seek to govern the shape of cucumbers or decree that the carrot must be classified as a fruit?

How absurd that EC policy ensures that surplus milk is poured down drains, while Cheddar cheese producers cannot get enough milk to produce their cheese because of EC rules, with the result we import £150 million worth of Cheddar cheese, thereby vastly adding to our balance of trade deficit? Nor is it purely in terms of arbitrary authority that the menace is manifest. The Commission, as the sole initiator of policy, gains immeasurably from the Treaty because virtually every facet of policy is brought within its purview. One of the benchmarks of a nation's independent status is its unfettered power to determine foreign policy. Particularly is this so with Britain. Herewith Title V, Article J(9) – "The Commission shall be fully associated with the work carried out in the common foreign and security policy field". There is not a shred of doubt that after Maastricht ratification the Commission is preparing to become the *de facto* Government of Europe, with Jacques Delors as Head of State and the 14 recently appointed Commissioners to senior government portfolios effectively in his Cabinet, with ever-increasing responsibilities. The way forward for those of us utterly opposed to the whole Maastricht edifice, and who would thus delight in its crumbling like a pack of cards, is to pressurise for a referendum in Britain and to assist the Danes as best we can in their new referendum campaign: the truth will ultimately come out and the Euro centralists will receive a rude awakening.

(ii) The Lisbon Treaty – its true nature

What part have conspiracies played in the evolution of political thought and action? Despite the risk that those uttering such sentiments may be thought appropriate candidates for internment in a mental institution, the question is a serious one: it has far more poignancy than those who would reject the idea out of hand may care to admit.

In the United States, the secretive meetings of shadowy bodies such as the Council on Foreign Relations, the Trilateral Commission and the Bilderberg Group are well documented. Indeed, it is not at all far-fetched to describe the deliberations of such groupings as "conspiratorial". More recently, we have witnessed the enormous power of the neo-con lobby, prompted by powerful unelected figures such as Paul Wolfowitz and Richard Perle, in formulating American foreign policy towards Iraq and Afghanistan with the pretty disastrous consequences evident for all to see. Both adventures have become prime illustrations of what the dissenting lobby in Vietnam in the 1960s, with every justification, used to call 'a no-win war'.

In the United Kingdom, we have had a fair share of criminal conspiracies: the Gunpowder Plot to blow up the House of Lords in 1605 during James I's state opening of parliament and the Cato Street conspiracy in 1820, involving a plot to murder four cabinet ministers just before George IV's accession to the throne readily come to mind.

Much more recently, in 1966, Harold Wilson, then Labour Prime Minister, described the seamen's strike of that year as being promoted by "a tightly knit group of politically motivated men" who organised that crippling stoppage over a six-week period. He was, in fact, referring specifically to the part played by the British Communist Party's (CPGB) industrial organiser, Bert Ramelson, from the party's headquarters in London.

Towards the end of his premiership, moreover, Wilson became convinced that there was an M15 plot to unseat him and reveal him as a Soviet agent (for which allegation there was minimal evidence).

Yet, by a fair distance the most far-reaching, damaging and significant conspiracy ("a secret plan or agreement to carry out an illegal or harmful act, specially with political motivation, a plot, the act of making such plans in secret" – Collins' dictionary) has been how the political élite have succeeded in dragooning the United Kingdom, through unrelenting lies and deception, into what is now known as the European Union.

Right back to the times of Jean Monnet and Robert Schuman in the late 1940s and early 1950s, the so-called 'European Construction' was the ultimate ambitious objective: that the countries of Western Europe should eventually come together in complete political and economic union. The setting up of a common market, itself never intended to be a free trade area but rather a highly regulated internal market protected against external competition by tariff barriers, was regarded as merely a first step along the political pathway, treaty by treaty, as dictated by circumstances, always moving us in the same direction towards that distant, never clearly defined goal of a federal European state.

A culture of deceit has permeated all decision-making. Our politicians and civil servants have sought to downplay the significance of "Project Europe" and to present it to the wider public as something essentially different from what it has come to be, and, more importantly, what they knew all along it would come to be. This, of course, meant that every time a fresh step towards the new state was being contemplated – and witness how, almost surreptitiously, the European Economic Community became the European Community and ultimately the European Union – British politicians of all the main parties have first expressed opposition as a tactical ploy to much of what their continental partners were proposing but then, with supine weakness and duplicity, fell in line and in doing so deliberately concealed from the British people just how much they had surrendered.

An appalling consequence, one of many, is the extent to which our entire political system has become enmeshed with that of the European project and how so much of the legislation which rules our lives now emanates from Brussels, through regulations and directives. Revealed knowledge from state papers explains the depth of this treachery and the long-term planning behind it. The Public Records Office in Kew has disclosed a number of extremely salutary documents which I have been able to examine.

When Edward Heath, then Minister of State for Europe, visited Professor Hallstein, then President of the European Commission, in November 1960, his report on that meeting noted how Hallstein had emphasised that joining the community was not just a matter of adopting a common tariff but an introduction to a new statehood. It would be necessary, insisted Hallstein, for any new entrant to accept the principle that the EEC was intended to evolve into something much deeper – "some form of federal state" which was what the Commission was working towards. [Source: PRO/FO/371/150369].

A particularly informative document was called the *Werner Report*. In 1969, the Council of Ministers had commissioned the Prime Minister of Luxembourg, Pierre Werner, to draw up a plan to move the Common Market forward to full economic and monetary union. This confidential report began circulating amongst Brussels bureaucrats in October 1970 just as Britain's negotiations to enter the EEC were getting underway.

It was at this time that a secret briefing note to Heath from Con O'Neill, the senior civil servant responsible for Europe, explained that, if implemented, Werner's proposals would have enormous political repercussions. O'Neill's memorandum described "a process of fundamental importance, implying progressive development towards the political union … going well beyond the full establishment of a common market". The Werner plan, it was claimed, would lead to "the ultimate creation of a European Federal State, with a single currency". All the basic instruments of national economic management (fiscal, monetary, income and regional policies) would be transferred to the central federal authority. The Werner report concluded that the radical transformation of present communities should be accomplished within a decade [PRO/FCO/30/789].

In the light of that assessment from Con O'Neill, Edward Heath's shameful behaviour disclosed the true extent of his political dishonesty and total absence of candour towards the British people. Just consider: In his *White Paper*, circulated to every household in the country in June 1971, Heath stated: "There is no question of Britain losing essential sovereignty" – a lie. And then, in a television broadcast to mark Britain's entry to the EEC in January 1973, Heath affirmed: "There are some in this country who fear that in going into Europe we shall in some way sacrifice independence and sovereignty. These fears, I need hardly say, are completely unjustified". Again, a lie, a particularly brazen one with revelatory consequences for the

British people insofar as Heath had always managed to project himself as a man of honour and integrity.

As the years have gone by so has the Eurosceptic antipathy to the whole construction been reinforced with incontrovertible justification. British life has become the victim of an implanted alien virus. The conflict between metric and imperial measures is merely one dramatic symbol of this conflict. Others present themselves at all levels of our involvement with politicised Europe: hideous costs; the destruction of our fishing waters; the corruption of the Brussels bureaucracy [the community's accounts, for instance, have been rejected by the Court of Auditors for three years]; the sheer waste inherent in the Common Agricultural Policy requirement of dumping surpluses in production.

The political dimension, to be sure, is that France and Germany are determined to assume dominance and ultimately hegemony of the continent of Europe. No doubt for them it would be hugely convenient if the history books could be re-written so that Henry V had lost at Agincourt in 1415 or that Nelson had failed at Trafalgar in 1805, or that Wellington had not triumphed against Napoleon at Waterloo in 1815. Painful memories, so let Britain, pipsqueak nation, perfidious Albion, disappear, sucked into a province of the giant octopus of Greater Europe (or Eurabia as it will come to be in fifty years time unless we collectively institute massive re-emigration of alien populations from our continent).

The sorry condition of politicised Europe, achieved within two generations through the betrayals of Rome, Maastricht, Amsterdam and Nice, just gets worse. The latest abomination, the Treaty of Lisbon, needs patient analysis. Of course the Euro-fanatics claim it to be something essentially different from the unlamented and failed constitution. Paradoxically, it was Ireland in the person of Bertie Ahern, its former leader, that secured agreement on the constitution while chairing the Brussels summit of 2004. Ireland itself had rejected the Nice Treaty of 2001. The pathway to the Lisbon Treaty began in May 2000 when Joscha Fischer, then German Foreign Minister called for a European constitution which was duly endorsed by EU leaders in December 2001 at Laeken, near Brussels, in the shape of a "constitution for European citizens". In July 2003, the text of the constitution, written by no less a personage than Valéry

Giscard d'Estaing, former French President, was handed over with appropriate pomp to the respective EU nations' governments. The Constitution was signed in Rome in October 2004. Spain ratified it by referendum with a 77% 'yes' vote in February 2005 after massive government propaganda unchallenged by a tepid Eurosceptic press, but the French rejected it by 54% - 48% in May 2005, while the Dutch gave it a 61% 'no' vote three days later. Something sturdy about the French and the Dutch! European leaders and the entire bureaucracy broke out in a hot sweat and flat panic. What to do?

Step forward Angela Merkel, German Chancellor. Democracy must not be allowed to get its way. She demanded and obtained an inter-governmental conference to propose a new text. This saw the light of day in October 2007. The new document was, in fact, an old style "amending treaty" rather than a replacement of previous agreements.

The relatively clear language of the 448-article constitution disappeared to be replaced by a legal jungle of cross-references, amendments, sub-texts, deletions and protocols. The formulators within the bureaucracy had triumphed. No one would be able to understand it or, if they did, have the patience to digest it. It was to be named the Lisbon Treaty, technically described as: "The Treaty amending the Treaty establishing the European Union and the Treaty establishing the European Community". Phew!

Ratification of the Treaty took place in Britain on 18 July 2008, in a cloak of secrecy, only made known to the public on the previous day. The instrument of ratification was signed by the Queen and delivered to the Italian foreign ministry on 20 July.

Not for us the opportunity of a referendum despite the promise of one made at the time of the last election on the constitution by Blair and later endorsed by Brown. Both have consistently denied (they would, wouldn't they?) that the Treaty is effectively the defunct constitution tidied up, yet there is an abundance of evidence, as I shall come to demonstrate, that essentially it is substantively the same. New Labour knew perfectly well that a referendum on Lisbon would produce a resounding 'no' vote: therefore, everything had to be done to scotch such an absurd idea.

Of course, the Irish referendum result should have scuppered the Treaty altogether in that all 27 countries have to ratify it.

President Sarkozy of France, King of the Europhiles, in a speech to the European parliament in early July 2008, put his own distinctive stamp on the Irish vote: "Irish voters have plunged the EU into crisis with their rejection of the Treaty. It is Europe's duty to act now".

Sarkozy's brilliant idea is that the Irish should have another referendum and if that goes the wrong way then another, and, if necessary, another. What cynicism!

Our own House of Lords has behaved with little less ignominy. It failed miserably on 11 June and then 18 June, respectively, in first declining to amend the Treaty Bill to provide for a referendum and secondly in refusing to delay ratification so as to debate the implications of the Irish vote.

In the aftermath of Ireland's vote the architects of the European conspiracy lost no time in strengthening their resolve. Giscard d'Estaing told *The Irish Times* newspaper on 21 July that the rejection would not kill the Treaty (as legally it should have done). "We're evolving towards majority voting because if we stay with unanimity we will do nothing".

At least the Czech government showed a degree of independent spirit. It postponed ratifying the Lisbon Treaty while its constitutional court decided whether approving the text was lawful. And the Polish President, Lech Raczyuski, refused to ratify the Treaty on 1 July. We must hope he too stands his ground.

The substantive content of the Lisbon Treaty is what is so crucial for the British people to grasp. It represents the biggest ever transfer of power to the European Union. The number of vetoes given away by the Treaty is more than twice the number given away at Maastricht in 1992 and five times more than in the creation of the single market in 1986. To be precise, the Treaty of Rome gave away 38 vetoes, the Single European Act 1986 12 (and it is worth here remembering that Mrs Thatcher claimed she had never appreciated its true effect); the Maastricht Treaty gave away 30 vetoes, the Amsterdam Treaty of 1998 24, the Nice Treaty of 2000 46 but the Lisbon Treaty surrenders 63 vetoes from British control to European Union control – that is to say, 63 areas of political action where our government cannot stop the EU from passing new laws on every facet of our British national life.

The context in which this shameful betrayal has been allowed to happen is there to see for all who wish to examine the texts.

Jean-Claude Juncker, Prime Minister of Luxembourg, put the essence of the matter clearly: "Of course there will be significant transfers of sovereignty", (*The Daily Telegraph*, 3 July 2007) while carefully adding that he would not want to draw the attention of the British people to too much specific detail. But he did give a clear overall perspective:

> "There is a single legal personality for the EU, the primacy of European law, a new architecture for foreign and security policy; there is an enormous extension in the EU's power; that is the Charter of Fundamental Rights."

Meanwhile, the European Commission waits patiently and malignly for more pliable British politicians who can be cajoled into abandoning the so-called "red lines" purporting to exempt Britain from a variety of Treaty commitments. In any event, these reservations will collapse anyway when the European Court of Justice gets to work on the Treaty. It is, perhaps, worth considering the true nature of the ECJ. It is not the sort of court which sits comfortably with or derives its authority from British legal structures or British jurisprudence. When the community's originators first established the ECJ their model was the Conseil D'Etat of France. It set the precedent for the EEC's legal procedures. As far back as 1964, in the case *Costa v Enel (Case 6/64)* the judgment concluded that "the transfer by the States from their domestic legal system to the community legal system of the rights and obligations under the Treaty carries with it a permanent limitation of their sovereign rights, against which a subsequent unilateral act at variance with community principles cannot prevail".

In essence, therefore, the ECJ is revealed as an administrative law court with competence to rule on any legal issue linked to, or arising out of, administrative actions. It is effectively now an arm of government – the government of the new state, the European Union – with no real judicial independence.

Reverting to the Lisbon Treaty, the true nature of its contents was declared in Parliament in July by Michael Connarty MP, the Labour Chairman of the European Scrutiny Committee:

> "Every provision of the Constitution, apart from the flags, mottos and anthems, is to be found in the Lisbon Treaty. We think they are fundamentally the same and the government have not produced a table to contradict our position?"

Speaking to the European Parliament on 27 June 2007, Angela Merkel admitted that:

> "the substance of the constitution is preserved. That is a fact."

Addressing the Constitutional Affairs Committee of the European Parliament on 17 July 2007, Giscard d'Estaing, in his capacity as chairman of the convention which drew up the EU Constitution had this to say:

> "In terms of its content the proposals remain largely unchanged; they are simply presented in a different way ... the reason is that the new text could not look too much like the constitutional treaty."

Meanwhile Bertie Ahern, then Prime Minister of Ireland, told *The Irish Independent* newspaper on 24 June 2007:

> "They haven't changed the substance – 90 per cent of it is still there."

And for Gordon Brown:

> "We will put the European constitution to the British people in a referendum and campaign wholeheartedly for a 'yes' vote." (Labour Party election manifesto).

What do these remarkable declarations from the political élite tell us? Nothing less than that a massive confidence trick has been perpetrated on the peoples of Europe so that they should never come to understand the treachery being practised upon them. For our own people, not once has Gordon Brown attempted to explain how he considers the Lisbon Treaty not to be the same contextual document as the constitution when all the accumulated evidence is that there are no differences and that, therefore, the denial of a referendum is a dreadful breach of a promise made in patently clear terms.

The entire New Labour collection of globalists, careerists and opportunity seekers know perfectly well that whatever 'red lines' may have been reserved in practice they will not be sustainable. They will be challenged in the European Court of Justice and, to be sure, the UK. will be placed in a situation where the whole treaty will apply to it because of a steady transfer of jurisdiction to the Council of Ministers, the Commission and the ECJ.

The devil's in the detail. So what are the crucial provisions of the Lisbon Treaty which will finally erode Britain's sovereignty and formalise its position as a vassal state in the new European order of federalism?

Article 4(2) has been added to the Treaty protocol giving the EU legal powers to influence the UK. into participating in EU plans to control our legal system and specifically to comply with EU rulings in areas of justice and home affairs.

Article 61(4) allows the EU to pressurise the UK. into recognising the judicial decisions of other EU member states. This is known as the reciprocity principle and will lead to a harmonisation of civil law and place severe constraints upon our common law principles and statute.

Article 69D(a) will give the EU Euro-just arm the power to initiate criminal investigations and the power to instruct national authorities to begin proceedings while **Article 69E(4)** makes provision for a European public prosecutor (who can override any decision by the Crown Prosecution Service) and for mandatory co-operation between the police forces of member states. Implicit in this is the exchange of information, training, research methods and investigation techniques (none of which would be exceptionable if done on a voluntary basis). **Article 69G** will expand the powers of Europol making it the EU police force.

Under **Article 68(3)** the Brussels institutions will have the power to force Britain to adopt identity cards and the Treaty will further exacerbate the disastrously porous condition of Britain's borders by permitting the EU to take full control over Britain's asylum and immigration policies.

All of these provisions will, of course, place more costs on the British taxpayer. The effect of **Article 63(b)** is that Britain will be expected to share the financial burden of immigration which in practice means we will be supporting asylum seekers in EU states that have a lower gross domestic product than the UK.

Article 62(l)(a) entrenches what we already know to be the *de facto* position: that there will be no controls on persons, whatever their nationality, when crossing internal borders – in other words, uncontrolled immigration from within Europe will continue.

A particularly sinister development (among many let it be said) is that by **Article 63(l)** the EU is given power to decide on who, and for how long, residents of non-EU states, even those from the Commonwealth, will be able to stay in Britain. The EU will also determine the border checks these people will face.

Article 46(A) confirms the EU's ability to sign international agreements that will be binding upon the UK, reinforcing the surely irrefutable argument that the EU is already a state in its own right.

Article 308 has a particularly far-reaching effect on our national life. It is that the Lisbon Treaty will be self-amending. It will allow more expansions in the EU without national parliaments and electorates having to agree such transfers. The Nice Treaty gave power to do this but only to assist the processes of the single market but **Article 308** deletes reference to the single market, thereby allowing the EU to expand beyond the limits of the Lisbon Treaty itself.

Nothing escapes the tentacles of the EU's grasp. Even energy provision. **Article 176(b)** could mean that the UK will become obliged to supply energy to another member-state if that state is having difficulties with its own networks. Furthermore, by **Article 100(l)**, Britain will be compelled to share its reserves at any time of crisis as adjudged by the Commission.

When concerns were raised by the oil and gas industry about the implications of **Article 100(l)** that proposal was removed from the final text of the then EU Constitution. Now, however, by subterfuge most cunning, it has found its way back into the text of the Lisbon Treaty threatening our energy resources.

Despite the so-called 'red line' over taxation that the government claimed it secured, the reality is different because much of our taxation is already controlled by the EU: for instance, indirect taxation (VAT) and business tax which has been dominated by decisions made by the ECJ. Then there is the EU taxation code of conduct which seeks to use stealth to harmonise taxes by eliminating tax competition: that is, the EU wants to stamp out low taxes and maintain unnecessarily high rates. What is more, as a result of the government's cowardly surrender of the rebate, the British taxpayer will be giving up £9.3 billion each year and, since the accounts are not properly audited – and what a scandal that in itself is – we do not know where the money ends up.

The government repeatedly claims there will be no EU foreign minister with control over foreign policy. The truth is the reverse. They don't actually use the designation "foreign minister" but the grandiose title "the High Representative of the Union for Foreign Affairs and Security Policy" – a post known to be coveted by the peripatetic Tony Blair no less. In any case, **Article 9E(l)** will abolish the UK veto over the appointment of the High Representative and under **Article 28(4)** the High Representative will also have authority to propose EU military missions.

EU interference even extends to our prison system in the UK. The Lisbon Treaty will endorse **Directive 2004/38/EC** which prevents the UK from deporting European criminals. The Human Rights Act 1998 has already caused havoc with the UK's efforts to fight crime. We can be sure that the ECJ will use the Charter of Fundamental Rights to further interfere with our legal processes.

The geopolitical argument that 'an ever-closer Europe' will bring to an end all European conflicts is a manifest absurdity. The history of the Balkans is a classic illustration of the opposite. In the early 1990s Germany was determined to bring about an independent Croatia but in so doing accelerated the break-up of Yugoslavia. The United States was an ally of Germany in this needless international meddling. The EU, being a federation, likes to smash up other federal states before swallowing them into its embrace. In co-operation with NATO it deliberately undermined Serbia and advocated the bombing of Serbian towns and cities in 2002. It is already taking great delight in recognising the illegal state of Kosovo, part of Serbian territory, where the Christian Serbs have been progressively depopulated over the last 15 years and seen their ancient monastic Christian heritage destroyed and replaced by an Albanian Islamic hegemony (see further my piece on the destruction of the Federal Republic of Yugoslavia on page 256).

In the ongoing climate of treachery and decadence, what needs to be the response to the political class whom history will judge harshly by their deeds? Above all, let us re-assert at every opportunity available to us that what constitutes nationhood is territorial integrity, national independence from internationalist cliques and unfettered parliamentary sovereignty achieved through national democracy.

As a corollary, let us make abundantly clear through all the organs of the media that are open to us that the European Union, the hostile vehicle of politicised Europe, is wholly at variance with our ideals.

Let us further re-assert that for us Europe is nothing more or less than a continent, a geographical entity. Certainly we rejoice being part of a European civilisation which has embraced most of the creative influences of the world; in writing, music, architecture, medicine, engineering and philosophy – compare the exact opposite from the continent of Africa and other backward regions of the world – but that we have no destiny to merge our nation with others into a monolithic structure.

People of nationalist disposition should commit themselves to working unremittingly for the implosion of the European Union, the likelihood of which is far less improbable than many may imagine; consider the sudden demise of the Soviet Union in 1989. More directly, we should strive to get as many like-minded candidates elected to the European Parliament in 2009 and ultimately to the national parliament at Westminster where, in concert with other Eurosceptic MPs, we can obtain a majority to repeal the European Communities Act 1972 in order to take our country out of the European Union.

In the meantime, on the economic front we should take every opportunity to challenge our political opponents to explain precisely how membership of the EU is profitable to us when all the evidence is that we would be far better off out, whereupon we would be free to enter bi-lateral trading arrangements, perhaps on most-favoured nation terms, with individual EU countries as well as the outside world as is the case with Norway, Austria and Switzerland. Outside Europe it is China and India which are becoming the economic power houses.

We must never forget that the European question, at heart an issue of identity, is inextricably linked with that of immigration. These two great issues of our time are ideologically complementary, reflecting the deepest aspirations of a nationalist philosophy which demands the return of *our* land to *our* people.

(iii) The great referendum debate – A chronological survey

10 April 2016

Free movement of people and labour is restated by the European Commission (effectively the government of the European Union together with the Council of Ministers), as one of the fundamental principles of the EU. Albania, Macedonia, Montenegro and Turkey are all bidding to join the EU. Yet the Remain campaign, through its propaganda leaflet, for that is what it is, costing over £9 million, asserts that immigration will, for the foreseeable future, be of the same order whether we stay or leave. This is the height of pessimism and almost certainly palpable nonsense, given that 47% of all immigration to the UK is from EU countries and the UK is powerless to prevent it.

Iain Duncan Smith of the Leave campaign makes the very evident and incontrovertible point that it is simply not true that the German government, for instance, would not export motor cars to Britain because Chancellor Merkel might disapprove; or that the French government would cease selling farming products to us, or that the Italian government would forgo the opportunity to sell its goods or services to us.

13 April

Chris Grayling of the Leave campaign takes a swipe, and rightly so, at Barack Obama for abusing his hospitality in Britain by making a thoroughly contentious speech in which he said that the UK would be placed "at the bottom of the queue" for trading deals with America. Grayling further states that Obama doesn't understand the nature of our relationship with Brussels and that Obama is asking the British people to accept a situation that he would not himself recommend for the American people. Further, Boris Johnson describes Obama as "downright hypocritical" with every justification, arguing that "for the United States to tell us in the UK ... to surrender control of so much of our democracy is a breathtaking example of the principle of 'do as I say but not as I do'. Well said Boris!

15 April

On the second day of his somewhat controversial visit to the UK, Obama stresses that while it is the British people's decision whether or not to leave the EU (how generous of him) it is right to make the case that the UK, and by extension its ally America, is stronger and more prosperous if the UK remains a member of a stable EU.

This is mere unsubstantiated waffle, devoid of serious substance. It ignores the reality that the UK would be far better off negotiating bilateral trade deals not only with America, but Brazil, China, India, Russia and Japan – markets as large or even larger than the EU, as well as individual EU countries who, individually, would benefit substantially.

Matthew Elliott of Leave makes the salient point that America zealously defends its own sovereignty even to the point of refusing to pay the congestion charge, yet Obama thinks the UK should hand more power over our affairs to the Brussels bureaucrats and EU judges.

19 April

Simon Heffer, esteemed columnist of *The Sunday Telegraph*, writes of "a torrent of exaggeration, distortion and forecasts based on apocalyptic assumptions" emanating from Cameron and his Downing Street propaganda machine.

As the campaign gets into full swing Heffer writes that the Leave campaign has made a somewhat dismal start, complaining that it seems reluctant to enter the fray on the issues that most upset the public: mass immigration and the vulnerability to international terrorism that it creates. He makes the point that Leave seems to represent little more than Tory 'outers' which sidelines excellent campaigners like Labour MP, Kate Hoey, and Nigel Farage of UKIP, a popular and articulate proponent of leaving.

I concur that the Leave campaign must become a broad church, something of vital importance to a successful outcome.

22 April

Theresa May, Home Secretary, who has nailed her colours to the Remain campaign mast, makes a highly unusual contribution to the debate by lambasting the Euro and proclaiming that staying in has major risks for the UK. I ask myself whether she is trying to position herself strategically so that she will be regarded as a Tory peacemaker in the inevitable troubles to come in the party. If so, she is making a pretty good fist of it.

As regards the economy, she states that it is nonsense to argue that Britain is too small a country to flourish outside the EU because we are the fifth biggest economy in the world and growing faster than any economy in the G7 countries, attracting nearly a fifth of all foreign investment in the EU.

Lord Howard from the Leave campaign presents a less sanguine perspective on Mrs May and immigration. "It is a humiliating spectacle to watch the Home Secretary admit that immigration is too high but there is nothing she can do to stop it".

How right is Michael Howard.

25 April

Kate Hoey, down-to-earth, excellent parliamentarian, in an article in *The Daily Express*, places the Remain/Leave divergence in perfect context:

> "Those campaigning to remain betray their lack of confidence in their own country. They say that the UK is too small, too weak to survive outside the bureaucratic colossus. They are so wrong. We know that, as the fifth largest economy in the world with a seat on the UN Security Council and ancient friendships including the Commonwealth, whom we so disgracefully abandoned, we would not just survive but would prosper as an independent power."

How comfortably that sits compared with the waffle and tendentious scare-mongering we have heard from David Cameron and George Osborne.

28 April

The deliberate exaggeration that all major financial companies, institutions and their executives support the Remain camp has been nobbled. More than 100 senior city figures sign an open letter calling for a Leave vote. Matthew Elliott, Vote Leave chief executive, declares: "It is clear that the City of London would not only retain its pre-eminence as the world's most important financial centre, but would also thrive after freeing itself from the EU's regulatory shackles".

Fat cats like Sir Philip Green, of Top Shop and the failed BHS, now know where to put their opinions. They are well on the way to losing the argument.

Meanwhile, Nigel Farage makes the crucial point on immigration that Britain risks a Turkish hegemony over the EU, whether that happens soon or in the distant future. With its 70 million Muslim population, Turkey's accession would lead to a serious conflict with Christian civilisation and its European heritage. Incidentally, since when has Turkey been located in Europe? It is an Asian country and should not qualify for membership of the EU.

8 May

The campaign warms up. Downton Abbey creator, Julian Fellowes, adopts a scholarly, philosophical approach to the issues. In calling for Britain to leave, Fellowes, an Oscar-winning dramatist, likens the EU to the Austro-Hungarian empire, the collapse of which plunged the continent into the First World War. Fellowes states: "I believe we should be out. It's about philosophy, it's about democracy versus autocracy. It's not just that I think they are important, because they are, but I think it's the wrong direction. History has for hundreds of years been moving towards government that is answerable to the people and yet suddenly we have done an about-turn and we've gone back to the Austro-Hungarian empire. I don't think that's the right direction.

9 May

Franklin D Roosevelt, former US President, once articulated the wise words: "Let me assert my firm belief that the only thing we have to fear is ... fear itself; nameless, unreasoning, unjustified terror". How apt as we contemplate David Cameron's ridiculous and patently untrue remark that by leaving the EU we place in jeopardy peace and risk starting a Third World War. So weak are Cameron's arguments that he can only resort to unutterable balderdash of a type which has no foundation in fact.

Meanwhile, the Japanese PM, Shinzo also trots out virtually the same words as Obama in calling for a Remain vote. The hand of Cameron is clearly detectable in the language used even if written for him by a Downing Street subordinate.

10 May

In an interview with Andrew Marr on BBC, Michael Gove, Justice Secretary, asserts that we should have access to the single market, but that we should not be governed by the rules that the European Court of Justice imposes on us, which are a cost to business and restrict freedom.

In particular, Mr Gove states that key markets would not be hit by tariffs because European countries are sensitive enough to appreciate that they would not wish to harm trade with the UK, Brexit or no Brexit, and specifically that no German finance minister would go to BMW Motors to tell them to lay off workers because Britain needs to learn a lesson and be punished, given that Germany sells more cars to us than we do to them; or that a French government would tell their farmers that they can no longer sell wine and cheese in the event of a Brexit vote.

Of course, Chancellor George Osborne, more technocratic than ever, waffles on about how wrong Gove has been.

The single market (introduced by the Single European Act 1986) only allows trade with non-European members if all 28 member states of the EU agree.

11 May

David Cameron makes reference to Britain's war dead from the First and Second World Wars in support of his vacuous and wholly irrelevant arguments in favour of remaining in the EU. He is becoming ever more desperate in his scaremongering tactics and is seeming to suggest that a Third World War could be the product of a Leave vote. Has he taken leave of his senses if he seriously believes the electorate will fall for this sort of nonsense?

Boris Johnson declares that the Remain campaign's latest attempt to win votes in next month's EU Referendum "has turned Project Fear into Project Armageddon".

In a keynote speech in London, Johnson successfully presents Britain as a country on the brink of a great escape from subjugation and condemns Cameron for his complete failure to curb immigration with hopeless, unattainable targets.

12 May

Colonel Richard Kemp, who commanded British forces in Afghanistan, accuses campaigners of putting words in the mouths of war veterans who have been wheeled out to support the Remain campaign on the basis of incomplete information. A spokesman for *Veterans for Britain*, supporters of Brexit, asks whether they realise they are signing up to a project that undermines the autonomy of the UK's armed forces.

Speaking at the Vote Leave's London Headquarters, Iain Duncan Smith attacks the social injustice of EU policies which have become a friend of the haves rather than the have nots. He emphasises that Cameron gave in to Angela Merkel's demand to drop his so-called EU membership renegotiation "red line" – an emergency brake on immigration – with the result that it vanished when Cameron revealed his very limited demands in November 2015.

The truth will always emerge. It is now indisputable that Cameron is much influenced by Merkel and that Germany has a major part in dictating British European foreign policy.

13 May

The cost of educating 700,000 children from the EU in British schools is revealed to have risen to £3.4 billion a year. This is a figure that has almost doubled since 2006 and is directly attributable to free movement of people rules within the EU. Employment Minister, Priti Patel, reiterates what all but Cameron and his advisers seem to know: that gross immigration is completely out of control and will continue to remain so unless we leave on 23 June.

A government study of the impact of immigration will not now be revealed until after the Referendum – a typical subterfuge to discourage Britons from voting to leave.

Meanwhile, Boris Johnson, who is having a powerful impact on the referendum debate, compares the EU's ultimate aim of creating a federal European superstate with the historic ambitions of Philip II of Spain, Frederick the Great, Napoleon and Hitler. Johnson is absolutely right and increasingly more and more people realise it.

14 May

Christine Lagarde, Head of the International Monetary Fund, delivers a ridiculous scaremongering report to the effect that Brexit will be an unmitigated economic disaster, for which highly dubious pronouncement she produces minimal accurate factual evidence. Madame Lagarde and her colleagues' opinions will prove to be trumped by the good sense of the British people, given the wildly inaccurate IMF economic forecasts over the past 15 years.

A government statistic that, between 2011 and 2015, 900,000 EU citizens moved to the UK is now revealed as untrue. The Office for National Statistics states that the true figure is 2.4

million immigrants. The ONS has also demonstrated that the discrepancy between the government figures and the number of EU citizens registered with a National Insurance number is understated by a quotient of 3:1. The British people are being deceived on a massive scale.

15 May

A Leave spokesman warns that if we vote Remain, "there is a parade of nasties being stored by the meddlesome EU Commission". We already pay Brussels £350 million a week subject to a later reduction of that figure according to the value of our rebate, quantified by the Commission. The bill is likely to go up because of the refugee crisis. The Commission has already delayed presentation of its mid-point review of the total EU budget from 2014 to 2020. It is expected to include proposals to increase spending by just less than £16 billion over three years. UK taxpayers handed over £13 billion to the EU in 2015 and its spending reached £110 billion in 2014.

MPs, including serving ministers, have joined migration experts in demonstrating that it is now clear that the levels of mass migration to Britain from the EU has been 'undercounted' for many years. The government somewhat fatuously insists that its statistics can be trusted because not all of the 900,000 arrivals stayed for at least a year (how can it know?) and that therefore not all of them can be counted in.

16 May

George Osborne demonstrates how total unreason has begun to afflict so many in the Remain camp – in particular senior ministers. Osborne labels campaigners who want to leave the EU as "a bunch of conspiracy theorists who will soon accuse the government of faking moon landings and covering up the existence of the Loch Ness monster".

Osborne claims that Britain could eventually forfeit £200 billion in trade and £200 billion in foreign investment within a year of being outside the EU – figures based on unsubstantiated claims and 15 years of no trade deals.

If this is the best Osborne can do, he reveals himself as a master of moronic utterance and unfit to hold high office. Cabinet Minister, Chris Grayling, a wonderful example of calm and rationality, puts the issue into clear perspective: "... the conspiracy theories around the European Union are there in black and white and while you don't need any hidden elements to it there is a clear plan to create a federation of the Eurozone".

17 May

A pact between Cameron and big business to scare Britain into staying in the EU is revealed. A leaked letter suggests the PM was plotting with a multi-national firm on how to hammer home the Remain case while still claiming he was prepared to campaign to leave. He had been telling the House of Commons that he "ruled out nothing" unless he won concessions from the EU. The secret strategy involved asking FTSE companies to put in their annual reports warnings about the dangers of Brexit. It was discussed in a letter from Serco boss, Rupert Soames, to Cameron 11 days before the renegotiation "deal" with the EU was complete.

Labour MP, Gisela Stuart, accuses Cameron of being knee-deep in conspiracy. Serco has multi-billion contracts with the government. Steve Baker, Tory MP, rightly declares: "This should come as no surprise. The corporates do well out of the EU because they can afford well-paid lobbyists and lawyers to stitch up the rules".

18 May

A Brussels report admits that there will be an increased terror threat as a result of visa-free access to Turkey. It will come from fanatics posing as Turks targeting European cities. Some 70 million Turkish citizens will be able to enter the European Schengen borderless zone as a concession to secure Turkey's support for a wider package of border control measures. The European Commission report admits that terrorists and gangsters will take advantage of compromised security.

This appalling news backs up ex-MI6 chief, Sir Richard Dearlove's warning against free access to the Turks when migration into Europe is expected to soar over the next five years. Visas permit fingerprints of people entering Europe to be logged on a single database which can be searched by counter-terrorist operatives. This extra level of security will be removed under the deal on condition that Turkey helps to stop migrants flooding into Europe over the Mediterranean.

Cameron continues his arrogance and stupidity. His latest dreadful gaffe is to declare that Islamic State (ISIL) leader, Al Baghdadi, would be pleased to support Leave.

19 May

The Governor of the Bank of England, Mark Carney, faces calls for his resignation following his highly pessimistic statement that a Leave vote could plunge Britain into recession. He warns of economic catastrophe after Brexit: that living standards will fall, unemployment will rise as will inflation and as will house prices. Worse still, mortgages will be much more expensive and there will be a slump in the value of sterling. This 'expert' earns £875,000 annually. He became Governor in July 2013 stating that he would serve for five years. He now wants to serve for eight years.

Notably, Iain Duncan Smith, one of Brexit's most effective analysts and communicators, declares that the Bank of England forecasts are scarcely worth the paper they are printed on. With unemployment in July 2013 (when Carney joined as Governor) at 7.8%, Carney said it would take over three years to fall below 7%. Six months later it stood at 6.9%!

20 May

A desperate attempt is made by Cameron in the Queen's speech to keep his EU referendum campaign on track by deliberately failing to include proposals for giving priority to Parliament over Brussels, to scrap the Human Rights Act and to ensure that the expected 'sovereignty' bill would not see the light of day, if at all, until well after the referendum.

Iain Duncan Smith rightly states that the sovereignty bill has been "tossed aside". Nothing must stand in the way of the referendum and the Remain camp's programme to deceive the public, so that it should not be allowed to focus on Cameron's miserable failure to bring back anything worthwhile from his pseudo renegotiation. Paul Nuttall, Deputy UKIP leader, says: "Cameron's EU renegotiation has been revealed for everything that it is – a complete con-job".

21 May

It is revealed that a trade war between European Union countries is causing severe damage to the British economy. This emanates from a secret government memorandum which Cameron and his friends in Remain were most anxious should not see the light of day. Its essence is that France in particular, but other EU countries as well, are hampering new free trade deals because they want to protect their farmers from extra competition.

Cameron has always claimed that the power of Brussels to negotiate such deals with the world at large, especially America, is a critical reason why the UK should not leave the EU. Of course, under the EU treaties we cannot negotiate our own trade arrangements unless all 28 member states are in agreement.

22 May

Simon Heffer, outstanding *Sunday Telegraph* columnist, reveals that there is truth in a story circulating around Westminster that in the event of a Remain vote victory Cameron will create 25 peerages for those "supportive" in the campaign. We know the form with Cameron. Some of his recent ennoblements have truly scraped the barrel, pitching into the Upper House, for reasons of tokenism, people who in earlier times would never have been raised to such distinction.

Cameron now has his eyes on the captains of industry. The louder they shout and the more fanciful their pretensions and claims the better their chances of climbing the greasy pole of preferment. His latest whiz is to urge company shareholders to vote Remain and to publicise this in annual reports. This is the sort of thing which has inspired Cameron to write to the chief executives of Serco (which has billions of pounds worth of government contracts, outlining his plans to ask for pleas to stay in the EU, in their annual report.

Cameron and Osborne seem prepared to stop at nothing to get their way.

23 May

Steve Hilton, Cameron's one-time close friend and former political adviser, nails his colours to the mast firmly declaring his adherence to the view that Britain must leave "the arrogant and unaccountable European Union". He considers that our country is "ungovernable" as a democracy and that if we vote to remain, it will be in a club that has been "corruptly captured" by a self-serving elite.

Brussels directives, says Hilton, have crept into every corner of Whitehall and that less than a third of the government's workload is the result of trying to fulfil its own promises and policies.

Hilton rightly warns that the tentacles of the EU have placed interminable constraints on everything from employment law to family policy and that whereas Cameron insists that Brussels is working in Britain's best interests and that leaving would affect incomes and house prices, Hilton dismisses all this as "nonsense" and describes the EU as being anti-trade and anti-enterprise, and that it is NATO and not the EU which makes us safer from terrorists and rogue states.

24 May

George Osborne's apocalyptic predictions for the economy and the pound if there is a Brexit have a familiar ring about them. The Europhiliacs made similar noises when Britain was catapulted out of the European Exchange Rate Mechanism (ERM) in September 1992. This was the precursor of the single currency when 13 years later the same harbingers of doom predicted that we would have perpetual crisis if we failed to join the Euro.

Our ejection from the ERM, while a humiliation for the government amidst dire predictions of economic humiliation, in fact turned out to be a great boost for the economy. The fall in the pound as Britain disengaged itself made goods and services competitive once again. Output grew and our trade deficit at the time was overturned. Indeed, the economy expanded at an average of 3½ per cent from 1998 to 2007.

A brilliant analysis by *The Daily Mail*'s Alex Brummer counterposes the reality against the claims made by the Treasury and Osborne. Here it is:

WE'VE HEARD THIS DOOM-MONGERING NONSENSE BEFORE

... and last time, when we were told leaving the ERM would spark disaster, our exit began a golden economic age

REALITY: The worst-case scenario presented by the Bank of England, which unlike the Treasury is highly regarded for its economic analysis, is for a 'technical recession'.

That would mean two quarters of negative growth, not the dramatic downturn predicted by the Treasury.

Latest forecasts from private sector economists show the UK economy is on the up, despite the impending vote. Goldman Sachs (which is financially supporting the

'Remain' campaign) puts quarterly growth at 0.5 per cent. What is certain is that two-year forecasts are often wildly wrong. The continued slump in the Eurozone economies is likely to be just as much of a drag on growth as any uncertainty caused by Brexit.

CLAIM: Consumer prices will rise by between 2.3 and 2.7 per cent.

REALITY: This forecast is based on the assumption that the pound will fall heavily (not necessarily the case) and this will lead to a sharp increase in import prices.

What this ignores is that the world is going through a period of disinflation (falling prices). Oil and commodity prices are spectacularly low, and any effect on import prices of weaker sterling would be minor. Even if the Treasury is right, inflation of 2.3 per cent – just 0.3 per cent above the Bank of England's target rate – can hardly be regarded as incendiary.

CLAIM: Unemployment will increase by 1.6 per cent or 520,000 jobs and in a worst-case scenario could rise by 2.4 per cent to 820,000.

REALITY: Even if this forecast could be relied on, a jobless rate that is 1.6 per cent higher than the current 5.1 per cent rate would still be relatively modest compared to the 10 per cent-plus rate across the Eurozone. The latest unemployment figures show that, despite the uncertainty over Brexit, the UK created 44,000 new jobs in the first three months of 2016 and the number of people on the dole fell in April.

CLAIM: Average real wages will drop by 2.8 per cent.

REALITY: Higher inflation obviously means a hit for real (inflation-adjusted) wages. But if the Treasury's assumptions on inflation aren't fulfilled, this forecast falls apart. What *has* proved a long-term dampener on real wages, irrespective of Brexit, is the influx of new people into Britain's workforce.

CLAIM: House prices will fall by at least 10 per cent and perhaps as much as 18 per cent.

REALITY: This is based on the assumption that interest rates – and therefore mortgage rates – will have to rise to counter higher inflation.

But the Bank of England has been warning that if the economy keeps on growing, interest rates would have to rise anyway.

In parts of the country, such as the over-heated South-East, a fall in house prices might be welcome and enable more people to climb the ladder.

Irrespective of the referendum, the Chancellor has already taken some of the steam out of house prices by higher stamp duties on expensive properties, removing interest rate relief on second homes and a clamp-down on mortgage lending for buy-to-let.

CLAIM: The pound will fall by 12 per cent and possibly 15 per cent.

REALITY: The pound has actually been rising against the Euro and hit a three-and-a-half-month high last week. A devaluation of the pound could be just the present that our exporters need.

It would make Britain's exports of goods and services substantially cheaper on all global markets. Historical experience suggests that devaluation is almost always a huge plus for Britain.

CLAIM: The budget deficit could soar by £24 billion or, in the worst case, £39 billion.

REALITY: Budget deficits are highly sensitive to economic forecasts. If the Treasury has its growth and unemployment numbers wrong, then almost certainly this forecast will be wrong too.

An alternative scenario is that the repatriation of our payments to the EU could lower the budget deficit. Higher exports could generate more tax income which would lower the deficit.

Remember that the budget deficit is the difference between two very big numbers – what the government spends and what it collects in taxes and charges. Forecasting for both is never on the mark.

26 May

David Cameron is photographed in the national media with Tessa Jowell, walking through a zebra crossing in Abbey Road, London NW8, treading a path familiar to the Beatles some 50 years ago. What, I ask, has this pathetic tomfoolery got to do with the EU referendum? Apparently, he considers the creative industries, including pop music, will be enhanced by a Remain vote for which there is not a scintilla of evidence!

The Cabinet Secretary, Sir Jeremy Heywood, is warned by several Leave campaigners against breaking electoral law by issuing propaganda plastered on government web sites. Both Iain Duncan Smith and Boris Johnson write to him that the sites be removed within seven days because they will otherwise be infringing the Ministerial Code and the official Whitehall "purdah" period.

If the Remain camp is so confident of its economic message the Leavers can point to three questions raised by Andrew Lilico of the Europe Economic Consultancy: 1) if the EU is so good for growth, why has the American economy grown six per cent faster than the EU over the past decade? 2) If it is so good for jobs, why is Spanish unemployment standing at 21 per cent?, and 3) If it is so good for trade, why are deals with Japan, America and Canada at risk of breaking down?

27 May

Brussels is shown to be hiding the truth about the rising cost of European Union membership. It is delaying next year's draft budget for major spending increases until after the referendum. EU budget proposals for 2017 were to be published by the European Commission on May 28th but, according to an internal Brussels document, this has been postponed to the end of June so that the increases would not be known at the referendum date. The increases would cover shortfalls in payments for regional projects and security upgrades to EU buildings. MEPs have also postponed a 15 June vote on plans to tear up spending caps negotiated by Cameron in 2013.

Further, despite being outside the Schengen borderless zone, British taxpayers are having to pick up bills for a crisis caused by the EU's failure to secure the passport-free travel areas' external frontiers.

28 May

The Remain campaign's duplicity and dishonesty is fully revealed with the release of 26 government statements on the same day as the publication of the most recent very high immigration figures. This has been done with the intention of concealing the truth. The move comes on the last day of the parliamentary sitting before the Spring recess, making it impossible for MPs to hold the government to account over the various issues involved.

David Davis, a former Europe Minister and a clear-thinking Brexiteer who would, in my view, have made a better Prime Minister than David Cameron when the position was up for grabs in 2005 (see my article on page 284) claims that the Whitehall structure was linked in with the EU with many British civil servants having worked in Brussels. Davis claims that this has left them with a vested interest in wanting to remain in the EU and communicate the importance of this to Cameron. "The same people the PM seeks advice from as to what we should do concerning tax or economic policy turn to him and say 'we don't want to take any risks' ", says Davis.

Following criticism, Boris Johnson declares he will accept a challenge from the President of the European Commission, Jean-Claude Juncker, and debate with him the EU's plans to create a federal superstate. I rather think that if this came near to fruition Juncker would find reason to duck the challenge.

Lord Owen, one of the most distinguished politicians of recent times, comments on the relentless "carpet bombing" by the Remain campaign's corporates, financial institutions and banking specialists such that Leave campaigners could be forgiven for experiencing some pessimism. But the good doctor tells Allison Pearson of *The Daily Telegraph*: "I think the great British public can see through all this nonsense ... The opinion polls show that the Leave campaign is level pegging with Remain". Lord Owen rightly accuses Cameron of abusing his position as PM and failing to conduct the referendum with a dignity befitting a national leader.

Immigration moves centre stage. A record number of jobless EU migrants moving to the UK to look for work has pushed immigration from the EU to an all-time high. The total number of EU nationals coming here under freedom of movement rules was 270,000 last year, according to the Office for National

Statistics, including 77,000 arriving without the offer of a job. A record number have arrived from Romania and Bulgaria.

Net EU migration, which takes into account the number of EU citizens leaving the UK, was 184,000, two and a half times the size of my home town, Watford. Overall net migration, including those from outside the EU, was 330,000 in the year to December 2015. Cameron's pledge to reduce net migration to the "tens of thousands, no ifs no buts", is revealed as a complete mirage and unattainable. No expression of regret from the government, let alone an apology to the British people for having to submit to this disastrous experiment in people management.

30 May

Penny Mordaunt, the excellent Armed Forces Minister, confirms that in the event of Britain remaining in the EU despite the dissimulations of the Remain campaign, Britain will be obliged to join an EU army. This is provided for in the Lisbon Treaty.

With deliberate timing, the day after the referendum an enabling provision will be tabled by the EU's foreign policy commissioner. It will be kept hidden from the British people until then. It will be set down by Federica Mogherina, leading Italian Eurocrat. The powers will allow a group of nine or more EU states to merge their forces. Germany and Holland have already agreed to do so. Even if there was a British veto (which is unclear from the Lisbon Treaty) pressure upon us would be overbearing. Andrew Bridgen MP, Brexit activist and authority on the treaties, states: "This blows out of the window the Prime Minister's claim that we have been excluded from 'ever closer union'. Voters are being hoodwinked once again".

Meanwhile, pensioners are coming to learn that they will lose some of their retirement incomes if we vote to remain. This is because a Brussels directive requires insurers to increase their cash reserves to guard against the risk of insolvency. This has already driven down the rates on annuities which millions of workers have to buy to turn private or company pension pots into an income for life.

This is the reality which pales into insignificance Osborne's extravagant claims, made with no foundation in fact, that pensioners could lose between 18,000 and 32,000 pounds under Brexit.

31 May

A week ago the Institute of Fiscal Studies launches a report on the public finance consequences of Brexit. Its director, Paul Johnson, writing in *The Times*, offers his opinion. "I cannot say it is a fact that the economy would do less well following a Brexit. What I can say is that the overwhelming weight of economic evidence suggests that that would be the case".

Brexit campaign is perfectly entitled to emphasise that given the established fact that IFS receives substantial funding from agencies associated with the EU, it must be somewhat tarnished in its claim to be independent, at least in this debate.

Meanwhile, a highly respected City figure launches a blistering attack on EU "corruption". Robert Hiscox, who chaired Lloyds of London for 43 years until his recent retirement, claims that Osborne's Treasury has published misleading and illegal propaganda and that so-called experts from Goldman Sachs downwards are in the business primarily out of self-interest.

1 June

EU President Donald Tusk has made a remarkable admission. He warns EU leaders in blunt terms that their utopian illusions are tearing Europe apart and that any attempt to seize upon a British exit to force through yet further integration would be a grave mistake.

Tusk, conscious of a nationalist revival in his native Poland (amen to that) has heavily criticised the EU establishment for pushing a Europe without nation states that fundamentally goes against the grain of European history.

President of France, François Hollande, holds a special meeting of his inner cabinet to work out a response to Brexit, concluding that the entire edifice of Europe's post-war diplomacy is at risk of collapse. Hasten the day that that should happen since it would usher in with maximum profit to all a new era of European co-operation.

Meanwhile, public opinion shifts dramatically towards leaving the EU according to ICM by 52 per cent to 48 per cent and this is so whether people are questioned on-line or by telephone.

2 June

A salutary revelation from the European Anti-Fraud Office shows that £670 million of EU spending was lost to fraud in 2015. This is profoundly shocking and serves only to confirm what many people already know, that the EU is corrupt with a rottenness at its core.

The false claims are concentrated in Romania, Bulgaria and Hungary. Examples include 1.3 million Euros of EU agricultural aid to modernise a vegetable chilling plant in Bulgaria and the sending of 2 million Euros in aid to an ecology project in Africa, the operators of which were billing different international donors for the same work by supplying systematically false information.

The figures also show that just less than 900,000 Euros was lost in 2015 to dishonest EU staff. Despite this, the fraud agency's boss, Giovanni Kessler, declares that he does not believe there is widespread corruption. What then is there I ask myself?

The peripatetic Boris Johnson tells Leave supporters in a speech in Preston that Cameron "doesn't believe in Britain because he is constantly talking the country down" – and so he is with his pessimism: a third world war and lengthy recession being just two good examples.

3 June

Cameron faces Sky TV political correspondent, Faisal Islam, a man who often asks questions and either answers them himself or leaves precious little time for a response. Dave deserves some sympathy in that regard but in all truth he was poor. He continues to make the absurd claim that net immigration could be reduced to "tens of thousands", as promised in the Tory election manifesto, given that the current yearly net intake of immigrants is 330,000.

Islam reminded Cameron that he had stated that a Brexit might "lead to a Third World War" and whether this would come before or after a recession? On his renegotiations Cameron considered he had secured "an enhanced special status" whereas in fact he had achieved precious little.

Elsewhere German chancellor, Angela Merkel (who persists in wearing jackets two sizes too short for her) stands accused of bullying Britain into staying in the EU by declaring that we would be "punished" if voters back Brexit. Let us hope they give this veritable frump of a woman a proverbial kick up her posterior in forthcoming German elections.

4 June

The two big referendum debates conclude. Michael Gove for Brexit clearly outpoints Cameron whose lack-lustre, rather feeble performance won him few plaudits whereas Gove put Faisal Islam firmly in his place, talking of the job-destroying machine which is the EU where wages are lower, access to public services restricted and where 33 million people are ensnared in an autocracy. Injecting a personal note Gove added: "I know myself how my father's fishing business was destroyed by EU regulation".

The Leave campaign seems to be characterised by a complete absence of vindictiveness whereas Remain, with their excesses, gross exaggerations and scaremongering, are steadily destroying their own case. Gove brings a degree of idealism to the debate in contrast to the technocratic approach of Remain with a whole range of statistical information flowing from the Treasury based largely on hypothetical suppositions, often wildly inaccurate, as was the case with the consequences of our withdrawal from the Exchange Rate Mechanism in September 1992 and the vaunting of the benefits of the Euro currency to our long-term prosperity.

5 June

Michael Gove and Boris Johnson warn that voters cannot trust Cameron and Osborne to honour their promises on Europe. The Leave campaign declares that the Prime Minister has put the British economy "in severe danger" by giving away the UK's veto during discussions in Brussels in February. Britain is now "dangerously exposed" to being forced to hand over more money as the migration crisis worsens with workers fleeing the stricken Eurozone and heading to Britain for jobs.

Equally damaging, they claim, has been the government's failure to protect taxpayers from funding new bail-outs for the Eurozone. This means, with justification, that the public can have little faith in government promises.

Increasingly, people are realising that it is not enough to be told that leaving is a risky venture. They want to know just as much what it means for them and the UK if we vote Remain and the European economy declines, which on present trends is more likely than not. What, for instance, if the UK is locked out of free trade agreements with the outside world because the EU takes too long to conclude them? Or where is the guarantee that we wouldn't be sucked into further integration, regulation and bureaucracy?

6 June

Sir John Major enters the fray describing the Leave campaign as 'deceitful' in a savage personal attack on Boris Johnson. Deceit is a failing that Major knows something about given that he deceived his wife for many years when prime minister during a lengthy affair with Edwina Currie. A little respectful silence from Sir John would not go amiss if he insists on using pejorative language in the way he has done.

Sir John was a brilliant Financial Secretary to the Treasury and in my view an underrated Prime Minister so I write of him unfavourably in this context with no pleasure at all. He also has the great merit of being an avid cricket fan and bon viveur.

Another of Sir John's contributions to this debate is his statement that the NHS "is about as safe with them (Michael Gove, Boris Johnson and Iain Duncan Smith) as a pet hamster would be with a hungry python". Phew!

It should be recalled that one downside of Sir John's government was his errors over Europe. In October 1990 when he was Chancellor, the UK joined the ERM which caused interest rates to rise 15 per cent, leading to millions of homeowners moving into negative equity and pushing unemployment to 2.9 million in 1993.

I note that Osborne is at it again. He releases figures claiming that a vote to leave would add between £920 and £1,470 to the annual mortgage bill, equating to £77 and £122.50 a month. Think of a number, double it … etc. George needs a break.

7 June

Cameron moves from one grotesque exaggeration to another. Is he losing his marbles, I wonder? At 10am he pontificates about: prices rising, house prices collapsing, mortgage rates increasing, businesses going bust and unemployment going through the roof. Add those things together and he is going into Armageddon mode declaring finally that a bomb is now being placed under the economy, marginally less threatening perhaps than his previously uttered prospect of a third world war.

Then, at 12.15pm, he declares: "I genuinely don't believe that there's any scaremongering on my side"!

Business Secretary, Sajid Javid, writes a letter jointly with Peter Mandelson on the alleged benefits of Remain. Javid has found it very convenient to convert himself from an ardent Eurosceptic to an enthusiastic Remainer. High Office no doubt beckons. Meanwhile some Remain MPs are plotting to ignore the people's will by voting to keep Britain in the single market even if the referendum results in a Brexit victory. That would necessarily mean continuation of free movement of labour, along with capital, goods and services and uncontrolled, limitless immigration.

8 June

The European Commission announces plans to tackle the migrant crisis, which has begun to dominate the debate, by inviting ever more people into the European Union. Specifically, migrants from Africa and the Middle East will be given US-style green cards granting them work rights, allowing them to bring their families. This move comes on top of the one million migrants who reached Europe last year and the 206,000 in the first five months of 2016. The thinking here is that it will curb illegal immigration but there is no evidence whatever to support this proposition. It is also proposed to hand £6.2 billion in aid to African countries with a view to repeating a £4.7 billion deal with Turkey.

On other matters, on BBC's Radio 4 programme, To-Day, an interview set a former steelworker, Mike Gilbert, against lifelong Europhile, Lord Heseltine. After 31 years as a steelworker, Gilbert was laid off when the Redcar works were closed down last year. He has since had to sell his house. Heseltine claimed that the Tees Valley would overcome the loss of 2,200 steel industry jobs to become "a bustling powerhouse of economic activity".

Gilbert responded that the type of jobs created under the Heseltine plan would be minimum wage or zero-hours contracts rather than the skilled, well-paid work found in the steel industry. "It is another industry we're losing. In the last 40 years the fishing industry has been destroyed, shipbuilding finished, coalmining finished, the steel industry decimated and the car industry destroyed or sold", said Gilbert. He went on, "I'm a great believer that we should leave the European Union. We give the EU £161 million a week after deductions. This money would be better spent helping the UK ... when the steel industry was struggling in Italy and France their governments stepped in, but we were told EU rules on state aid meant nothing could be done in Redcar".

Heseltine could not have an answer and was truly humbled by this very sad tale.

9 June

Vote Leave campaigners accuse the government of trying to rig the referendum result by forcing through a last-minute extension to voter registration. This seems a cynical ploy made with the purpose of encouraging younger voters who are considered more likely to vote Remain. Given, sadly, the lack of interest among so many young people in buckling down to absorb the detail of the EU experiment and the pretty feeble excuse that they are not being given the facts, when patently they are, it has been thought appropriate to give them more time to register.

The rush to beat the original deadline has probably been dictated by Nigel Farage's clear points victory over Cameron in their recent TV debate. Bernard Jenkin, prominent Leave campaigner and Chairman of the Commons Public Administration and Constitutional Affairs Committee, warns that the government is "dicing with legality" in moving the voting deadline.

Contrary to Remain propaganda expectations it is reported that the prospect of a Leave vote has led to the biggest boom in British exports in 13 years showing that we would prosper departing the EU. The figures from the Office for National Statistics show that exports jumped from 9.1 per cent between March and April to hit 26.1 billion, the fastest month-on-month growth since January 2003. The trade balance is now favourable to the UK securing a free trade deal with the EU.

10 June

One of the more extravagant Remain claims is that British business supports staying in because it fears economic meltdown if we leave. Say that to one of our most successful businessmen,

Lord Bamford, founder of JCB, who has written to his 6,500 British employees to tell them that the Remain camp's prediction of economic collapse is very far wide of the mark. Cameron won't like this since over the past 15 years JCB has given £3.7 million to the Tory Party. Lord Bamford emphasises that the UK is a trading nation, the fifth largest economy in the world and perfectly capable of standing on its own two feet. Significantly, Carlos Ghosh, Chief Executive of Renault-Nissan, has declared: "Whatever is the decision of the UK, we will adapt to it. I don't think there is a reason to worry. We knew for many years that an exit was possible. So we'll deal with it".

11 June

German finance minster, Wolfgang Schauble, warns untruthfully that if Britain leaves the EU it would be a decision "against the single market". This comment, made to *Der Spiegel* magazine, is really an opportunity to engage in trading arrangements with some of the largest markets in the world. Schauble also predicts that Britain would be forced "to crawl back to the EU within years" whereas the more likely scenario is that the EU will have either imploded or bankrupted itself and become defunct. Could Schauble's outburst have anything to do with *Der Spiegel*'s English headline: 'Please don't go – Why Germany needs the British'?

Under Freedom of Information rules, statistics released recently show that 84,000 detentions were made at our borders last year. This is equivalent to 230 a day. The number of illegal immigrants captured has risen fivefold since 2013 when 16,008 were seized. This, of course, ignores the many thousands of stowaways thought to have made it across the channel. Beyond a shadow of doubt the EU has utterly failed to tackle the crisis while our own Home Office has tried to hide this information until after the referendum. I am shocked, but not surprised, to learn that demographic forecasters reckon that by 2065 white people will be in a minority in England. Anyone suggesting such a thing thirty years ago would have been laughed out of court. Is the prospect of this what we fought two World Wars for?

12 June

Penny Mordaunt, Conservative MP and doughty Leave campaigner, as well as being a very fine-looking woman – whoops

I've upset the politically correct brigade – declares in a piece in *The Sunday Express* that the thought of taking back control of our own destiny is all too terrifying a prospect to contemplate for the Remain camp. Their irresponsible scaremongering is now turning to national security issues, she argues.

We are told that border checks at Calais would cease if we leave the EU. This is despite the French interior minister's confirmation that, because of a separate bilateral agreement (the Treaty of Le Touquet) they will stay in place. We are told there are no plans for an EU army even though a draft strategy has been drawn up by Germany and the EU Battlegroup exercises on Salisbury Plain and we are warned that a Brexit will trigger civil unrest and extremism in Europe but this is happening not because of Britain's referendum, but because of the economic and social harm caused by the Eurozone.

Our real dangers come from remaining in a wholly dysfunctional European Union which has no solution to its Eurozone crisis and fails to allow member states to control immigration.

13 June

Two matters are worthy of record. The first is the sight of Amber Rudd, a woman promoted, like Nicky Morgan, well beyond her capabilities, laying into Boris Johnson in an ITV debate with a venom and vindictiveness which was disgraceful. Boris kept his cool and outpointed the ineffectual Rudd with aplomb.

The second is contained in a little-known provision which I myself uncovered in the Lisbon Treaty (2007) which manifests the grandiose designs of interference at every level which the European Commission has at its disposal. The provision in question known as 'the rule of law mechanism' permits the Commission to determine whether elected governments are "deviating from the common constitutional traditions of all member states". Quite how the Commission sets about its dictatorial mandate in this regard is unclear but these unelected bureaucrats have powers to decide whether or not an elected government is legitimate. If they come to the conclusion that it is not they can block the voting rights and funding to that country. This would no doubt have raised the legitimacy (quite wrongly) of the Austrian candidate of the Freedom Party if he had not narrowly lost the election last month as indeed it would if Marine Le Pen were to be successful in the 2017 French Presidential election.

14 June

David Cameron, Remain's joint scaremonger-in-chief (a wholly inappropriate role for a prime minister) with George Osborne is at it again. He now claims that pensions could be substantially reduced if Britain quits the EU. In his most recent contribution Cameron claims that economic turmoil could easily result in a £40 billion black hole in the public finances. This apparent funding crisis would lead to swingeing austerity measures not only cutting state pensions but scrapping free bus passes and free television licences.

Cameron's attempts to terrify a significant proportion of our population has met with a very severe reaction given that it is tantamount to blackmail. "...vote for us or take the consequences". The reality is that the latest polls are putting the Leave campaign six or more points in front.

Former chancellor, Lord Lamont, declares that non-members of the EU profit more from trade deals than its members do and that arguing for the single market on the grounds you can avoid a 3 per cent tariff by actually paying a 7 per cent fee is mis-selling "on a scale that dwarfs the PPI scandal", says Lamont.

15 June

With just over a week to go it is worth contemplating what some distinguished Labour Party voices from the past have had to say from their own historical perspective:

> "No socialist party with the prospect of forming a government could accept a system by which important fields of national policy were surrendered to a supranational European representative authority"
> – Denis Healey, 18 October 1950.

> "If you are going to have a democratic Europe, if you are going to control the running of Europe democratically, you've got to move towards some form of federation and if anyone says different to that they're misleading the public".
> – Hugh Gaitskell, 29 September 1962.

> "Britain's continuing membership of the European Community would mean the end of Britain as a completely

self-governing country and the end of our democratically elected Parliament as the supreme law-making body in the United Kingdom".
– Tony Benn, 18 June 1974.

16 June

The civil war in the Tory Party continues unabated and reaches a new degree of ugliness, with Brexit-supporting Conservative MPs expressing their contempt after Chancellor Osborne declares that he would hold an austerity budget in the event of an exit vote. This would include manifesto-breaking spending cuts and tax rises. Michael Gove, for his part, declares that he would not vote for such a punishment budget which is opposed by 65 colleagues including seven cabinet ministers. In a joint statement they say they would bring down the Brexit budget and that the chancellor's position would be untenable if he tried to deliver it. "We find it incredible that the chancellor can seriously be threatening to renege on so many manifesto pledges. It is absurd to say that if people vote to take back control from the EU that he would want to punish them. We do not believe he would find it possible to get support in parliament for these proposals to cut the NHS, our police forces and our schools".

Chancellor Osborne seems to consider that after a Brexit vote he would need to show the world that the UK has a 'credible plan' to deal with any deterioration in its public finances that would follow.

There is absolutely no evidence of deterioration but confirmation that Osborne, like Cameron, is more concerned with Merkel, Obama, Juncker and the massed ranks of corporate business than he is with the British people. Surely it is the case that Osborne has blown the last vestiges of his credibility to pieces with his shameless abuse of office.

17 June

Left-winger John Cryer, chairman of the Parliamentary Labour Party, declares that he is breaking rank to back Brexit because the EU in his view, as with so many others, is anti-democratic. I could have told him that 40 years ago! Still, better late than never. Cryer, MP for Leytonstone and Wanstead, exposes the serious divisions among Labour left-wingers, many, it seems, believing Corbyn doesn't have his heart in the job. Cryer Says: "The EU is not Europe but a political construct imposed on many countries ... undermining democratic governments, weakening national governments and handing powers to the markets and the corporate world".

At the same time Boris Johnson accuses Mark Carney, governor of the Bank of England, of talking Britain down while four senior Tories, Lord Howard, Lord Lawson, Lord Lamont and Iain Duncan Smith accuse Carney of "peddling phoney forecasts and doom-laden warnings.

Meanwhile, following Osborne's threatened harsh budget, *The Daily Mail*'s authoritative economics analyst, Alex Brummer, declares that in the event of a Brexit the UK should cut taxes, not raise them, pointing out that the last senior politician foolish enough to 'pre-announce' that there would be income tax increases in a future budget was the late Labour Shadow Chancellor John Smith, ahead of the 1992 election. It paved the way for a dramatic victory for John Major and the Tories.

18 June

The Eurozone is on the brink of another, possibly steeper, financial crisis and according to the International Monetary Fund's latest analysis it is in danger of being torn apart by political tensions. The IMF declares that it is being racked by high unemployment and bad debt.

Eurosceptic economists, very many of them, argue that Britain will be able to slash tariffs to zero on all imports if it leaves the EU, cutting the price of goods and making households better off. The IMF itself grudgingly concedes that this "would make UK consumers better off all else being equal even if it might be difficult to achieve in practice".

Christine Lagarde, boss of the IMF, has implied that Eurosceptic voters are narrow-minded. She increasingly looks like an Osborne stooge. Her insinuation that British voters who have concerns about immigration and want to leave the EU should have a wider perspective has met with a hostile response from many Tory MPs. One of them, John Redwood, declares his deep resentment at Lagarde's remarks. "Clearly Madame Lagarde believes that the true nature of the EU is not as a trading arrangement for independent countries but a political union with ever more central control in Brussels".

19 June

A little-considered poll commissioned by ITV's *Good Morning Britain* finds 44 per cent would vote to leave the EU compared with 42 per cent preferring to remain. I have a strong intuitive sense that this poll more accurately matches the people's will than some of the recent pro-Remain indicators. We shall see – only four days to go.

Research by the Eurosceptic Bruges Group banking expert, Bob Lydon, establishes that Britain has more than £80 billion at risk in the European Union. We could be compelled to pay for bad loans and unwise decisions made by both the European Investment Bank and European Central Bank. Additionally, all member states could be called upon to share the burden of debt arising from the 4.9 billion Euros unaccounted for to the satisfaction of the Court of Auditors.

Surveying the state of Euroland I perceive that at the present time France is a deeply unhappy land beset by strikes, demonstrations and in many places riots and all that on top of the terrible terrorist outrages. Austria, in defiance of EU law (which has no sanction to prevent it) has erected a border control on the Brenner Pass motorway from Italy. Meanwhile, Greece remains dangerously close to bankruptcy trying to manage its severe debt programme demanded by Germany. Our own people should bear these sort of issues in mind when they come to cast their votes.

20 June

The shocking murder of Jo Cox MP has evoked an inappropriate response from some of the leaders of the Remain camp seeking to gain political advantage from this tragedy. The executive director of Britain Stronger in Europe, Will Shaw, discloses to his supporters details of a new closing argument for the final hours of the referendum campaign. A leaked private telephone conference call posted on the internet declares: "We need to recognise that people have been pulled up short by Jo Cox's death .... and to emphasise now how the other side have stirred up division and resentment in the UK".

Andrew Bridgen MP, resolute Brexit campaigner, got it exactly right: "I thought that the Remain campaign had plumbed the depths of political campaigning but this is the pits. How low can they go?"

Not surprisingly, Cameron gets in on the act by referring on Twitter to an article by Mrs Cox in which she argues that Britain could deal with the issue of immigration more effectively by remaining in the UK. This is untrue as Cameron must know.

Meanwhile, union boss Len McCluskey admits that the enlargement of the EU into Eastern Europe has been a malign experiment conducted at the expense of British workers leading to sustained pressure on living standards. Honest and welcome but a long time in coming.

21 June

A counsellor to Turkey's president declares that Cameron is his country's principal supporter in its quest to join the European Union. In fact, Cameron has been playing down the prospect of Turkey's 77 million citizens getting free movement to the UK by joining the EU, suggesting that it will be as far away as the year 3000 before that eventuality. (How can he be so ridiculously precise, one wonders?)

In May 2014 Cameron declared that he very much supported Turkish membership of the EU thereby indicating that he had no objection to 70 million muslims entering the UK if that was their wish. This is nothing short of treachery against our Christian national civilisation. Aside from that, 90% of the land mass of Turkey is in Asia and not in Europe.

In yesterday's referendum debate Labour MP Gisela Stuart queries: "I would like the real David Cameron to step forward ... On the one hand he tells us they will join in the year 3000 or is it now 30 years?. And on the other hand we are spending £1.9 billion of your money to accelerate accession of Turkey. Which David Cameron are we to believe?"

22 June

Energy minister Andrea Leadsom is accused by Ruth Davidson, Scottish Tory Leader, of lying over Leadsom's claim that 60 per cent of British laws come from the EU. Not for the first time Davidson is plain wrong. The House of Commons library, which is the most authentic source of statistical accuracy, has collated all the acts of parliament and statutory instruments since 1993. 13.2 per cent have been EU related but when subsidiary regulations are added to the mix, 62.4 per cent of British law can accurately be described as originating from the EU.

Whereas President Hollande of France and others have lined up to threaten Leave voters that Brexit would necessarily lock Britain outside Europe's single market, Markus Kerber, head of the BDI, the federation of German industry, has given a sharp warning against a "regressive" introduction of tariffs in conflict with WTO rules. More than 5.5 million jobs in Europe are linked to exports to the UK and last year Britain imported £68 billion more in goods and services than it sold to the EU. Mr Kerber declares: "we would urge politicians on both sides to come up with a trade régime that enables us to maintain and uphold the levels of trade we already have."

23 June

And so to the vote.

24 June

The result is conclusive. The people of our country have made it known by 52% to 48% that they want this country to leave the European Union, its bureaucratic institutions and dictatorial processes and restore our parliamentary sovereignty and democracy. It is a marvellous day for all who believe in freedom. What other countries choose to do is up to them, but let there be no shadow of doubt the British people have spoken. There is no case at all to prolong the invoking of Article 50 of the Lisbon Treaty. The quicker we actually trigger the appropriate mechanisms the easier it will be to recover our independence.

Postscript to referendum result:

At the time of writing this postscript, in late January 2017, the Remain camp are increasingly seeking to find ways to water down the result of the people's will and to obstruct the recovery of Britain's national independence. Mrs May hasn't helped matters by allowing such an unnecessarily long time, nine months, to take the crucial steps to activate Article 50 Lisbon Treaty (2007). The purpose behind this delay is unclear and unexplained. Mrs May will have up to two years afterwards (too long anyway) to effect a beneficial settlement. A maxim of the Law of Trusts is spot on: "delay defeats equity" or, as rather nicely written, "*vigilantibus non dormientibus jura subveniunt*" – equity aids the vigilant, not the indolent. The Remain camp knows this. The longer they can drag talks out, muddy the waters and, through their propaganda, disseminate untruths and irrelevancies, the greater their chance of wrecking Brexit and a constructive European settlement.

Let us be clear. The nonsense about a "soft" Brexit being better than a "hard" Brexit needs to be demolished. The only Brexit is that of a clean break from the European Union. The negotiation of bi-lateral free trade agreements with the world is the way forward and eminently achievable within World Trade Organisation (WTO) rules and much lower time-limits than those often cited. Implicitly, it means leaving the single market, disowning the customs union, controlling our borders and stopping free movement of labour (thereby contradicting the EU Commission's belief that Europe is already a nation), ceasing immediately to pay financial levies (except the very limited ones already agreed upon), rejecting emphatically all welfare benefits for EU migrants and informing, by government decree, the European Court of Justice that, from the appointed day, its jurisdiction shall no longer extend to the United Kingdom.

That is what is needed. No messing about. No equivocations.

Index

[Only those names which are an essential part of the narrative are included]